Y0-DOU-361

"*Essentials of Middle and Secondary Social Studies* is a thoughtful introduction into the practice of teaching middle and secondary social studies. As a true methods book, Russell and Waters focus on an array of approaches to teaching. For anyone interested in a book that is built around the practical aspects of teaching social studies, this is a must-read book."

Bonnie Bittman,
Assistant Professor of Teacher Education,
The University of Hawaii

"The strength of *Essentials of Middle and Secondary Social Studies* is in its ability to provide reader with practical applications of research-based instructional strategies. Filled with illustrative vignettes, activities, and lesson plans, this book would be valuable for pre-service teachers who are just entering the classroom, as well as in-service teachers who may be looking for new ways to enliven their instruction."

Wayne Journell,
Professor of Secondary Social Studies Education,
University of North Carolina at Greensboro

"Too often, methods texts are rich in the 'why' of teaching the content. This book is outstanding in that it focuses upon the 'how' as well as the 'why'. Education student will benefit greatly from the wide and diverse research-based strategies to teach all students in today's educational world. Indeed, this book truly covers the 'essentials' of social studies instruction today."

Dr. Brad Burenheide,
College of Education, Kansas State University

Essentials of Middle and Secondary Social Studies

Building on the success of the of previous editions, *Essentials of Middle and Secondary Social Studies Third Edition* focuses on the key issues central to the teaching of middle and high school social studies, including lesson planning and instructional strategies. Written in an engaging, conversational style, the text encourages teachers in their development as professionals and enables them to effectively use creative and active learning strategies in the everyday classroom.

New to This Edition

This third edition has been refined with new and relevant topics and strategies needed for effectively teaching middle and high school social studies. New features include:

- An expanded chapter on the decision-making process in secondary social studies. This chapter provides additional discussion about the importance of helping middle and high school learners better understand the decision-making process and offers strategies for helping teachers make connections between choices, values, character development, and social justice.
- An updated chapter on technology designed to better prepare secondary social studies teachers to effectively incorporate technology into their instruction. Focus is given to virtual teaching and learning, media literacy, teaching with film, and numerous other ways to improve teaching and learning in the digital age.
- Updated further readings and helpful resources for all chapters to include supplemental digital and video sources related to various topics throughout the chapter. These resources were specifically curated to be impactful for preservice and in-service teachers, as well as anyone teaching secondary social studies methods courses.
- Added a "Checking for Understanding" section of questions at the end of each chapter that focuses on comprehension, application, and reflection on key concepts throughout the chapters.
- An expanded discussion of the Common Core Standards and C3 Framework and how it impacts teachers.
- An updated chapter titled "Experiencing Social Studies". This chapter focus on topics such as teaching with drama, role play, field trips, and service learning.
- Each chapter includes a "Helpful Resources" section that details various websites and online resources for further discovery.

William B. Russell III is Professor of Science Education at The University of Central Florida.

Stewart Waters is Associate Professor of Social Science Education at The University of Tennessee, Knoxville.

Essentials of Middle and Secondary Social Studies

Third Edition

William B. Russell III and Stewart Waters

Routledge
Taylor & Francis Group
NEW YORK AND LONDON

Cover image: © Getty Images

Third edition published 2023
by Routledge
605 Third Avenue, New York, NY 10158

and by Routledge
4 Park Square, Milton Park, Abingdon, Oxon, OX14 4RN

Routledge is an imprint of the Taylor & Francis Group, an informa business

Second edition published by Routledge 2018
First edition published by Routledge 2013

Library of Congress Cataloging-in-Publication Data
Names: Russell, William B., author. | Waters, Stewart, author.
Title: Essentials of middle and secondary social studies / William B.
Russell III & Stewart Waters.
Description: Third edition. | New York, NY: Routledge, 2022. | Includes
bibliographical references and index.
Identifiers: LCCN 2021056802 (print) | LCCN 2021056803 (ebook) | ISBN
9781032107905 (hardback) | ISBN 9781032107899 (paperback) | ISBN
9781003217060 (ebook)
Subjects: LCSH: Social sciences—Study and teaching (Elementary)—United
States. | Social sciences—Study and teaching (Secondary)—United
States.
Classification: LCC LB1584 .R86 2022 (print) | LCC LB1584 (ebook) | DDC
372.89—dc23
LC record available at https://lccn.loc.gov/2021056802
LC ebook record available at https://lccn.loc.gov/2021056803

ISBN: 978-1-032-10790-5 (hbk)
ISBN: 978-1-032-10789-9 (pbk)
ISBN: 978-1-003-21706-0 (ebk)

DOI: 10.4324/9781003217060

Typeset in Bembo
by SPi Technologies India Pvt Ltd (Straive)

Contents

List of Illustrations xiii
Preface xv

1 Becoming a Professional Social Studies Teacher 1

Looking Ahead 1
Can You? Do You? 1
Focus Activity 1
Influences and Experiences 2
Professional Certification, Conduct, and Ethics 2
Professional Organizations 6
Professional Development 6
Looking Back 10
Extension Activity 11
Reflective Questions 11
Helpful Resources 11
Further Reading 11
References 12

2 Contemporary Social Studies 13

Looking Ahead 13
Can You? Do You? 14
Focus Activity 14
The Goals of Social Studies 14
Why Is There Controversy in Social Studies? 16
Incorporating Themes from the Standards 19
Social Studies and the Common Core 20
College, Career, and Civic Life Framework and Social Studies 22
NCSS National Standards for the Preparation of Social Studies Teachers 23
Constructivism and Social Studies 24
A Problems Approach to Social Studies 24
Problems Approach in the Classroom 25
The Social Science Disciplines 27
Looking Back 31
Extension Activity 32
Reflective Questions 32

Helpful Resources 32
Further Reading 33
References 34

3 Planning Social Studies Instruction 35

Looking Ahead 35
Can You? Do You? 35
Focus Activity 36
Why Is Planning Important? 36
Setting the Stage: Creating the Environment 37
Why Don't Teachers Plan? 37
Long-Range Planning 39
Textbook-Centered Units 39
Types of Planning for Social Studies Units 41
Expanded Textbook Units 41
Deciding on Unit Topics 43
Developing the Unit Plan 45
Instructional Objectives 46
Content Outlines and Flowcharts 46
Concept Webs 46
Moving Toward the Development of Activities 48
Unit Elements Format 49
Finding and Using Prepared Units 55
Planning for Shorter Instructional Sequences 56
Looking Back 63
Extension Activity 63
Reflective Questions 64
Helpful Resources 64
Further Reading 64
References 65

4 Assessment and Evaluation 66

Looking Ahead 66
Can You? Do You? 66
Focus Activity 66
The Role of Assessment in Social Studies 67
Principles of Assessment 68
Guidelines for Assessment 69
Authentic Assessment and Portfolios 71
Assessment through Tests 72
Assessing Projects and Reports 75
Subjective Assessment 75
Peer Assessment and Self-Assessment 76
Checklist and Rubric Assessment 76
Analytical Assessment 76
Teacher Observations and Anecdotal Records 78

Looking Back 79
Extension Activity 80
Reflective Questions 80
Helpful Resources 80
Further Reading 81
References 81

5 Reading and Writing in Social Studies 82

Looking Ahead 82
Can You? Do You? 82
Focus Activity 83
Every Teacher Is a Reading Teacher 83
Reading and Writing Assignments in Social Studies 83
Reading Skills Needed in Social Studies 84
Helping Students Read Social Studies Materials 85
Extended Teacher Definitions 89
Teacher-Provided Experiences 89
Student-Centered Experiences 89
Less Can Be More: Quality Reading in Social Studies 91
Reading Textbooks 93
Reading Questions and Task Statements 96
Reading Social Studies-Themed Trade Books 96
Connecting Writing to Both Social Studies and Reading 99
Organizing to Write 100
Developing Research and Reporting Skills 102
Writing Creatively 103
Classroom Episode #1 104
Looking Back 106
Extension Activity 106
Reflective Questions 107
Helpful Resources 107
Further Reading 107
References 108

6 Social Studies and Diverse Learners 109

Looking Ahead 109
Can You? Do You? 109
Focus Activity 110
Multiple Intelligences 110
Multicultural Directions in Social Studies 111
Social Studies and English Language Learners (ELLs) 112
Social Studies and Exceptional Education Students 114
Looking Back 116
Extension Activity 116
Reflective Questions 117
Helpful Resources 117

Further Reading 117
References 118

7 Thinking, Problem Solving, and the Acquisition of Skills 119

Looking Ahead 119
Can You? Do You? 119
Focus Activity 120
Thinking Skills 120
Logical Thinking and Analyzing Skills 121
Critical and Creative Thinking 122
Problem Solving and Inquiry 122
Promoting Critical Thinking with Modules 127
Promoting Inquiry with Case Studies 128
Incorporating Thinking and Learning Skills in Social Studies 129
Building the Desire to Master Study Skills 129
Finding Information 130
Historical Thinking 132
Maps and Globes 133
Using Maps 135
Mapping a School Activity 137
Charts, Graphs, and Maps 138
Economic Skills 139
Looking Back 140
Extension Activity 141
Reflective Questions 141
Helpful Resources 141
Further Reading 142
References 142

8 Cooperative Learning in Social Studies 143

Looking Ahead 143
Can You? Do You? 144
Focus Activity 144
Social Factors in Cooperative Learning Groups 144
Different Approaches to Grouping 145
Cooperative Learning, Collaborative Learning, and Curricular Goals 146
Organizing Cooperative and Collaborative Learning Groups 147
Student Roles in Cooperative Learning 150
"Minds-On" Learning Inquiry 151
Projects and Problem Centered Group Activities 152
Cooperative Centers 153
Cooperative Learning and Technology 154
Looking Back 157
Extension Activity 158
Reflective Questions 158
Helpful Resources 158

Further Reading 158
References 159

9 Experiencing Social Studies 160

Looking Ahead 160
Can You? Do You? 160
Focus Activity 161
The Importance of Drama in Social Studies 161
Drama through Reading 162
Dramatic Reading 166
Role Plays and Other Structured Drama Techniques 169
Art- and Story-Related Dramatic Techniques 171
Reenactment 172
Interactional Drama 173
Drama Units 174
Storytelling in Social Studies 174
Process Drama in Social Studies 175
Effective Use of Drama in Social Studies 175
Simulation Games 176
Mock Trials 185
Field Trips 186
Service Learning Experiences 189
Looking Back 189
Extension Activity 190
Reflective Questions 191
Helpful Resources 191
Further Reading 191
References 191

10 Issues-Centered Learning and Decision-Making 193

Looking Ahead 193
Can You? Do You? 194
Focus Activity 194
Issues-Centered Learning 194
Case Studies 197
Inquiry Learning 198
Decision-Making Skills in Relation to Values 203
What Values Do You Teach? 205
Developing Values 208
Character Development and Citizenship 212
Character and Values: A Worldview Perspective 212
Social Justice Issues, Decision-Making, and Values 212
Looking Back 213
Extension Activity 214
Reflective Questions 214
Helpful Resources 214

Further Reading 215
References 215

11 Technology and Media in Social Studies 217

Looking Ahead 217
Can You? Do You? 217
Focus Activity 218
Getting Started: Technology as a Productive Tool 218
Technology and Standards 219
Online and Virtual Teaching 220
Enhancing Instruction with the Internet 220
Teaching with Film 227
Social Media 230
Challenges to Technology Integration 230
Looking Back 232
Extension Activity 232
Reflective Questions 233
Helpful Resources 233
Further Reading 233
References 234

12 Lesson Plans for Secondary Social Studies 235

Looking Ahead 235
Can You? Do You? 236
Focus Activity 236
Economics 237
Geography 245
Notes/Additional Resources 253
Circle Your Assigned Topic 254
Psychology 255
Sociology 262
Notes/Additional Resources 268
World History 269
Notes/Additional Resources 274
U.S. Government 280
U.S. History 288
Notes/Additional Resources 291
Looking Back 295
Extension Activity 295
Reflective Questions 296
Helpful Resources 296
Further Reading 296

About the Authors 297
Index 298

Illustrations

Figures

3.1	Example of a Content Flowchart	47
3.2	Concept Web for a Unit on Native Americans	48
9.1	What Do We Need in the Neighborhood?	182
12.1	World History Lesson Plan One: Graphic Organizer	274

Tables

1.1	Annotated List of Professional Organizations for Secondary Social Studies Teachers	7
1.2	State/Local Social Studies Organizations	8
1.3	List of Professional Journals	9
1.4	Professional Conferences	10
2.1	Curricula for Grades 5 Through 12	18
2.2	Expanding Environments Model and Contemporary Curricula	18
2.3	Descriptions of NCSS's Ten Themes for Social Studies	20
2.4	Examples of Thematic Units for Each Grade Level	21
2.5	C3 Framework Organization (NCSS, 2013, p. 12)	23
3.1	Curriculum Map	40
3.2	Examples of Behavioral and Non-Behavioral Objectives	47
4.1	The Extent to Which the Tool Is Used in Student Assessment	69
4.2	Example: Checklist	77
4.3	Example: Rubric	77
4.4	Example: Observational Checklist	79
5.1	Frayer Model Version A	87
5.2	Frayer Model Version B	87
5.3	Frayer Model: Example of Version A Completed	87
5.4	Frayer Model: Example of Version B Completed	88
5.5	Classifying Chart: Example 1	88
5.6	Classifying Chart: Example 2	88
5.7	Example of a Diamonte	90
5.8	Example of a Descriptive Paragraph	90
5.9	Examples of Trade Books: Biography	97
5.10	Types of Fiction and Poetry Related to Social Studies	98
5.11	Examples of Trade Books: Fiction	99
5.12	Story Starter Examples	105
5.13	Collaborative Writing: Sample Topic Sentence Set	105

6.1 Gardner's Multiple Intelligences 110
7.1 Thinking Skills and Activities 121
7.2 Functions of the Mind 122
7.3 Successful Strategies for Approaching Difficult Problems 123
7.4 Sample Guidelines for Problem-Solving Activities 124
9.1 Types of Interactional Drama 173
9.2 Possible Field Trip Ideas 186
9.3 Possible Service Learning Ideas 190
12.1 Handout A 239
12.2 Budget Expenses 239
12.3 Economics Lesson Plan Two: Handout A 245
12.4 Geography Lesson Plan Two: Appendix C 255
12.5 Geography Lesson Plan Two: Appendix D 255

Preface

Welcome to *Essentials of Middle and Secondary Social Studies, Third Edition*. This book is intended for pre-service and in-service social studies teachers and for social studies teacher educators. The book is designed to accomplish one primary goal. We seek to help middle and secondary teachers develop the knowledge and skills necessary to effectively teach students to become effective problem-solving citizens. This text offers a problem-solving approach to social studies. Included in the text are various examples of lesson plans and effective teaching methodologies.

The text includes 12 chapters and each chapter includes a focus activity to prepare readers for the chapter content; a self-test, which can be used to assess the readers' understanding of the chapter content; an extension activity for extending the learning experience beyond the reading of the text; and a resources section that provides readers with a list of relevant readings for individuals interested in furthering the knowledge base.

This text contains discussions of relevant topics and strategies needed for effectively teaching middle and secondary social studies today, including the following:

- A chapter on lesson plans designed to provide teachers with 12 classroom-tested lesson plans. The chapter includes two classroom-tested lessons for each social science discipline.
- Each chapter includes a "Helpful Resources" section. The resources section provides various resources for further development.
- Each chapter includes an "Extension" activity. The extension activity provides readers with the opportunity to extend the learning experience with relevant and meaningful scenarios. Instructors can also use the extensions as a class activity.
- Each chapter includes a "Focus Activity". The focus activity provides readers with the opportunity to prepare for the learning experience with relevant and meaningful scenarios. Instructors can also use the focus activity as a class activity.

Thanks to the students, teachers, and professors that have provided valuable feedback through the development of this book. Additionally, the authors would like to thank our respective families and friends for support and encouragement.

William Russell
University of Central Florida

Stewart Waters
University of Tennessee

1 Becoming a Professional Social Studies Teacher

Looking Ahead

The purpose of this chapter is to help you understand what it means to be a professional social studies teacher and what is required. As you will read, becoming a professional social studies teacher takes dedication and commitment by the individual. This chapter will help you understand that teaching social studies is more than just lecturing in front of students. It will also help you understand what you can do to make the most of your profession. There is an entire field that many social studies teachers, unfortunately, never experience. A field filled with professional social studies teachers who care about the content and pedagogy and about making a difference in students' lives. The field of social studies is full of rich resources, journals, and conferences designed to help you become and remain an effective teacher and professional educator.

Can You? Do You?

Can you …

- name at least two professional journals for social studies teachers?
- describe the principles of your state's professional code of ethics?
- list at least two types of professional development?

Do you …

- know the principles of your state's professional code of conduct for educators?
- know the qualifications of a highly qualified teacher?
- know the names of two professional organizations for social studies teachers?

Focus Activity

Before reading this chapter, try the focus activity below.

Becoming a professional social studies teacher takes years of dedication and professional training. At this point, most of you have decided that you want to teach middle and/or high school social studies. Why? Write down the reasons why you decided to become a secondary social studies teacher. Remember there are no wrong answers. Share and discuss your reasons with classmates. Do you share similar reasons with peers?

DOI: 10.4324/9781003217060-1

Influences and Experiences

> **FYI**
>
> This phenomenon is known as the "apprenticeship of observation," meaning teachers often resort to teaching in the way that they were taught as students. Critical reflections about your experiences as a student, both good and bad, are vital to becoming a strong teacher and continuing professional growth.

Your experiences as a middle and secondary student influenced how you approach social studies and what you consider to be effective means of educating. Not only do your educational experiences impact your teaching, but so do your social, economic, and political experiences. No matter your beliefs and background, keeping an open mind toward the teaching of social studies is ideal. Throughout this book and throughout your career, you will learn new methods and strategies for engaging students. A willingness to change and to try new ideas is a necessity for the professional social studies teacher.

For many of you, the reasons you want to become a social studies teacher are tied directly to your life experiences. Many of you might have had a dynamic teacher who influenced you, and you want to have the same impact on students. Others might have had a negative experience as a student, and you want to make sure that does not happen to future students. Whatever the case, you have had influences and experiences throughout life that have made an impact on your career decision.

Unfortunately, not all students have had ideal experiences in middle and secondary classrooms. Many of you probably had a teacher who did not motivate you to learn and/or engage you in the learning experience. Reflect for a moment about all the teachers you had as a middle and secondary student. Now, pick three of the best teachers you ever had and three of the worst teachers you ever had. Compare the good teacher's qualities to the bad teacher's qualities. Are there any similarities? Differences? Are there common themes among the good teachers and among the bad teachers? What are they? In Box 1.1 you will find a list of teachers and their respective qualities.

Professional Certification, Conduct, and Ethics

Certification

According to the No Child Left Behind Act (NCLB) Act of 2001, all teachers must be highly qualified. A highly qualified teacher is a teacher with a college degree, teaching certificate, and

> **Box 1.1 Real Examples of Teachers and Their Respective Qualities**
>
> **Effective Teachers**
> Mrs. R.A. Teacher – Caring, passionate, encouraging, great lessons
> Mr. Stud – Energetic, motivating, engaging, awesome activities, authentic assessments
> Dr. Awesome – Brilliant, approachable, high expectations, real-life application
>
> **Ineffective Teachers**
> Dr. N.O. Clue – Unclear expectations, sexist, dry, not engaging, non-authentic assessment
> Mr. Hitler – Yelled a lot, no classroom management, boring
> Mrs. S.A. Tan – Lots of busy work, rude, seemed to hate students and her job, unprofessional

competence in a particular subject area. Measuring competence in a subject area is typically demonstrated by passing a standardized test in the subject area (e.g. Praxis or Florida Teacher Certification Examination). Requirements for becoming certified vary depending on the state in which you inhabit. Many states have reciprocity and allow you to carry your certification from one state to another. For more information on certification guidelines and policies specific to your state, contact your state department of education.

Professional Conduct

FYI

Remember that professional conduct extends to your online and/or social media presence. Teachers can and do lose their jobs for social media activity, so always approach these platforms with extreme caution.

Every teacher must adhere to a professional code of conduct. Typically, each state provides its teachers with a professional code of conduct for the state. A professional code of conduct is simply a list of principles/rules that a professional teacher must abide by. Failure to adhere to the code may often result in suspension/termination and/or loss of one's professional teaching certificate. In Box 1.2, you will find an example of the professional code of conduct from Florida. For more about your state's professional code of conduct for educators, contact your state department of education.

Ethics

There is a large variety of professional codes of ethics for teachers developed by state departments, unions, professional organizations, and other non-profits. Most professional codes of ethics incorporate the same core principles; these include the educator's relationship with the students, with colleagues, and with the community. In Box 1.3, you will find an example of the professional code of ethics from Florida. For more about your state's professional code of ethics for educators, contact your state department of education.

Box 1.2 6B-1.006 Principles of Professional Conduct for the Education Profession in Florida

1. The following disciplinary rule shall constitute the Principles of Professional Conduct for the Education Profession in Florida.
2. Violation of any of these principles shall subject the individual to revocation or suspension of the individual educator's certificate, or the other penalties as provided by law.
3. Obligation to the student requires that the individual:
   a. Shall make reasonable effort to protect the student from conditions harmful to learning and/or to the student's mental and/or physical health and/or safety.
   b. Shall not unreasonably restrain a student from independent action in pursuit of learning.
   c. Shall not unreasonably deny a student access to diverse points of view.
   d. Shall not intentionally suppress or distort subject matter relevant to a student's academic program.

e. Shall not intentionally expose a student to unnecessary embarrassment or disparagement.
f. Shall not intentionally violate or deny a student's legal rights.
g. Shall not harass or discriminate against any student on the basis of race, color, religion, sex, age, national or ethnic origin, political beliefs, marital status, handicapping condition, sexual orientation, or social and family background and shall make reasonable effort to assure that each student is protected from harassment or discrimination.
h. Shall not exploit a relationship with a student for personal gain or advantage.
i. Shall keep in confidence personally identifiable information obtained in the course of professional service, unless disclosure serves professional purposes or is required by law.

4. Obligation to the public requires that the individual:
   a. Shall take reasonable precautions to distinguish between personal views and those of any educational institution or organization with which the individual is affiliated.
   b. Shall not intentionally distort or misrepresent facts concerning an educational matter in direct or indirect public expression.
   c. Shall not use institutional privileges for personal gain or advantage.
   d. Shall accept no gratuity, gift, or favor that might influence professional judgment.
   e. Shall offer no gratuity, gift, or favor to obtain special advantages.
5. Obligation to the profession of education requires that the individual:
   a. Shall maintain honesty in all professional dealings.
   b. Shall not on the basis of race, color, religion, sex, age, national or ethnic origin, political beliefs, marital status, handicapping condition if otherwise qualified, or social and family background deny to a colleague professional benefits or advantages or participation in any professional organization.
   c. Shall not interfere with a colleague's exercise of political or civil rights and responsibilities.
   d. Shall not engage in harassment or discriminatory conduct which unreasonably interferes with an individual's performance of professional or work responsibilities or with the orderly processes of education or which creates a hostile, intimidating, abusive, offensive, or oppressive environment; and, further, shall make reasonable effort to assure that each individual is protected from such harassment or discrimination.
   e. Shall not make malicious or intentionally false statements about a colleague.
   f. Shall not use coercive means or promise special treatment to influence professional judgments of colleagues.
   g. Shall not misrepresent one's own professional qualifications.
   h. Shall not submit fraudulent information on any document in connection with professional activities.
   i. Shall not make any fraudulent statement or fail to disclose a material fact in one's own or another's application for a professional position.
   j. Shall not withhold information regarding a position from an applicant or misrepresent an assignment or conditions of employment.
   k. Shall provide upon the request of the certificated individual a written statement of specific reason for recommendations that lead to the denial of increments, significant changes in employment, or termination of employment.

l. Shall not assist entry into or continuance in the profession of any person known to be unqualified in accordance with these Principles of Professional Conduct for the Education Profession in Florida and other applicable Florida Statutes and State Board of Education Rules.
m. Shall self-report within forty-eight (48) hours to appropriate authorities (as determined by district) any arrests/charges involving the abuse of a child or the sale and/or possession of a controlled substance. Such notice shall not be considered an admission of guilt nor shall such notice be admissible for any purpose in any proceeding, civil or criminal, administrative or judicial, investigatory or adjudicatory. In addition, shall self-report any conviction, finding of guilt, withholding of adjudication, commitment to a pretrial diversion program, or entering of a plea of guilty or Nolo Contendre for any criminal offense other than a minor traffic violation within forty-eight (48) hours after the final judgment. When handling sealed and expunged records disclosed under this rule, school districts shall comply with the confidentiality provisions of Sections 943.0585(4)(c) and 943.059(4)(c), Florida Statutes.
n. Shall report to appropriate authorities any known allegation of a violation of the Florida School Code or State Board of Education Rules as defined in Section 1012.795(1), Florida Statutes.
o. Shall seek no reprisal against any individual who has reported any allegation of a violation of the Florida School Code or State Board of Education Rules as defined in Section1012.795(1), Florida Statutes.
p. Shall comply with the conditions of an order of the Education Practices Commission.
q. Shall, as the supervising administrator, cooperate with the Education Practices Commission in monitoring the probation of a subordinate.

Specific Authority 229.053(1), 231.546(2)(b) FS. Law Implemented 231.546(2), 231.28 FS. History – New 7-6-82, Amended 12-20-83, Formerly 6B-1.06, Amended 8-10-92, 12-29-98.

Box 1.3 6A-10.080 Code of Ethics of the Education Profession in Florida.

1. The educator values the worth and dignity of every person, the pursuit of truth, devotion to excellence, acquisition of knowledge, and the nurture of democratic citizenship. Essential to the achievement of these standards are the freedom to learn and to teach and the guarantee of equal opportunity for all.
2. The educator's primary professional concern will always be for the student and for the development of the student's potential. The educator will therefore strive for professional growth and will seek to exercise the best professional judgment and integrity.
3. Aware of the importance of maintaining the respect and confidence of one's colleagues, of students, of parents, and of other members of the community, the educator strives to achieve and sustain the highest degree of ethical conduct.

Rulemaking Authority 1001.02, 1012.51, 1012.53 FS. Law Implemented 1012.32, 1012.34, 1012.51, 1012.53, 1012.795, 1012.796 FS. History-New 3-24-65, Amended 8-9-69, Repromulgated 12-5-74, Amended 8-12-81, 7-6-82, Formerly 6B-1.01, 6B-1.001.

Professional Organizations

> **FYI**
>
> Membership in professional organizations dedicated to the advocacy of social studies education is crucial for social studies educators in order to fight against marginalization of the field on the state and national levels.

As a professional social studies teacher, the best way to stay current in the field of social studies education is to become an active member of a professional social studies organization. Actively participating in professional social studies organizations allows you to network with other teachers; obtain valuable teaching ideas and content knowledge via publications and conferences; and promote social studies education and its importance to students, teachers, parents, principals, superintendents, politicians, etc. There are a number of professional organizations that are valuable to secondary social studies teachers. See Table 1.1 for an annotated list.

Each state also has a professional social studies organization that is affiliated with the National Council for the Social Studies. See Table 1.2 for a list of state social studies organizations and web addresses.

Professional Development

> **FYI**
>
> Most states require a certain number of professional development hours to maintain an active teacher license. Consult with your district- and state-level board of education in order to make sure you meet the expectations to maintain or renew your professional licensure.

Professional development is a common aspect of being a professional social studies teacher. Professional development is required by most certification boards to maintain professional certification. Professional development comes in many forms, such as college/university classes, online seminars and training, in-service training, professional journals, and professional conferences. Many of the organizations mentioned above provide various types of professional development opportunities for classroom teachers. However, some of the most common professional development comes in the form of professional journals and conferences. As a professional educator, reading professional social studies journals and attending and/or presenting at professional conferences are great ways to stay abreast of contemporary social studies.

Professional Journals

There are a number of journals devoted to social studies and middle/secondary education. As a teacher, subscribing to all of them might not be practical. However, many of the journals are included with membership to their sponsoring organization. Many school/district libraries also subscribe to journals. See Table 1.3 for an annotated list of journals that secondary social studies teachers will find useful.

The journals listed in Table 1.3 are not a comprehensive list but will serve as a great starting point. Teachers should also check with local/state social studies organizations, for many have journals that are not included on this list.

Table 1.1 Annotated List of Professional Organizations for Secondary Social Studies Teachers

The Association for Middle Level Education (www.amle.org)	Since its inception in 1973, the Association for Middle Level Education (AMLE), formerly the National Middle School Association, has been a voice for those committed to the educational and developmental needs of young adolescents. AMLE is the only national education association dedicated exclusively to those in the middle grades. With more than 30,000 members representing principals, teachers, central office personnel, professors, college students, parents, community leaders, and educational consultants across the United States, Canada, and 46 other countries, AMLE welcomes and provides support to anyone interested in the health and education of young adolescents.
The Council for Economic Education (www.councilforeconed.org)	The Council for Economic Education (CEE) is the leading organization in the United States that focuses on the economic and financial education of students from kindergarten through high school. For the past 60 years, its mission has been to instill in young people the fourth "R"—a real-world understanding of economics and personal finance. It is only by acquiring economic and financial literacy that children can learn that there are better options for a life well lived, will be able to see opportunity on their horizon line and, ultimately, can grow into successful and productive adults capable of making informed and responsible decisions.
The International Society for the Social Studies (www.TheISSS.org)	The International Society for the Social Studies (ISSS) is a non-profit, professional society devoted to the social studies. ISSS is an international interdisciplinary society for individuals striving to promote and enhance the importance of social studies education across the world. Its members include both U.S. and international teachers, professors, students, scholars, and others who support social studies education across the globe.
The National Council for Geographic Education (www.ncge.org)	The National Council for Geographic Education (NCGE) is a non-profit organization, chartered in 1915 to enhance the status and quality of geography teaching and learning. NCGE supports geography teaching at all levels—from kindergarten through university. Its members include both U.S. and international teachers, professors, students, businesses, and others who support geographic education.
The National Council for History Education (www.nche.net)	More than 20 years ago, the National Council for History Education was founded to bring together historians, teachers, education specialists, university faculty, community leaders, museums, archives, libraries, and historical societies to ensure not only that history was being taught in our schools, but that excellence of instruction and learning occurred. The National Council for History Education builds bridges between K–12 teachers, college and university faculty, and museums/libraries/historical societies who all share a common passion for teaching history.
The National Council for the Social Studies (www.ncss.org)	Founded in 1921, the National Council for the Social Studies (NCSS) has grown to be the largest association in the country devoted solely to social studies education. NCSS engages and supports educators in strengthening and advocating social studies. With members in all the 50 states, the District of Columbia, and 69 foreign countries, NCSS serves as an umbrella organization for elementary, secondary, and college teachers of history, civics, geography, economics, political science, sociology, psychology, anthropology, and law-related education.

Organizations are listed alphabetically.

Table 1.2 State/Local Social Studies Organizations

Alabama Council for the Social Studies	http://alsocialstudies.org
Alaska Council for the Social Studies	www.akcss.org
Arizona Council for the Social Studies	www.azsocialstudies.org/
Arkansas Council for the Social Studies	www.arsocialstudies.org
California Council for the Social Studies	www.ccss.org/
Colorado Council for the Social Studies	http://cosocialstudies.org/
Connecticut Council for the Social Studies	www.ctsocialstudies.org/
Delaware Council for the Social Studies	http://dcss.edublogs.org/
Florida Council for the Social Studies	www.fcss.org/
Georgia Council for the Social Studies	www.gcss.net/
Great Lakes Regional Council for the Social Studies	www.wiu.edu/users/mffci/
Illinois Council for the Social Studies	www.illinoiscss.org/
Indiana Council for the Social Studies	http://indianacouncilforthesocialstudies.shuttlepod.org/
Iowa Council for the Social Studies	www.uni.edu/icss/
Kansas Council for the Social Studies	www.kcss.info/
Kentucky Council for the Social Studies	www.kcss.org/content/
Louisiana Council for the Social Studies	http://lcss1812.org/
Maine Council for the Social Studies	www.memun.org/MCSS/
Maryland Council for the Social Studies	www.mdcss.org/
Massachusetts Council for the Social Studies	www.masscouncil.org/
Michigan Council for the Social Studies	www.mcssmi.org/
Minnesota Council for the Social Studies	www.mcss.org/
Mississippi Council for the Social Studies	www.mcss.org.msstate.edu/
Missouri Council for the Social Studies	www.mosocialstudies.com/
Nebraska Council for the Social Studies	www.nebraskasocialstudies.org/
Northern Nevada Council for the Social Studies	www.nvsocialstudies.org/
Southern Nevada Council for the Social Studies	http://sites.google.com/site/sncssweb/home
New Hampshire Council for the Social Studies	www.nhcss.org/nhcss/default.cfm
New Jersey Council for the Social Studies	www.njcss.org/index.php
New Mexico Council for the Social Studies	www.unm.edu/~nmcss/
New York State Council for the Social Studies	www.nyscss.org/
North Carolina Council for the Social Studies	http://ncsocialstudies.org/
Ohio Council for the Social Studies	http://ocss.wordpress.com/
Oklahoma Council for the Social Studies	www.okcss.org/
Oregon Council for the Social Studies	www.oregonsocialstudies.org/
Pennsylvania Council for the Social Studies	http://pcssonline.org/
South Carolina Council for the Social Studies	www.sccss.org/
South Dakota Council for the Social Studies	www.southdakotasocialstudies.net/
Tennessee Council for the Social Studies	www.tncss.org/
Texas Council for the Social Studies	http://txcss.org/
Utah Council for the Social Studies	www.ucssblog.com/
Vermont Council for the Social Studies	http://vermontsocialstudies.org/
Virginia Council for the Social Studies	www.vcss.org/
Washington Council for the Social Studies	www.wscss.org/
West Virginia Council for the Social Studies	http://wvcss.edublogs.org/
Wisconsin Council for the Social Studies	www.wcss-wi.org/

Organizations are listed alphabetically.

Professional Conferences

FYI

Not only is presenting and attending professional conferences great for your growth and development as a teacher, but many schools/districts also will count these experiences as professional development hours toward your licensure renewal. Check with your local administrators for details.

Table 1.3 List of Professional Journals

The Clearing House: A Journal of Educational Strategies, Issues, and Ideas (www.tandfonline.com/VTCH)	*The Clearing House* offers informative, practical articles on teaching and administration in middle schools and junior and senior high schools. In peer-reviewed articles, educators report their successes in teaching as well as present articles on administrative procedures, school programs, and teacher education for the secondary level.
The Geography Teacher (www.NCGE.org)	*The Geography Teacher* provides a forum for educators and scholars to present innovative teaching strategies and essential content for K–12 geography, AP Human Geography, introductory college geography, and pre-service methods classrooms and courses. It also offers a forum for discussion of state, national, and international trends in geography education.
The History Teacher (www.societyforhistoryeducation.org)	*The History Teacher* is the most widely recognized journal in the United States devoted to the teaching of history. Published quarterly (released in November, February, May, and August), it features informative and inspirational peer-reviewed analyses of traditional and innovative teaching techniques in the primary, secondary, and higher education classroom.
The Journal of Social Studies Research (www.TheISSS.org)	*The Journal of Social Studies Research* (JSSR) is an internationally recognized peer-reviewed journal designed to foster the dissemination of ideas and research findings related to the social studies. JSSR is the official publication of the International Society for the Social Studies (ISSS) and is one of the most widely read journals in the field. JSSR is published four times a year: Winter, Spring, Summer, and Fall.
Middle Ground (www.AMLE.org)	*Middle Ground* magazine is the practitioners' magazine of the Association for Middle Level Education. It provides a voice and a resource for those committed to the educational and developmental needs of young adolescents. The magazine's readership includes more than 22,000 principals, teachers, central office personnel, professors, college students, parents, community leaders, and educational consultants across the United States and internationally.
Middle Level Learning (www.NCSS.org)	*Middle Level Learning* brings together lesson ideas and theoretical content focused on social studies in the middle grades. MLL is published online three times a year: September, January/February, and May/June.
Middle School Journal (www.AMLE.org)	*Middle School Journal*, a refereed journal, is an official publication and membership benefit of the Association for Middle Level Education (AMLE). Published five times per year in September, November, January, March, and May, the journal offers articles that promote quality middle-level education and contribute to an understanding of the educational and developmental needs of youth between the ages of 10 and 15.
Social Education (www.NCSS.org)	*Social Education* contains a balance of theoretical content and practical teaching ideas. The award-winning resources include techniques for using materials in the classroom, information on the latest instructional technology, reviews of educational media, research on significant social studies-related topics, and lesson plans that can be applied to various disciplines. Departments include Looking at the Law, Surfing the Net, and Teaching with Documents. Social Education is published six times per year: September, October, November/December, January/February, March/April, and May/June.
The Social Studies (www.tandfonline.com/VTSS)	*The Social Studies* is a peer-reviewed journal that publishes articles of interest to educators at all levels. Suitable topics include those concerned with the social studies, the social sciences, history, and interdisciplinary studies. The journal welcomes articles that present new directions, options, or approaches.

Journals are listed alphabetically.

Table 1.4 Professional Conferences

The Association for Middle Level Education Annual Conference (www.amle.org)	The Association for Middle Level Education holds an annual conference. Every year the conference is located in a different region. The annual conference is an excellent professional development opportunity for middle level educators.
The Council for Economic Education National Conference (www.councilforeconed.org)	The Council for Economic Education (CEE) hosts a national conference every year in a different location. The annual conference is an excellent professional development opportunity for middle and secondary teachers interested in economic education.
The International Society for the Social Studies Annual Conference (www.TheISSS.org)	The International Society for the Social Studies (ISSS) Annual Conference is located in Orlando, FL every February/March. The conference is an excellent professional development opportunity for middle and secondary social studies teachers.
The National Council for Geographic Education Annual Conference (www.ncge.org)	The National Council for Geographic Education (NCGE) hosts a conference every year in a different location. The annual conference is an excellent professional development opportunity for middle and secondary teachers interested in geographic education.
The National Council for History Education National Conference (www.nche.net)	The National Council for History Education hosts a national conference every year in a different location. The annual conference is an excellent professional development opportunity for middle and secondary teachers interested in history education.
The National Council for the Social Studies Annual Conference (www.ncss.org)	The National Council for the Social Studies hosts a conference every year in a different location. Every five years, the conference is held in Washington, DC. The annual conference is an excellent professional development opportunity for social studies teachers.

Conferences are listed alphabetically.

There are a number of professional conferences that social studies teachers should attend. As a teacher, attending all of them is not practical. However, conferences are professional development opportunities that allow teachers to obtain new teaching ideas and information as well as network and share ideas. Many of the professional organizations discussed previously host professional conferences. See Table 1.4 for a list of conferences useful to professional social studies teachers.

The professional conferences listed in Table 1.4 are not a comprehensive list, but will serve as a great starting point. Teachers should also check with local/state social studies organizations, for many have annual conferences.

Looking Back

Becoming a professional social studies teacher takes commitment and dedication. As you embark on your teaching career, always remember why you became a teacher. Continuously reflect to ensure that you are still teaching for the betterment of the students.

Be aware of and follow a professional code of conduct and a professional code of ethics for the state in which you live. Furthermore, become an active member of a professional organization/s. Also, stay abreast of current trends and effective teaching strategies using professional journals. These professional development opportunities along with professional conferences will help you continue to grow as a qualified social studies teacher.

Extension Activity

Scenario

You are in the process of applying for a few social studies teaching positions in YourTown School District. As you examine the various job openings, you notice that all of the applications require a personal goals statement. As you begin to draft your personal goals statement, you realize that your letter could be the difference between getting an interview or not.

Task

For this activity, draft a personal goals statement. Be sure to detail what it means to be a professional social studies teacher and your professional goals.

Reflective Questions

1. What is a highly qualified teacher?
2. What are the names of two professional journals for social studies teachers?
3. What are the names of two professional organizations for social studies teachers?
4. Can you name two types of professional development?

Helpful Resources

Visit the National Council for the Social Studies website for up-to-date information on conferences and developments in the field.
www.socialstudies.org

Visit the following site to read the National Council for the Social Studies Revised Position Statement on Ethics.
www.socialstudies.org/position/ethics

Watch the video below of a group of classroom teachers working together to develop a professional learning action plan to improve performance.
www.teachingchannel.org/videos/professional-learning-action-plan

Further Reading

American Federation of Teachers www.aft.org
The American Federation of Teachers is a union of professionals that champions fairness; democracy; economic opportunity; and high-quality public education, healthcare, and public services for our students, their families, and our communities. This website will provide readers with a great deal of information that they may determine to be valuable and important throughout their professional social studies career.

National Education Association www.nea.org
The National Education Association (NEA), the nation's largest professional employee organization, is committed to advancing the cause of public education. NEA's three million members work at every level of education—from preschool to university graduate programs. The NEA has affiliate organizations in every state and in more than 14,000 communities across the U.S. Being familiar with the NEA and its beliefs and practices could be beneficial for professional social studies teachers.

Strike, K.A. & Soltis, J.F. (2009). *The Ethics of Teaching* (5th Edition). New York, NY: Teachers College Press.
This book is a great resource for both new and seasoned teachers. The book is written directly for teachers and addresses pertinent issues for today's teachers. The book uses realistic case studies of ethical dilemmas to examine topics such as multiculturalism, religious differences, and professional conduct.

Wong, H.K. & Wong, T.R. (2005). *The First Days of School.* Mount View, CA: Harry K. Wong Publications.
This book is written for pre-service teachers wanting to become effective professional educators. The book details what it means to be an effective teacher and professional. It covers topics such as classroom management, ethics, and effective planning.

References

Florida Department of Education. (1982). Code of Ethics of the Education Profession in Florida. Available at: www.fldoe.org/edstandards/code_of_ethics.asp.

Florida Department of Education. (1998). Principles of Professional Conduct for the Education Profession in Florida. Available at: www.fldoe.org/edstandards/code_of_ethics.asp.

United States Department of Education. (2001). No Child Left Behind. Available at: www2.ed.gov/nclb/landing.jhtml.

2 Contemporary Social Studies

Looking Ahead

The purpose of this chapter is (1) to help you understand the concept of social studies, its purpose, and what it includes; (2) to see why social studies is needed in school; and (3) to suggest an overall approach to social studies curriculum and the teaching of the curriculum. To achieve these goals, you need to understand what social studies is and how it springs out of a need in society.

To understand social studies, you must first understand the purpose that it serves in the total school curriculum. That purpose, stated in simple form, is to develop good citizens for the democratic society in which we live. Becoming a good citizen is sometimes referred to as developing civic virtue, and there is, of course, a wide interpretation of exactly what either term really means. Even so, we can say that we want students to feel positive about themselves and have a desire to be positively contributing members of the various communities of which they are a part. It also means that students will develop the desire and the ability to be economically independent, to be informed about and involved in the decision-making that goes on in their communities, and to be aware of and knowledgeable about the world around them. We want students to be free from prejudice and to be fair minded in dealing with others, to believe in a system of justice and law, to take leadership roles, and to give reasoned and fair support for legitimately appointed or elected leaders.

FYI

"Decision making is the heart of social studies instruction." Shirley Engle, 1960.

Since society is changing rapidly, teaching social studies is even more of a challenge today than it was in the past. Teachers really need to think about different approaches to teaching social studies. They need to work more effectively with students who have different cultural backgrounds. They need to teach in ways that involve active learning and to find approaches that focus on solving problems. The final section of this chapter addresses the goals of social studies as perceived by different groups. Social studies itself is a product of the changing society, prevailing approaches to its teaching, and the varying conceptions that social studies teachers have of its goals.

Recognizing that social studies has a strong knowledge base, we will also look at the social science disciplines. These disciplines all examine the world from a different perspective, with different emphases and foci, often using different scholarly tools. The social scientists working in these disciplines provide the scholarship, methods, concepts, and information that are the basis for social studies curriculum in schools. The better we understand them and their relationship to one another, the better we can utilize and select from what they have to offer.

DOI: 10.4324/9781003217060-2

Can You? Do You?

Can you ...

- identify reasons why there is controversy in social studies?
- identify and explain the various social science disciplines?
- explain the goals of social studies?

Do you ...

- know all the social science fields that are included in social studies?
- have an understanding of a problems approach to teaching social studies?
- think of social studies simply as history and/or geography?

Focus Activity

Before reading this chapter, try the focus activity below.

Take a scrap piece of paper and draw a picture of social studies. Be sure to use images and not words. Share drawings with classmates. Discuss the details of the drawings. Compare drawings for substance with classmates. Does your drawing share common themes/elements with classmates? If so, what are the themes/elements?

The Goals of Social Studies

What is social studies? What is the purpose of social studies? Like many questions, the answers are not always clear or simple. Within the field of social studies the questions are not the issue, but instead it is the answers to the questions that are the issue. These two questions or the answers to these two questions have contributed to social studies literature and its identity or lack of one. Social studies is a unique field. It is a field that has been searching for a clear and cohesive identity. The search for this cohesive identity has been challenged by the various definitions and rationales for social studies.

What is social studies? The National Council for the Social Studies (NCSS) defines the social studies as:

> the integrated study of the social sciences and humanities to promote civic competence. Within the school program, social studies provides coordinated, systematic study drawing upon such disciplines as anthropology, archaeology, economics, geography, history, law, philosophy, political science, psychology, religion, and sociology, as well as appropriate content from the humanities, mathematics, and natural sciences.
>
> (NCSS, 2010)

What is the purpose of social studies? The NCSS states that "the primary purpose of social studies is to help young people develop the ability to make informed and reasoned decisions for the public good as citizens of a culturally diverse, democratic society in an interdependent world" (NCSS, 2010).

Although the National Council for the Social Studies' definition and purpose statements are the most commonly used and accepted, there are alternative definitions and purpose statements that are common to many of the critical areas of social studies. Throughout the history of social studies numerous scholars have provided differing definitions of social studies and statements regarding the purpose and approach of social studies.

Barth (1993) has said that one of our most basic beliefs is that "Social Studies is citizenship education." Hartoonan (1993) has added that "our work should be to illuminate the essential connection between social studies learning and democratic values" and thus be a "liberating force in the lives of citizens." Put another way, the two primary jobs of schools are to help the society by producing effective, contributing citizens and to help the students lead happy lives in which they are enabled to achieve their potential. That is what social studies is all about and why social studies is so needed in school.

Though social studies educators disagree as to priorities, the following list identifies those purposes that are most often associated with social studies programs:

- Preparing responsible citizens for the nation, the state, and the local area
- Preparing students to have the knowledge and skills in social studies needed for college
- Developing awareness and understanding of contemporary social issues
- Developing healthy self-concepts
- Teaching the methods of social scientists
- Motivating students to want to learn about the social studies
- Developing the ability to solve problems and make decisions
- Developing culturally responsive "global" citizens.

FYI

Democratic decision-making is considered a foundation of the C3 Framework.

Whatever we do as teachers is certainly done for the present, but it has to be done with an eye to the future. In trying to help you become an effective social studies teacher, it is important for you to consider what happens if you succeed as a teacher. The students you teach will, in due course, become adults themselves. They will obviously be living in a different kind of society, one that you must try to anticipate and prepare them for. However, beyond that, the kind of impact that you will have on students and the kind of people they become are critical outcomes of education. The following are just a few of the areas where you, as a middle or secondary social studies teacher, will have an impact when your students become adults:

- The jobs they have and the way they do their jobs
- The way they feel about themselves
- The way they handle responsibility
- The way they treat other people
- How they meet and resolve problems and difficulties
- Their motivation and overall attitudes
- What they value and how they treat the things they value
- How they relate to their heritage
- How they relate to their environment
- How they relate to and deal with people of other cultures, nationalities, and ethnic groups.

In each of these and in other areas where teachers influence students, it is safe to say that most of us would happily accept a broad variety of outcomes and still feel that we had made a positive impact in a student's life. The question is, "just how much in each area can we expect of ourselves?"

That is not a question that can be left unanswered. A good analogy is putting together a jigsaw puzzle. It is always easier to do a puzzle with a picture of what it is going to look like when put together. The same holds true for teaching. From an attitudinal standpoint, it is useful to envision students five to ten years into the future and imagine them in the most positive light.

Why Is There Controversy in Social Studies?

Social studies has been, and will continue to be, constantly under attack by critics. The content taught in social studies is constantly being examined. The root reason for this is that learning social studies is a lot more complex than developing an ability or skill such as reading and mathematics. It is almost without boundaries or borders. With this richly varied array of curricula, which may at times be contradictory, there are factors that contribute to the controversial nature of social studies. Those factors include:

- Anything that human effort produces is, by definition, imperfect. Before we even get a curriculum together, we and others begin to see the flaws and problems. When we put something into use, those flaws become glaringly apparent to us.
- Cultural change is constant. We live in an era of immense societal complexity and rapid change. As soon as we develop a program, changes occur that require adjustments. Social studies curricula are responsive to changes in the social climate. Changes in emphasis are likely to reflect the times. Wars, depressions, periods of prosperity, international relationships, and a host of other things that influence the public climate impact social studies.

FYI

Remember to always be cautious, purposeful, and thorough whenever addressing any controversial content in the classroom.

- People have differing values, priorities, and viewpoints. Social studies is not just a skill subject. In a democratic society, there is little likelihood of long-term consensus and none at all of universal agreement on what ought to be taught and from what viewpoint.
- Special-interest groups influence curriculum. In our society, there are pressure groups with their own agendas and expectations. They want to influence or even control what is being taught in the schools.
- Social studies represents an enormous changing body of knowledge. Social studies curriculum simply defies coverage or even adequate sampling. We can never have enough depth or breadth.

Goals and objectives should be the first and most important concerns of a social studies teacher. They complement one another. Goals are distant, immeasurable, and even unattainable. They give direction to our efforts and, if we are goal-oriented and goal-driven, we constantly work toward them yet never reach a point when they are achieved. How can one reach the goal of becoming an effective problem solver, for example, or the even broader goal of being a good citizen? The essence of goals is that they describe the person we are constantly in the process of becoming (Moore et al., 1989).

Objectives, however, are short term, attainable, often measurable, and very specific. We can know when we achieve them, so they become for us milestones and markers of our progress. Goals determine the directions we want to go, but the accomplishment of objectives lets us know that we are getting there.

In education, we generally begin planning by defining our goals. Once goals are set, we try to describe the specific teaching and learning outcomes (objectives) for short periods of instruction that will move students toward the goals. Goals without objectives remain as only dreams. Objectives without relationship to goals are purposeless. Objectives for social studies tend to be decided on the basis of the specific content being taught and the group to which it is being taught. The broadest goals for the field have been centrally determined and defined in the U.S. by various groups, given authority by still larger organizations. Regardless of the group, throughout this century and the next, social studies has been, and will be, invariably linked to goals of citizenship education. The frameworks developed in the reports of the various commissions, task forces, and committees have served as models for textbook curricula and for those developed for state and local school districts. Reports impacting school social studies in the twenty-first century include the NCSS Task Force on Creating Effective Citizens (2001) and the Task Force of the National Commission on the Social Studies (1989).

The introductory statement of the goals section of the report of the NCSS Task Force on Creating Effective Citizens (2001) set a problem-solving focus for the social studies and emphasized thinking skills. The Task Force stated the students should have the skills necessary to "solve real problems in their school, the community, our nation, and the world." Additionally, effective citizens should use "effective decision-making and problem-solving skills in public and private life." The responsibility of social studies is to prepare young people to identify, understand, and work to solve problems in an interdependent world.

The Task Force of the National Commission on the Social Studies was funded by the Carnegie Foundation, the Rockefeller Foundation, the MacArthur Foundation, and the National Geographic Society. It enjoyed the sponsorship of the NCSS and the American Historical Association. Over two years in preparation, the Task Force's report, titled *Charting a Course: Social Studies for the 21st Century* (1989), formulated the following goals that the social studies curriculum should enable students to develop:

1 Civic responsibility and active civic participation
2 Perspectives on their own life experiences so they see themselves as part of the larger human adventure in time and place
3 A critical understanding of the history, geography, economics, politics, social institutions, traditions, and values of the United States as expressed in both their unity and diversity
4 An understanding of other peoples and of the unity and diversity of world history, geography, institutions, traditions, and values
5 Critical attitudes and analytical perspectives appropriate to analysis of the human condition.

Social Studies Curriculum

The term *social studies* is, to a great extent, a product of the twentieth century. It was officially adopted as the name for the curricular area in 1916 by the Committee on Social Studies, a subgroup of the Commission to Reorganize Secondary Education, which had been set up by the National Education Association. The committee reported the conclusions in the *1916 Report*, which outlined the good citizenship concept and also recommended the curricula for Grades 5 through 12 (see Table 2.1).

In the late 1930s, Paul Hanna proposed a sequence of instructional topics that was to revolutionize social studies. This framework, known as the Expanding Communities Model or Expanding Environments curriculum, was based on a theory that students' ability to understand their world

Table 2.1 Curricula for Grades 5 Through 12

Grade 5	American History
Grade 6	World History (Western Civilization)
Grade 7	Geography/European History
Grade 8	American History
Grade 9	Civics
Grade 10	European History
Grade 11	American History
Grade 12	Problems of Democracy (Economics/Politics/Social)

Table 2.2 Expanding Environments Model and Contemporary Curricula

Grade	*Expanding Environments Model*	*Contemporary Curricula*
6th	The World (Western Civilization)	World Cultures
The Western Hemisphere		
7th	World Geography	World Geography
8th	History of the United States	American History

progresses through a series of developmental stages and that social studies programs should be structured to coincide with those stages (Hanna, 1957, 1963). The progression began with a study of the students themselves and their homes and families and moved through increasingly larger communities that were more remote and abstract to students' thinking.

In spite of all the pressure for change, the Expanding Environments concept has been the major influence on social studies curriculum for over 50 years. Grades 6 through 8 of the Hanna model are shown in Table 2.2. Alongside each grade level is shown the dominant pattern of curriculum organization currently used in textbook and school curricula.

The beauty of the Expanding Environments model was its logic. It made sense to a lot of people both from the standpoint of its reflection of a reasonable pattern of child development and as a logical way to organize social studies curriculum. Hanna's model was developed at a fortunate time in many ways. The social climate of the nation was ideal, with America coming through a depression and a world war from which it emerged as the leading power in the free world. Technology and communication as well as the economic conditions were also right. Hanna's model was soon adopted by many school systems and by textbook publishers. It is, to this day, the most common model used in schools in the U.S.

From the 1960s to the 1970s a spirit of reform known as the New Social Studies gripped the social studies (Fitchett & Russell, 2011; Byford & Russell, 2007). It manifested itself in a series of well-warranted criticisms of the Expanding Environment curriculum as it was by then represented in textbook series and school curricula across the country and in the development of new curricula, many of which were closely tied to the various social science disciplines. Critics pointed out that social studies teachers relied too heavily on textbooks and that there was too much memorization of facts. But there was major curricular criticism as well. Critics charged that social studies lacked sufficient substantive content; that African Americans, Hispanic Americans, women, and other groups were insufficiently represented, stereotypically represented, or misrepresented; and that significant issues and content topics of controversy were avoided. The New Social Studies movement was spurred in part by federal funding and in part by the social consciousness and concerns of the period. The lasting changes injected into social studies by these reform efforts during this era included:

- A greater sensitivity to the representation of various ethnic groups and women in social studies material
- Focus on inquiry and values

- Greater global consciousness
- Focus on social sciences other than history and geography as sources of insight and methods of inquiry about the world
- Greater awareness of and ability to deal with controversy in the social studies classroom
- An emphasis on learning concepts and generalizations rather than isolated facts.

Efforts to set the direction for social studies have reaffirmed the importance of history and geography. Perhaps the most prestigious of the groups to examine the future of social studies have been two curriculum task forces. The first of these was the Curriculum Task Force of the National Commission on the Social Studies in the Schools, which published a report, *Charting a Course: Social Studies for the 21st Century*. The task force outlined the following characteristics of content in the social studies:

> History and geography should be the unifying core of the social studies curriculum and should be integrated with concepts from economics, political science, and other social sciences.
>
> Social studies should be taught and learned consistently and cumulatively from kindergarten through grade 12.
>
> The curriculum should impart skills and knowledge necessary for effective citizenship in a democracy.
>
> The curriculum should balance study of the United States with studies of other cultures.
>
> Superficial coverage of content should be replaced with in-depth study of selected topics.
>
> (NCSS, 1989)

The task force envisioned three courses being taught in Grades 4, 5, and 6, including, in no specified order, (1) United States history, (2) world history, and (3) geography. In Grade 7 the task force called for the study of the local community, along with state history and geography. American history would be taught in Grade 8, followed by world and American history and geography to 1750 in Grade 9. Grade 10 would continue with world and American history and geography from 1750 to 1900. Grade 11 would culminate the study of world and American history and geography. Grade 12 would include the study of government and economics (1989).

The second group, set up by the National Council for the Social Studies, was called the Task Force on Standards for the Social Studies. It worked over a period of three years before coming out with its original report in 1994, *Expectations of Excellence: Curriculum Standards for Social Studies*. This report established ten themes for social studies and was intended to influence and guide curriculum design and overall student expectations for Grades K–12. In 2010, the task force released a revised and updated report titled, *National Curriculum Standards for Social Studies: A Framework for Teaching, Learning, and Assessment*. The updated report provides a description of the ten basic themes for social studies (see Table 2.3).

Incorporating Themes from the Standards

The focus themes identified by the standards task force, to some extent, are taken from the social science disciplines and represent their essential lines of inquiry. Following a kind of candlewick principle, these themes can run through topics of study and across grade levels, drawing essential content and skill development to themselves.

FYI

Inquiry is considered a foundation of the C3 Framework.

Table 2.3 Descriptions of NCSS's Ten Themes for Social Studies

1. Culture	Social studies programs should include experiences that provide for the study of culture and cultural diversity.
2. Time, Continuity, and Change	Social studies programs should include experiences that provide for the study of the past and its legacy.
3. People, Places, and Environments	Social studies programs should include experiences that provide for the study of people, places, and environments.
4. Individual Development and Identity	Social studies programs should include experiences that provide for the study of individual development and identity.
5. Individuals, Groups, and Institutions	Social studies programs should include experiences that provide for the study of interactions among individuals, groups, and institutions.
6. Power, Authority, and Governance	Social studies programs should include experiences that provide for the study of how people create, interact with, and change structures of power, authority, and governance.
7. Production, Distribution, and Consumption	Social studies programs should include experiences that provide for the study of how people organize for the production, distribution, and consumption of goods and services.
8. Science, Technology, and Society	Social studies programs should include experiences that provide for the study of relationships among science, technology, and society.
9. Global Connections	Social studies programs should include experiences that provide for the study of global connections and interdependence.
10. Civic Ideals and Practices	Social studies programs should include experiences that provide for the study of the ideals, principles, and practices of citizenship in a democratic republic.

Thematic units represent one approach to implementing the standards. Such units are integrally related to literature-based programs and unify the content of social studies with other curricular areas. In non-graded settings, thematic units can be part of an internal structure.

Examples of thematic unit topics at each grade level are detailed in Table 2.4. The list is not presented as a sequential model curriculum and certainly will not precisely reflect any particular school or textbook curricular program. These unit topics are presented to give an idea of topics that might be taught, suggest connections to the standards and to a specific discipline, and illustrate the notion of thematic threads.

Social Studies and the Common Core

When discussing standards in education during the era of accountability, certainly one of the most popular and emerging topics revolves around the Common Core Standards (www.corestandards.org). These standards represent a state-led effort coordinated by the National Governors Association Center for Best Practices (NGA Center) and the Council of Chief State School Officers (CCSSO) to provide a list of standards for K–12 schools in order to help students prepare for college and the workforce (Kenna & Russell, 2014). The standards were developed by a variety of contributors, including teachers, administrators, and other content specialists, and informed by all of the current state standards of education as well as standards from other top-performing countries around the world. One of the primary purposes behind the Common Core Standards is to help provide a more clear and consistent set of expectations for student learning at each grade level across the United States. Attempting to clarify and identify high-achieving expectations for student learning across the states has become increasingly important because not all states go through the same process of adopting state standards and, thus, what states deem important for academic and personal growth can vary greatly.

Table 2.4 Examples of Thematic Units for Each Grade Level

Unit Topic	Possible Theme(s)	NCSS Themes
6th Grade		
Common Social Science Subject: World History/Western Civilization		
Unit Topic	Possible Theme(s)	NCSS Themes
Models of Ancient Governments	Citizenship Authority	2, 6, 9
Castles and Moats	Adaptation Cause and Effect	2, 5, 6
Renaissance and Reformation	Cause and Effect Individual Impact	6, 9, 10
7th Grade		
Common Social Science Subject: Geography		
Unit Topic	Possible Theme(s)	NCSS Themes
Africa	Location Culture	1, 3, 9
China	Culture Location	1, 3, 9
Developing Countries	Culture Scarcity	1, 3, 7
World Resources	Distribution Supply and Demand	7, 8, 9
8th Grade		
Common Social Science Subject: American History		
Unit Topic	Possible Theme(s)	NCSS Themes
Coming to the Americas	Adaptation	2, 3, 6
Building a New Nation	Cause and Effect Authority	2, 6, 9
Civil War	Conflict Cause and Effect	2, 3, 5
Industry and Power	Production Science	6, 7, 8
Age of Technology	Change Technology	8, 9
9th Grade		
Common Social Science Subject: Geography		
Unit Topic	Possible Theme(s)	NCSS Themes
Introduction to Geography	Five Themes of Geography Human Geography	1, 3, 5
North and South America	Resources and Regions Government and Global Economy	7, 8, 10
Europe	Population and Tourism European Union	3, 8, 9
Africa	Colonization Challenges of Developing Countries	1, 3, 6
Asia	Religion and Culture Globalization and Trade	1, 2, 3
Australia and Antarctica	Resources and Regions Environmental Concerns	2, 7, 9
10th Grade		
Common Social Science Subject: World History		
Unit Topic	Possible Theme(s)	NCSS Themes
Origins of Civilization	Culture Society	1, 2, 3
Classical Greece and Ancient Rome	Famous Philosophers Forming an Empire	4, 8, 10

(*Continued*)

Table 2.4 (Continued)

Religions of the East	Confucius Buddha	3, 5, 6
Traditional Societies	Asian Cultures Africa and the Muslim World	7, 8, 9
Dynasties and Empires	Italian Renaissance China and Japan in the Middle Ages	2, 5, 9
11th Grade Common Social Science Subject: American History		
Unit Topic	Possible Theme(s)	NCSS Themes
Early Exploration	Natives and Immigrants Colonization	1, 3, 9
American Revolution	Representative Government Taxation	5, 6, 10
United States Expansion	Manifest Destiny Imperialism	1, 3, 9
The Progressive Era	Capitalism Government Regulations	4, 7, 8
Civil Rights Movement	Discrimination Equal Opportunity	5, 6, 10
12th Grade Common Social Science Subject: Government and Economics		
Unit Topic	Possible Theme(s)	NCSS Themes
Philosophical and Historical Foundations of Democracy	Representative Government Natural Rights	2, 3, 6
Creating the Constitution	Branches of Government Federalism	3, 5, 6
Politics and the American People	Political Parties Mass Media and Public Opinion	1, 4, 8
Public Policy	Foreign Policy Tariffs	6, 7, 9
Individual Rights	Civil Rights Civil Liberties	2, 3, 10
Money and Banks	Fiscal Responsibility Taxation	5, 7, 10

The Common Core Standards emphasize English language arts (reading/writing) and mathematics. The Common Core Standards for other specific content areas have not been developed and, according to the Common Core Initiative (2012) (www.corestandards.org/faq), there is no plan to develop standards for other content areas. Nonetheless, the current language arts standards include standards for literacy in history/social studies, science, and technical subjects. Since most states have dedicated standards or strands for each content area at every grade level, teachers might indeed find the Common Core Standards to be a more manageable and practical resource than current state standards.

College, Career, and Civic Life Framework and Social Studies

In 2013, the National Council for the Social Studies developed the College, Career, and Civic Life Framework for Social Studies Standards (C3 Framework). The C3 Framework was designed "for states to upgrade their state social studies standards and for practitioners—local school districts, schools, teachers and curriculum writers—to strengthen their social studies programs" (www.ncss.org/c3).

Table 2.5 C3 Framework Organization (NCSS, 2013, p. 12)

Dimension 1: Developing Questions and Planning Inquiries	*Dimension 2: Applying Disciplinary Tools and Concepts*	*Dimension 3: Evaluating Sources and Using Evidence*	*Dimension 4: Communicating Conclusions and Taking Informed Action*
Developing Questions and Planning Inquiries	Civics	Gathering and Evaluating Sources	Communicating and Critiquing Conclusions
Economics			
Geography History	Developing Claims and Using Evidence	Taking Informed Action	

The C3 Framework has three primary objectives:

> enhance the rigor of the social studies disciplines;
> build critical thinking, problem solving, and participatory skills to become engaged citizens;
> align academic programs to the Common Core State Standards for English Language Arts and Literacy in History/Social Studies.
>
> (www.ncss.org/c3)

The C3 Framework foundation is inquiry learning, and the framework hopes to better strengthen social studies instruction. According to the NCSS website,

> The C3 Framework, like the Common Core State Standards, emphasizes the acquisition and application of knowledge to prepare students for college, career, and civic life. It intentionally envisions social studies instruction as an inquiry arc of interlocking and mutually reinforcing elements that speak to the intersection of ideas and learners.

Furthermore, the C3 Framework is organized into four dimensions. The four dimensions (See Table 2.5) center on the use of questions to spark curiosity, guide instruction, deepen investigations, acquire rigorous content, and apply knowledge and ideas in real-world settings to help students become active and engaged citizens in the twenty-first century (www.ncss.org/c3).

NCSS National Standards for the Preparation of Social Studies Teachers

Building on the C3 Framework, in the Spring of 2018 an NCSS task force published a set of standards for the preparation of social studies teachers. This document highlights five core competencies (or standards) for social studies teacher education. The standards include (1) Content Knowledge, (2) Application of Content Through Planning, (3) Design and Implementation of Instruction and Assessment, (4) Social Studies Learners and Learning, and (5) Professional Responsibility and Informed Action. Additionally, there are six assessment types outlined in the document that offer guidance on how to actually collect evidence and data for teacher education programs to demonstrate proficiency in the preparation of social studies teachers. While all components of this document might not relate directly to pre-service teachers, we believe the standards are important for prospective and current social studies teachers to consider for a variety of reasons. These standards illuminate some of the many skills, dispositions, and competencies expected of quality social studies teachers. Whether one has been teaching for 20 years or is just preparing to enter the field, it is important to be aware of the standards, expectations, and vision of what quality social studies instruction looks like from the perspective articulated by the leading organization in the field.

We encourage all readers to take the time to read the standards in their entirety. They are available for free online on the NCSS website. See the Helpful Resources section at the end of this chapter for the direct website link.

Constructivism and Social Studies

Social studies educators have given a great deal of attention to theories and research about how students learn. A teacher's concept of the way in which students acquire and retain knowledge should influence teaching methodology. The last generation of teachers has largely rejected the notion that they could simply present information and it would, somehow, be absorbed and learned. They have also pretty much cast aside behaviorism, with its view that learning occurs through systematic stimulus and response, punishment and reward. These explanations of learning have simply been inadequate descriptions of how knowledge is acquired and understood.

The learning theory that most social studies educators subscribe to is called constructivism. Constructivist thought dominates the thinking of most scholars and writers in social studies. This means that constructivist beliefs influence the development of curriculum materials and ideas about how best teaching can be achieved.

The basic concepts of constructivism were expressed by John Dewey, and later by psychologists Jean Piaget and Jerome Bruner. The idea is that learners have to construct their own meaning. They do this individually and socially. Learning is an active process in which sensory input is used. The major article of belief of constructivists is that knowledge is something that the learner builds or constructs for him/herself. To put it another way, knowledge is the result of assimilating any new information, ideas, and experiences encountered to give them meaning. This new information has to make sense with and tie into what that learner already knows for it to have any meaning. That is why the term *constructivism* is used; the learner literally constructs his or her own knowledge by combining new impressions and information with existing perceptions and conceptions.

Von Glasersfeld (1987) has suggested that constructivism has two major principles that are paraphrased below:

1. Knowledge is actively constructed by the learner, not passively received from the environment.
2. What the learner knows is constantly adapting and being modified by experience.

To put it another way, we make sense of the world by fitting new information and new ideas with what we already know. We construct meaning or explain what we encounter. An oversimplified example is found in our love of the use of analogy in explanation and definition. We are always trying to find some basis of comparison that our audience already understands.

A Problems Approach to Social Studies

There is no doubt about it, social studies is far different today than it was years ago. Society has changed. Schools have changed. Students' lives keep changing. Even the problems that students face are different. For example, there has been a constant increase in the number of students involved in child abuse, divorce, domestic violence, gangs, substance abuse, single-parent homes, and crime. Schools are preparing students for an ever and rapidly changing world with new and unique demands for citizens. There have also been changes that influence students' present and future lives in other ways. There has been a dynamic, complex revolution in technology, information, and communication. There have been major shifts in society, including sweeping changes related to gender roles and ethnic and cultural relationships. There have also been major changes in the governmental and economic makeup of the United States and the world.

In a world in which change has become the norm and we have to constantly face dilemmas for which there is no precedent, social studies is needed more than ever to help students learn to deal with problems. Teachers need to take a problems approach. Though the word *problems* may be defined in many ways, we are going to define it as any task or situation for which a solution is required or desired and for which a method of solution is not provided or immediately apparent. Problem solving is more than the situation itself. Often problems involve moral dilemmas; persisting issues; and/or difficulties, dangers, or curiosities for which there is no verifiable solution. Problems require that existing knowledge be retrieved and used to resolve new or different difficulties. Most importantly, intrinsic to problem solving is the ability to deal with failure and with the inability to identify easy or quick solutions in constructive ways.

Problem solving is the most pervasive skill from a curricular standpoint. It is the one skill that is most needed throughout life. Almost all situations we face as a society and nearly all the decisions demanding personal actions may be best described as problems. If students (and teachers) can develop the requisite mindset, attitudes, and skills of problem solvers, they will be equipped to meet the needs of the future. If they do not, their education becomes obsolete almost before it is complete. Problem solving is the essential skill for each of the disciplines. That is, a person with a problem-solving mindset will be a more successful student. This is an ability that teachers need to emphasize if every student is to become an independent learner. Problem solving is also the essential survival skill for school. Each teacher, each class, each student, each school day, each assignment presents a unique intricacy of circumstances and demands. It would not be an overstatement to say that the essential life role is problem solving.

Problems Approach in the Classroom

Secondary students can deal with problems and content that is much more distant and removed from their own experience. These students need to be more involved in the systematic development of questions and problems. Since secondary students have more skills, knowledge, and experience, they can be involved in a greater variety of research activities. They are more peer-oriented and less teacher-oriented, so group problem solving can be structured into the activities. The emphasis remains on an environment where curiosity is encouraged and stimulated. The teacher in such an environment is going to be constantly leading students to events and ideas that will set them thinking. The students in this setting are going to be "on the learn."

A teacher who uses the problems approach is going to be constantly asking questions, trying to arouse curiosity, and having the students make decisions. The teacher will be encouraging students' questions and helping them to find ways of seeking answers. The entire environment of the classroom becomes fixed on learning how to learn. Students' awareness of problems and their ability to generate alternative solutions is heightened in this kind of environment. Perhaps the best way to look at how the problems approach works is to look at how one teacher used this approach.

Classroom Episode #1

A 6th-grade teacher has launched into a study of the medieval period in European history. The teacher began by trying to get the students to systematically examine their existing concepts of the period. They talked about movies and television programs that they had seen as well as some things that had been picked up from cartoons, comic books, and games. Some of the students also had some knowledge that came from children's literature. There was as much, if not more, fantasy as reality in what they thought they knew about the period.

At about this time the class was surprised by a visit from two people in medieval clothing. One of these men told the students that he was an architect and that he was involved in designing and building castles. The other man said that he was a knight. The men described a situation they were involved in on the coast of England near the Welsh border. King Edward had sent them there to build a castle. Now they had to decide exactly where to build it, but it was not all that easy. While the men were in the classroom, they talked with the students about the reasons for castle building, about all the problems that might be involved, and about the rudiments of castle defense.

By the time the men left, an idea had evolved. Soon the students had developed a hypothetical map of what the region would be like. At the teacher's insistence the map was quite large. In addition, the students were urged to orient their map to some real area on the English coast. The map itself was not altogether fiction because the students did some reading about the geography of the area. The completed map showed a seacoast, the Welsh border, three villages for which the students made up names, and a monastery. It also showed a river, some fens or swampy land, a forest area, and a few roads. Other features were added as the students continued to read and discuss. They learned something about feudal land division and tried to reflect it in the map. Other landmarks, including a ruined castle and some churches, were added. The villages themselves began to take on detail and show differences in size and complexity. As the students researched, they decided that there had to be a feudal manor or two in the area with some kind of fortifications; these were added.

The people came last. The students' research began to reveal the different roles and social statuses that the various people at the monastery and in the villages would have had in all likelihood. The class developed a set of characters, each of whom they tried to describe in some detail. They gave them names and described where they lived, what they did and how they did it, how they dressed, and what their lives were like. They were particularly fascinated by the diet of the common people during this period. The study of daily life, clothing, and customs evolved through group work over about a week.

The students then drew names so that each could "become" one of the characters. Once more in groups, this time according to where they "lived," they continued researching their characters. The groups also began talking about where they wanted the king's castle to be built. They looked into the dangers and fears that faced the lives of the people of this period.

Nearly three weeks after their first visit the two medieval men returned. For this visit, the students had planned and worn costumes of their own and the questions were almost unstoppable. The students eagerly told the visitors what they had been doing. Then each group made a presentation in which they introduced themselves in their medieval roles. The groups each made a case for one particular site for the king's castle. Some of the groups, especially the one representing the monastery, did not want the castle built right in their area. Others had noticed not only the protection that the castle offered, but also the commercial possibilities that a garrison of soldiers would have for the nearest town. When the groups were finished, the architect and the knight explained where they thought the king's castle should be built. Most importantly, they showed that they had listened to the students' reasoning as they presented their case.

This was the beginning rather than the end. The study went on into the actual building of the castle and to several follow-up activities. However, this beginning had laid a foundation of interest and reason for research on which the teacher could continue to build. The students were exploring nearly every major theme and concept of medieval life as they created scenarios and solved problems as they arose.

The Social Science Disciplines

The focus of social studies is on the student learning to understand, interpret, and live in his or her world. Social studies is also an inclusive term for that broad field of study that includes courses that focus specifically on history, geography, sociology, economics, psychology, government, anthropology, and related subjects. Some people use the phrase "the seamless web" to describe the relationships among all these subjects. They like to see social studies as an interdisciplinary curricular area that draws its content from what scholars in a variety of disciplines know about the social world.

The disciplines themselves would more correctly be called social sciences, and each of them offers different content emphases and different methods of inquiry than the others. When social scientists start counting off the social sciences, different numbers are likely to be given. This is partly because there are some disciplines, such as philosophy and religion, that some people accept as social sciences and that other people see as humanities or even natural sciences. An additional factor is that each social science keeps dividing as specializations develop. As a specialization gathers more scholars and knowledge, its perspective and methods of scholarship change too. Over time, it becomes as different from its parent discipline as that discipline is from every other one. Some see archaeology as a part of anthropology, and others see it as a branch of sociology.

For our purposes, let us admit to eight social sciences, while recognizing that someone else might have a longer or shorter list. The eight we will look at are, in alphabetical order: anthropology, economics, geography, history, political science, psychology, religious studies, and sociology. We will look at each of them in turn, basically to refresh our memories and clarify our thinking about the chief concerns of these disciplines and the essential roles each plays in social studies. While we need to keep in mind that each of the social sciences utilizes concepts from all of the other disciplines, we also need to recognize that each discipline has unique contributions.

Anthropology

Anthropology is the study of culture, especially human culture. *Culture* may be defined as a system of beliefs and values, behavior patterns, and customs that is shared by a society of people. A sense of sharing and oneness with others in this society is often part of what defines and distinguishes particular cultures. Scholars in the field generally like to think of their approach as holistic because they are interested in everything there is to know about a culture. Anthropologists study everything from ancient ruins and human remains to existing cultures. There are numerous and varied specializations within the field, including archaeology and ethnography. Because cultural change is a major concern of anthropologists, technological development within a culture has immense importance in many of these specializations.

FYI

Consider the contemporary relevance of this field in the classroom regarding discussions of "cultural appropriation" in the U.S.

Anthropologists look for cultural generalizations. They want to know what defines a culture and what makes it fit together. Anthropologists look carefully at a process they call enculturation, which has to do with how young people learn about their own culture, and the influences that cultures have on one another, especially those that result in acculturation, or the cultural exchange that occurs when there is long-term contact. Like geographers, they are concerned with the natural environment. However, anthropologists have a different perspective, their concerns being mostly with how culture is influenced by environment and what part culture plays in how humans adapt.

Anthropologists attempt to immerse themselves thoroughly within a culture, often becoming very personally involved. From this experience, they expect to gather immense amounts of data about that culture for further study. There is continual concern about how much anthropologists will be influencing a less technologically advanced culture even as they study it.

The concept of culture is essential. Students need to become less ethnocentric and learn more about other cultures. An anthropological focus can be an important part of interdisciplinary programs, but the focus of many primary units is on comparing cultures. Social studies educators have also found that some of the investigative techniques of anthropologists, chiefly archeological site excavation and interviewing and observation, are highly adaptable for use with students.

Economics

Economics deals with resources and with the production, exchange, and consumption of goods and services. Economics is perhaps the most problem-centered of the social sciences since its basic concept is scarcity. The resources are scarce and are always likely to be exceeded by human needs and wants.

Economists try to analyze the use of and demand for various resources in order to make recommendations about the problems that relate to scarcity. Economics is often mathematical and quantitative. Economists continually try to predict the future and to recommend courses of action that will create a more fortunate situation in the future. Therefore, they are continually trying to find ways to look at quantities produced, exchanged, and consumed. Because some medium of exchange (money) is going to exist in societies where there is specialization, economics is also concerned with money and other forms of capital and with related areas such as banking, taxation, and investment.

The real importance of economics to students is that throughout their lives students will be playing the roles of worker (producer of goods or services), consumer (user of goods and services), and citizen (part of a society that operates under some economic system). They need to learn a number of economic consumer skills and develop economic values that can be embedded in social studies. These have to do with such diverse areas of their lives as handling money, banking, budgeting, buying and selling goods and services, and choosing a way of making a living. They also will need to learn to deal with how scarcity relates to and impacts their own lives. There is also some important economic content for students both as future citizens and as students studying other countries. In both roles, students need at least some understanding of how the economy operates and how this affects people's lives.

Geography

Though maps and globes are among the major tools of geographers, and a particular branch of geography—cartography—is devoted to the science of mapping, the field of geography is far broader, encompassing the study of the earth's surface and how that relates to human beings. Geographers are interested in how humans adapt to various living conditions and how humans alter the geography. Physical geographers tend to focus on the earth's natural features (topography, landforms, climate, bodies of water, vegetation, animal life, etc.). Cultural geographers are concerned with people and with the factors that influence their location as well as how humans use and impact resources.

Basic to geographic understanding is some knowledge of where places are located in the world. Many students and teachers lack very basic information about their world. With the great variety of colorful, interesting, interactive, and/or electronic maps available to use with students today, there is little excuse for not drawing students into map study. In a world where people have become much more mobile and where people are drawn closer by communication and transportation revolutions, it seems fairly clear that students need more place-location knowledge than ever before.

Geographic knowledge is basic to understanding and knowing about the world and its people, and problems related to geography are among the most important facing the world today. Students are aware of many of these problems and need to be informed and knowledgeable about their impact on their world. Students often have heard only enough to frighten them about geographic problems ranging from overpopulation to pollution, from the depletion of the ozone layer to the destruction of the rainforests, from the rapid consumption of fossil fuels to world famines and droughts.

As defined by the National Council for Geographic Education and the Association of American Geographers in 1984, geographic education is focused on five themes:

1 Location: Position on the earth's surface
2 Place: The characteristics that distinguish and define each place
3 Relationships within places: Advantages and disadvantages for human settlement
4 Movement: Interacting of humans
5 Regions: Areas that display unity in terms of selected criteria.

The questions that geographers ask deal with where people live and why. They are interested in the factors that make the earth habitable. They are also concerned with how variations in geographic factors influence economic development, culture, and sociopolitical organization.

Students can easily be drawn into a study of other settings and other people. Everything has a geographic setting, and the realization that we understand events and people's actions better when we know more about that geographic setting makes the study of geography important to every subject students study throughout life. The flora and fauna or minerals and rocks they study in the sciences, stories and poems they read in literature, and the people and events they study from the past all relate to numerous geographic factors.

History

History is the study of the past, or at least the surviving record of the past. Generally, we limit our study to the human past, but that in itself is very broad. There is a history of scholarship, of military events, and of economic, cultural, and social phenomena. History examines, in fact, the whole spectrum of humans in interaction with one another and with the earth.

The problem of history is that the record of the past is always incomplete, full of bias, and distorted. This problem has produced two schools of thought regarding historical inquiry. On the one hand, narrative historians, sometimes called humanist historians, suggest that the inadequacies of the record and the complexity of the past defy any attempt to make generalizations. They conceive the historian's job as one of basically describing the past more accurately, insightfully, and fully. Scientific historians, on the other hand, attempt to use scientific methods, often with quantitative data.

Historians study documents, records, personal letters, diaries, business inventories, legal papers, wills, bills of sale, newspapers, and government papers. Historians also study and compare the physical remains of the past from buildings, roads, and walls to the smallest of objects either preserved through time in someone's safekeeping or found in such places as ruins and tombs. Historians also look at such things as paintings, recordings, photographs, and, for most recent times, video recordings. Finally, historians use people as a resource through approaches such as interviews and observations.

Middle and high school curricula usually includes the learning of historical facts. Involving students in the narrative or the story and drama of history and in the quest for historical knowledge is essential if history is to be learned effectively. Historical fascination is the key to historical learning.

History deals with questions through which a picture is reconstructed of how events actually occurred, why they occurred, and how/if they impacted subsequent events. Teachers can stimulate a genuine interest in what life was like in the past. When students are led to examine history as a series of mysteries and problems, they can be naturally led to look at some of the primary resources that historians use. It is really exciting to watch when a student experiences an "Aha!" moment (a moment when a student discovers and understands something new). Once students begin seeking new knowledge, concepts like historical change, cultural bias, civilization, colonization, and cause and effect begin to be perfectly logical to them and to come with the learning.

Political Science

> **FYI**
>
> Preparing students for civic life is a central component of both the C3 Framework and the NCSS National Standards for the Preparation of Social Studies Teachers.

Political science is the study of government and all that is associated with the governing process. It deals with human behavior throughout the entire political system and includes the study of the legislative, the judicial, and the executive process. Political scientists study governmental organizations, political parties, pressure groups, voting and elections, and other related parts of the process. They also study different types of government and different types of roles performance by those involved in governing.

Political science attempts to give an accurate and complete picture of the way that the political process works both generally and at particular points in time. Certainly, the basic tools of the political scientists are analyses of documents, court cases and governmental acts, and media coverage of political events. However, political scientists also attempt to make predictions based on the notion that when conditions are similar, it is likely that outcomes and results will tend to repeat.

Students are in the process of becoming aware of the forms and functions of government prior to middle school. Their political awareness is often closely linked to their geographical and historical understanding. Students are typically politicalized by the age of 12. Throughout middle and high school, students are reevaluating and developing numerous political concepts, including right and wrong, justice, authority, power, security, and politics. They become aware of their own exposure to vast barrages of propaganda.

Political science offers students a great deal of useful information and concepts in the process of learning about government. Since political science is largely based on questioning the process, in looking analytically at every event, the methods of the discipline are useful for middle and secondary students.

Psychology

Psychology is the study of the behavior and thinking of individuals, especially humans. One branch of psychology, social psychology, is devoted to behavior in groups. Psychologists study development across the entire lifespan. They are interested in a number of factors that relate to the social studies, including individuality and self-concept, motivation and attitudes, learning and cognition, human personalities, and behavior of individuals in groups.

Psychology provides insight into social behavior in the classroom and into several elements related to learning. As students learn about other people and other times, they need to understand why people behave as they do. They also need to understand something about the kinds of actions taken by different types of leaders.

Religious Studies

Religious studies examines the systems of beliefs and the various practices associated with the various faiths of the world. It is an extremely broad field. Scholarship in religious studies reaches from large formal religions such as Buddhism, Islam, Christianity, Hinduism, and Judaism to small, relatively obscure cults. Likewise, the spectrum goes from ancient religions that have not been practiced for centuries to modern religions with both ancient and recent origins. Religious studies scholars also have great interest in political philosophies that contain substantively religious ideas and have important ramifications that impact on religious practices. Confucianism and communism are examples of such.

The importance of religious studies to middle and high school curricula relates to the importance of religious beliefs in people's lives. As students study other times and other places, they need some understanding of the religious context. Geography and history are at least partly attributable to religious factors. It is important to remember that religious studies is not teaching a religion, but teaching about various religions.

It may also become important for students to understand that religious views may impact some of the activities of the classroom as well. Students need to understand the difference between studying religious views and advocating them. There may be families represented in the class with religious beliefs that will not allow the students to participate in some school activities. In the last half-century, a related issue has been the place of religious beliefs in the schools. Several questions have been raised about traditional school practices that are related to religious beliefs. These questions have brought about a number of constitutional controversies involving infringement on freedom of religion and the concept of separation of church and state.

Sociology

Sociology is the study of how people act in groups. Sociologists are interested in different kinds of groups, both formal and informal, and how these groups operate and interact with other groups. They are interested in individuals only with regard to the roles they have within groups. They are very much aware of the influence that societal values and norms have on individuals. An essential assumption of sociology is that individuals need groups in order to survive.

Sociologists study many groups that are very important to students. They examine the family, the classroom, the school, the community, and numerous types of organizations and groups around the world. Sociology's important contributions to social studies have to do with what the discipline tells us about group behavior. Sociologists offer perspectives about how people act in different institutional and community settings. Sociologists also examine how changes in the institutions occur. They look at social order and influence and authority within groups. They examine the different roles people play and social relationships, as well as the impact of technological change on social institutions.

Looking Back

Social studies is constantly changing because of the variety of influences and pressures for change. Social science disciplines have had a continued and important role as the source of content of the social sciences. Each of the social sciences—history, geography, anthropology, sociology, economics, political science, psychology, and religious studies— offers a body of knowledge, a unique perspective about the world, and a method of inquiry from which students can learn. As a social studies teacher, you must be prepared to teach all of the subject areas because you will most likely be certified to do so and because they all intertwine and overlap with each other.

Extension Activity

Scenario

You are searching for a teaching position in Yourtown School District, which is a very difficult district to "get your foot in the door." Just as you had lost hope you receive a phone call from Dr. Russell, the principal of Yourtown High School (YHS). Dr. Russell invites you for an interview. During your interview, an enthusiastic committee member asks you, "What do you believe to be the goals and purpose of social studies?" Your response could be the difference between being offered the teaching position and not being offered the position.

Task

For this activity, write down how you would answer the enthusiastic committee member. Be sure to clearly discuss the goals and purpose of social studies.

Reflective Questions

1 What is the C3 Framework?
2 What are the Common Core Standards?
3 What factors contribute to controversy over what is taught in the social studies?
4 How would you characterize the problems approach to social studies?
5 In what ways did the NCSS task force groups referred to in the chapter stress the role of thinking skills in social studies?

Helpful Resources

Watch this video of NCSS executive director Susan Griffin defining social studies and the connection with the C3 Framework.
https://youtu.be/3HD9apVNq0I
Visit this website for a direct link to the NCSS National Standards for the Preparation of Social Studies Teachers.
www.socialstudies.org/sites/default/files/media/2017/Nov/ncss_teacher_standards_2017-rev9-6-17.pdf
Watch the video below to see Sarah Brown Wessling discuss the integration of the Common Core Standards into the classroom curriculum.
www.teachingchannel.org/videos/how-to-read-common-core
Visit this website to explore the Common Core State Standards.
www.corestandards.org
This video provides an overview of the Common Core Standards, including what they are and what they are not.
Watch https://youtu.be/NxRg__r9HLg
This video provides an overview of the Common Core Standards.
Watch https://youtu.be/5s0rRk9sER0
This video is hosted by Michelle Herczog. She interviews and discusses the C3 Framework with a variety of social studies scholars from across the country. Includes a discussion with C3 project director Kathy Swan.
Watch https://youtu.be/AESqr-vGgLEWatch this video from NCSS, which details how the C3 Framework aligns with the Common Core Standards.
https://youtu.be/kb0QW6GwNbg
For a full-text copy of the C3 Framework visit www.ncss.org/c3

The Council for Economic Education (CEE) is an organization for economic education. The CEE publishes numerous books and resource materials for the economics classroom.

www.councilforeconed.org

Watch the following Flocabulary video on the Three Branches of Government for examples of creative ways to share political science content with students. Also, feel free to share this video directly with your students!

www.flocabulary.com/unit/3-branches-of-government/

Watch the following Flocabulary video on George Washington Carver as an example of how to get students excited about historical figures.

www.flocabulary.com/unit/george-washington-carver/

Watch the following Flocabulary video on the major world religions. Also, feel free to share this video directly with your students!

www.flocabulary.com/unit/major-world-religions/

Further Reading

Barr, R., Barth, J. & Shermis, S. (1977). *Defining Social Studies.* Silver Spring, MD: National Council for the Social Studies.

This book discusses the various perspectives and issues that surround social studies and its identity. The book includes five chapters analyzing the nature of social studies, its goals and objectives, and the issues surrounding the lack of a constant definition.

Engle, S. (1960). Decision making: The heart of social studies instruction. *Social Education, 24*(7), 301–306.

This article discusses the role of decision-making in social studies and emphasizes its purposes as the central and vital aspect of social studies instruction. This seminal article outlines decision-making as an approach to social studies and played a significant role in the way social studies was viewed.

Kenna, J. & Russell, W. (2014). Implications of common core state standards on the social studies. *The Clearing House: A Journal of Educational Strategies, Issues, and Ideas, 87*(2), 75–82.

This article discusses the Common Core Standards and the impact they have on social studies instruction.

National Council for Geographic Education. (1994). *Geography for Life: The National Geography Standards.* Washington, DC: National Geographic Society Committee on Research and Exploration.

This book is the framework for geography education. The book outlines the goals and purpose of geography education. In addition, the book outlines the themes and national standards and presents readers with possible products students will produce and the process in which the students work to obtain the geographic knowledge.

National Council for the Social Studies. (2010). *National Curriculum Standards for Social Studies: A Framework for Teaching, Learning, and Assessment.* Silver Spring, MD: National Council for the Social Studies.

This book is the framework for social studies educators. The book outlines the goals and purpose of social studies. In addition, the book outlines the themes and national standards and presents readers with possible products students will produce and the process in which the students work to obtain the knowledge.

Ochoa-Becker, A. (2006). *Democratic Education for Social Studies: An Issues-Centered Decision Making Curriculum.* Charlotte, NC: Information Age Publishing.

This influential book, originally published in 1988, was written by the iconic social studies educator Shirley Engle. This volume includes a rationale for an issues-centered decision-making curriculum for the social studies classroom.

Russell, W. (Ed.) (2011). *Contemporary Social Studies: An Essential Reader.* Charlotte, NC: Information Age Publishing.

The field of social studies is unique and complex. It is challenged by the differing perspectives related to the definition, goals, content, and purpose of social studies. This volume discusses the contemporary issues surrounding social studies education today. This volume encourages and inspires readers to think. The 28 chapters included in this volume are written by prominent scholars in the field of social studies. The collection inspires and provokes readers to reconsider and reexamine social studies and the current state of the field. Readers will explore the various critical topics that encompass contemporary social studies.

Thornton, S. (2003). From content to subject matter. *The Social Studies, 92*(6), 237–242.

This article discusses the purpose and goals of social studies. It also examines the relationship of verbiage and terms between social studies and the various social science disciplines.

References

Barth, J.L. (1993). Social studies: There is a history, there is a body, but is it worth saving. *Social Education*, 57(2), 56–57.

Byford, J., & Russell, W. (2007). The new social studies: A historical examination of curriculum reform. *Social Studies Research and Practice*, 2(1), 38–48.

Common Core Initiative. (2012). Common Core FAQ's. Available at: www.corestandards.org/faq.

Fitchett, P., & Russell, W. (2011). Reflecting on MACOS: Why it failed and what we can learn from its demise. *Paedagogica Historica: International Journal of the History of Education*, 47(1), 1–16.

Hanna, P.R. (1957). Generalizations and universal values: Their implications for the social studies program. In *Social Studies in the Elementary School: Fifty-Sixth Yearbook of the National Society for the Study of Education* (pp. 27–47). Chicago, IL: University of Chicago Press.

Hanna, P.R. (1963). The social studies program in the elementary school in the twentieth century. In G.W. Sowards (Ed.), *The Social Studies* (pp. 42–78). Glenview, IL: Scott Foresman.

Hartoonan, M. (1993). A guide for redefining the social studies. *Social Education*, 57(2), 59–60.

Kenna, J., & Russell, W. (2014). Implications of common core state standards on the social studies. *The Clearing House: A Journal of Educational Strategies, Issues, and Ideas*, 87(2), 75–82.

Moore, C., Bryant, D., & Furrow, D. (1989). Mental terms and the development of certainty. *Child Development*, 60(February), 167–171.

National Council for Geographic Education. (1984). *Guidelines for Geographic Education: Elementary and Secondary Schools*. Washington, DC: Association of American Geographers/National Council for the Geographic Education.

NCSS (National Council for the Social Studies) Task Force on Creating Effective Citizens. (2001). *Creating Effective Citizens*. Available at: www.ncss.org/positions/effectivecitizens.

NCSS. (2013). *The College, Career, and Civic Life (C3) Framework for Social Studies State Standards: Guidance for Enhancing the Rigor of K–12 Civics, Economics, Geography, and History*. Silver Spring, MD: NCSS. Available at: www.ncss.org/c3.

Task Force of the National Commission on the Social Studies in the Schools. (1989). *Charting a Course: Social Studies for the 21st Century*. Washington, DC: National Commission on the Social Studies in the Schools.

Task Force on Standards for the Social Studies. (1994). *Expectations of Excellence: Curriculum Standards for Social Studies*. Washington, DC: NCSS.

Task Force on Standards for the Social Studies. (2010). *National Curriculum Standards for Social Studies: A Framework for Teaching, Learning, and Assessment*. Washington, DC: NCSS.

Von Glasersfeld, E. (1987). Learning as a constructive activity. In C. Janvier (Ed.), *Problems of Representation in the Teaching and Learning of Mathematics* (pp. 3–17). Hillsdale, NJ: Lawrence Erlbaum.

3 Planning Social Studies Instruction

Looking Ahead

The aim of this chapter is to help you become a better planner. To do this, we begin with the problems that teachers have in planning. We then move to the structures of different teaching plans. As you read the chapter you need to consider these questions:

- What are your strengths and weaknesses as a planner?
- What do you need to be able to do to plan a teaching unit?
- Are you likely to rely heavily on a textbook?
- How can you effectively plan long term?
- Are you planning to meet the needs of all your students, including those with special learning needs and those whose cultural background is different from your own?

Effective planning is a necessary and essential ingredient of effective teaching. Obviously, there is more to teaching than planning, but imagine a teacher who does not plan. Such a teacher has no sense of what is to go on in the classroom and quickly loses efficacy and impact. Fortunately, many teachers do at least some planning, but many do far too little. Too often, teaching plans consist of cryptic notes in lesson-plan books referring to pages in the textbook. These kinds of plans can hardly lead to exciting, creative classrooms.

Can You? Do You?

Can you …

- plan an instructional social studies unit?
- identify and describe different types of units?
- write instructional objectives?
- establish a "set" in a lesson?
- identify the basic components in a lesson plan?

Do you …

- have experience in collaborative planning?
- know how to go about choosing a unit topic?
- know how to create a curriculum map/guide?
- know what is meant by the term *webbing* when referring to planning?
- understand instructional objectives?

DOI: 10.4324/9781003217060-3

Focus Activity

Before reading this chapter, try the focus activity below.

Think back about your educational experience. What was the most memorable lesson/unit you experienced as a student? What makes the lesson/unit memorable? Share experiences with classmates. Discuss the details of experiences and compare. Do your educational experiences share common attributes with others? If so, what attributes? Do you think these experiences will have an impact on how you plan for instruction? If so, how?

Why Is Planning Important?

Planning has special importance in broad content areas like social studies where there is so much information. Because of the breadth of the field, even the best and most experienced teachers will not have comprehensive knowledge. All teachers need to use numerous resources. The resource possibilities are constantly growing. The Internet and a growing variety of computer software packages alone have increased the possibilities astronomically. One of the major elements in good planning is finding and collecting the best resources and organizing them in a purposeful way.

Most teachers are likely to start their planning with a textbook because many schools/districts set a guideline or require a specific curriculum. Teachers may also get help from mentor teachers in some schools, or from a team leader, a lead teacher, a department chair, or an entire group of grade-level colleagues. Since state governments are legally responsible for the public schools, there are state guidelines containing frameworks, rules, standards, and/or regulations regarding what is taught. National teacher organizations also provide input about what should go on in the social studies. (The NCSS (1994), the Association for Supervision and Curriculum Development, and the National Education Association are among the largest of these organizations. The NCSS alone publishes two useful journals for social studies teachers, *Social Education* and *The Social Studies*.)

One problem with having all these resources, and, remember, these are only the beginning points for planning, is that they end up as mountains of pages of print telling the teacher what to do—far more than he or she can cope with. By its very size, the accumulation of resource guides, instead of helping, intimidates and confuses new teachers. Teachers feel they can only retreat to the safety of that first resource, the textbook. Staying strictly with that safe resource soon becomes a comfortable and safe pattern. It is a natural thing to do. It reduces uncertainty and confusion and leaves the difficult decisions of planning to the so-called experts. However, it prevents these teachers from reaching their own potential.

FYI

While non-reliance on textbooks may seem obvious on the surface, there is no denying that textbook-based instruction still takes place all over the country. Do better, be better!

There are some good reasons why long-term, total reliance on textbooks is not the best course:

1 Following this route means that the teacher, the social studies curriculum, and the classroom are not likely to be very exciting, interesting, or enjoyable for students. If the whole point of schooling is to produce involved, independent learners, then this is surely the last kind of environment one would want to foster.

2 "Read and answer the question" social studies, which is the type of teaching the textbook approach is likely to produce, is not likely to be very meaningful or seem very purposeful to students. Though it is almost a corollary to reason #1, not only are students not going to enjoy this kind of approach, they also are not going to learn from it or understand why they are doing it.
3 There is little teacher satisfaction gained from such an approach. What makes teaching exciting is seeing what you have planned come alive in the classroom and seeing student learning result from your plans. When you repeatedly use a "canned" plan, teaching soon becomes boring and unrewarding.

Setting the Stage: Creating the Environment

If you are the kind of teacher who wants to avoid the textbook pitfall, how do you begin to plan? Curiously, both the planning process and the actual planning product that flows out of this process involve a good deal of scene setting. Doing social studies in the classroom is almost like doing theater. We are trying to create a dramatic climate, one with just the right kind of tension and sufficient excitement for learning to occur. With effective planning in social studies, that climate is there and it can be identified by some predictable hallmarks.

These hallmarks include the following:

- *A sense of anticipation or expectancy on the part of the student audience*: They know that something special is going to happen and they have a fairly good idea of what it is, with just enough uncertainty for the sake of anticipation and suspense.
- *A feeling of purpose and direction*: Students know why they are there and what the class is all about.
- *An awareness that is more than knowledge of continuity*: What is done today relates to yesterday as well as to tomorrow.
- *An atmosphere of involvement or participation in the planning process itself and how the plans flow into the doing*: There is a sense of community or even family that acknowledges that "we are in this together."
- *An awareness of leadership*: To a degree, this seals off or at least pulls the reins to control conflict. It keeps a sense of urgency, allowing flexibility, but keeps at the job.

Why Don't Teachers Plan?

FYI

"Failing to plan is planning to fail." Alan Lakein

It may seem negative to approach planning from a "why don't teachers plan (even the experienced ones)?" perspective, but if we look at some of the reasons teachers do not plan or at least do not plan well, you may see why planning is so difficult yet so important. This may be helpful when we examine some of the planning tools that are used in social studies. We first must recognize that we must deal with teachers' perceptions of their reasons as much as the reasons themselves. How teachers feel about what they do and do not do and how they look at themselves is very important. There is a growing belief that time management is an area in which simply understanding the problems and deterrents may help the teacher in overcoming them. Here are a few reasonable conclusions about the factors involved in teachers' failure to plan.

- *Not enough time*: Teachers have crowded days often filled with unavoidable trivialities, both planned and unplanned. Clerical tasks, students demanding attention, classroom accidents, discipline situations, paper grading, and many others compete to more than fill every minute.
- *Failure to set time priorities or give priority to planning*: Because teaching is time-intensive, teachers must be very careful to choose which tasks get high priority and which get less attention.
- *Dependence on previous material*: Once teachers have taught a topic a few times, they begin to accumulate a quantity of "stuff that works." There are obvious advantages to this, and the old adage, "if it ain't broke, don't fix it," comes to mind. But there are also dangers, including staleness and a tendency to get behind the times.
- *Procrastination*: For some of us, the whole problem is reduced to being slow about getting around to things.

FYI

Benjamin Franklin once said, "You may delay, but time will not." (*Poor Richard's Almanack* by Benjamin Franklin, 1914; 1758)

- *Failure to communicate*: There is a cooperative element even in teacher planning. Good planning means letting involved people (parents, resource people, school officials, other teachers, etc.) know what they need to know and what they need to do in advance.
- *Experience*: Experience itself may stand in the way of effective planning. Teachers can develop patterns and habits very quickly that are counterproductive, and these may persist and transfer.
- *Lack of interest or enthusiasm for the content*: Some teachers will say that they do not like social studies.
- *Fear of the content*: Some teachers do not have the content knowledge to teach social studies effectively and comfortably.
- *Low energy*: Many teachers say that they just do not have the energy, psychological or physical, to plan.
- *Inability to deal with peer pressure*: Teachers want to be approved and liked by other teachers. They model their behavior on experienced teachers.

There are no easy ways to deal with all these forces that work against planning. Obviously, self-discipline, resolve to plan well, and a firm sense of purpose are qualities that teachers need. However, beyond these difficult and elusive acts of will, there are some concrete strategies that teachers can use to improve planning habits and skills. Not all of the following suggestions will work for everybody, but they are worth a try.

a Schedule your time to include a specifically designated planning time and stick to the schedule as though a planning time were a meeting with the president.
b Make lists of planning jobs and prioritize the lists.
c Examine and change your patterns of behavior to avoid distractions.
d Do the worst first, meaning, complete that which you most dread and want to put off before you do the easier or more satisfying things.
e Learn to "say no" without feeling guilt, turning off and away those who would interrupt your planning time.
f Record and celebrate your planning successes in ways that you can remember and then repeat (if it works, make sure you can do it again).

Long-Range Planning

Long-range planning starts well before the school year begins, at which point the teacher creates a curriculum map/guide for a specific subject for the upcoming school year/semester. In some cases, curriculum maps are centrally created at the district or state level. In other cases, your school's adopted textbook may include a prescribed curriculum map. However, in some cases it the responsibility of the teacher or grade-level team to prepare a curriculum map. A basic curriculum map will include curriculum content and standards and a time frame for which the material will be covered. An example of a social studies curriculum map can be seen in Table 3.1.

> **FYI**
>
> Curriculum maps or guides can sometimes be called a scope and sequence or a pacing guide.

Long-range unit planning is more detailed than a curriculum map. The word *unit* is used with a lot of different meanings. Basically, a unit includes everything a group of learners do to explore a particular topic. What unifies the study or makes it a unit is the topic itself. This is true whether that topic is a general category type (such as Transportation), a concept (such as Democracy), a time period or event (such as The Age of Exploration), or a question (such as What can be done to reduce pollution?). When we talk about units in teaching, we are usually talking about the teaching plan for that topic. Such plans vary in length, in amount of detail, and even in their source of creation. A unit may attempt to plan for a week or for six weeks of work. Some people think that students need to learn more about each topic, while others are convinced that more topics need to be covered. For most teachers, a unit plan will include two to three weeks of instruction. A minimalist unit plan includes the unit objectives, curriculum standards, assessments, and daily lesson plan sequence. A more advanced unit plan will include a detailed curriculum calendar along with detailed daily lesson plans.

Textbook-Centered Units

Textbook programs dominate classrooms (Educational Market Research, 2012; Ball & Feiman-Nemser, 1988). Using textbooks does not eliminate the need for preparation but does reduce the amount of preparation and does, to some extent, take the responsibility for making decisions about what students need to learn out of the teacher's hands.

Textbook units offer some important instructional advantages. For teachers who use textbook-centered units, there is common reading material containing the same information for all students. This is of tremendous advantage, for it makes it possible to give single assignments and to unify instruction. Another important positive about this type of teaching is the security of knowing that those who have prepared the material have knowledge and expertise in the field, have done a good deal of research into content, and have given thorough professional attention to the preparation of the text. There is added teacher peace of mind in knowing that modern technology has made it possible to keep the reading level of textual material more precisely at the intended grade level than at any point in educational history.

Textbook-centered units emphasize, usually above all else, getting information from print, most specifically from the textbook. Assignments involving reading pages, portions of chapters, and entire chapters to answer sets of questions or do other types of written exercises are most common.

Table 3.1 Curriculum Map

Teacher: David Householder
Unit 1: Foundations of Government Time Frame: 3 Weeks
Essential Questions: What is government? Are what are the foundations of government?

Standards	*Resources/Technology*	*Objectives*	*Assessment*
GC.1 Cite textual evidence and evaluate multiple points of view to analyze the influence of ancient Greek, Roman, and leading European political thinkers, such as John Locke, Charles-Louis Montesquieu, Niccolò Machiavelli, Jean-Jacques Rousseau, and William Blackstone on the development of United States government. GC.2 Determine the central ideas in passages from *Democracy in America* to examine the character of American society, including its religious, political, and economic character, as articulated by Alexis de Tocqueville. (H, P) GC.3 Describe the purposes and functions of government as outlined in the Preamble to the Constitution and demonstrate an understanding of current application of those purposes and functions by identifying current government actions related to each of the six purposes. (P) GC.4 Explain how the Constitution reflects a balance between the promotion of the public good and the protection of individual rights. (H, P) GC.5 Summarize (CC) with supporting evidence why the Founding Fathers established a constitutional system that limited the power of government. (H, P) GC.6 Describe the systems of enumerated and shared powers, the role of organized interests (*Federalist* Number 10), checks and balances (*Federalist* Number 51), the importance of an independent judiciary (*Federalist* Number 78), implied powers, rule of law, federalism, popular sovereignty, and civilian control of the military. (P) GC.7 Analyze how the Bill of Rights limits the powers of the federal government and state governments. (P) GC.8 Assess the claims, reasoning, and evidence of various authors to analyze the tensions within our Republic and the importance of maintaining a balance between the following concepts (H, P): majority rule and individual rights, liberty and equality, state and national authority in a federal system, civil disobedience and the rule of law, freedom of the press and censorship, relationship of religion and government, relationship of legislation and morality, government regulation and free enterprise GC.35 Analyze the meaning and importance of each of the rights guaranteed under the Bill of Rights and how each is secured (e.g., freedom of religion, speech, press, assembly, petition, and privacy). (P)	McClenaghan, William A. *American Government*. 2002 ed. Prentice Hall: Massachusetts. Smith, Jane Wilcox. And Sullivan, Carol. *United States Government*. 2005 Teacher's Ed. AGS Publishing: Circle Pines, MN. Primary Sources: excerpts from the Magna Carta; Mayflower Compact; English Bill of Rights; *Two Treatises of Civil Government*, John Locke; Declaration of Independence, Thomas Jefferson; excerpts from *The Federalist Papers* – 1, 9, 10, 39, 51, 78; excerpts from the Constitution; excerpts from *Democracy in America*, Alexis De Tocqueville; "The Social Contract" by Jean Jacques Rousseau https://www.icivics.org/teachers http://constitutioncenter.org/learn/educational-resources/lesson-plans http://www.loc.gov/teachers/classroommaterials/themes/civics/lessonplans.html http://www.sharemylesson.com National Archives http://www.christina.k12.de.us/literacylinks/elemresources/lfs_resources/activating_strategies.pdf	-Students will examine the foundations of American government as seen through the eyes of the Founding Fathers. Students will make connections between American government origins and the present situation. -Students explain the fundamental principles and moral values of the American government as expressed in the Constitution and other essential documents of American federalism.	-Students are given a "Bellwork and Daily Questions" handout at the beginning of each week. This acts as their entrance and exit ticket for each lesson. They turn this in on quiz/test day or as deemed by the teacher. -Students will read the Declaration of Independence and decipher it in order to understand its meaning in modern-day English. -Students will analyze various political cartoons dating back to the 1760s. -Students will go on a "Constitutional scavenger hunt" to understand how the document was set up and established. -Students will found their own country and base their country's giving principles from the U.S. Preamble. -Students will be given one quiz per chapter and given one unit exam for each unit. -Students will write an editorial to the *Pennsylvania Gazette* in the year 1783, outlining the core problems of the Articles of Confederation. -Ch. 1 quiz -Ch. 2 quiz -Ch. 3 quiz -Ch. 4 quiz -Unit 1 exam

(*Continued*)

Table 3.1 (Continued)

Teacher: David Householder
Unit 2: Political Behavior: Government By the People Time Frame: 3 Weeks
Essential Questions: What is the role of media in politics? How do people act politically?

Standards	*Resources/Technology*	*Objectives*	*Assessment*
GC.25 Analyze the origin, development, and role of political parties. (H, P) GC.26 Explain the history of the nomination process for presidential candidates and the increasing importance of and difference between primaries, caucuses and general elections. (H, P) GC.27 Analyze appropriate textual evidence to evaluate the roles of polls and campaign advertising, and examine the controversies over campaign funding. (P) GC.28 Describe the means that citizens use to participate in the political process (e.g., voting, campaigning, lobbying, filing a legal challenge, demonstrating, petitioning, picketing, and running for political office). (P) GC.29 Explain the features of direct democracy in numerous states (e.g., the process of initiatives, referendums, and recall elections). (P) GC.30 Examine information in diverse formats and media to analyze trends in voter turnout and the causes and effects of reapportionment and redistricting. (P) GC.31 Analyze the function of the Electoral College. (H, P) GC.32 Cite textual evidence to defend a point of view about the meaning and importance of a free and responsible press. (P) GC.33 Describe the roles of broadcast, print, and electronic media, including the Internet, as means of communication in American politics. (P) GC.34 Explain how public officials use the media to communicate with the citizenry and to shape public opinion. (P)	-Political cartoon analysis from the Library of Congress -The textbook -iCivics -Library of Congress -National Constitution Center -Share My Lesson -PBS	Students evaluate issues regarding campaigns for national, state, and local elective offices. Students evaluate the influence of the media on American political life.	-Students will create a graphic organizer describing the core beliefs of the Democratic and Republican parties. Students will also create one for conservatism and liberalism. -Students will write a letter to their local congressman or woman. - "Bellwork and Daily Questions" handout -Ch. 5 quiz -Ch. 6 quiz -Ch. 7 quiz -Ch. 8 quiz -Ch. 9 quiz -Unit 2 exam

Types of Planning for Social Studies Units

Textbook teaching is an easy pattern to set and a difficult routine to break. One reason it is so prevalent is that nearly all teachers have to do it. However, there are some positive ways a teacher can make use of this pattern to take control of their own teaching. The simplest of these is to use the textbook as a base but expand from that textbook. In this section, we will look at using and adapting different planning units, beginning with expanded textbook units.

Expanded Textbook Units

Social studies textbooks are structured into units that consist of single chapters or, in many cases, a series of two or more chapters. Teacher editions provide such material as vocabulary lists, activity ideas, day-by-day lesson plans, questions, and even lists of additional resources. Publishers may also provide numerous supplementary materials, including student handouts, project planning procedures, posters, maps, charts, PowerPoint presentations, videos, and so on.

Teachers who rely heavily on textbooks need to be especially concerned about purposeful teaching. A regimen of careful planning with a focus on how to use the textbook creatively can help reduce, if not totally avoid, the pitfalls usually associated with textbook teaching. The following steps should be considered by teachers:

1 Try to get the "big picture." Be sure that you understand what the goals of the textbook are and how each book is organized and fits into the entire series.
2 Create a scope and sequence or curriculum map (what you teach and when you teach it) for the school year. As you do this, be sure to consider unequal treatment (giving more time to some topics than others) and omission of some topics.
3 For each unit, use the teacher edition judiciously to plan activities to introduce the topic and to help students achieve the objectives and reach a holistic understanding of the topic.
4 Maintain a high level of sensitivity to reading difficulties students may encounter and be ready to accommodate the individual learning needs of students.
5 Remember, the textbooks and their provided materials are only one of a variety of resources available for effective instruction. Try to think of alternatives to the textbook's suggested activities that address the goals and objectives of each unit in a student-centered way. Try to establish a balance of new versus repeated instructional activities from chapter to chapter. This gives students both the security of being able to learn a set of expectations about how to do things and the motivational freshness of activity variety.
6 Examine evaluation materials provided with the textbook carefully, and use them only after seeing their relationship to the teaching objectives. This usually means that you see what information, concepts, and basic skills are being assessed.

Collaborative Units

In many schools, teachers work in teams to prepare units. The arrangements for doing this vary. In some cases, there are structured formal efforts across entire school districts by appointed groups of teachers. Other formal arrangements may involve grade level teaming or subject area/discipline teaming.

FYI

Depending on the organization of your school, you will most likely be organized into subject matter teams or grade-level teams. Subject matter teams are more common in Grades 9–12 and grade-level teams are more common in Grades 6–8.

The kinds of social studies units produced and the ways that teachers are expected to use them are almost as varied. In most instances, the aim is to combine talents and save individual teacher's planning time while producing some consistency throughout the school or system in the content that is taught. The units may, in some instances, even be developed to ensure that all teachers will be following the same sequence of activities. It is more common, though, for team planning to produce resource units that can be shared among teachers. Resource units systematically delineate common objectives, identify the most appropriate and useful available resources for teacher and student use, and create and share plans for teaching strategies and activities. Resource units may also include common tests and other evaluation procedures.

Some units that are planned by collaborative effort may be regarded as teaching units. These will not offer the same number and variety of activities as resource units, but they will have specific activities or lesson plans. Only a few, if any, alternative activities will be provided. Teachers may be expected to follow such units entirely, or they may have the option of doing the prescribed lessons or developing their own plans.

Teachers who are making a move into a grade level and school where such collaborative units are used may want to consider the following as guidelines:

1 Find out what degree of conformity and collaboration is expected from you as well as the extent to which you are expected to use units already prepared. At this step and all others, it is good to establish an advice-seeking relationship with a mentor teacher or the lead teacher if possible. (At the same time, you can find out how much creativity is encouraged.)
2 Become familiar with available units, paying attention to the goals and objectives. (Make sure that you understand and follow the pattern of intent.)
3 See how the collaborative units relate to the textbooks that are in the classroom (if there are any).
4 Browse through the activities looking for the overall motivational and teaching quality as well as particularly outstanding ideas and plans.
5 Look for ways that you can put your own creativity into existing activities. Simply by adding details, embellishing, and improving the focus of activities and lessons in existing collaborative plans you may enliven your own teaching.
6 If the school allows, plan alternative activities and lessons to substitute for those that you see to be weaker.
7 Work through and implement the plans provided. Keep an open mind, but review effectiveness and possible alternatives.

Teacher-Developed Units

When and how should teachers develop their own teaching units? The prevailing pattern for many social studies teachers is to stick to the textbook, partially because teachers have the feeling that this is what they are supposed to do and partly because it is easy and safe. We have already said that textbook teaching is an easy pattern to set and be stuck with. Nearly all teachers, pressured with too much to do and too little time, find it necessary to use textbook-centered units or some other prepared instructional plans.

Teachers should, however, develop new units whenever possible. Teaching is a creative profession and creative teachers will want to be constantly developing new ideas themselves. However, given the amount of time required to find, adapt, and develop resources, developing new units is an ongoing task.

Teacher-made units may take any form, but whatever form they take is almost certainly going to mean more work for the teacher compared to simply following a prepared unit plan. The major purpose of developing unit plans is that planning such units will mean more effective and impactful teaching. Teacher-made units are worth the effort because they can be made to fit the specific needs and abilities of your students. Teacher-made units can consider resources that are the teacher's personal possessions as well as those that may be part of a school and/or classroom collection. Such units can also reflect a teacher's individual abilities, talents, personality, and teaching style. Most important, perhaps, is the argument that planning a teaching unit can be creatively and personally satisfying. It can provide teachers with that sense of accomplishment that is so important for retaining a positive attitude and avoiding burnout in any profession, especially one like teaching.

Individual teaching units have the tailor-made quality of being uniquely suited to achieving what the teacher thinks to be most important in the very ways that seem most suitable for the people most directly involved.

Deciding on Unit Topics

Teachers do not usually have total freedom in choosing unit topics. The teacher may be expected to follow a set of curriculum guidelines, a scope and sequence, or a curriculum map where a course of study is outlined. In some instances, teachers are required to stick to the topics described in these systems or state guides, but sometimes they have the freedom to develop their own interests as well. A second option that teachers may have is to plan in conjunction with other teachers on their team (either grade level or some other configuration) so that all students are exposed to similar topics or themes. In a few cases, teachers have the flexibility of doing teacher-guided group planning through which interests, needs, and problems identified by the students are explored.

Whether the teacher is planning the unit or helping students to plan, a similar process occurs. Sometimes a wonderful, exciting idea seems to almost jump out. The teacher or the class experiences some stimulating, motivating event that generates enthusiasm and curiosity. For example, something in the news, an event on the calendar, a happening in the neighborhood, or something someone reads or sees on television grabs your attention and makes a topic seem like the perfect study for the class. More often the teacher may be searching for a topic. For such searches, thinking goes through four stages:

1 Coming up with a menu of possible topics
2 Narrowing the field and finding a broad focus
3 Identifying a topic and refining that selection into a title that adds zest and uniqueness (taking it out of the boring and mundane class)
4 Deciding on the direction and structure that studying that topic ought to take.

The teacher first needs to have an idea of which topics are appropriate for a unit in social studies. It would be true, but not very helpful, to say that the range of topics almost defies description. Looking at one or several textbooks may give some idea of the types of topics that might be appropriate. This is going to provide a limited notion, at best, and probably an unimaginative one. To get a broad picture it might be suggested that, among the possible unit topics, the following are typical: countries or groups of countries, regions, civilizations, specific places or types of places, eras, specific time periods, events or a series of related events, processes, phenomena, problems, historical figures, historical developments, and issues.

To show how the evolution of selection can take place, it might be useful to examine an example of a 6th-grade teacher who has already gone through the process of selecting a unit topic.

Planning Episode #1

Mrs. Conner, a 6th-grade teacher at Hart Middle School, has selected the topic of the Middle East for her next unit. The topic is timely, but greater focus is needed.

At this point, Mrs. Conner uses a few resources and discusses her ideas with colleagues. Eventually, this produces a list of possibilities that vary in quality, focus, usefulness, appropriateness, and appeal. The list is:

Middle Eastern Folk Tales
Islam and the Middle East
Leaders of the Middle East Today
From Mohammad to Saladin to Sulieman: People of Influence in Middle Eastern History
European Colonies in the Middle East
The Countries of the Middle East Today
What It Is Like to Live in the Middle East
The Riches and Resources of the Middle East
Cities of the Middle East

Once a satisfactory list has been formed, the narrowing process begins. The individual topics are weighed in the balance of questions such as:

- How does this fit in with the other units that are being taught?
- How does this relate to the overall goals and purposes for the class?
- Is this something that this class might really get excited about?
- Is this broad enough (or narrow enough)? Is it too general (or too specific) in the focus it allows?
- Are there resources available?
- How does this approach fit in with the way we are handling other topics in the class?
- How exciting is this topic for students? For me?

After deliberation, the list is reduced to two or three possible titles and at last Mrs. Conner decides on "What It Is Like to Live in the Middle East" as the focus. It seems provocative, creates curiosity, and yet leaves room for some of the geographic focus she wants. It is precisely because of that openness that more thought is necessary.

Mrs. Conner then starts to flesh out some sense of direction. For example, she considers areas where students lack accurate knowledge about the Middle East. She also identifies a series of problems related to the topic:

- The belief that the people in the Middle East all have the same culture
- The belief that all of the Middle East is a desert
- The idea that all Middle Easterners support terrorism
- Ignorance about how modern Middle Eastern people live.

Developing the Unit Plan

Once a focus has been found, effort can be directed at developing one of three types of units. Teachers may decide to develop a resource unit. The kind of work that this involves is mainly creating, collecting, gathering, and ordering materials, teaching ideas, and activities, much as a team of teachers would do in developing a collaborative resource unit. One major difference is that the teacher can include personal resources that would not be available to everyone in a collaborative unit. The other two options, sketch units and teaching units, differ from one another most in the extent of development and in the amount of attention that is given to detail. Sketch units are of greatest use to teachers who are trying to form a broad overview of the teaching content, sequence, and activities and who then use the sketch unit as a basis to gather resources and do more specific planning later. These outline plans are also useful to teachers who find it convenient to rely heavily on textual materials but who want to have the control of doing their own basic planning.

Teaching units are more thorough and fleshed out in greater detail. They offer teachers the advantage of a plan of study that needs only calendar and success/failure adjustments. That is, the teacher does very little planning once the unit is complete other than making adaptations when teaching sequences utilize a different amount of time than originally allotted or where careful monitoring indicates a need for additional activities.

Whether the teacher is doing a sketch unit or a teaching unit, the next step in planning is to get a clear and specific picture of the desired learning outcomes. This is going to help in two ways: It will give directional focus and it will help limit the scope. This targeting tells us what to teach while, at the same time, keeps us from the pointless and sometimes frustrating activity of trying to teach everything about often broad unit topics.

There are several ways to attack the problem. The teacher may choose to begin by developing a set of instructional objectives. Another starting place is the content itself. Some teachers prefer to start with a content outline or a content organizational chart in which a list of generalizations can serve as headings. Another idea is a kind of visual representation called a web, which shows the interrelationships of the different concepts and/or elements to be covered in the unit. Planning webs allow teachers to examine objectives, content outlines, and webs.

Instructional Objectives

At some point in planning, a teacher needs to be concerned with the learning outcomes that he or she wants to occur as a result of the instruction. Educators usually refer to the outcomes that are given special focus as objectives. A social studies-centered unit will have multiple objectives. In fact, most social studies activities have several objectives in addition to much incidental learning.

Objectives are targeted gains in knowledge or skills or desired changes in affective areas like aspirations, attitudes, values, and feelings. Since they are targets, objectives need to be identified as specifically as possible. A well-stated set of objectives should give clear direction to the teacher and be of help in planning activities. Specific objectives are also helpful to teachers and students in evaluating learning. By clearly identifying what the outcomes should be, everyone can tell when they are achieved.

For this reason, many school systems insist that teachers use what are referred to as behavioral objectives. Behavioral objectives are even more precise. They identify specific acts that students can perform that will demonstrate that the desired learning or change has occurred. Such objectives are observable, and the standard of successful achievement is identified.

Language is very important in writing behavioral objectives. Words and terms that suggest that the teacher would have to know what was going on inside a student's mind are simply unacceptable. A properly stated behavioral objective would never suggest that the student would "know" or "understand" something. Parallel examples of behavioral and non-behavioral objectives are detailed in Table 3.2. In each set, the first objective uses acceptable behavioral objective language while the second does not. It should be noted that behavioral objectives cannot be written simply by referring to some word list of strong specific action verbs. Teachers who do this may fall into the trap of focusing on trivialities or identifying activities rather than desired learning outcomes. Words and phrases in isolation may be deceptive. The specific identification of an observable action that shows learning defines an objective as behavioral. It should also be noted that an objective can be very specific, important, and valuable for teaching, yet not be behavioral.

Content Outlines and Flowcharts

Content outlines help the teacher determine what is most important to teach. They help teachers and students discover the structure of the topic being studied. An outline may be a simple content flowchart, as detailed in Figure 3.1, which identifies the key subtopics in a unit on Egypt and the order in which they will be taught. A flowchart not only identifies the areas of study but also begins to suggest the order of the teaching itself.

Concept Webs

A visual device that teachers can use to frame the big picture of a unit is called a web because its appearance bears a strong resemblance to a spider's work. Basically, a web shows how the various

Table 3.2 Examples of Behavioral and Non-Behavioral Objectives

Example Set #1	
Behavioral	Given a cup of multiple colored candies, students will be able to correctly make a graph showing the distribution by color.
Non-Behavioral	Kindergarten students will learn to graph using one criterion.
Example Set #2	
Behavioral	After studying the community and the people who work in it, the students will be able to match pictures of ten community helpers they have studied with their place of work on a pictographic map of the community.
Non-Behavioral	Students will become aware of the workplaces of community helpers.
Example Set #3	
Behavioral	After a study of the Middle Ages in Europe, students will be able to list three provisions of the Magna Carta.
Non-Behavioral	Students will realize the significance of the Magna Carta.
Example Set #4	
Behavioral	Students will be able to correctly identify areas of high population density on a population map.
Non-Behavioral	Students will understand how to use a population map.
Example Set #5	
Behavioral	After a study of the maps of Africa, the student will be able to name five countries in Africa.
Non-Behavioral	Students will know that Africa is a continent made up of over 40 nations.

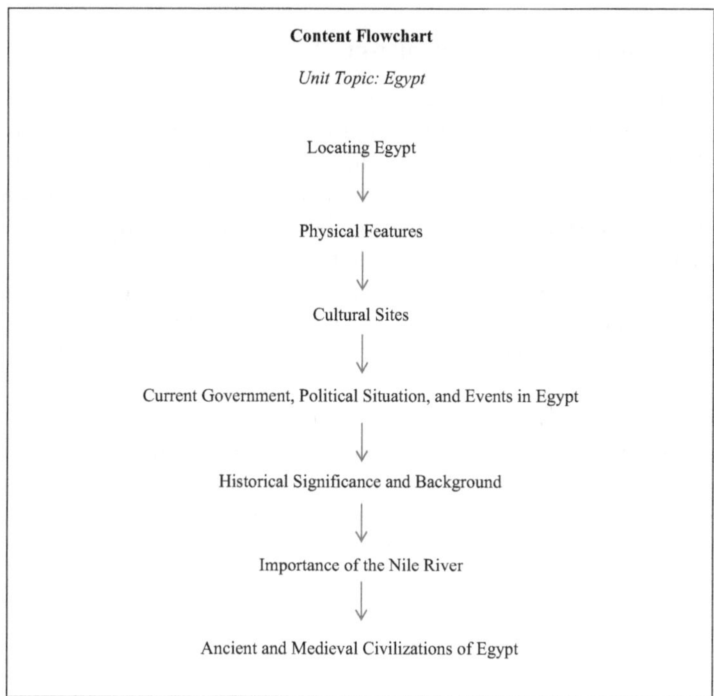

Figure 3.1 Example of a Content Flowchart.

concepts covered in a unit are linked or interrelated. Near the center of the web are the broad topics and most important ideas. Peripheral layers show the subordinate and less important ideas. Unit webs are best evolved in two stages. The first stage is simply brainstorming and choosing topics to study. The second stage arranges these topics according to priorities (importance) and relationships. Webbing is a better tool when the teacher has a comfortable familiarity with the unit topic and therefore knows the content. Figure 3.2 details a concept web for a unit on Native Americans.

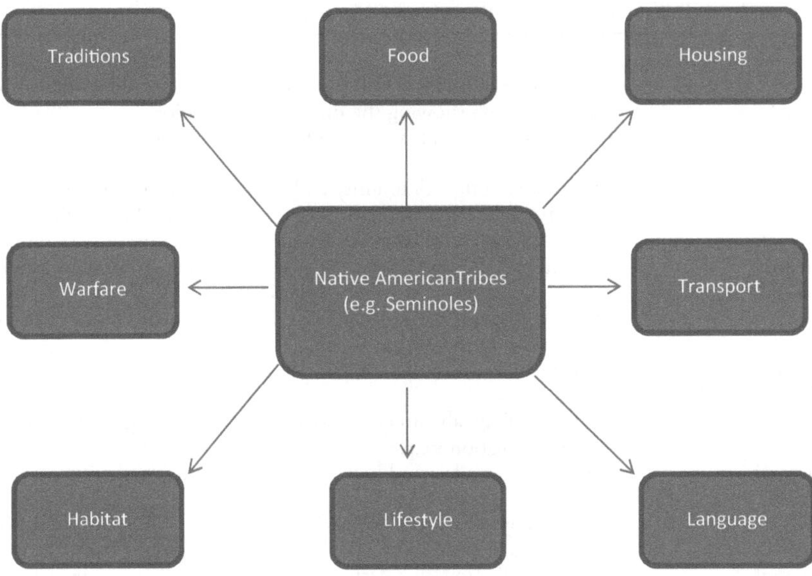

Figure 3.2 Concept Web for a Unit on Native Americans.

Moving Toward the Development of Activities

As the teacher is building toward this mental picture of the unit, a lot of other work and thinking needs to be going on simultaneously. One thing that is very important is that the teacher needs to be constantly on the lookout for resources. The possibilities can be overwhelming. Among the available resources are books and magazines with good teaching activities, fiction and nonfiction books and stories that students will want and be able to read, and other resources such as films, streaming video, digital resources, computer programs, music, and artifacts.

The possible tools of teaching often accumulate until there is a problem of selecting the best, most appropriate, and most useful. The resources, along with the overview of the content and the development of the objectives, begin to shape the kind of learning activities that will form the unit itself.

The dramatic element of the classroom was alluded to earlier. The sequencing of the teaching-learning activities in a unit is very much like structuring a drama itself. Much like a play or a movie, if you can imagine a very long drama, the unit unfolds over several days or weeks. Like a drama, the earliest stages of the unit must grab the students' attention (set); provide a sense of direction and purpose (objectives); create excitement, interest, and suspense; and give a great deal of background information. This is often referred to as the initiation stage of the unit, and teachers usually have just one or, at best, two days to accomplish everything described.

Once the unit is launched, the body of the unit can be built of activities that are aimed at developing the objectives and maintaining and extending interest. These activities, which form the greatest part of the unit, are sometimes referred to collectively as the developmental phase of the unit. Most of the research, information gathering and sharing, problem solving, and extension and enrichment of the unit goes on during this developmental period.

The final phase of a unit, called the culmination phase, serves multiple functional purposes. At this point, it is obvious that closure is needed—some activity or activities that will give students a sense that they are finished with this particular study. A unit needs a climax and the culminating activities need to provide this. It may be that students will show what they have learned by sharing their knowledge with someone else: parents, the principal, other classes, or even each other. So, one type of culmination activity might be a program, a festival or cultural celebration, the making of a movie by the class, or some similar activity. The culmination of the unit also serves as a summative overview and a drawing together of all that has been learned. It should be, in fact, the time when the teacher helps students to comprehend the significance of what they have been studying. If students have been working on a problem or a group of problems, this is the point where solutions are offered and findings and conclusions are reached. Not surprisingly, the culmination of a unit is also the place where the teacher needs to take stock or make the final evaluation of what has been learned. Of course, evaluation should be ongoing and present in every activity, but it is again at this culmination level that the teacher needs to make the final assessment. One last function that the culmination of a unit may serve is that of maintaining or even stimulating interest in the topic that has been studied while providing a transition to some new area of study. While it may seem strange to try to create interest just as you are leaving an area of study, this is the very point at which we want to be saying to students, "We've spent all the time we can, but there are a lot more interesting and exciting things for you to learn if you want to go on your own. Now here are some other ideas for you to consider and here are some great resources you can use." The transitional function is equally logical when you think about how students learn. Basically, they understand new experiences by comparing them to things they already know about. So, the transitional aspect of the culmination is simply the beginning of showing relationships, similarities, and dissimilarities with the new area of study.

The format of a unit may be developed in many ways, with no single format being *the* correct method. To mention a few of the alternatives, units may be organized as sequenced daily lesson plans with lessons of varying duration each structured around one or more specific objectives; as a set of lessons, each teaching specific concepts, generalizations, or subtopics; or as subsets of activities reflecting the various curricular areas from which the activities are drawn (art, music, language arts, etc.). Regardless of the format that shapes the unit, all unit plans need to show reflection on certain necessary elements. These are shown in the format that follows. A brief (one week) unit follows, illustrating how this format may be used.

Unit Elements Format

1 Descriptive and identifying information
   a A title (this may be in the form of a statement, a problem statement, an issue description, or a descriptive and appealing title)
   b Grade level(s) of students toward whom the unit is directed
   c Estimated or allotted duration (the time in weeks with some description of how much time is to be spent each week)
2 Rationale
   a Overview statement of the importance of the area of study regarding both content and the approaches used
   b Arguments and assertions regarding the significance and the appropriateness of the topic of study
3 Unit objectives
   a A list of the most important targeted learning outcomes of the entire unit (these may be categorized in some way, the most common classification being cognitive or knowledge objectives to include facts to be remembered, concepts and generalizations to be understood, etc.; affective objectives to include values and attitudes to be developed, beliefs and aspirations to be gained, appreciations to be cultivated, etc.; and psychomotor or skills objectives)
4 Content description: This may be embodied in the objectives and not needed as a separate entity. A content description may be presented in several ways, including the following:
   a A list of generalizations
   b A sequenced content outline

   c A concept web of the unit
   d A list of concept definitions.
5 Activity sequence: There is more than one way to present this area, including the following:
   a An ordered set of lesson plans with initiating, development, and culminating activities in order
   b Parties arranged according to the subject area with which the social studies is being integrated (art, music, language arts, etc.)
   c Unit activities organized into subunits each representing a subtopic, a generalization, a key concept, or some other content heading
   d Unit organized around key activities with contingency alternatives stemming from each of these
   e Unit organized into key activities with enrichment activities and skill and background activities planned on a needs basis (often this will be done in the form of Learning Centers).
6 Description of the unit evaluation process: Development of the evaluation or assessment design as it is built into individual lessons and activities. Ways of assessing to what extent learning outcomes have been achieved, detailing evaluation strategies, including any unit test(s).
7 Accommodations: Be sure to plan various accommodating activities and strategies for students with different learning needs.
8 Resources: This cataloging effort may take the form of a simple bibliographic listing or a more useful but more time-consuming series of annotated bibliographic entries. One convenient organization pattern for resources is division into teacher-resource and student-resource sections. It is also useful to create subcategories based on resource type (e.g., audiovisual materials, games and computer resources, reference materials, enrichment trade books, etc.).

Planning Episode #2

Unit Title: The Acquisition of the Louisiana Territory
Grade Level: 6th grade
Allotted Time: Five 50-minute class periods

Rationale

FYI

A rationale is justification for teaching the content in narrative form. This may include real-life applications or other reasons for covering the material in the manner you are planning. For example, is the topic mandated by state law? Is the topic relevant in local news? etc. Justification for teaching the content in narrative form. Real-life applications or other reasons for covering the material in the manner that you are planning, i.e. is it mandated by state law? Is the topic relevant in local news? etc.

This unit deals with the acquisition of the Louisiana Territory by the United States and the subsequent exploration of that territory. Since the class is studying the history of the United States throughout the year, the study of a particular historic episode in more detail is especially useful to show the human side of history. The Lewis and Clark expedition shows the hazards and some of the difficulties faced by pioneers, without violence or sensationalism. The journal of the expedition is a complete and detailed primary resource that students can read with understanding. The members of the expedition exemplify courage, resourcefulness, a sense of responsibility and duty, and other desirable character traits. The purchase and the exploration of the Louisiana Territory nearly doubled the territorial size of the United States, thus having tremendous impact on the young nation.

Objectives

> **FYI**
>
> To help you write objectives, answer the following question. What skills will the students acquire from this unit/lesson?

> **FYI**
>
> When planning a unit, you are outlining the objectives you hope students will meet by the end of the unit.

The students will be able to:

- identify the importance of the Louisiana Purchase
- explain the major details of the purchase
- identify purposes for the Lewis and Clark expedition
- name several of the difficulties that the expedition encountered
- trace the approximate route of the expedition on a map and explain how long Lewis and Clark spent on the trip
- make comparisons to other explorations.

Content Outline

> **FYI**
>
> When planning a unit, you are outlining the content you hope students will learn by the end of the unit.

1 Events leading to the purchase:
   a. the need of Americans on the western frontier to use the port of New Orleans
   b. the acquisition of Spanish territories by France and the closing of the port of New Orleans
   c. Monroe and Livingston appointed by President Jefferson to go to France
   d. the personality and motivations of Napoleon:
      i. need for money to finance his military efforts
      ii. lack of desire to defend large distant territories against a powerful British navy
   e. the vision and opportunism of Monroe and Livingston to exceed their authorization
2 The Lewis and Clark expedition:
   a. purposes of the expedition:
      i. gathering of scientific information
      ii. contact with the native peoples
      iii. proving the feasibility of travel
      iv. exploring and mapping
   b. Difficulties and dangers
      i. environment and weather
      ii. travel hardships and problems (including the danger of being lost)
      iii. possible encounters with hostile natives and wild animals
   c. Impact of the expedition

Initiating Activity

FYI

When planning a unit, this section is a summary of what you hope students will learn by the end of the unit. You have yet to create daily lesson plans. The daily lesson plans will provide much more detail.

Procedure

Present the background to the Louisiana Purchase as a series of problems in a storytelling context, getting students to respond.

Problems

If you are in a business, what do you have to do? (Sell goods or services.)

Now, if you have something to sell and you and your product are one place and the people who want it are hundreds of miles away, what is your problem? (To get it to market as quickly and cheaply as you can. Give the background on the furs and other goods Americans had to take down river to New Orleans.)

Well, what happens when the officials in New Orleans will not let you bring your goods through any longer? (Guide discussion to the eventual involvement of President Jefferson.) What do you think the president will do?

The next step leads into a role-play activity in which two students portraying James Monroe and Robert Livingston are given their commission by the president and Congress to buy New Orleans and Florida from France for $2,000,000. They meet the Emperor Napoleon who was, so the story goes, in his bath at the time of the interview (Napoleon should be portrayed by the teacher, another adult, or a very well-coached student). At the point where Napoleon makes his offer, interrupt the role-play to discuss with the class the implications and the reasoning of all parties. Explain to the students that the final terms were worked out not by Napoleon himself, but by the French Foreign Minister, whose name was Talleyrand Perigord, and by the Treasury Minister, Barbe-Marbois. Tell them that these two ministers got more money out of the Americans than Napoleon expected. Have students guess how much more money. (It was $5 million.) Ask the students about who they think got the better deal. Then bring closure.

Tell the students that Jefferson and the United States had bought "a pig in a poke" (a deal that is foolishly accepted without being fully examined). Hold up a cloth or leather bag and explain the expression. Tell them that Jefferson knew there was a big river involved (pull a long-crooked strip of blue paper out of the bag) and an important port city (pull out many Monopoly-type houses and tiny toy ships). But all Jefferson or anyone else knew about the rest of that purchase was that there was a lot of it. (At this point, empty the bag, which is filled with the jigsaw puzzle pieces representing the current states that were eventually carved from the Louisiana Territory.) Tell the students that Jefferson was not the kind of man who would leave something like this alone. Lead into the commissioning of the Lewis and Clark expedition and its purposes. Close by announcing the objectives of the rest of the unit and then reviewing the details of the purchase, using a large wall map and tracing the expedition's route very quickly.

Developmental Activities

Review the Louisiana Purchase. Tell the students that this amounted to a cost of about 2 cents per acre. Have them figure the number of acres and square miles. Possibly have them figure cost using inflation.

Explain the purposes of the Lewis and Clark expedition by reading or having students read portions of the Lewis and Clark journals. Discuss the importance of the expedition.

Using journals and maps, have students make a carefully measured timeline of the 28-month journey. Also, have them use string measures (pieces of string cut and marked to fit map scale) to measure various segments of the journey. Discuss the reasons some distances would take longer.

Discuss the hardships, dangers, problems, and difficulties that students imagine the expedition might have encountered. Then have students do the following in-basket activity, which is based on actual incidents during the expedition.

In-Basket Activity: Up the River with Lewis and Clark

Students will be able to:

- explain the dangers and difficulties faced by Lewis and Clark.
- recognize differences in significance and urgency among frontier situations, where outside help could not be available.

Have students work in pairs playing the roles of Lewis and Clark. The role-play activity should be done in the following steps:

1. Let students examine a map showing the route of the Lewis and Clark expedition. Explain the reasons and purposes of the expedition.
2. Have students work through 15 situations prioritizing the need for action and finding solutions. You may want them to write down their solutions. Some will be obvious, others will require some creativity.
3. Discuss the various ways students have ordered the situations and compare solutions.
4. Have students compare their solutions with what Lewis and Clark actually did.
5. Have students discuss how their priorities differ and compare with a historian's views. (Note: you may prefer to use only a teacher copy and present them orally.)
6. Have students discuss what they learned from the activity. You might discuss why most Native Americans were so friendly (this is very different from the picture painted by movies and television), other dangers that might have come up, the length of the journey, and the time it took. Tell students there is, of course, no correct order for the problems to be solved. Then, discuss with them the logic that they used in their own sequencing of the tasks.

As a follow-up activity, give students a list of other explorations that they might like to read about and study:

- the voyages of Columbus
- LaSalle's trip down the Mississippi River
- NASA space explorations, including Neil Armstrong's moon landing
- Leif Eriksson's voyages.

Have students discuss how these were similar to and different from the Lewis and Clark expedition.

Culminating Activity

FYI

When planning a unit, this section is a summary of potential assessment activities you hope students will be able to complete by the end of the unit. You have yet to create daily lessons plans. The daily lesson plans will provide much more detail. At this stage, you will also start to prepare detailed rubrics, checklists, and tests.

Have students put on a program consisting of:

1. a reenactment of Jefferson's decision to send emissaries to France and the meeting between Napoleon and Monroe and Livingston
2. a Living Time Line in which students costume themselves as events in the Louisiana Purchase and Lewis and Clark expedition, each describing his or her own event
3. a floor-map activity in which guides lead guests along a large floor-map representation, showing guests the route of the expedition.

Evaluation

Evaluation is built into every activity in some way. A final unit test might consist of the following questions:

- From what country did the United States purchase the Louisiana Territory and what was the price?
- Name two dangers faced by the Lewis and Clark expedition.
- Give one reason the Louisiana Purchase was important.
- Give one aim of the Lewis and Clark expedition.
- On an unlabeled map, trace the route of the Lewis and Clark expedition, naming the rivers they traveled.

Finding and Using Prepared Units

Teachers may feel that they do not have the time, energy, or ingenuity to prepare elaborate and extensive units of their own for the entire school year. At the same time, they may not want to fall into the pattern of teaching directly from the textbook.

There is an alternative available to teachers even if there is no established district or school curriculum guide complete with authorized, already prepared units and even if there is no easy collaborative planning or sharing going on in the school in which they teach. That alternative is to "borrow" premade units from some source outside the school.

The maxim of unit "borrowing" ought to be, "If you are going to 'borrow,' then take the best!" How does a teacher with little time to search (if you had the time, you would have planned your own unit in the first place) find the best?

First, you should search the most prominent of resources—the Internet. Searching Google or Yahoo for lesson plans will ensure a plethora of options. However, you need to ensure that the lesson plans are adapted to meet the needs of your students and instructional objectives. Second, you should search professionally or even commercially prepared materials that have already undergone the scrutiny of selection and the polishing of rewrites and editing. A starting place among these are the commercial teaching magazines such as *Instructor, Teacher, Learning*, or *Mailbox*. Professional journals such as *Social Education, The Social Studies, The History Teacher, The Clearing House, Middle Level Learning*, and *Social Studies Research and Practice* will be worth a look through, too. A trip to a university library or searching through electronic databases could be very fruitful. You can also examine other textbook series teacher editions. The teacher editions may hold some pleasant surprises. Certainly, any gems found in these outside textbooks will require some adaptation, but that will be true of almost any "borrowed" material. One other resource worth a look through in a university library will be other methods textbooks in social studies. Some of these contain provocative unit ideas.

Third, you should "always be on the lookout for materials for teaching." At conferences, in the rooms of other teachers, at the teacher center (if your system is lucky enough to have one), browsing online, or even in the dentist's office, the very thing needed may be waiting for the alert person who takes the initiative and the time to nose through the available material. One of the resources for teacher-prepared units is the Association for Supervision and Curriculum Development, which publishes a list of available units and curriculum materials available for school systems.

To use prepared units effectively, the key concern is adaptation. The focus in adaptation must be on the intended learning outcomes and the students' needs. If the teacher begins with concern for how a unit plan can bring significant learning, then all other kinds of needed changes fall into place. A second and related focus should be on the vitality and motivational appeal of the activities for students. Will students be excited, interested, and stimulated by these activities? A third related concern to the teacher is whether the resources are available. This may have to do as much with a realistic self-assessment of time, energy, and initiative as with material resources, but both are needed.

Planning for Shorter Instructional Sequences

The most useful and important among shorter instructional sequences is the lesson plan or daily lesson plan. A lesson plan is in many ways a unit in miniature, and lessons contain similar key elements such as objectives, procedural descriptions of activities, and identification of resources. A lesson plan is a detailed outline of what and how you plan to teach a given topic on a day and/or over several days.

Any lesson plan design that is going to be particularly useful will be one that is structured to help students better retain what they are taught. Where a unit is examining a broad topic, a lesson plan is examining a specific subtopic of the unit. The format of a lesson plan will depend on your school/district. In the standards and accountability era we live in, a basic lesson plan often includes the information shown in Box 3.1.

Teachers should consider answering the following questions at the start of planning a lesson. These questions can help organize and "kick-start" the lesson-planning process.

1 What do you want the students to learn from the lesson? (goal, rationale)
2 What skills will the students acquire from the lesson? (objectives)
3 What is the best way to get the information across to the students? (procedures)
4 Do I have the materials needed to effectively teach this lesson? (materials)
5 How I can I make sure the students understand what I am teaching? (evaluation)

Box 3.1 Russell's Basic Components of a Lesson Plan

1. Lesson Topic
2. Objectives
3. Rationale
   A. Standards
   B. Real Life Application
   C. Other
4. Content
5. Materials/Resources (books, maps, tests, rubrics, etc…)
6. Procedures
   A. "Hook"/Involvement Strategies
   B. Sequential Lesson Steps with Time Allotment
   C. Remediation/Enrichment Strategies
   D. Closure/Preview
   E. Assessment and Evaluation (e.g. observation, test, project, etc…)
7. Accommodations
   A. ESOL Accommodations
   B. Special Education Accommodations
   C. Other (Learning Styles, etc…)

Besides Russell's Basic Components of a Lesson Plan format given in Box 3.1, there are variations of lesson planning. The Hunter (1990–1991) lesson sequence has been a helpful model because it is structured in a series of distinctive, easily constructed steps. A lesson design developed from the elements in Hunter's sequence follows.

1 Get the students' attention and prepare them for what they are going to learn. The teacher needs to think of ways of capturing and focusing interest on the topic of study. This part of the lesson may also review previously studied related material, making a transition and aiding understanding by relating new material to the old. The major purpose is to develop readiness for learning the new topic.
2 Explain the objective(s) or purpose(s). A key element in the Hunter approach is that the students have a good idea of the ends the teacher has in mind. This step includes a clear communication of what the teacher intends to accomplish. In a sense, though, it is something more than that; if possible, the teacher and the students need to reach a consensus so that there can be shared goals that are understood by both.
3 Do direct teaching. In this step, the teacher is communicating the new information of the lesson, teaching concepts, and so on, using a variety of techniques.
4 If it is appropriate, model what you want the learners to do. Though not all lessons require this step, in many it is essential. Basically, it involves demonstration or the completing of examples by the teacher. The teacher shows students how each step in a process is completed (e.g., finding a location using map coordinates).
5 Check for understanding. This is sometimes referred to as the monitor and adjust stage. It is a point at which the teacher determines if the students understand what the lesson is all about. It requires some activity in which students give and receive feedback. This may involve a signaling device in which all students participate, a questioning technique using selected students, or individual responses from every student.
6 Provide guided practice. The teacher gives students a chance to use new skills or concepts. Again, the emphasis is on monitored practice with feedback from the teacher.
7 Provide opportunity for independent practice.

Though this lesson-planning model will not and should not be suited to every lesson, it can provide a useful pattern for many. As a model, the seven steps in the lesson plan show very clearly the importance of developing detail, specificity, and sequence in the procedure of a lesson plan. The following is an example of a plan developed along the lines of the Hunter model.

Planning Episode #3

Teacher: Joshua Kenna
Grade: 6th Grade
Unit Topic: Japanese American Internment Camps
Lesson Topic: Justice Prevails?

Objectives

FYI

Ideally a lesson plan will include two to three objectives.

- Students will be able to identify the prejudice that Japanese Americans experienced during WWII.
- Students will be able to explain how the internment of Japanese Americans was wrong.
- Students will be able to express empathy toward internees by writing a letter of apology on behalf of the American government.

Standards

FYI

This lesson plan aligns with the national standards. Your lesson plan should also align with your state standards.

- NCSS Standard 2: Time, Continuity, and Change: *Social studies programs should include experiences that provide for the study of the past and its legacy.*
- NCSS Standard 3: People, Places, and Environments: *Social studies programs should include experiences that provide for the study of people, places, and environments.*
- Common Core CCSS.ELA-LITERACY.CCRA.SL.1-Prepare for and participate effectively in a range of conversations and collaborations with diverse partners, building on others' ideas and expressing their own clearly and persuasively.
- Common Core CCSS.ELA-LITERACY.CCRA.SL.2-Integrate and evaluate information presented in diverse media and formats, including visually, quantitatively, and orally.

Daily Planner

FYI

This section should list activities and provide the estimated time needed.

- Spectrum Vocabulary: 5–10 minutes
- Read *Japanese American Internment Camps* by Gail Sakurai: 20–30 minutes
- Brainstorm activity: 5–10 minutes
- Ranking Injustices and Accomplishments: 10–15 minutes
- Example Letter of Apology: 5–10 minutes
- Letter of Apology homework

Activating Strategy

> **FYI**
>
> The activating strategy should engage students and "hook" them into the lesson.

Whole Group Instruction

The teacher will ask students to look at the white board and recite the two written words, "Injustice" and "Prejudice" as a group *(Visual, Auditory).*

Then the teacher will complete a "Spectrum Vocabulary" activity.

- Spectrum Vocabulary: Students will be asked to stand along a spectrum based on their knowledge of a given vocabulary word (i.e., they will stand either at the "I know" or "I don't know" spot or anywhere in between, which means they heard of the word but don't know it well enough to define it). This is a great activity as it requires students to move; also the teacher can gain a visual of who does or does not know a vocabulary word. The teacher will also ask every student standing in the "I know" section to define the word for the class *(Kinesthetic, Auditory, and Visual).*

Once the students have completed the activity for both words, the teacher will ask students the following essential questions, which should also be written on either the white board or in a PowerPoint: "Was it right to place Japanese Americans in Internment Camps during WWII? Explain." and "What relationship exists between injustice and prejudice?" *(Auditory).*

Instruction

Small Group Instruction/Collaboration

> **FYI**
>
> This section will detail the instructional procedures.

- The teacher will have students read the book *Japanese American Internment Camps* by Gail Sakurai in small groups, meaning students will take turns reading small passages until the book is completed in its entirety. However, a teacher could read the book with the students or have students sit in small groups but read silently and periodically discuss what they read *(Visual, Auditory, Intrapersonal, and Interpersonal).*
- Upon completing the book, the teacher will ask the students how they felt about the treatment of Japanese Americans *(Auditory).*

Guided & Independent Practice

FYI

In this section, the teacher is detailing how he or she will guide students and allow them to work independently.

Small Group Instruction/Collaboration

The teacher will have students start a "Brainstorming" activity and students will not have the aid of the book *(Visual, Auditory, and Interpersonal).*

- Brainstorming: Students, as a small cooperative group, will try to list all the injustices Japanese Americans endured and accomplishments they achieved during the Internment Camp time period *(Visual, Auditory, Kinesthetic, Interpersonal).*

Once students have finished compiling the list of injustices and accomplishments they will have a small group discussion. Each group must rank the injustices and accomplishments from the highest degree to the lowest degree. Groups will then share their ranked lists with the whole class and justify their rankings *(Visual, Auditory, Kinesthetic, and Interpersonal).*

Closure

FYI

Here the teacher is wrapping up the lesson and bringing everything together, thus providing closure to the students' learning experience.

Whole Group Instruction

Following the presentations of the ranked lists the teacher will ask students, "What can one do after an injustice has been committed?" There are various answers but one answer that the teacher should be looking for is to apologize *(Auditory).*

The teacher will ask students what are some necessary components for writing a letter of apology. The students should list the following:

- Name of recipient
- An apology
- Acknowledgement of wrongful actions with supporting details
- Name of offender

Visual

Once students have listed all the necessary components of a letter of apology, the teacher will show an example of an apology letter and go over the homework, where students will have to write an apology letter on behalf of the U.S. government (*Intrapersonal*).

Assessment/Evaluation

FYI

This section details the assessment procedures that will be utilized.

Individual Assessment

Students are to write a letter to Japanese American internees apologizing on behalf of the U.S. government. Students are expected to include at least two specific injustices and two accomplishments of Japanese Americans. They must also express why they feel the actions taken by the U.S. government was in fact an injustice. Students could complete this as homework if desired (*Intrapersonal*).

Materials/Technology

FYI

All teachers want to make sure all required materials are obtained prior to the lesson. You don't want to start baking a cake only to find out halfway through that you have no flour.

- White/chalk board and markers/chalk
- Projector and PowerPoint or document camera
- Book: *Japanese American Internment Camps* by Gail Sakurai
- Butcher paper and markers/crayons

Cross-Curricular Connections

FYI

Cross-curricular connections are more common in today's classroom than ever before and are a main theme in the Common Core Standards.

- *Reading/Literacy*: Students will read a nonfiction book entitled *Japanese American Internment Camps* by Gail Sakurai.
- *Writing*: Students will write an apology letter to Japanese American internees on behalf of the U.S. government.

Meeting Individual Needs of Diverse Learners

FYI

Meeting the individuals needs of all learners should be standard practice. Here you want to plan appropriate accommodations for your students.

- *Multiple Intelligences*: This lesson fosters auditory, visual, kinesthetic, interpersonal, and intrapersonal learning through the small cooperative grouping and the various activities and the assignment. The parts of this lesson that relate to these learners are highlighted throughout the lesson.
- *Students with Disabilities*: These students will be given all the accommodations as required from their Individual Education Plans, including but not limited to: preferential seating, extra time on assignments, clear agenda, checking for comprehension beyond what is normally required, etc. Plus, this lesson utilizes small cooperative learning groups whereby students with learning difficulties can be assisted by high-achieving students.
- *English Language Learners*: Visuals will be used to aid ELL students (i.e., when telling students to get out a piece of paper, the teacher should literally pull out a piece of paper as the directions are given). Also, the teacher should try to translate the key vocabulary words in a student's native tongue if possible. Furthermore, the teacher can have these students complete their work by writing in their native language and then attempting to translate it at a later date.

Character Education Connection

FYI

Character education is considered a foundational goal of public education and is mandated in many states. Here you want to detail how you will be addressing character-related traits/topics/themes.

- Tolerance: This lesson teaches that prejudices are wrong.
- Respect: Students are encouraged to treat everyone regardless of ethnicity or skin color with respect.
- Responsibility: Students are apologizing for the actions taken by an earlier generation of Americans. This will help students learn from previous mistakes and learn to apologize for future wrongdoings that they may be responsible for.
- Caring: Students are encouraged to care for others who may not have a voice or who face prejudices.

Looking Back

The quality of planning makes a difference in the quality of teaching. Teachers fail to give adequate time to planning for a variety of reasons, but by determined systematic effort, planning can add to teaching effectiveness and satisfaction.

The term *curriculum map* is most often used to describe the long-term planning a teacher does to outline the curriculum for an entire year/semester. The term *unit* is used to describe the planning a teacher does to teach a large topic to a group of students. The teacher editions of textbooks use the term to describe the activities provided for teaching particular content, usually chapters. Whether a textbook unit or a teacher-made unit, considerable planning is involved. Teacher-made units may be of several types, including collaborative or team units, which are usually resource units.

Short-term planning most often takes the form of daily lesson plans. The format of lesson plans varies depending on your state/district. Russell's Basic Components of a Lesson Plan format and Hunter's lesson sequence are two different formats for planning a lesson. In the standards and accountability era we live in, lesson plans typically have common attributes including lesson topic, objectives, standards, materials, procedures, evaluation, and accommodations.

Extension Activity

Scenario

Even on a Friday afternoon, the front office at Yourtown High School (YHS) was a circus of activity as you emerged from your meeting with your principal, Dr. Russell. Before you could even make it to your classroom, the word had spread among the faculty about the social studies committee, and you heard quite a few teachers express interest in being on the committee. Some teachers seemed excited about helping reform social studies at YHS. Others seemed interested in protecting the status quo. You were relieved to get to your classroom, grab your stuff, and head off for the weekend. After all, Monday would be more than the start of a new week, it would be a new beginning for social studies at YHS.

Questions

1. Dr. Russell charged you with a task of forming a social studies committee to advise him on planning/reforming the curriculum. What are the advantages/disadvantages of having a committee like this in a school?
2. Do you think having teacher input on curriculum planning/reform would produce better curriculum for the students? Why or why not?
3. What are the qualities a teacher should possess to be on this committee? Of these qualities, which are the most important? How should these teachers be selected?

Task

Once the committee has been formed and organized, the teachers get to work. Imagine your group is the committee. Create a curriculum map (what will be taught and when) for your grade level's social studies curriculum. Be sure that you meet all required state standards. The scope and sequence should be detailed and be for the entire school year.

Reflective Questions

1 What are some reasons why teachers cannot always plan as effectively as they should?
2 What is a curriculum map?
3 What is the difference between long-range planning and short-term planning?
4 What is a collaborative unit?
5 What are the necessary elements in a unit plan?
6 What are the basic components of a lesson plan?

Helpful Resources

Volusia County School District has an array of curriculum maps online.
http://myvolusiaschools.org/K12-Curriculum/Pages/ElementaryCurrMaps.aspx
Watch this video of an experienced teacher detailing how she maps the curriculum and aligns it with standards and the C3 Framework.
https://youtu.be/Cq0Z06xzQTQ
Watch this video discussing unit planning versus daily lesson planning.
www.youtube.com/watch?v=UZdTmnMByQ8
Check out this video about writing learning objectives based on Bloom's Taxonomy.
www.youtube.com/watch?v=4DgkLV9h69Q
Watch this short video about writing objectives.
www.teachertube.com/video/writing-learning-objectives-introduction-423152
Federal Resources for Educational Excellence (FREE) is a U.S. Department of Education website that houses more than 1,500 federally supported teaching and learning resources. The website includes a great deal of primary sources and photos, along with ideas and suggestions for instruction.
www.free.ed.gov
Watch this first-year teacher explore how to write effective lesson plans.
www.teachertube.com/video/new-teacher-survival-guide-planning-423156
PBS Teachers provides teachers with complete lesson plans with free media spanning multiple subjects for all grades. Resources for the Classroom:
www.pbs.org/teachers.
The Gateway to 21st Century Skills. The Gateway is one of the oldest publicly accessible U.S. repositories of education resources on the web. The Gateway contains a variety of educational resource types from activities and lesson plans to online projects to assessment items. The Gateway is supported by the National Education Association.
www.thegateway.org.

Further Reading

Chandler, P. & Hawley, T. (Eds.). (2017). *Race Lessons: Using Inquiry to Teach About Race in Social Studies*. Charlotte, NC: Information Age Publishing.

This book addresses practical considerations of teaching about race within the context of history, geography, government, economics, and the behavioral sciences. The book provides teachers and teacher educators with concrete lesson ideas for how to engage learners with social studies content and issues of race.

Hickey, G. & Clabough, J. (Eds.). (2017). *Digging Deeper: Activities for Enriching and Expanding Social Studies Instruction K–12*. Charlotte, NC: Information Age Publishing.

This book includes research-based lessons and activities that enrich and expand social studies instruction while building K–12 students' critical and creative thinking. Throughout the book readers will find teacher-tested lessons/activities that link social studies content and concepts to the standards and recommendations of the National Association for Gifted Children (NAGC) and the National Council for the Social Studies (NCSS).

Lintner, T. (Ed.). (2013). *Integrative Strategies for the K–12 Social Studies Classroom*. Charlotte, NC: Information Age Publishing.

This book provides educators with insights and strategies into how to integrate social studies with other discipline areas. The book features multiple examples of integrative opportunities, and each chapter offers a series of grade-specific integrative lesson plans ready for implementation.

Roberts, P. & Kellough, R. (2006). *A Guide for Developing Interdisciplinary Thematic Units* (4th Edition). New York, NY: Prentice Hall.

This book provides a step-by-step approach to using interdisciplinary thematic units to help students acquire the knowledge and develop the problem-solving skills required for today's changing—and challenging—times.

References

Ball, D.L., & Feiman-Nemser, S. (1988). Using textbooks and teachers' guides: A dilemma for beginning teachers and teacher educators. *Curriculum Inquiry*, 18(Winter), 401–423.

Educational Market Research. (2012). *The Complete K–12 Report: Market Facts and Segment Analysis*. Rockaway Park, NY: Educational Market Research.

NCSS. (1994). *Expectations for Excellence: Curriculum Standards for the Social Studies*. Washington, DC: NCSS.

4 Assessment and Evaluation

Looking Ahead

Assessment is essential to effective social studies teaching, not because politicians say so or because there is so much stress on grades and test scores, but because it informs teachers and learners. Effective assessment tells what we are doing right and what we need to improve. Assessment, at its best, should reflect what teachers and schools are trying to accomplish.

This chapter focuses on the tools that teachers use in assessing students. We want to stress that all assessment in social studies should be firmly based on the goals and objectives of the social studies program. We also want to stress that the students need to be involved in the assessment process.

A lot has been written about authentic assessment over the past decade. Authentic assessment means that the focus is on what students do and produce rather than on test scores. The notion of authentic assessment is consistent with the problems approach. Solid authentic assessment involves students in the evaluation process, making them aware of what needs to be accomplished and learned.

Can You? Do You?

Can you ...

- explain why grades and test scores are so emphasized in schools?
- explain how teachers go about determining grades?
- explain authentic assessment?

Do you ...

- know why evaluation is always comparative?
- know how evaluation should be different in the problems approach?
- know the strengths and weaknesses of objective and subjective tests?

Focus Activity

Before reading this chapter, try the focus activity below.

Think back about your educational experiences. What was your favorite social studies assignment/project when you were a student? Why? Share experiences with classmates. Discuss the details of the assignment/project and make comparisons. Does your favorite social studies assignment/project share common attributes with others? If so, which attributes?

DOI: 10.4324/9781003217060-4

The Role of Assessment in Social Studies

Teachers and students tend to equate terms such as *assessment* or *evaluation* with grades. This is like thinking that art is a paint brush or that music is a voice or a piano. Grades and standardized tests are tools by which assessments are done. They are indicators of student progress and learning, of the degree of teaching success, and of areas of strength and weakness. Teacher-made tests, teacher observations, and the various kinds of work that students produce provide teachers with indicators. It is extremely important that teachers not lose sight of the purpose of evaluation in social studies, which, as in any other area of instruction, should be to improve student learning.

FYI

Assessments often carry a negative connotation surrounding "standardized tests," but assessments can be crucial to understanding student learning when designed and implemented properly.

Assessment, especially achievement test scores as well as summary grade evaluations on report/grade cards, takes on special importance to administrators, teachers, students, and parents. Grades and tests are important because they are the major form of feedback to students and parents. In addition, they are a concrete and permanent record based on performance data.

Feedback is only part of the reason for student assessment. Student assessment is also related to finding out how well a teacher has taught, how well a student has learned and performed, and what still needs attention. At best, evaluation guides and improves teaching and learning.

All types of student assessment involve comparison of student performance. Many people like grades and test scores because they provide the easiest comparisons and have many bases of comparison. Student performance can be compared in a quantitative way to some particular criteria of success built into school or teacher objectives, to a performance standard, to classmates, to the whole school, to a national average, or to personal past performance or perceived potential. Normative performance, for example, is the basis on which most standardized test scores are analyzed. Norms or averages can be computed and used to compare the performance of one person or group to average performance of either an age or grade group or even among all people who have taken a particular test.

Another basis of comparison is criterion-based assessment. Criterion-based assessment is the extent to which an individual can meet indicators of success that relate to particular characteristics. Levels of performance are set in advance based on some preconceived notions of what constitutes mastery.

When a teacher plans instruction, a criterion-based assessment is often useful. The preselected criteria of success identified for a lesson or a unit are called objectives. Objectives describe the specific knowledge or skills that are expected to result from the teaching/learning activities. Objectives identify the desired learning outcomes. Objectives can be more clearly defined and evaluated if they name a behavior that might be an indicator that the objective has been achieved, known as a behavioral objective.

Assessment and teaching will be more effective if based on objectives or desired learning outcomes that we can then use as indicators of the degree of success we have had in teaching. When the learning outcomes provide direction, both teaching and evaluation are more focused and purposeful learning is more likely to occur. One approach to teaching, often referred to as mastery learning, is based entirely on the notion that instruction about any basic learning needs to continue until that standard has been achieved.

Social studies has been struggling for a long time with some particular dilemmas that educators in other curricular areas may just now be starting to see. One of these dilemmas has to do with the overall evaluation of students, but especially with the assigning of grades. Social studies learning outcomes involve the acquisition of knowledge; the development of skills; the variables of interpersonal relationships; very complex and often subtle changes in personal values, philosophies, and beliefs; and other criteria that relate to performance and to the development of products that are often intricate and elaborate. For some of these outcomes, it is very easy to design ways of assessing that can be easily measured. For what may be considered the most important learning outcomes, though, measurement and assessment are much more difficult and subjective.

Principles of Assessment

Assessment is important to teaching and learning when it helps teachers, students, parents, and administrators improve on what is already being done. Well-constructed assessment gives students and parents, as much as teachers, ownership in the learning process. This can only be accomplished if all are involved in deciding what the assessment will be and how it will be used.

Alleman and Brophy (1999) discuss the changing nature of assessment in the social studies. They point out that assessment should be focused on curricular goals and objectives and be used as a means of improving both the curriculum and the instructional program. They go on to assert that "evaluation of student achievement should be used solely to improve teaching and learning" (p. 336).

The standards movement in social studies has had a profound influence on how social studies teachers view assessment. Historically, success in the traditional classroom was based on the ability to remember specified information and the mastery of particular technical skills. The job of assessment has become much more complex. Information and skills are now viewed differently, with emphasis on students learning how to obtain information and how to learn skills. Learning to learn and becoming an independent learner are stressed. The foci of evaluation are expanded to include such factors as the ability to identify and define problems, flexibility to handle new situations, ability to apply knowledge in different settings, and openness to many ideas and solutions. The real concern is the ability of students to handle problems.

An illustration of how the tools of evaluation and grading have changed is shown in Table 4.1. The table is hypothetical, but reflects observed differences in general.

Social studies educators argue that assessment can be important to teaching and learning when it helps everyone involved think about and better understand how they are doing and how they can improve in relation to the goals of social studies (Alleman & Brophy, 1998; NCSS, 1990). Authentic assessment gives students as well as teachers ownership in the learning process (Avery, 1999). Both goal-centered assessment and authentic assessment can only be accomplished if we consider at least five major principles:

1 The aim or purpose of all assessment in education is to improve learning by:
   a Making sure the curricular goals are understood by all.
   b Identifying specific areas of student strengths and weaknesses.
   c Identifying effective and ineffective teaching practices.
   d Being sure that assessment tasks themselves involve organization of information and decision-making.
   e Identifying the need for additional and/or different instruction.
   f Bringing about self-assessment and independent learning.
2 To be authentic, assessment must be an ongoing process, and a variety of tools must be used with understanding.
3 Everyone must realize that all assessment is imperfect and that flaws are inescapable. Types of errors include:

Table 4.1 The Extent to Which the Tool Is Used in Student Assessment

0 Not Used at All
1 Used Sparingly/Occasionally
2 Used Frequently
3 Of Critical Importance in Evaluation

Evaluation Tools	*Traditional Teaching*	*Standards-Based Teaching*
Daily assignments	2–3	1
Short quizzes, review	2–3	1
Short quizzes, problems	1	2–3
Objective tests, recall	2–3	1
Objective tests, application	2–3	2
Essay tests, informational	2	1
Essay tests, problems	1	2–3
Individual projects	1–2	3–4
Reports, written	1–2	3–4
Reports, oral	1	3–4
Group/collaborative		
Projects	1–2	2–3
Reports, written	1–2	2–3
Reports, oral	1	3–4
Teacher observation	1	2–3
Self-assessment	0–1	1–3
Journals	0–1	1–3
Stories and other writing	0–1	1–3
Games and active discussion	0–1	1–3
Problem-solving activities	0–1	1–3
Dramatic activities	0–1	1–3
Participation in community service projects	0	1–3
Personal portfolios	0	2–3

  a. Sampling error: What we choose for assessment does not allow us to effectively identify what the student knows and does not know, what the student can do and cannot do. (This could be a bad test item or an unrepresentative sample of the student's work.)
  b. Assessor error: The person doing the assessment makes the wrong assumptions and/or inappropriate interpretations, and/or incorrect judgments.
  c. Communication error: The assessment message sent to and/or received by the student is incorrect, misunderstood, or otherwise constructed so that it does not result in learning improvement.

4. Students need to develop ownership of the goals of assessment.
5. All assessment should relate to the goals of the curriculum and classroom assessment should be directly connected to soundly conceived and well-stated objectives.
6. Classroom evaluation should be based on what you intend to teach, what you teach, and what you intend for students to learn from that teaching.

Guidelines for Assessment

Assessment may require many different types of instruments and forms in social studies, including quizzes, tests, examinations, observations, oral examinations, interviews, conferences, checklists, self-evaluations, portfolios, holistic evaluation of projects and papers, and a host of others. Even if we limit our concern to just grading and the other formal ways of providing students and parents feedback, the complexity of the assessment process is sometimes overwhelming. That complexity might be illustrated by looking at a typical six-week grading period. A social studies teacher, even a traditional one, might have the following variety of information on which he or she would like to base grades:

> **FYI**
>
> Remember to always offer a variety of assessments throughout your instruction to offer students multiple opportunities and avenues to demonstrate learning.

- Scores/grades on one or two unit tests plus quiz grades
- Scores/grades on homework and/or seatwork completed
- Evaluations of student map work of different types
- Grades from several pieces of evaluated written work (stories, poems, essays, reports, outlines, questions answered)
- A holistic evaluation of a group project involving working together to produce a group report and some display (diorama, mural, table scene)
- Grades for an individual research project given both in writing and orally with artifacts made by the student
- Observations of participation in class activities and discussion
- Notations on volunteer projects, including some very elaborate ones showing a great deal of energy and interest
- Student self-evaluation and peer evaluation of projects.

The first obvious problem is that if some numerical averaging is to be used to determine a grade, this teacher has more than one option for determining each of the various numbers to plug into the grade mix. The second problem has to do with coming up with an overall formula that accounts for or weighs differences in importance and effort for each activity. Subjective decisions are made about the relative value or percentage of a grade to be allotted for different tasks and performances. A third and even more important difficulty, though, is that only some of the activities on the list may be evaluated in such a way as to yield definitive and objective grades. Some of the most important student work simply has to be evaluated in very subjective ways. Even checklists, which can produce questionable quantitative information, just will not provide any true evaluation of this work.

The point is that assessment, even the small part of it that we call grading, is never easy and never without flaws. Teachers have to make difficult decisions. These decisions can be, and probably will be, questioned and debated. To provide at least a small help in the decision-making, we want to offer ten broad principles or guidelines for assessment:

1 Both the form and the substance of assessment tools can best be defended if based on teaching objectives. Think through in advance what learners are to accomplish and ways to effectively evaluate these accomplishments.
2 We need to assess what we teach, not what we should teach; both teaching and assessment should reflect what we want as learning outcomes.
3 We need to focus assessment on what is important rather than on what is easy to measure.
4 Ongoing assessment is preferable to endpoint; we need to incorporate evaluation into regular activities.
5 Assessment of teaching should be based on what students learn rather than on what they already know and can do; therefore, we need to find out what they already know before we teach.

6 If we give students a clear understanding of the purposes of any assessment and the reasons for the assessment, they will perform a lot better.
7 Students need to perceive the assessment as fair and honest, not tricky or directed at "catching" them.
8 Assessment procedures should be built around the notion of finding ways of improving instruction.
9 Effective assessment involves the student in self-evaluation, thinking about how he or she can do better, and taking responsibility for his or her own learning.
10 A teacher should always remember that assessment is, at its very best, a subjective and risky affair:
    a Anyone can be wrong about a grade or any kind of assessment and everyone is sometimes wrong.
    b Anyone can make mistakes about the information upon which evaluation is based.
    c Anyone can misjudge a student or a student product.
    d Anyone can be wrong about what they should be evaluating and teaching.

Everyone will be guilty of faults (a) through (d) above on a regular basis. Many of the approaches, techniques, and tools of assessment are well known because we have experienced them as students ourselves. Even so, an overview of the various tools of evaluation can help teachers find a more purposeful and fair personal approach to grading and evaluation.

Authentic Assessment and Portfolios

FYI

Authentic assessment is a foundational construct of the C3 Framework and the NCSS National Standards for the Preparation of Social Studies Teachers.

Educators have become more concerned in the last decade about how well the various means of assessment are working. One issue is that tests alone are inadequate as measures of ability and learning. Educators can easily identify students who do poorly on tests and produce and do wonderful things in class or show great knowledge and skill in conversation. They see the same kind of discrepancies with students who have high test scores and do poorly outside the tests. There are many questions about the validity of the tests themselves, since scores seem to be influenced by reading ability and cultural background.

Then, of course, there is real concern that the quality of learning simply does not lend itself to being quantified. Going beyond issues relating to testing to the broader one of giving grades, many educators feel that students need to take an active part in the evaluation instead of having the traditional receptive and even passive roles. In even the best situations in the past, students have taken part in only a limited number of in-class experiences where they have graded their own work or that of other students. Students have been given few, if any, experiences where they have had the opportunity or the need to examine their own thinking and work reflectively and diagnostically.

The term *authentic assessment* describes a broader approach to student evaluation that tries to bring teachers, parents, and students together to look at the whole body of work that reflects student ability and potential. The term *authentic* is used because the basic premise of the approach is that we need to look at all types of real work that students do in order to see their accomplishments and potential. Types of assessment that have been used in the past, especially tests, simply do not have any relation to the ways that skills and knowledge are used in the real world and in jobs later in life. Educators involved in this effort are looking more to methods of evaluation, which involve all kinds of performance and products of performance that show what students can do, particularly what they can do over more extended periods of time.

Authentic assessment is an approach that relies on authentic or alternative means of assessment, such as individual portfolios or collections of student work assembled over time. The student takes an active and important role in the development and organization of the portfolio. Students usually help decide what goes into the portfolio. Students may also be responsible for organizing and record keeping with regard to the contents of the portfolio. Emphasis may be given to student initiative in conferences with the teacher. The individual items in the portfolio become the basis for student–teacher conferences and the base of comparison for future work. Students who learn to gather and organize material for a portfolio, and to select the best material for it, are not only more active in evaluation but also are learning skills that will be of benefit in the world of work.

One way that a teacher can control the size of a portfolio and insure that students actually do some selective decision-making is to limit each portfolio to a certain number of pieces/artifacts. Another way is to require that the portfolio include examples of particular types of work (e.g., book reports, essays, answers to comprehension questions, poems, stories, maps, pictures, problem-solving activities, and group reports). The form that portfolios take can also help the teacher manage the size in order to make them meaningful, evaluated work instead of unorganized collections. In some cases, the portfolios may be physical, organized scrapbooks, but they can also be electronic portfolios.

Ideally, portfolios bring teachers and students together in ways that help students improve work. Even so, there are obvious problems when it comes to how they are used in evaluation. The success of portfolios depends upon several factors:

1 The students, teacher, and others have to see them as important and purposeful.
2 Time has to be spent between the teacher and student, both in the development of the portfolio and in its evaluation.
3 Acceptable procedures for organizing and evaluating the portfolio have to be developed.
4 There have to be clear-cut ties between the portfolio assessment and traditional grades.

Portfolios can be evaluated in several ways, including group and individual conferences, written descriptive feedback, and diagnostic and evaluative checklists. The evaluation, whatever form or forms it takes, should make the best sense to the teacher and student.

Assessment through Tests

In a world of high-stakes testing, the very first thing many people think of is standardized tests when the subject of assessment is mentioned. Tests always involve performance and are used because they are an efficient method of finding out what people know or can do. Nationally normed standardized tests, though not as well known in social studies as in reading and mathematics, are given system-wide and statewide because they have been viewed as a way of comparing and evaluating students as to their mastery of information and skills. Though many educators are dissatisfied with standardized tests and the way the data are used, there currently is a movement toward national testing programs.

In social studies, the most widely used forms of tests are written ones that involve answering questions or performing specified tasks. Generally, tests that involve little or no judgment in grading are called objective measures. Included in this group are true–false tests, multiple-choice tests, labeling of diagrams and maps, matching, and some short-answer and fill-in-the-blank tests. Most of these tests can also be called "high-cue" tests because they contain a lot of clues and may even supply the correct answer (e.g., matching). The kind of thinking that is required may involve recognizing and basic rote memorization of information.

The advantages of objective-type measures mostly relate to the unchanging quality of the test items. The correct answers are thought to be verifiable and absolute. Except when the teacher makes a detectable and documentable error, there is little or no danger of misinterpreting or wrongly grading an answer. In addition, such questions can cover the material to be tested by sampling what is important in a very equitable way based on preestablished criteria, and performance data can be gathered to establish the value of individual items. Once such tests are established, the teacher can correct them fairly quickly.

However, there are many criticisms of objective tests. These criticisms help point out that these tests are really not objective at all. Many criticisms deal with test-item construction. Here are some criticisms of objective tests:

- Insufficient information is given to call for one specific answer (multiple-choice stems and completion or fill-in-the-blank: e.g., All of the ___ were ___).
- Items are written deliberately to be tricky or misleading (e.g., True or False: Cortez conquered the Incas in Mexico).
- Test items tend to concentrate on the less important and even trivial aspects of a topic of study (e.g., Short answer: How many Pilgrims survived the first winter in Plymouth?).
- Test items require the students to share an opinion (e.g., True or False: The greatest woman of the nineteenth century was Florence Nightingale).
- Questions are often long, wordy, and confusing.
- More than one alternative is plausible as an answer.
- It is difficult to write objective items that involve creativity, evaluation, and application, and few objective tests include such items.
- Objective tests often work to the advantage of lucky guessers, and chance plays too large a role.

Social studies teachers are still going to find objective tests useful. First, there is no doubt that objective tests are efficient. They can be taken and graded quickly. Students easily learn the skills needed to answer objective-test questions. Furthermore, the skills developed taking these tests are useful for future standardized tests.

Social studies teachers who use objective tests can improve the quality and usefulness of the tests over time. First, they need to make sure that every question relates to some important objective or learning outcome. They also need to realize that high success on the test is their goal because if most students do poorly, it is an indicator that they have not taught effectively. If many students miss a particular question, something is wrong. It probably means that the question was worded in a way that was vague or difficult to understand, that the material was not taught, or that the information was either not understood or had no impact.

Tests that require value judgments in evaluation are described as subjective measures. Subjective measures include nearly all types of essay and problem-solving work, where the process is as important as (if not more important than) the answer and where thought and creativity are often part of the judgment. These can be called "low-cue" test items because they depend almost wholly on the ability of students to understand and retain information relative to the question and use it. Little or no information is supplied.

Subjective tests require students to think and to structure thinking, recalling the appropriate information and applying the information. They also allow different students to use different arguments and information. There are as many common criticisms of essay tests as an objective measure. Critics claim the following:

- There is no fair and consistent way of grading an essay test.
- Students who do not write well do not do well on essays.
- Many students are able to be too creative in their answers.

- The kind of thinking required in essay tests is beyond the ability of most students, so the measures are unfair indicators of what they know.
- Essay tests can only sample a small amount of the material covered, not all of the objectives.
- Essay tests take much more time to grade and must be graded by someone who both knows the material and how it was taught.

An answer to the criticisms above is called holistic evaluation. In this approach, the preparation procedure includes supplying students with thorough descriptions of various performance levels for essays. These descriptions range from descriptions of characteristics of poor answers on up to the attributes of superior essays. These criterion-based descriptions become the basis for the grading, which is the process of categorizing essays into levels. They are generally referred to as rubrics.

Holistic evaluation has been a way of responding to legitimate recognition of a testing problem. It is a good way to show that simply by knowing the pitfalls of any form of test or test question, it is possible to avoid or at least reduce the dangers. The form of a test and the kind of test questions that a teacher uses should be a matter of sense and judgment. Some tests provide information specifically to help planning and teaching (formative evaluation); some are merely diagnostic; and others are intended to be final, exit evaluations (summative). Any good test for social studies, whether it includes subjective or objective questions or both, and regardless of its intended use, is going to do the following:

- Measure what it is supposed to measure (prerequisite knowledge, what is important, what has been taught and learned, etc.).
- Require the thinking skills that the teacher wants students to use.
- Allow the teacher to evaluate how well the objectives have been achieved.
- Be an additional learning experience for students.
- Be constructed and evaluated with fairness.
- Be carefully and clearly worded and understandable to students.
- Not be a test on which students fail because of the lack of reading ability.
- Be constructed so that students can be expected to complete it in the time allowed.
- Relate to all objectives in an equitable way.
- Be of a length and type that is appropriate to students, the material covered, and the way the material was covered.

Developing a test and even deciding to use one that has been prepared to go with a textbook or other educational material should be a thoughtful and purposeful procedure. The first consideration should be the purpose that the test is going to serve. Several additional steps are needed, which might include the following:

1 Think about your specific purposes in the evaluation. What are you trying to find out about what the students have learned or what they can do with that knowledge?
2 Consider how much time you want the test to take, accounting for attention span, ability level, the breadth and depth you want in the evaluation, and the importance attached to the particular evaluation.
3 Decide what kind(s) of activities or behaviors you want the test or quiz to include.
4 Develop a plan for dividing the test into its component parts. This may take such forms as outlines, sets of objective statements, and organizational plans allocating percentages.
5 Prepare the individual items.
6 Carefully check the items for content, wording, clarity, readability, and so on.
7 Have someone else read the items to see if that person understands them as you intended them and to see if there is any ambiguity, the possibility of multiple interpretations, trickiness, and so on.

8 If possible, have someone take the test to see how that person interprets it and answers the questions and how long it takes to complete. (As a rule of thumb, multiply adult time by three to get an estimate of student completion time.)
9 Observe students as they take the test to note ease or frustration, commonly experienced difficulties and individual problems, and differences in rate of completion.
10 When grading tests, become aware of instances where student answers consistently vary from the correct answer.

Assessing Projects and Reports

Projects are extremely difficult to assess. They often involve art ability or other abilities outside of those that are directly related to social studies learning and thinking; sometimes reflect parent help and/or differences in financial and other resources; and, even for a similar assignment, vary immensely in type, complexity, and learning value. When projects are done by cooperative learning groups, various members may make vastly different contributions. All of this is almost an essential part of the nature of this type of activity. Project work, at its best, involves a tremendous amount of thought and effort in conceptualization that may not be reflected to the evaluator in the finished product. One of the problems of project work is that students may turn it into copy work, reflecting almost no thought or originality. The teacher may or may not detect this when it happens, depending on how carefully the material is read, how familiar the teacher is with the resources and/or the style of the language used in them, and what the teacher expects from a style. Flashy and impressive projects may, finally, reflect little learning or teaching; unimpressive projects, on the other hand, may be the result of much more time and thought.

Even so, it is within the very qualities that make projects difficult to evaluate that the true value of project work is found. Projects involve students; they make them think and apply what they learn; they require conceptualizing, problem solving, and solution finding; they provoke research and questioning; they necessitate planning and organization; and, in the case of cooperative learning projects, they involve group interaction skills and teach some valuable lessons about how other students operate and think.

Reports, whether oral or written, present all the same evaluation difficulties. They involve language abilities of different types, and the student's self-confidence and ability to communicate to and/or in front of others may influence how good the report seems as much as, or more than, the actual thought and work involved. Availability of resources may also be a factor, as may the nature and form of the assignment. A well-structured report assignment, for example, should produce successful results.

Projects and reports may be evaluated in several ways. The most common of these are any number of types of subjective evaluation with or without comment, checklist evaluation, analytical evaluation, rubrics, peer evaluation, and self-evaluation.

Subjective Assessment

The teacher's overall subjective judgment has always played a role in assessment. It is authoritarian in style and relies almost entirely on the teacher's professional judgment. The reasoning is that the teacher observes a project or report through its development, has an intimate knowledge of individual students, and has had a great number of past experiences with student projects and reports. Subjective assessment assumes the authority of the teacher and his or her right to be the judge. Students are discouraged from questioning any grade or judgment from the very beginning. At least an unconscious reason for this discouragement is that the criteria for judgments is not easily verbalized and is not very consistent. In fact, a teacher or student could bring almost any factor into a justification argument. It is very difficult to give instructive and useful diagnostic feedback in this approach. When instructional suggestions and comments are made, they tend to be interpreted by the student as the teacher's rationale for the grade given. This may not actually be true.

Flaws in writing mechanics (or the absence of such flaws) and the appearance of projects sometimes influence teachers' judgment of substance and ideas. Often ideal models/examples are used to show students in advance what a good report or project looks like. This may or may not have positive effects. Seeing the models/examples may reduce creativity in some cases or even cause student frustration at not feeling able to complete equivalent work. It may also cause students to simply repeat or copy the model/example, making minor changes. On the other hand, models may provide students with clarification about expectations.

Peer Assessment and Self-Assessment

Peer assessment and self-assessment by students represent the aim of all evaluation. Social studies teachers need to be constantly working toward the point where they can develop constructive ideas about what constitutes good work and make adjustments to achieve it. The basic process, whether involving peer assessment or self-assessment, begins with educating students to think of first efforts as preliminary stages. The process also means that students develop high standards, a desire to produce quality work, and an acceptance that such work can be achieved through revision. Students become involved in actively seeking to understand what it takes to produce good work. This is always a goal, and the process of moving students in the direction of the goal is at the center of standards-based teaching as well as the problems approach. Students perceive success in terms of work that they can take pride in; intrinsic goals replace extrinsic ones.

The process is one in which students learn to judge their own reports and projects as well as those of their peers, to know what they need to contain, and to have a refined concept of the features that distinguish outstanding efforts. Obviously, this is an ideal and, as such, is something that teachers need to work toward, not expect at the outset. Teachers need to carefully structure instruction so that students learn how to make judgments. Follow through is needed, and a developmental approach is an absolute requisite to achieve more than superficial assessment.

Checklist and Rubric Assessment

Using checklists or rubrics to assess produces an assessment that is criterion-based. A checklist or rubric may identify the features that the project or report is to include and the characteristics that the teacher expects in a report or project. When checklists and rubrics are given to students in advance, they help students clarify the teacher's expectations and provide a sense of security about how they can be successful in meeting expectations and getting a good grade. Such thinking may produce regimented work and cause students to work too much on meeting the criteria and too little on creative problem solving.

An example of a checklist that might be used with a third-grade reporting activity is detailed in Table 4.2. The items on the checklist might be treated with a simple check mark to indicate acceptability or might be rated in some way to show how well each criterion has been met.

Items on a rubric will be marked to indicate the level of acceptability or might be rated in some way to show how well each criterion has been met. Table 4.3 depicts an example of a rubric that was used to assess a project on monuments around the world. The rubric is suitable for Grades 5 or 6.

Analytical Assessment

Analytical assessment is based on careful examination of student behaviors or products in the light of clearly identified criteria. This approach may take several forms. When projects or reports are evaluated analytically, the teacher usually examines them very carefully and gives a detailed

Table 4.2 Example: Checklist

The report…

- __Has a clear, creative, descriptive title.
- __Attempts to solve a problem or answer a question.
- __Deals with an important topic.
- __Is well organized with at least three subtopics.
- __Has a list of references (in correct form).
- __Shows that the references have been used.
- __Covers the topic completely.
- __Is presented in an interesting way.
- __Shows that the writer or presenter is knowledgeable about the topic.
- __Uses visual material (pictures, charts, maps, etc.).
- __Shows concern for mechanics (grammar, punctuation, and spelling).
- __Has a good summary and conclusion.

Table 4.3 Example: Rubric

	Unsatisfactory 0–1	*Satisfactory 2–3*	*Excellent 4–5*	*Points Earned*
Location	–The monument was not located within the assigned country. City and significance of location was not provided.	–The monument was located within the assigned country. City and significance of location was briefly discussed.	–The monument location, city, and significance of location were all addressed clearly and accurately.	
Demographic Information	–The project does not include demographic information.	–The project included some of the demographic information, but with a few errors.	–The demographic information was accurate and useful.	
Historical Monument	– No background information or analysis of the monument was provided.	–The monument was located within the assigned country and some background information was provided, but with little analysis.	–The monument location, background information, and analysis were all clear and informative.	
Rationale for Visiting Monument	– Did not provide a rationale.	–The rationale was somewhat detailed.	–A detailed rationale was provided.	
World Monument and Cultural Guide	–The guide was not completed and/or contained multiple examples of incorrect information.	–The guide was completed, but some of the information was inaccurate or irrelevant to the project.	–The guide was fully completed with accurate and useful information.	
Presentation	–The information was not shared with the class.	–The presentation was too brief and difficult to follow.	–The presentation was clear and informative.	
Technical Aspects and Grammar	–There were multiple misspelled words or grammatical errors.	–There were a few misspelled words and/or grammatical errors.	–There were no misspelled words and/or grammatical errors.	
Comments:			Total /35 pts.	

reaction. Sometimes this is a preliminary evaluation after which the students can revise, change, and improve their work. This view treats the work that has been done as a phase in the process of learning how to do this type of project. It is a draft. Whether the analysis is merely a step in the process or comes as a final feedback session, it can take one of two basic forms. One approach is for the teacher to begin with no criteria, basically letting the work itself dictate how it is analyzed. The idea is to give feedback of the strengths and weaknesses that will allow students to improve. Another analytical approach involves the examination of a report or project to see how well it meets a few standards. Comments would then be made relative to each of these standards. For example, the following categories might be the basis for evaluation of a project:

- Topic (What thought is evidenced in the selection of the basic idea?)
- Approach (How unique and interesting is the approach?)
- Effort (Does the project show industry and care?)
- Purpose (Is the project purposeful and instructive?)
- Visual quality (Does the project attract attention and interest?)
- Mechanics and content (How well does the project reflect research and knowledge, and is it done with a care for correctness?)

Teacher Observations and Anecdotal Records

FYI

"If we teach today's students as we taught yesterday's, we rob them of tomorrow." (John Dewey, p. 167)

Descriptions of your observations of students do not easily translate into a form that can be considered in grading. Teacher observations are considered informal assessments compared to formal assessments like tests, projects, etc. Nonetheless, teacher observations are an invaluable tool in evaluation. One of the reasons is that the development of the student is full of subtleties and nuance. Teachers need to be reminded that the essence of an individual is not really something that can be quantified.

The best social studies teachers are those who are reflective educators. The records of day-to-day actions of students often give teachers the best substance on which to reflect. In addition to the paper trail of students, these records are of two broad types: criterion-based quantitative observations that usually take such forms as checklists; and qualitative observations that take the form of narrative descriptions. If either type is used, it needs to be done in a systematic and regular way, and it needs to be kept up over a long period of time. This record keeping cannot be done when teachers are presenting to the class; the logical times for such record keeping are when students are engaged in activities that allow the teacher to quickly reflect and make notes and when students are not present, such as during lunch, planning, and recess and at the end of the school day.

What becomes obvious with only a little knowledge of the techniques of teacher observation is that they incorporate checklist techniques in a particular way. In observation, checklists are shortcuts to developing systematic records of how students are behaving and progressing. They give the teacher a record that helps him or her make sense of the class, and they do so with very little time spent outside class, beyond determining and setting up what qualities the teacher is seeking. Checklist assessment also relates well to determining the actual accomplishment of at least certain kinds of objectives.

Table 4.4 Example: Observational Checklist

Name	*Works without conflict*	*Gets on task*	*Problem solves*	*Shows leadership*	*Behavior is appropriate*
Group 1					
Billy					
Maria					
Heather					
Eric					
Name	*Works without conflict*	*Gets on task*	*Problem solves*	*Shows leadership*	*Behavior is appropriate*
Group 2					
Jason					
Freddy					
Michael					
Starla					

Observational checklists may take many forms. One of the most common is a list of very specific competencies or knowledge (e.g., knows the cardinal directions). When a student masters an item on the list, his or her name is checked. A checklist might be set up to keep systematic track of group activity as well. The teacher might carry the checklist outlined in Table 4.4 about the room during an independent cooperative learning activity.

While checklists save time, anecdotal teacher observation records demand a lot of time. Anecdotal material may reflect specific observations during the day. It is narrative in form and describes actual behavior. Such comments may not need to be lengthy or provide a lot of detail, but they do need to be complete. The teacher may or may not want to create categories for such notes prior to observation. Some may be behavioral, for example: "When John lost his place in line at lunch, he shoved several students and made threatening remarks." Others may reflect participation, for example: "Caroline raised her hand for several questions in discussion. On two occasions that I called on her she answered correctly and completely."

The time required by anecdotal observation approaches to evaluation demands that such observations be focused on particular problems or particular students. The data can be very helpful in instances where faculty are going to meet and discuss a student or where reference material is being gathered to recommend special attention for a student. This type of information may also help a teacher deal with a classroom management issue.

Looking Back

Assessment is an important and complex part of social studies. Assessment tools allow teachers to examine their own effectiveness as well as the learning of their students. Sound evaluation begins by comparing what has been learned to what the teacher intended to teach. In other words, achievement is measured against objectives.

Teachers assess this learning through student behaviors and student products. They need to be constantly aware of the need to focus on what is important, not just on what is easy to measure. Authentic assessment advocates argue that tests and other traditional measures do not measure in a "real" way what a child is capable of doing. One approach to authentic assessment is through student portfolios. The most traditional assessment tools are tests, quizzes, and papers, but evaluation based on these tools alone does not give a true or authentic picture of student capability. Other student activities are as important, or more important, than tests and written papers. Teachers may attempt more complete assessment by using observational tools including checklists and criterion-based rubrics for projects and other assignments.

Extension Activity

Scenario

Currently you are teaching at Yourtown High School (YHS) and everything is going wonderfully. However, on Monday morning you arrive at YHS and you are inundated with students giving you flak about their grade on a social studies project. You explain to the students why they received the grade and the day goes on as normal. It is almost 5:00 and you are preparing to leave school for the day, but just as you are about to leave the principal of YHS, Dr. Russell, comes in and wants to meet. He has received numerous complaints regarding your grading procedures from parents and students. Unaware of your grading procedures, he asks to see your assessment plan for the assignment receiving the complaints; however, you do not have one. He explains that all effective teachers have an assessment plan and he expects you to create assessment plans in the future. Embarrassed, you apologize and agree to create an assessment plan from now on. Furthermore, you promise to complete an assessment plan for the next social studies lesson you teach and email it to him by tomorrow morning.

Task

For this activity, an assessment plan is simply a plan for assessing students' learning and is a basic component of any effective social studies lesson plans. Your assessment plan should have measurable learning objectives and multiple forms of assessment. The learning objectives and forms of assessment must align.

Select a social studies lesson topic and create an assessment plan. The assessment plan should include learning objectives and forms of assessments to measure those objectives. Create assessments that align with learning objectives.

Reflective Questions

1. What does the term *basis of comparison* mean in assessment?
2. Why are both the method and the content of assessment based on the teaching objectives?
3. What is *authentic assessment* and how should it be implemented?
4. What are the criticisms of both objective and subjective tests?
5. Can you describe an example of an informal assessment?

Helpful Resources

Watch this video created by Teachings in Education about authentic assessment.
https://youtu.be/rQPCk27tM4U

Watch this video from NCSS about authentic assessment and the C3 Framework.
https://youtu.be/Ci0KF35ENII

Internet 4 Classrooms. Former classroom teachers created this website as a forum for educators to gain up-to-date and relevant information about assessment and evaluation issues and ideas in public schools. Teachers will find useful updates about social studies testing, curriculum developments, and evaluation processes for states all over the U.S.
www.internet4classrooms.com/index.htm

Watch this video that briefly highlights the pros and cons of standardized texting.
https://youtu.be/tUyjJEY3o6A

Watch this video that highlights various teachers and their utilization of formative assessments in the classroom.
https://youtu.be/mMDVzRy8bJU

Watch this video that clearly outlines summative and formative assessments and how they can be utilized.
https://youtu.be/rJxFXjfB_B4
Watch this video, which highlights a history fair and how the social studies projects impacted students.
https://youtu.be/cpkQZYF7jY4
Watch this video explaining the foundation of project-based learning.
www.youtube.com/watch?v=LMCZvGesRz8&list=PLvzOwE5lWqhSgJVgg7VfRkBisbmm-BFUL&index=9
Rubistar for Teachers. This valuable and free website allows teachers to construct rubrics for classroom assignments in a clear fashion. The site is very user-friendly and walks teachers through the step-by-step process of creating rubrics to enhance classroom instruction and assessment.
http://rubistar.4teachers.org/
Watch this video by Teachings in Education, which outlines and explains rubrics and a rationale for utilizing rubrics in the classroom.
https://youtu.be/b4shMaSel00.

Further Reading

NCSS. (1991). Position statement: Testing and evaluation of social studies students. *Social Education, 55* (September), 284–285.
This position statement issued by the National Council for the Social Studies analyzes how testing and evaluation of social studies students can contribute to the development of more engaged citizens. The organization addresses how testing and other kinds of evaluation can help teachers weigh the appropriateness and effectiveness of social studies instruction while also providing recommendations for evaluation instruments and student achievement evaluations.

Pearcy, M. (Ed.). (2017). *Best Practices in Social Studies Assessment.* Charlotte, NC: Information Age Publishing.
This book details various adaptive assessments. Furthermore, the book highlights the essential role of teachers in creating assessments that blend higher-order critical thinking, complex content knowledge, and an understanding of their own students.

Vinson, K.D., Ross, E.W. & Wilson, M. (2011). Standards-based educational reform and social studies education: A critical introduction. In W. Russell (Ed.), *Contemporary Social Studies: An Essential Reader* (pp. 153–172). Charlotte, NC: Information Age Publishing.
This book chapter examines contemporary social studies curriculum and assessment within the context of standards-based educational reform. The authors discuss the impact of curriculum standards on social studies assessment, evaluation, and instruction.

References

Alleman, J. & Brophy, J. (1998). Assessment in a social constructivist classroom. *Social Education*, 62(January), 32–34.

Alleman, J. & Brophy, J. (1999). The changing nature and purpose of assessment in the social studies classroom. *Social Education*, 63(October), 334–337.

Avery, P.G. (1999). Authentic assessment and instruction. *Social Education*, 63(October), 368–373.

NCSS. (1990). *Social Studies Curriculum Planning Resources.* Dubuque, IA: Kendall/Hunt.

5 Reading and Writing in Social Studies

Looking Ahead

If we were to imagine social studies as a huge monument, the very base on which the weight rested would be an area called information and communication skills. Social studies at any level cannot stand without these skills. We simply have to be able to find, process, and use information in order to problem solve and/or make decisions. When we have questions to answer, our success depends on either knowing or being able to find the specific information that those questions require. In addition to all of these information skills, social studies requires us to interpret information and create from it. What this all means is that students' ability to deal with information is a critical one.

This chapter deals with the development of those information skills most essential in the social studies. It focuses on some of the types of materials and assignments that teachers traditionally have found to be useful as well as on types of materials that have become available in this age of technology. The chapter also speaks to the pitfalls and problems that teachers and students encounter in using these tools.

Can You? Do You?

Can you ...

- name the four basic purposes for reading and writing assignments in social studies?
- identify the specific reading abilities students need in social studies?
- explain how to use textbooks with students who cannot read?
- think of ways to use fiction books in social studies?
- help students use the Internet for research?

Do you ...

- know what students dislike most about using references?
- know how to break students out of "copy from the Internet"?
- know how to make social studies book reports interesting?
- know how to help students learn to organize their writing?
- know several ways to teach new concepts and new vocabulary?
- know some ways to actually shorten what students have to read?
- know why it is important for students to understand the organization of reading material?

DOI: 10.4324/9781003217060-5

Focus Activity

> Before reading this chapter, try the focus activity below.
>
> Think back about your educational experiences. What was your favorite book(s) as a teenager? Why? Do you remember reading or having it read to you by a parent or teacher? Even as an adult do you like hearing people read aloud? Share experiences with classmates. Discuss the details of the books and how you might use them in your classroom.

Every Teacher Is a Reading Teacher

Every middle and high school teacher must be, in some sense, a reading teacher. To begin with, reading is one of the essential ways in which we get information and directions in social studies. So a social studies teacher has to deal with the particular reading skills that are useful in learning history, economics, government, etc. Social studies teachers are instrumental in helping students acquire the specific reading skills needed in the content area.

Middle and high schools often still offer separate skills-based reading instruction for students. The reality is that many middle and high school students have not developed the level of reading skills that they need. Even an average secondary class may have students who are nearly non-readers in the same room with those able to read on a college level. In some schools and classes, poor readers may compose over half the class. Because of this wide range of reading ability among students, as well as several other factors, many schools require social studies teachers to infuse reading strategies, reading standards, and reading requirements into the social studies curriculum.

Reading and Writing Assignments in Social Studies

Reading and writing have long been important and necessary skills for learning in the social studies. Obviously, students need to read to obtain information, background, and detail, as well as to discover arguments and opinions. In addition, many different social studies activities require writing. Students must often write to demonstrate that learning has occurred. Writing can even be conceived as a way of speaking.

> **FYI**
>
> "If we encountered a man of rare intelligence we should ask him what books he read."
>
> —Ralph Waldo Emerson

Both teachers and students need to first understand the purpose that a particular reading and/or writing assignment serves in order for it to be completed in an effective, meaningful way. An effective assignment will exhibit several traits. It will be:

- Interesting and/or provoke the curiosity of students.
- *Teacher-facilitated.* Though students need to overcome difficulties and solve their own problems, the difficulties and problems cannot be so great as to cause students not to do the assignment. Make work challenging without making it impossible.

- *Devised to be accomplished in an amount of time that is appropriate to the age and the ability of students.* Students need to believe that they can accomplish the tasks. Sometimes we have to break large assignments into segments in order to accomplish this.
- *Clearly organized and understandable.* A lack of clarity is the most common problem of assignments. Students need to have a clear and complete understanding of what and how to accomplish the assignment.

Reading Skills Needed in Social Studies

A number of identifiable reading activities and skills are important if students are going to get meaning from textbooks and other reading materials. Kent and Simpson (2008) have suggested that social studies is a vehicle to teach phonemic awareness, phonics, and vocabulary. To assume that students have successfully mastered these skills in earlier grades is a major mistake. It is also a mistake to assume that students are motivated to read. McLaughlin (2012) has stressed that teachers need to have a sound understanding of reading comprehension itself. Skills may not have been learned at all, and if they were they are often forgotten if unused. The following is a list of some of those activities and the skills involved:

1. Recognize the organization of reading materials:
   - Remind students about how to use boldfaced headings as cues to content organization and how to use the headings to make the content more meaningful.
   - Help students learn to recognize topic sentences, and show them how to use these in skimming and scanning.
   - Review with students how one identifies main idea(s).
   - Model and give students experiences in finding supporting ideas and facts that relate to main ideas.
2. Bring meaning to reading:
   - Help students learn vocabulary and concept meaning by recognizing and using context definitions and identifications. Social studies is always introducing new concepts and terms.
   - Review with students how to use glossaries and outside resources to find the meaning of vocabulary.
   - Give students experiences that help them learn to use structural analysis and context clues to obtain vocabulary meaning.
   - Help students to relate what they read to personal experiences, observations, and past learning.
   - Relate new material to previous studies.
   - Teach students to recognize and follow relationships in text (e.g., sequence, chronology).
   - Help students to relate what they read to particular problems and purposes brought to the reading.
3. Read for a purpose:
   - Before they read, help students understand questions and problems so that they will recognize appropriate solutions when they encounter them.
   - Teach students how to skim for overall meaning.
   - Teach students to scan for specific information, answers to questions, and useful related ideas.
   - Help students develop the habit of using the table of contents and index to find specific information.
   - Show students how to obtain information from maps in the text and how this can contribute to overall understanding of the reading material.
   - Teach students how to use and interpret charts and graphs in the text.

4 Read critically:
  - Help students learn to recognize author bias.
  - Teach students to recognize discrepancies, contradictions, and missing information.
  - Teach students to identify relationships among elements (e.g., cause and effect).
  - Help students learn to distinguish opinion from fact, description from interpretation, and so on.

Helping Students Read Social Studies Materials

There are a variety of strategies and techniques for helping students read social studies-related material. Some are simple and direct, while others are complex. What you want as a teacher is for students to be able to get maximum use of social studies material of all types. We would like to suggest a four-step strategy:

> **FYI**
>
> Always remember to check the reading levels of primary sources utilized in the classroom as many of these documents might have challenging or unfamiliar vocabulary as well as advanced reading levels.

1 Pre-teach the meaning of words and terms that may be new prior to giving reading assignments.
2 Reduce the length of independent reading tasks, especially with students who read below grade level.
3 Provide specific, clear purposes for reading. This cannot be stressed too much. Students need to know why they are reading.
4 Help students get a sense of the "story" that the reading material is telling, developing their predictive skills so that they can use features of the text (such as context and boldfaced headings) and features of tasks (such as key-in question words) to anticipate more accurately.

By specifying a series of steps, we are not suggesting that these teaching procedures should always be the same, following a lockstep sequence. The precise order of the steps as well as the decision to include or omit specific steps may change greatly according to individual teaching style, the topic of study, and other individual and classroom factors. More importantly, we do not want to give the impression that these steps can only be carried out in one way. We want to suggest general approaches, not specific techniques. Some notion of the range of possibilities is indicated in the examples that are given in the following sections describing each step, but the possibilities are far greater.

Strategies for Developing Vocabulary

The single most important factor in reading comprehension is vocabulary meaning (Gregg & Sekeres, 2006; Shanahan, 2001; Gersten & Baker, 1999). As Brunner (2009) has commented, "Students won't want to read text that contains a lot of words that they don't know." Every student develops and extends four basic vocabularies throughout his or her education: reading, listening, speaking, and writing.

> **FYI**
>
> Don't take vocabulary development for granted! Spend time helping students develop skills and strategies necessary to be successful.

Social studies deals with world cultures, historical times, social and governmental processes, and an endless variety of often unique names of people and places. This makes the field vocabulary-rich. Many words are introduced for which students have few, if any, related experiences or concepts. Proper nouns, particularly names of people, places, and events, are abundant. Many complex and abstract concepts are also given word labels in social studies. The new words that students encounter in social studies reading materials are terms that are entirely new to them—terms that are not in their speaking or listening vocabularies. Teachers are responsible for providing enabling experiences and building necessary concepts and vocabulary. New vocabulary to be understood by the student must be fitted into perceptions and experiences that form the student's existing view of the world (Smith, 1975). New concepts then become part of the student's worldview only when they can be related to that view as it already exists.

If students are to be successful in understanding or making sense of social studies reading tasks, they must learn to think about new words before they read. Pre-teaching of essential new words and the concepts they represent prior to any reading task will save both teacher and student frustration. Many types of activities and techniques can be used for developing vocabulary meaning prior to reading. A few ideas are suggested and described.

Teacher Explanation of Meaning

Often the most efficient way of introducing vocabulary words is for the teacher simply to explain the meanings of crucial terms prior to reading. If several terms are involved, sharing a PowerPoint of the words and definitions or providing student with copies of a vocabulary list may help. A list may even be provided in the text, but unless the teacher pays attention students will most likely ignore it. For individual assignments, the teacher should provide a vocabulary list before material is read. However the new vocabulary is introduced, teachers need to help students see each word in context, relating the importance of the term to the particular reading assignment. The words need to be seen and heard by students.

At its simplest, the teacher explanation involves pointing out to the students where the text uses and defines particular terms. Teacher definitions might point out pictures, maps, and charts in the text that illustrate the concepts involved in particular terms. For some words, actual objects can be used from which students might get term-related multisensory experiences.

Though it is the most efficient way to introduce vocabulary, direct teaching may also sometimes be an ineffective method. Students will not always feel a need to listen or look, particularly if the routine of the explanations becomes too tedious and regular. When the teacher uses this approach, presentations of words and definitions need to be varied, exciting, and reinforced with student involvement. This way of teaching vocabulary should be interspersed with other approaches to vocabulary development.

Frayer Model

The Frayer Model is a graphical organizer used for concept development and vocabulary building. The model requires students to think about and describe a concept. The model is designed to have students analyze a concept, synthesize the concept, and apply the information. The Frayer Model was designed by Dorothy Frayer and colleagues (Frayer et al., 1969) at the University of Wisconsin. Using the Frayer Model is an extremely valuable tool for helping students grasp the meaning of a new concept and truly understand it. Concept development is key for understanding social studies content. For example, if a student does not understand the concepts of abolitionists, slavery, freedom, and/or equality, they may have a difficult time understanding and meeting the learning goals surrounding a unit on the Civil War. There are two versions of the Frayer Model that teachers will find valuable. Table 5.1 depicts Version A and Table 5.2 depicts Version B.

Table 5.1 Frayer Model Version A

Definition (In Own Words)		*Characteristics*
	CONCEPT	
Examples (Personal)		Non-Examples

Table 5.2 Frayer Model Version B

Essential Characteristics		*Non-Essential Characteristics*
	CONCEPT	
Examples		Non-Examples

FYI

The Frayer Model is a quick and easy way to check for understanding during your instruction. Consider opening your lesson by having students complete the graphic organizer, then continue into your lesson and instruction. Close the lesson by having students complete the graphic organizer again. It is a very simple and efficient way to assess student learning.

As a class or individually, students complete the Frayer Model to obtain a deeper understanding of a concept. Common steps for implementing the Frayer Model are below.

1 Describe and explain the Frayer Model to the class.
2 Give an example of how to use the model. Use a simple and common concept to demonstrate the sections of the model.
3 Assign a new concept(s).
4 In collaborative groups, pairs, or individually, have students complete the model with the assigned concept(s).
5 Have students share their conclusions.

Table 5.3 depicts an example of Version A of the Frayer Model that can be used to help students gain a better understanding of the concept of culture. Table 5.4 depicts an example of Version B of the Frayer Model that can be used to help students gain a better understanding of the concept of dictatorship.

Table 5.3 Frayer Model: Example of Version A Completed

Definition (In Own Words)		*Characteristics*
The ideas, values, beliefs, and ways of doing things that I share with the people who live in my area.		• Shared ideas • Shared beliefs • Shared practices
	CULTURE	
Examples (Personal)		Non-Examples
• What I wear • What I eat • How I speak		• My hair • The weather • My eye color

Table 5.4 Frayer Model: Example of Version B Completed

Essential Characteristics	*Non-Essential Characteristics*
• State exerts control • Central planning • Autocratic ruler (one person in control) • Power to govern without consent of those being governed	• Violent transition • Genocide • Inequitable distribution of goods and services
DICTATORSHIP	
Examples	Non-Examples
• Cuba • North Korea • Germany (Hitler) • Russia (Stalin)	• U.S. • United Kingdom • Mexico • Canada

Classifying Experiences

Using classifying charts helps students see how terms fit into various systems of concepts. Charting is an effective way to help students categorize and see relationships among words and terms. Though such charts are more often used in reviewing after reading, they can also help students build a conceptual framework for new words. For example, the terms *bayou* and *canal* might be understood better if depicted using Tables 5.5 and 5.6.

Other classifying experiences may simply involve students in sorting and prioritizing terms and words or a series of questions that bring out previous associations that will enable them to classify the terms.

Table 5.5 Classifying Chart: Example 1

Term	*Features*	*Natural or Constructed*	*Examples*	*Related Geographic Features*
Bayou	Shallow; sometimes navigable	Natural	Bayous in Louisiana delta	Low-lying marshlands; May drain into ocean/river
Canal	Shallow; navigable; may have locks to change elevations; often connects two bodies of water	Constructed	Erie Canal Suez Canal Panama Canal	Major transportation route links

Table 5.6 Classifying Chart: Example 2

Waterways	*Landform*	*Types of Vegetation*
Bayou	Isthmus	Deciduous trees
Canal	Delta	Savannah
Lake	Cape	Taiga
River	Island	Desert

Extended Teacher Definitions

If one or two terms are central to understanding total reading selections, then the teacher may need to give a more extended definition, including illustrations. For example, the terms *pioneer* and *frontier* are both abstractions. Both would be crucial to understanding entire units and entire chapters of text in the study of American history. Since the terms have several meanings and describe very complex and involved ideas, with both positive and negative connotations, the teacher may want to go to elaborate lengths to develop the depth of understanding needed. The teacher may want read aloud descriptions of features of pioneer life, show audiovisual materials and websites, and provide a wide range of real experiences prior to reading. An extended discussion to reach a group consensus about the definition would be still another way to introduce terms.

This in-depth approach might need to be used with many critical abstractions. The following questions might serve as a guide for developing a consensus definition of the abstract term *democracy*:

- What are your first thoughts about the meaning of democracy? (This might start a round of association play.)
- What are the features or characteristics of a democracy? (Prepare a list on the board.)
- Do all leaders in this country have the same concept of democracy? (Depending on student knowledge, you might ask about particular contemporary or historical individuals and their differences.)
- Does democracy mean equal opportunity? Participation in government? Equal wealth? Freedom (what freedom)? Equality?
- If a country has democratic ideals, does this mean it will have democratic practices?

Teacher-Provided Experiences

Some terms may be better understood if the teacher can provide real or vicarious experiences to illustrate the concepts involved. Names of articles of clothing, such as a dashiki from West Africa or utensils such as an Egyptian shadoof or a medieval trebuchet, for example, may be better understood if students see the objects and try to use or wear them. Foods that can be tasted may leave a more lasting impression.

Where real experiences are impossible, vicarious experiences may also be useful in developing concepts. These experiences may include hearing or reading fictional stories, seeing and hearing audiovisual presentations, or taking part in other activities where students can identify with the people involved.

Student-Centered Experiences

Finding meanings for new words can be an exciting new adventure for students if the teaching is well planned. However, it can also be routine, unpopular "busywork." The number of words must be limited, with special thought to the age and ability of the students. Student involvement and participation in the discovery of new definitions will slow the instructional process but help ensure a greater understanding. The techniques are numerous and only a few can be described here.

- *Students teaching students*: Each student is responsible for just one word or, at most, two that appear in a unit to be studied. The job of the *authority* is to become so knowledgeable about that word that if any question about its meaning is raised, he or she will feel comfortable in attempting to answer.
- *Picture definitions*: The students are responsible for the meaning of a term or word in visual form. Posters, collages, and rebuses are among the many possible forms these defining visuals

may take. Collages may be especially useful in depicting abstract concepts such as democracy, as well as in developing a concept of a particular person, their character traits, and accomplishments.

FYI

The use of visuals is essential in quality social studies instruction. This will help make the content and class more interesting and accessible to struggling readers.

- *Sound pictures*: A few particular social studies terms lend themselves to sound pictures as a way of vocabulary introduction. In some cases, a student may have to use some type of audio recorder to collect the total sound picture. For example, the call of a muezzin or the singing of a cantor might be ways of gaining concepts of what these individuals do in a study of religion. A foreign language or dialect, a musical instrument, a type of song or dance melody, and other similar concept words can be defined through experiencing the sound.
- *Word look-outs*: Each student is responsible for finding one or two words and their meanings. During class activities over a period of several days, every word will come into discussion. When an individual's word comes up, that person is responsible for noticing, defining, and writing the word on the chalkboard or on a classification chart.
- *Contextual locating*: Many terms are defined either directly or indirectly by the reading context. As a skimming exercise, have students look for and read definitions of words and terms as the text defines them.
- *Creating context*: Often the best way to learn what a word means is to use it. In this technique, students demonstrate that they know the meaning of a word by inventing a context where the word can be used properly. The particular context required of the student may vary greatly from a story, a descriptive paragraph, a single sentence, a poem, a poster or cartoon caption, a bumper sticker, a picture title, and/or a type of poem. These and many others can be creative applications of words through written contexts. Examples of a *diamonte* (a diamond-shaped poem) that defines the word *scimitar* can be found in Table 5.7, and a descriptive paragraph for the word *senators* can found in Table 5.8.

Table 5.7 Example of a Diamonte

Scimitar
Keen
Curved blade
Defense of Islam
Saracen
Sword

Table 5.8 Example of a Descriptive Paragraph

Senators
No matter how big your state is or how many people it has, there are always two Senators. Senators are elected every six years. There are fewer Senators than there are Representatives.

Less Can Be More: Quality Reading in Social Studies

Reading is the means not the end of dealing with social studies materials. Understanding and being able to understand the content is the goal. Therefore, more comprehension can be achieved by cutting the number of actual pages of reading. For some students, a reading assignment of two pages versus one of 10 or 20 pages of reading may mean the difference between doing and not doing the reading.

One of the most creative ways a teacher can help a student read is to control the amount of material that the student has to read. The trick is to find ways of focusing the student's reading effort on the particular information that he or she absolutely needs to know. Since social studies materials are most often written at or above grade-level reading ability, reducing reading may be helpful for many students. Following are several ways of reducing the reading load:

- Use student-written summaries instead of the text.
- Use teacher-written summaries instead of the text.
- Use textbook cut-ups.
- Try textbook highlighting.
- Experiment with question write-ins.
- Cooperate with class divide-ups.

Using Student-Written Summaries

One way to reduce reading is to collect, over a period of several years, student-written summaries of chapters or sections of printed material. These can be put in binders or folders with illustrations and/or saved as electronic files on a computer and then used as reading material for students. The time needed to collect good summaries puts the beginning teacher at a disadvantage. A teacher may need several classes before a sufficient number of good summaries can be assembled. Cooperation from a teacher and class in a higher grade may be one way of overcoming this difficulty temporarily. Good student-written summaries have several advantages:

- They are usually closer to the language that students speak and hear daily, both in sentence structure and vocabulary, than are other materials.
- They reflect digested rather than raw content. That is, they include the message that one student has received from the readings.
- They are usually brief and to the point, leaving out many things a teacher would include.

Before student summaries are used as a substitute for textual materials, the teacher must do some careful editing. This can be very time-consuming. Summaries may be duplicated and used with an entire class, with groups of students, or with individual students with special reading problems. A 6th-grade student wrote the following example in Box 5.1. The teacher read and corrected the paper, and, after a conference, the student rewrote it. This summary is a student's view of an entire chapter of a textbook.

Using Teacher-Written Summaries

Well-prepared teacher summaries of materials also take a great deal of time to produce. Such summaries are especially useful because they may be written to include all specific facts and ideas that the teacher especially wants students to understand. Vocabulary can be specifically controlled and limited. The teacher should have a clearer and more complete understanding of the conceptual content of the material than students and be able to give the purposes and themes more emphasis. Clear references to pictures, diagrams, and other features of the text can be inserted.

Box 5.1 Example of a Student Summary

The first industry to grow in the United States was the textile industry. This happened after Samuel Slater brought the idea of cotton spinning machines to the United States and Francis Lowell built machines for making cotton cloth. Eli Whitney came up with the idea of mass production and interchangeable parts.

After the Civil War, more money went into industries and many industries grew. Andrew Carnegie built the steel industry into an empire. When he was 66, he sold all his companies and retired. Other industries that grew were the banking industry and the oil industry. Industries got so big that they became monopolies.

There were also new farm machines and scientific developments during the industrial revolution. One famous scientist was George Washington Carver. People moved off the farms and into the cities. Many people also emigrated from other countries to the United States. In the cities, people began having problems because of houses with poor safety and sanitation.

Because of the time that summaries require, the teacher usually should not try to write summaries for all readings. Summaries may be duplicated and used with an entire class, with groups of students, or with individual students with special reading problems.

Box 5.2 is a teacher's summary of the same selection covered by the student write-up. Similarities and differences in style and completeness can be noted, but the one crucial quality of shortening the material read is the same. Thus, both make good substitute reading materials.

Box 5.2 Example of a Teacher Summary

The Industrial Revolution brought changes to life in the United States. This "revolution" began in the first half of the 18th century with the textile industry in New England. Two men made this happen-Samuel Slater and Francis Lowell. Slater was an Englishman who built the first cotton spinning machines. Lowell built factories with weaving machines that made cotton cloth. The Industrial Revolution was also aided by Eli Whitney, the inventor of the cotton gin, who introduced the ideas of mass production and machines with interchangeable parts.

After the Civil War, the development of a national market due to transportation developments made more money available for industry. Among the great industrialists was Andrew Carnegie who built the large steel making industry and J.P. Morgan, who built a large banking industry and later bought Carnegie's steel empire. Another leader was John D. Rockefeller who founded Standard Oil. This was one of the businesses that grew so large that it could put competition out of business. The government became so concerned about such businesses that it tried to regulate them through a law called the Sherman Antitrust Act (1890).

New farm machines and scientific developments revolutionized farming and caused many people to move to the cities where jobs were available in factories. Large numbers of immigrants also came from Europe and Asia to the cities. Cities grew so quickly that they developed problems due to crowded areas and poorly built buildings. Sanitation and safety in tenement (apartment) buildings was very bad.

Attempts to deal with the problems were called reforms. Limits were set on immigration. Laws were passed to improve housing and sanitation. Settlement houses were founded to provide services. One of the reformers was Jane Addams who founded a settlement called Hull House in Chicago.

Textbook Cut-Ups

Textbook cut-ups require that the teacher have a free rein with the materials. It also demands extra copies of materials and a ruthlessness in destroying books and similar materials that repels many teachers automatically. It may be an especially good way of salvaging texts no longer in use.

Two copies of each page to be used may be needed for every cut-up version unless the material is printed on only one side or careful editing is done. The teacher cuts out only the most important sentences, pictures, and other things appearing on the pages and glues or pastes them in order on a clean sheet. A textbook chapter can usually be reduced to a few pages. Textbook cut-ups eliminate the overpowering and discouraging number of pages that may keep many students from ever attempting to really do an assignment.

Textbook Highlighting and Write-Ins

Go through the chapter before the students do and highlight the parts that they really need to pay attention to, or have the students highlight as they read. Warn students about what is important and what is not. Make sure the students know what has been done and why before they read the material.

Writing in the text is something that students have done and that teachers have discouraged. This technique causes a breaking of the taboo. It is a technique that is easier if only a few problem readers are involved and the teacher aids them by marking up their texts.

The teacher draws attention to major points and to questions answered by writing notes in the text. If textbook questions are used, they may even be cut out and taped directly next to the answers. Arrows can be drawn to maps, pictures, and charts from the descriptive references to where they are discussed in context.

Class Divide-Ups

Instead of having every student read every part of the text, assign only portions of the text to each student for reading. All can still have the benefit of the information in the entire reading. One student might be assigned half the chapter, for example, and a partner assigned the other half. The partners then have to prepare each other with the important and useful information in each half. Another way to work this is to have various groups assigned certain sections. After reading the section, members of the group meet to decide what they need to teach the class from their section and how this can be done most effectively. Until students become good at this, it will be necessary and helpful for the teacher to sit in on group meetings to provide guidance.

Reading Textbooks

Reading is an interactive process. Real reading is not taking place unless the reader is finding meaning. For that to occur, the reader has to be making a conscious, purposeful effort to be mentally engaged and involved and is showing at least a small amount of interest. Effective reading involves coupling decoding and comprehension skills with background knowledge and an awareness of the interrelationships of elements in the text (Vacca et al., 2010). The questions that a teacher needs to ask before using textbooks with students in social studies include the following: How can we make textbook assignments have the most meaning and usefulness to the greatest number of students? How can we aid students in relating background and in seeing the interrelationships of parts of the text? How can we maximize interest in the reading? The fundamental issue is making any work that students do with the textbook meaningful, important, and purposeful.

If textbook units are to be used effectively, students have to view work as something more than a series of tasks to be completed, and teachers have to see curriculum as more than a number of pages to cover (McCutcheon, 1981). This is going to be true of any social studies approach in which students are using any kind of print or non-print materials to get information or ideas. Let us look at what teachers need to do to use textbooks and similar reading materials effectively:

- Give specific purposeful assignments. Not only does the teacher need to have clear and important purposes for having students read material, the students need to understand what those purposes are. Talking with students about why they are reading should be as important as telling them what to read. It also means that the teacher will need to have a fair degree of certainty that the students can actually accomplish those purposes.
- Stimulate interest in the reading. Fortunately, teachers have several ways available to arouse interest; most of them involve creating curiosity. The teacher can, for instance, ask questions that can be answered by the reading material, point out curious and interesting illustrations that are explained or further described in the text, start and leave incomplete stories that are finished in the assigned reading, or give thumbnail sketches of people, places, or events in the text.
- Make sure that students have the skills needed to do the assignment. Many reading skills are needed in the social studies. A partial list of these appears on pages 89–90. If the teacher does not know the mastery level of a needed skill, it is a good idea to provide at least a review demonstration and monitored practice before the students do the assignment.
- Provide supervision, monitoring, and help where needed. Monitoring is important for a number of reasons. First, it is an effective form of teaching and, at least in some instances, allows the teacher to keep students from deep learning of incorrect ways of completing assignments. Second, it helps teachers easily spot cases of "frustration" so that directions can be clarified or help given to students who do not understand assignments. Such help, particularly the right kind of help, is not always available to a student outside the classroom. Third, monitoring gives the teacher feedback about the effectiveness of the pre-teaching, the clarity of the assignment, and the ability of the students.
- Follow up on reading assignments. If students are required to read and complete tasks associated with reading, it should be because this will help them learn important things. What they learn needs to be applied and used in ways that make learning from print important.

Helping Students Develop a Sense of the "Story" by Aiding Predictions

Every reading, textual or otherwise, has a message or story. Knowing the story and getting a sense of its purpose, organization, and direction before we read helps us better understand. Effective previewing or surveying of reading material helps in the following ways:

- It provides purposes for reading in the form of expectations.
- It heightens anticipation and interest.
- It helps determine in what way materials relate to particular interests, questions, hypotheses, and so on.
- It provides advance organizers for thinking about what is read.
- It aids in predicting.

According to Smith (1975), greater accuracy in prediction is highly important to reading comprehension. That is, if the individual has a better idea about the nature of the reading content before reading, he or she will understand it better. The SBR3 technique (Herber, 1978) is a five-step procedure consisting of steps labeled: Survey, Question, Read, Recite, and Review. Of these steps, surveying or previewing the material seems to be most important because effective surveying helps all other phases. If the student can predict, he or she can follow the direction of the writer and anticipate his or her thoughts. A number of teaching techniques, including the following, can help students predict more accurately the content of reading materials:

- Point out the headings and boldface type so students recognize them as organizers.
- Have students discuss speculations from titles and headings about what content is logical.
- Point out pictures before reading and discuss them. From the pictures and the captions, intelligent guesses are possible about the accompanying written material.
- Point out specific references in the text to maps and illustrations so students will know to look for these during reading. For example, the text might refer to stone ruins that an illustration will show.
- Provide an outline or introduction overview and discuss it. A simple outline for the selection involved in the student and teacher summaries used previously might be:
  I The textile industry grows in the United States.
  II Transportation aids the growth of industry after the Civil War.
  III Machinery revolutionizes farming.

Purposeful Reading

If asked, "Why are you reading this?" most students respond with a shrug of the shoulders or, at best, answer, "Because the teacher told me to." However, the most effective readers are very aware of their purposes for reading and when and how they need to find very specific types of information. This alertness to the purposes of reading allows students to read material more rapidly, use context and format clues in locating information, access and use such features as an index or table of contents, and even determine appropriateness or inappropriateness of the material. Reading to achieve specific purposes aids in developing predictive skills, as described earlier.

To help readers use their social studies textbooks and other reading materials with a better sense of purpose, teachers need to set purposes for students that are specific and clear, guide them so that they read to understand those purposes, and follow through to emphasize the importance of those purposes.

The major learning students need for purposeful reading is that the objective of reading in social studies is not simply to read the material. In fact, reading is incidental and only a tool by which students gain the necessary information. Some very common procedures of social studies textbooks focus on providing purpose for reading regardless of whether the teacher is aware of this purpose. These procedures include:

- Providing guide questions before reading that identify specific types of information and understandings the student is to gain.
- Providing study questions that ask the student to identify the ways an author thinks and to go beyond the author's thoughts. For example, after reading material on historical periods, questions might be asked to get the student to explain how people in those eras might think about the way we live in the present.
- Alerting the student prior to reading to follow-up tasks that will employ particular knowledge and concepts. For example, in the chapter on industrial change in America, the student might be asked to build one model of a farm before industrial changes were made and another after to show how farming was revolutionized.

When tasks related to reading are given to students, the purposes need to be made clear. It should not be assumed that students understand why they are reading or know what to look for.

Practice exercises such as skimming and summarizing for particular facts, details, or headings can help students become more aware of the importance of purposes in guiding how and what they read.

Reading Questions and Task Statements

Many students have difficulty reading social studies materials simply because they do not make effective use of question clues that could help them be more purposeful in their reading and more accurate and correct in the way they respond. Teachers can incorporate direct teaching about question clues into social studies or reading study skills instruction. One of the most fundamental skills in dealing with questions has to do with getting an immediate idea of what a question is asking and being able to relate that to the reading material. One of the ways that effective readers do this is by being sensitive to the nature of question words and to the nature of the answers these words demand.

Question words such as who, what, where, and when call for particular kinds of answers. One does not have to have any knowledge at all of the reading material itself to know that the answer to "Who was the English king and leader in the Third Crusade?" will not be, "The Long Bow," "The Battle of Agincourt," or "The Holy Roman Empire." "Who" dictates a particular kind of answer, including the name or description of a person or group of persons. Therefore, we know the answer to be Richard the Lionheart. Any question, in fact, offers clues to the length and nature of acceptable answers by the question words that appear in it. Many students intuitively learn this as they develop their skills in reading and the social studies. For some, though, it is crucial that teachers develop their sensitivity to the influence of key words on question meaning.

Even alerting students to organizational features of textbooks related to questions may be useful to them. For example, students should realize that answers to lists of questions in the text are usually found in the same sequence that they are asked. As simple and logical as this may seem, there are many students who may need to be reminded often.

Another feature that students should recognize is question reversal and parallel structure. These both refer to questions that are written in exactly the same language as the text but with a change in sentence order. A question such as, "What was the ruler of Ancient Egypt called?" will probably be answered in the text with a statement such as, "The ruler of Ancient Egypt was called the Pharaoh."

Teachers constantly grapple with problems students have in grasping and retaining social studies content through reading. Teachers need to remember that the objective of social studies is not to have students read so much as it is to have them learn to use reading as one way to master concepts, learn new content, and obtain information relative to problem solutions.

Reading Social Studies-Themed Trade Books

FYI

Teachers should also take the opportunity to communicate and coordinate with English/Language Arts teachers to explore cross-curricular connections.

Students need to learn how to identify, use, and appreciate trade books. Trade books are common in the classroom and are written at various levels. Trade books include a variety of reading topics and formats, including biographies, fiction, and poetry. An excellent resource for teachers regarding social studies-related trade books is the NCSS annotated bibliography *Notable Trade Books for Young Readers*. The books that appear in the annotated book list are evaluated and selected by a Book

Review Committee appointed by the NCSS and assembled in cooperation with the Children's Book Council (CBC). The annotated bibliography is published annually and includes:

> books that emphasize human relations, represent a diversity of groups and are sensitive to a broad range of cultural experiences, present an original theme or a fresh slant on a traditional topic, are easily readable and of high literary quality, and have a pleasing format and, when appropriate, illustrations that enrich the text.
>
> (NCSS & Children's Book Council, 1997)

Visit www.NCSS.org for the *Notable Trade Books for Young Readers* annual list for the last few years.

Reading Nonfiction

Increasing numbers of nonfiction books that are bold, exciting, and informative are being written for students. Biographies are written at many levels. Some nonfiction books have real depth and feeling as well as interesting information that will arouse students' curiosity. Such books can be used in a lot of ways in addition to being displayed on standard classroom "interest" tables and used for report activities.

Well-written, carefully researched, often colorfully illustrated nonfiction picture books of high quality are abundant. Some are good enough to read aloud, and even secondary students do not mind being read to if the reader is expressive and fluent in his or her reading. Some of these books describe other cultures or life in other places. Others richly describe events and the details of life in different times. The accurate illustrations add to the delight that students experience and to the learning value.

The best biographies are full of anecdotes and stories. Some of the best ones are spiced with humor that humanizes their subjects and makes the books more enjoyable. Table 5.9 lists some recently published biographies that middle school and secondary teachers may find useful when teaching social studies. The list includes title, author, publisher, grade level, and connections to various NCSS themes.

Table 5.9 Examples of Trade Books: Biography

Title (Year)	*Author*	*Publisher*	*Grade Level*	*NCSS Themes*
Balcony on the Moon: Coming of Age in Palestine (2017)	Ibtisam Barakat	Macmillan Children's Publishing Group	6–12	1, 3, 4
Blood Brother: Jonathan Daniels and His Sacrifice for Civil Rights (2017)	Rich Wallace and Sandra Neil Wallace	Boyds Mills Press	9–12	2, 10
Florence Nightingale: The Courageous Life of the Legendary Nurse (2017)	Catherine Reef	Houghton Mifflin Harcourt Books for Young Readers	6–12	3, 4
WHOOSH!: Lonnie Johnson's Super-Soaking Stream of Inventions (2017)	Chris Barton	Charlesbridge	6–8	8, 3, 4
Women in Blue: 16 Brave Officers, Forensics Experts, Police Chiefs, and More (2017)	Cheryl Mullenbach	Chicago Review Press	6–8	5, 6, 10
All We Have Left (2017)	Wendy Mills	Bloomsbury	9–12	1, 3, 5

Reading Fiction and Poetry

Another way that social studies learning can occur is through fiction that students encounter in the reading and language arts curriculum and as recreation. Fiction is about people, events, and places—often about real ones. Even animal characters in stories often personify human qualities. Fiction deals with solving problems and often centers on values and emotions. Fiction is often culturally routed, and story forms such as myths, tall tales, and folk tales tell much about the culture of their origin.

Poetry also offers social studies learning opportunities. We can learn and remember a lot about the beginning of the American Revolution, for example, by doing a readers' theater based on Longfellow's *Paul Revere's Ride*. Poetry is the most economically worded, intense, and focused form of verbal communication. The basic job of poetry is to express personal feelings and thoughts either in song or story form. What this means, in effect, is that the content of all fiction and poetry can be called social studies.

One reason for using fictional material in social studies is that fiction is most often more appealing to students than nonfiction. Good stories just read better than textbooks, where the task of covering specific content controls the writing. Fictional characters and plots are imaginative, exciting, and appealing to the emotions, while bare fact material of any sort is not always so interesting. Many students who give only minimum effort to textbooks and other nonfiction materials are avid fiction readers. They can often be led to discover history, geography, and other social studies content through fiction. In fact, many grow to love the social studies after first having their interest stimulated by fiction.

What kind of fiction do you want to guide students to? We often think a book is going to be good social studies material if it meets some, but not necessarily all, of the following conditions:

- It tells a good story well.
- It develops strong, real characters who are confronted with important and believable problems.
- It contributes something to the reader's knowledge and understanding of the world (other people, other places, other times, oneself).
- It provokes the reader to think and feel about some human problem or situation.
- It helps the reader deal with his/her own problems.

There are many types of fictional and poetry books that relate to social studies. Though far from complete, Table 5.10 provides a fair sampling of the varieties of story types that can be used as part of social studies.

Some excellent teachers make it a daily practice to find time to read aloud to classes, exposing students to at least a portion of some really powerful and interesting books with solid social content. One reason for doing this is that students really enjoy it. In addition to the motivational value,

Table 5.10 Types of Fiction and Poetry Related to Social Studies

Story or Poetry Type	*Social Studies Function*
Historical fiction	Makes past lifestyles more real and relatable
Myths and legends	Show the values of other cultures and times
Fables	Show moral reasoning
Porquois tales	Show non-scientific reasoning
Tall tales and other hero tales	Show occupations and valued qualities
Folk tales	Show cultural values, customs, and fears
Lyric and concrete poetry	Mirrors values and ideals
Narrative poetry, historic	Provides a way of examining hero qualities
Narrative poetry, non-historic	Provides a look into worldviews

Table 5.11 Examples of Trade Books: Fiction

Title (Year)	*Author*	*Publisher*	*Grade Level*	*NCSS Themes*
Saving Wonder (2017)	Mary Knight	Scholastic, Inc.	6–8	2, 8, 10
It Ain't So Awful, Falafel (2017)	Firoozeh Duma	Houghton Mifflin Harcourt	6–12	1, 3, 4, 5
It Looks Like This (2017)	Rafi Mittlefehldt	Candlewick Press	9–12	4, 5
River Runs Deep (2017)	Jennifer Bradbury	Simon & Schuster/ Atheneum Books for Young Readers	6–12	1, 2, 4, 8
Ghosts (2017)	Raina Telgemeier	Scholastic, Inc./ GRAPHIX	6–8	1, 4
The Honest Truth (2017)	Dan Gemeinhart	Scholastic, Inc.	6–8	3, 4

reading aloud to students is good modeling; students see the teacher, who they admire and look up to, reading. Students can often listen with understanding, memory, and appreciation to books and stories that are too difficult for them to read themselves.

Fictional books and stories as well as poems are usually rich in drama and can be turned into skits, role plays, pantomimes, and other acting-out experiences. Some poetry lends itself to choral reading and independent read-aloud activity. Fictional books are an alternative to topical assignments for students to practice reporting skills.

Table 5.11 lists some recently published fictional trade books that secondary teachers may find useful when teaching social studies. The list includes title, author, publisher, grade level, and connections to various NCSS themes.

Connecting Writing to Both Social Studies and Reading

Another language skill, writing, is equally important to the social studies. Through writing, teachers can better discover not only what students know but also what they think. Writing is a way of thinking. It requires that students process and use knowledge, solving problems and doing synthetic creative thinking. However, writing assignments can be difficult and meaningless if they are not carefully planned and imaginative themselves. By way of example, something as routine as a written theme or book report, often cobbled together from copied dust jackets and abstracts, can challenge the imagination and thinking skills of students. Here are eight alternative and unique book activities that can be more effective and have much more impact on the reporter and on the audience:

1 *Economic reports*: For a book or a topic, draw two circle graphs. On one, show the "expenditures" of the main character or subject. On the other, show that character's "income." Of course you are not told this directly, so you need to use problem-solving and inferencing skills. The circles should be segmented, estimating the percentage of the total budget the character would have had to pay on today's market for the goods and services received in the story and the sources of income.
2 *Archaeology reports*: Create a shoebox dig for a book or topic. Having read the material, try to imagine that archaeologists are digging into the site of the main events about which you have read hundreds of years after it happened. In the shoebox create in miniature the artifacts they might find at the site.
3 *Museum reports*: Create a miniature museum exhibit commemorating the people, places, and events depicted in the reading material. This can be done as a diorama or through a series of drawings.
4 *Comic book reports*: Create a comic book for the person, place, or event you have read about using cartoon drawings.

5 *Historical creation reports*: Create documentary evidence that traces the history of a book or topic. You need to create "faux" documents that support the facts. Use your imagination.
6 *Story geography*: Map a book or an event showing the location of the episodes and events described. Then give a map talk taking the major character(s) involved through these events step by step.
7 *Sociometries of books*: Develop diagrams showing the relationships of people in a book or the people involved in an event. Small circles represent individuals, dotted lines show kinship ties, and solid lines with arrows stand for positive feelings of like or love. The oral report consists of explaining the diagram.
8 *Publicity and review reports*: Create a promotion for a book or an event as it might be sold in a television commercial or news report, or develop a review that might be given on a television review program if the book were a movie.

Organizing to Write

Reading and writing activities or assignments in social studies may take several forms. The follow-up of a class or group reading assignment might include having students do any of the following activities:

- Answer questions
- Write a summary
- Write a solution to a problem using information from the reading material
- Make up a story involving the time or place described
- Write a description
- Write book reports on single books read independently (e.g., biographies, books about events, "You are there" books, viewpoint books, etc.)
- Write summaries of articles in magazines and newspapers
- Make written plans for a project or activity
- Write letters requesting information or materials (often done in role)
- Write letters of appreciation to historic individuals or book characters
- Imitate literature types from other cultures or times (e.g., Japanese Haiku poetry, tall tales, ballads, etc.)
- Do in-role writing activities in which the student pretends to be in another culture, place, time, or position
- Write dramas and skits related to unit topics being studied
- Write narrative reports of library research on a topic or of an experiment conducted, a series of observations, an interview, or a conversation
- Make up rules, generalizations, hypotheses, cause and effect statements, etc.

Students experience two major kinds of difficulties with writing assignments in social studies. The first has to do with the clarity of the assignment. The teacher simply needs to be sure to explain an assignment clearly and completely. The teacher needs to cross-check, asking students to repeat and even paraphrase and explain in their own words the expectations. The second difficulty has to do with how well prepared students are for an assignment. Avoiding this difficulty involves being assured that students have the ability or readiness to do the assignment. It also means that they have been taught how to do the assignment.

The base or prerequisite skills needed for many, if not all writing jobs include note taking, writing answers to questions, and outlining. All of these skills involve having the ability to see what is most important and the ability to discern what is relevant for particular purposes. For students to develop these abilities, they have to, first, be able to see the essential purpose of the writing job itself. Second, as they read, listen, or observe, they must be able to pick out central messages. Third, they need to be able to scan for messages related to particular criteria.

Do not assume that students have already developed the necessary skills. Once you have determined the skills they do and do not have, you can set about to gradually develop the needed abilities. Note taking, question asking and answering, and outlining can be boring, especially if students do not understand the assignment or if the content is dry. All are learned skills, and most middle and high school students are far from mastering them (Boyle, 2011; Donohoo, 2010). Utilize interesting and relevant topics to help students learn the skills. Outline the sports section of the newspaper or the lyrics of a pop song, for example, or take notes on a comic book or a travel brochure. Be absolutely sure that students understand what it is they are supposed to do. One procedure to try is the following:

1 Define the skill that you want students to have and analyze the steps they will have to go through in performing that skill.
2 Find out what students can do by giving them a very simple and short supervised task involving the skill.
3 Model the skill, using a question and answer format to get students to look at what you are doing analytically.
4 Repeat the model, going step by step with new content, allowing students to do the work as a class. Monitor to make sure that they are all with you.
5 Supply exercises in which part, but not all, of the structure is in place.
6 Gradually withdraw the structure until students can perform without it.

Such a systematic procedure sounds simple and logical, but the majority of teachers seldom follow this kind of procedure. Research indicates that teachers rarely make certain that students understand the questions in textbook assignments (Anderson & Burns, 1987) and that there are often major comprehension problems inherent in the questions themselves (Cooper, 1986). The questions may be unclear in their wording. Students may lack the background knowledge needed to understand them or may be unable to see just what it is that the questions are seeking.

In spite of these problems, research supports post-reading questions as contributing to learning (Walberg, 1986). This would seem to indicate that if teachers would be more careful about assignments and about preparing students for them, such assignments could be beneficial.

Plan to keep an assignment within reach of a particular group of students. By "within reach" we mean that the assignment is one that students can do in a reasonable amount of time. Reducing assignment length (the number of questions to be answered) while providing more guidance and feedback is beneficial (Barron et al., 1998; Slavin, 1987). Mechanisms for doing this include dividing work among students, segmenting assignments, and identifying assignment mentors (Turner, 1989).

Following are guidelines that may make textbook question assignments more meaningful:

- Assign questions only after reading them carefully.
- Give clear, complete directions both in writing and orally, taking time to explain and answer questions.
- Call attention to special problems and trouble spots students are likely to encounter.
- Point out where questions call for the student to evaluate, be creative, or give interpretation.
- Teach the students about question words and that questions in texts are answered in the order that they are asked.
- Follow up completed assignments by going over them in a meaningful way.
- Wherever possible, use visual graphic organizers.

Developing Research and Reporting Skills

Students are often asked to write and present reports in social studies. Such activities can serve several purposes, including but not limited to the following:

- Writing both necessitates and helps thinking. By asking students to complete a report we are giving them valuable practice in thinking skills.
- Writing is developed by practice. By involving students in writing activities, we help them develop their writing skills.
- Reporting activities allow students to pursue individual interests and work at their own levels.
- Giving a report empowers a student with a sense of authority. He or she becomes an expert and gains ownership of a unique and special knowledge.
- Reporting can help a student develop and improve self-expression.
- Presenting a report can be an application of the entire spectrum of language skills.
- Reports can give oral and visual displays of writing and/or speaking.
- Reporting can be structured to foster social interaction.
- Reports provide checkpoints where student learning is observable and in a form where such learning can be evaluated.

Reports can be written, oral, or both. Reading, writing, and oral language skills are combined in reporting. Among the most common problems associated with reporting assignments are wholesale copying from books and the Internet, students' lack of comprehension of their own work, stumbling and stiff presentation of oral reports lacking in meaningfulness or purpose, and inattention of students to one another's reports. It is easy to see that all of these problems are somewhat related. Fortunately, they are also avoidable.

None of the problems associated with student reports is attributable to the nature of reporting itself. They seem to be more related to the lack of thought by teachers relating to the clarity of reporting assignments and the readiness of students for particular types of reporting assignments. Problems also come due to the failure of teachers to teach students how to prepare and write a report and presentation.

Let us first look at the assignment stage. Reporting assignments may be set in several contexts:

1 As an assignment all students complete (everyone reports on the same thing).
2 As parts of sets of assignments from which all students choose (students may choose among two or more projects).
3 As a form of recognition or distinction to better students (reporting activity is done only by students the teacher sees as capable and likely to put forth the effort).
4 As volunteer activities that are encouraged and rewarded (History Fair, extra credit, praise).

None of these forms is inherently better or worse than any of the others. What is important is that students know and understand which rules are being used. A logical rule of thumb is to keep the system simple.

There are a number of types of reporting assignments. Earliest reporting activities in school begin with sharing or show-and-tell activities and with language experience approaches. Sharing activities are important because they develop students' ability to talk in front of an audience and can help them learn to distinguish important and appropriate things from those that have less significance and relevance. Language experience approaches, which are a form of teacher-led corporate reporting, have similar value and teach students sequencing and ordering skills as well.

One type of individual reporting is experiential reporting. "What I Did/Learned/etc. on My Summer Vacation," the most trite example of this kind of report, gives this type of assignment a bad name. At its best, an experience report is a positive learning experience. It involves having students give true accounts of events that have reality to them. There is a natural narrative and sequence and an opportunity to learn the importance of supporting detail, noting cause and effect relationships, and drawing conclusions.

The same can be said for observational reports that are accounts of events witnessed and sometimes staged and orchestrated by the student. Observational reports can be made about movies, television programs, YouTube and other online videos, dramas, field trips, and other events witnessed by students both as individuals and as groups. They may even be done collaboratively.

Face-to-face phone and/or Skype interviews can be the basis of interesting reports. Students need to be given a structure of questions to ask in the interview. This can be provided by the teacher or developed in a guided class discussion. Audio or video recordings of the interview can be useful both in report write-ups and in segments as part of oral reports.

Reports may also take the form of demonstrations. Students can show either directly or by simulation how something was or is done in a culture. They may also use drama as the vehicle for the report.

A real danger in reporting is that of mindless, copied reports. This danger can be averted by clear directions that specify how the report is to be organized. Whatever form of reporting or writing students may be asked to do, success rather than failure can be expected if the teacher follows certain principles:

1 Assignments should be stimulating, interesting, and challenging to students.
2 Writing assignments need to be clear. Teachers need to provide both a written description and an oral explanation of the assignment and seek feedback about how well students understand the expectations.
3 Assignment length and complexity need to be within the capabilities of students. This can be achieved by:
   a limiting the length of the assignment
   b segmenting the assignment into logical steps or components.
4 Provide a structure for the report. Among the many structuring devices that might be used are outlines, sets of questions, dramatic devices (e.g., job applications for biographical reports on historical characters), a list of key points, or chronologies.
5 Successful writing assignments result from embedding the teaching of necessary directions and skills development into the writing assignment process. The assignments should:
   a specify and direct length by specifically defining length (number of words or sentences or pages) or space provided;
   b embed the teaching of such skills as summarizing, paraphrasing, skimming, and scanning into the development of the assignment;
   c provide a structure of steps to follow in doing the assignment;
   d specify and provide the resources to be used and direct students on how to use them.

Writing Creatively

Writing can actually make social studies more engaging. The variety of creative-writing tasks that can relate to any social studies topic is really limited only by the teacher's imagination. Any idea used needs to be tested with three questions before it is tried:

FYI

Creative writing is a wonderful way to make the task of writing social studies content more interesting, relevant, and exciting to students who might not traditionally enjoy the class.

1 Is doing this task really going to serve a purpose related to understanding what is being studied?
2 Can students do this task and in a reasonable amount of time?
3 How is this task going to affect or relate to the other activities that we are doing?

A number of beneficial writing activities can be described as in-role writing. In-role writing means that the writer is pretending to be someone else as he or she writes. One kind of in-role writing involves trying to go through an authentic writing exercise from a particular time period, such as writing letters, songs, wills, and epitaphs for famous and non-famous historical characters.

An alternative type of in-role activity involves imagining how a historical character might deal with some of the paperwork we deal with today. For example, how would that character fill out a job application or a questionnaire? What about Attila the Hun applying for a job as a school teacher, Clara Barton seeking a school nurse position, or Thomas Jefferson trying to get the media coordinator's job. Students can also write in-role autobiographies in story, rap, or poetry form.

Classroom Episode #1

This is a simple song about Cleopatra sung to 6th graders, titled "Float Your Boat Down the Nile" (to the tune of "Home on the Range"):

Floating north on the Nile, watching crocodiles smile,
And the bull hippopotami play.
With the Sphinx you can kid, see the Great Pyramid
Abu Simbel, it's huge, so they say.
Row, row down the Nile
Ride like Cleopatra in style
See a fierce lion pride, or an asp slither slide
And the camels race by single file.
Alternative Chorus
Row, row down the Nile
Shave your head, it's the old Egypt way.
And if you should die, you can be mummified
Then you'll see just how much your soul weighs.

Creative-writing strategies can involve imitating a writing form of a particular culture. Students studying Japan can, of course, write Haiku poems. The study of Germany and France invites fairy tales, the American West suggests tall tales, ancient Greece and Rome might produce myths and fables, and the New England colonies bring sampler messages and Horn Book sayings and stories. Reading stories or poems that come from any culture can provide models for meaningful creative writing.

Other kinds of creative writing can offer exciting promise, including problem-solving stories where the solution is not easily available or is, at least, a challenge. Usually the teacher provides a story starter that is a problem scenario. Table 5.12 lists a few story starter examples.

Students then write a story in which the central characters try to solve the problem. For example, an 8th-grade class was given a scenario about two students from the North who found themselves deep in the heart of the Confederacy at the outbreak of the Civil War. They had to write a story in which the students figured out how to find their way back.

Table 5.12 Story Starter Examples

Julius Caesar is sending messages to his troops and fears that his messenger might be captured by the Germani.
America is gripped by the Great Depression and Franklin Delano Roosevelt wants to do something dramatic and visible to reassure the American people.
After President Lincoln is assassinated and the secretary of state severely wounded, national leaders want to assure the country that the conspirators are all caught and punished.
Thomas Alva Edison has invented the gramophone or record player and wants to control the kinds of recordings available so that quality and taste are maintained.

One activity utilizes simple stories that students make up about fictional students they imagine in the cultural setting they are studying. It may sometimes be difficult to get adolescents involved to the extent that they feel that they are actually doing research in order to write the story. However, if this can be achieved, it gives them what amounts to a real scholar's purpose for studying. This might be in the form of a diary in which they make daily entries. These could involve such events as traveling with Columbus, Marco Polo, or any explorer, going on a cattle drive with cowboys, taking a wagon train or a railroad train west, going on a modern trip to a set of preselected sites, or any one of a host of other journeys.

Collaborative writing is another effective strategy. This is where students write a story as a group. Their story is structured by the skeleton story in a series of topic sentences. Each student or pair of students independently writes a paragraph beginning with one topic sentence. When finished, the group works together to smooth out the inconsistencies and write in transitions. Table 5.13 provides an example of a set of topic sentences that might be used for students to collaboratively write a "Robin Hood" story.

Table 5.13 Collaborative Writing: Sample Topic Sentence Set

Many a good and honest man had turned outlaw, because of the greed and the cruelty of the Norman nobles. These outlaws roamed the king's forests foraging what they could. The most famous of all the outlaws was Robin of Locksley, better known as Robin Hood. Robin was himself of noble blood, but had been dispossessed of his land and titles by trickery. Along the roads that led though Sherwood Forest, no rich Norman traveler was safe from Robin's merry band of outlaws. According to legend, Robin Hood robbed from the rich and gave to the poor. You can help to build yet another story to add to the Robin Hood legend.

1. The Sheriff of Nottingham, unable to catch the outlaw known as Robin Hood, at last had hit upon what he thought would be a foolproof plan.
2. Disguised as peasants, the Sheriff and three of his archers slipped into Sherwood Forest quietly.
3. As they passed through a glade in the forest, an arrow whistled through the air, missing the Sheriff's ear by little more than an inch.
4. The Sheriff did not realize that Robin Hood had seen though his disguise immediately and told a story of how he and the others had been forced off of their land in the north.
5. Blindfolded, the four strangers were led through a twisting, turning way to a secret glen.
6. Secretly, the Sheriff left a trail of white pebbles for his soldiers to follow.
7. When the blindfolds were removed, the Sheriff's men were amazed at the great group of busy and happy people they saw.
8. The outlaws treated their visitors royally, feasting and toasting them through the late afternoon.
9. With a mischievous grin, a small man came strolling through the boisterous crowded tables to pour out a bag of white pebbles in front of the Sheriff.
10. As Robin and a half dozen or so men surrounded them, Sir Guy and the archers looked at each other fearfully.
11. The Sheriff and his men, relieved of the weight of their purses, their weapons, and their shoes, wandered in the forest for days before they were found, and the Sheriff was not a happy man.

Looking Back

Social studies is knowledge-based, and that knowledge has been most readily communicated through print and the Internet. Students need reading and writing skills to succeed in social studies. Teachers give reading and writing assignments for the purpose of reviewing information, preparing for new studies, extending what goes on in the classroom, and developing creativity.

There is a growing unity of purpose between social studies and the language arts as the literature connection becomes more apparent in social studies with the Common Core Standards. Writing skills are emphasized in all content areas and are requirements of most state assessment tests. Educators know that reading and writing ability grows through practice and that reading and writing is linked to thinking.

When students have problems reading content material, there are several strategies that teachers can use. Among the most important of these is pre-teaching vocabulary, reducing the actual length of reading assignments, providing sufficient and clear purposes for reading, and developing predictive skills.

Extension Activity

Scenario

Wednesday, the middle of the week and an early release day, arrived quicker than normal at YHS. As students are leaving school for the day, you have a brief conversation with your principal, Dr. Russell. As you are talking, Dr. Russell asks if you are ready for trade book adoptions. Knowing that you have not started working on the adoption list, you explain that you are planning to start this week. Dr. Russell reminds you that trade book adoptions are due next Wednesday.

Feeling a little stressed about the trade book adoption timeline, you consider alternatives. In the end you decide you only have two options. Option One: Develop your own list of 20 books you could use in your classroom to help teach social studies. Option Two: Partner with other teachers and develop one list of 20 books that all the teachers involved in your grade or course will utilize to help teach social studies.

Questions

1. What are the advantages and disadvantages of having other teachers' input and adopting one set of trade books?
2. What are the advantages and disadvantages of selecting your own list of 20 books for adoption?
3. What qualities, topics, etc. would you seek in the new books?

Task

Select either Option One or Two, and once an option has been selected get to work developing a trade book adoption list. The list should include at least 20 recently published trade books. The list should include all bibliographic information, summaries of the books, a discussion of how you could use the books in the curriculum, and possible state and national standards addressed.

Reflective Questions

1 What are the four basic purposes for which reading and writing assignments are used in independent seatwork?
2 What are the qualities that you need to look for in a nonfiction book?
3 What are some different kinds of fictional materials that can be used in social studies?
4 What are the purposes of learning research and reporting skills?
5 How are guidelines useful in making textbook questions more meaningful?
6 Why do teachers have students write reports and present them orally?
7 What ways can you teach concepts and vocabulary to students?
8 What is SQ3R?
9 What is meant by the term *purposeful reading* and why is the concept important?

Helpful Resources

Watch this video, which explores a 6th-grade teacher and how she teaches scaffolding for reading comprehension.
https://youtu.be/gleNo8dqHb8
This video details the importance of literacy in the history/social studies curriculum and how it can be effectively incorporated.
https://youtu.be/sF0BpowS4Gg
Watch this video about how to use the Frayer Model.
https://youtu.be/AdjN09VouaU
This video, created by the National Council for the Social Studies, explores informational text and how to make text more readable and enjoyable.
https://youtu.be/8UE3b2N16zk
Visit The Great Books Foundation, which is a useful website for teachers looking to incorporate reading into their classroom instruction. Books are recommended for a variety of topics, including social studies, with additional ideas on how to create meaningful activities and assessments from the suggested books.
www.greatbooks.org/
Visit the NCSS *Notable Trade Books* site, which contains links to past years' lists of the National Council for the Social Studies *Notable Trade Books for Young People*. The list contains books about a variety of social studies topics for multiple reading levels. It is a good place for teachers to find supplemental readings for units or to build a classroom library.
www.socialstudies.org/resources/notable
Visit Repositories of Primary Sources, which contains a vast hyperlinked database to over 5,000 web pages containing holdings of manuscripts, archives, rare books, historical photographs, and other primary sources for teachers, researchers, and scholars. Teachers could find this site useful in locating primary resource reading materials for class or for student research projects where students need to locate primary resources.
www.uiweb.uidaho.edu/special-collections/Other.Repositories.html
Watch this video about mastering essay writing.
https://youtu.be/oegC9JWi2xw?list=PL96_6089u0OWHB5KhnHRp7MTU2fNa-dP8.
This video details the R.A.C.E. strategy to writing short essay responses.
https://youtu.be/mPnt9AFaTd
Watch this video, created by the National Council for the Social Studies, highlighting how teachers can teach argument writing in the social studies.
https://youtu.be/7GRnQviAshM

Further Reading

Ogle, D., Klemp, R. & McBride, B. (2007). *Building Literacy in Social Studies*. Alexandria, VA: Association for Supervision and Curriculum Development.

This book presents both the underlying concepts and the research-based techniques that teachers can use to engage students and build the skills they need to become successful readers, critical thinkers, and active citizens. The authors provide various strategies, teaching models, graphic organizers, and step-by-step instructions.

Vacca, R.T., Vacca, J.L. & Mraz, M.E. (2010). *Content Area Reading: Literacy and Learning Across the Curriculum.* Boston, MA: Allyn and Bacon.

This book addresses the valuable and inclusive topic of literacy and learning through reading in all content areas. The authors present practical examples and research-based practices to increase literacy for students in all content area courses.

References

Anderson, L.W. & Burns, R. (1987). Values, evidence, and mastery learning. *Review of Education Research*, 57(2), 215–223.

Barron, B., Schwartz, D., Vye, N., Moore, A., Petrosino, A., Zech, L., Bransford, J. & The Cognition and Technology Group at Vanderbilt. (1998). Doing with understanding: Lessons from research on problem and project-based learning. *The Journal of the Learning Sciences*, 7, 271–311.

Boyle, J.R. (2011). Thinking strategically to record notes in content classes. *American Secondary Education*, 40(1) (Fall), 5–65.

Brunner, L. (2009, May). The kids can't read. Principal Leadership: *Middle Level Education*, 9(9), 18–22.

Cooper, D. (1986). *Improving Reading Comprehension.* Boston, MA: Houghton Mifflin.

Donohoo, J. (2010, November). Learning how to learn: Cornell notes as an example. *Journal of Adolescent and Adult Literacy*, 54(3), 224–229.

Frayer, D., Frederick, W.C. & Klausmeier, H.J. (1969). *A Schema for Testing the Level of Cognitive Mastery.* Madison, WI: Wisconsin Center for Education Research.

Gersten, R. & Baker, S. (1999). *Reading Comprehension Instruction for Students with Learning Disabilities: A Research Synthesis. Executive Summary.* New York, NY: National Center for Learning Disabilities.

Gregg, M. & Sekeres, D.C. (2006). My word: Vocabulary and geography learning. *Journal of Geography*, 105(2), 53–58.

Herber, H.L. (1978). Teaching Reading in Content Areas (2nd ed.). Englewood Cliffs, NJ: Prentice Hall.

Kent, A.M. & Simpson, J.L. (2008). Social studies and literacy integration: Making the most of our teaching. *Social Studies Research and Practice*, 3(1), 142–152.

McCutcheon, G. (1981). Elementary social studies teachers' planning for social studies and other subjects. *Theory and Research in Social Education*, 9(Winter), 45–66.

McLaughlin, M. (2012). Reading comprehension: What every teacher needs to know. Reading Teacher, 65(7), 432–440.

National Council for the Social Studies & Children's Book Council. (1997). Notable children's trade books in the field of social studies. *Social Education*, 61(April/May), 1–15.

Shanahan, T. (2001). *The National Reading Panel: Teaching Children to Read.* Newark, DE: International Reading Association.

Slavin, R.E. (1987). *Cooperative Learning: Student Teams.* Washington, DC: National Education Association.

Smith, F.A. (1975). *Comprehension and Learning: A Conceptual Framework for Teachers.* New York, NY: Holt, Rinehart, and Winston.

Turner, T.N. (1989). Using textbook questions intelligently. *Social Education*, 53(1), 58–60.

Vacca, R.T., Vacca, J.L. & Mraz, M.E. (2010). *Content Area Reading: Literacy and Learning Across the Curriculum.* Boston, MA: Allyn and Bacon.

Walberg, H. (1986). Synthesis of research in teaching. In M. Wittrock(Ed.), *Handbook of Educational Research: A Project of the American Educational Research Association* (3rd ed., pp. 214–229). New York, NY: Palgrave Macmillan.

6 Social Studies and Diverse Learners

Looking Ahead

Social studies as a subject is diverse, as are the students in your class. Teaching diverse learners can be a challenge if not properly equipped. Teaching an array of students who are from different countries, speak different languages, have different cultural beliefs and values, and learn and retain information differently, are some of the many requirements of a social studies teacher.

This chapter begins by discussing the various learning styles you will see in your classroom. The chapter then moves into a discussion regarding multicultural education and what it means to be a culturally responsive teacher. From there, the chapter focuses on teaching English Language Learners (ELLs) social studies and various teaching techniques that can be utilized to accommodate the needs of English learners. The chapter concludes with a discussion of teaching exceptional education students and details various strategies social studies teachers can utilize to accommodate social studies instruction. It should be noted that the techniques and strategies detailed in the chapter can be utilized and have been found to be effective with many, if not all, student populations.

Can You? Do You?

Can you ...

- identify Howard Gardner's multiple intelligences?
- describe the common characteristics of a culturally responsive teacher?
- identify the ideals of multicultural education?

Do you ...

- understand what it means to be a culturally responsive teacher?
- know how to adapt instruction to meet the needs of English Language Learners?
- know two strategies to accommodate instruction for exceptional education students?

DOI: 10.4324/9781003217060-6

Focus Activity

Before reading this chapter, try the focus activity below.

Think about your various learning experiences. Think about how you learn. Do you know how you learn best? If so, move to option one; if not, move to option two.

1. Option one: How do you learn best? When did you become aware of how you learn best? Share your answer with classmates.
2. Option two: Since you are unaware of how you learn, try to discover how you learn best. Think of things you have learned and how you have gone about learning the information. For example, maybe you remember making flash cards for a test that you aced. Maybe you remember building a birdhouse that helped you understand measurement. Spend time reflecting about how you learn. Once you realize how you learn, it will make learning more meaningful, enjoyable, and efficient. Share your experience with classmates.

Multiple Intelligences

Since the beginning of the twentieth century, the concept of intelligence has been carefully studied. Intelligence tests, conceived early in the century, have continued to be developed and refined. Early psychologists generally believed that intelligence could be defined as overall intellectual capacity and potential. Toward the end of the century, the most widely used intelligence tests were challenged as being culturally biased. However, the concept of a single quality of intelligence remained largely intact. The psychologist who has offered the greatest challenge to this idea when it comes to learning is Howard Gardner (1983). Gardner discounts the idea of considering intelligence in the limited dimensions assessed by the kinds of tests that have been used in education. In fact, he argues that schools often fail because they have concentrated exclusively on verbal and mathematical ability; Gardner contends that individuals have different kinds of intelligence and that schools should provide learning activities that allow students to learn as they learn best. Originally seven in number, Gardner's list of intelligences has possibilities for expansion.

Currently, eight intelligences are being considered in many teacher education programs. Table 6.1 shows Gardner's eight intelligences (1999) and presents an abbreviated explanation of each.

In sum, Gardner's work relating to multiple intelligences demonstrates the need to diversify instruction to meet the students' individual learning needs. It is essential, since students learn in different ways, that teachers utilize a variety of teaching techniques, strategies, and methods of instruction.

Table 6.1 Gardner's Multiple Intelligences

Intelligence	*Explanation*
Linguistic-Verbal	the ability to read, write, and communicate with words
Logical-Mathematical	the ability to reason and calculate in a logical, systematic way
Visual-Spatial	the ability to think "in pictures"
Musical	the ability to make or compose music
Interpersonal	the ability to work effectively with others
Intrapersonal	the ability for self-analysis or reflection
Bodily-Kinesthetic	the ability to use the body to solve problems or to create products
Naturalist	the ability to recognize flora and fauna, to make other distinctions in the natural world

Multicultural Directions in Social Studies

Multicultural education has been a transforming force in social studies since the 1960s, yet even its strongest advocates differ widely about what exactly multicultural education should be. Beginning in the 1980s, scholarship emerged related to multicultural education. Agreement has emerged about the ideals of multicultural education. Gorski (2000) asserts that the ideals of multicultural education include:

- All students should have equal chances of achieving their full potential.
- Students must be prepared to live and work in an increasingly intercultural society.
- Teachers should be enabled to effectively facilitate learning for every individual student, no matter how culturally similar or different.
- Schools have to be active in ending oppression and prejudice—first within their own walls, then by developing all students to be socially and critically active and aware.

> **FYI**
>
> Social justice and advocacy are becoming an increasingly important and visible component of contemporary social studies instruction.

- The role of schools is essential to laying the foundation to change society and eliminate oppression and injustice.
- The goal of multicultural education is to effect social change.

Multicultural education goes beyond teaching tolerance and "advocates the belief that students and their life histories and experiences should be placed at the center of the teaching and learning process and that pedagogy should occur in a context that is familiar to students and that addresses multiple ways of thinking" (NAME, 2003, p. 1). Multicultural education means reaching comfort levels with curricular issues that give us discomfort, raising and addressing issues that are difficult, and asking questions that challenge thinking and beliefs. To bring about the changes advocated for multicultural education, these ideals must be embodied in all social studies curricula. Teachers themselves need to become more sensitive and aware of both obvious and subtle incidents of prejudice, bias, and/or intolerance. Educators need to become culturally responsive teachers. Culturally responsive teaching requires all educators to develop an understanding of students' learning contexts (Gay, 2000). Culturally responsive teaching is a pedagogy that recognizes the importance of including students' cultural references in all aspects of learning (Ladson-Billings, 1994). Common characteristics of culturally responsive teaching are:

Positive perspectives on parents and families
Communication of high expectations
Learning within the context of culture
Student-centered instruction
Culturally mediated instruction
Reshaping the curriculum
Teacher as facilitator

(Educational Alliance at Brown University, n.d.)

FYI

Exploring the experiences and perspectives of traditionally marginalized groups is a best practice for any effective social studies teacher concerned with presenting multiple perspectives.

Culturally responsive teaching is much more than teaching the notable and iconic figures of color. It requires teaching alternative perspectives inclusive of gender and race (Ladson-Billings, 1995).

Social Studies and English Language Learners (ELLs)

Non-English-speaking students are a reality in the contemporary classroom. The most popular and accepted term for non-English-speaking students is English Learners (ELs) or English Language Learners (ELLs). However, depending on your state and district, ELLs are also referred to as English as a Second Language (ESL) students, Limited English Proficient (LEP) students, or English Speakers of Other Languages (ESOL).

According to the National Clearinghouse for English Language Acquisition, the number of English Language Learners (ELLs) across the U.S. increased by 51 percent to over 5.3 million students between 1998 and 2009 (2011). Furthermore, ELLs are considered to be the fastest-growing segment of the student population when compared to other subgroups in U.S. schools (Cruz & Thornton, 2009).

California, Florida, and Texas are a few of the states in the nation that face an enormously large ELL population. Nonetheless, teaching ELLs is not limited to those states. No Child Left Behind (NCLB) (2002) requires adequate yearly progress across all student populations. This means that attention must be given to the needs of ELLs. It can be extremely challenging for ELLs to demonstrate progress in an English-only curriculum. According to the NCLB guidelines, ELLs are required to be tested in English within two years of entering a U.S. school. In 2005, only 4 percent of all 8th-grade ELLs achieved proficiency on the National Assessment of Educational Progress (Short & Fitzsimmons, 2007).

Communicating With ELLs

When communicating with ELLs in an social studies classroom, speak clearly. However, you do not need to speak louder; they are not deaf. When communicating with ELLs use props, pictures, drawings, gestures, signals, objects, graphic organizers, etc., to help explain the directions and/or the social studies content information. If you are communicating in written form, be sure to print legibly or type information. Sloppy handwriting and/or cursive add an additional challenge for ELLs. In all forms of communication, be sure to avoid slang terms (e.g., "cool"), colloquialisms (e.g., "y'all"), and idioms (e.g., "kick the bucket") (Szpara & Ahmad, 2007).

Managing the Classroom

As with any efficiently and effectively run classroom, students need to be aware of requirements and expectations. Develop classroom rules, procedures, and routines for everything from using the restroom to turning in assignments to getting make-up work, etc. Just as you would teach the American Revolution or any other topic, be sure to teach the class rules, procedures, and routines. Post your rules in English and in your respective ELLs' language/s. For translating, try the school/district foreign language department. Classroom structure will help ELLs to function in the classroom environment. Furthermore, involve ELLs in day-to-day activities. Do not isolate them. However, be sure to foster an environment that allows all students to feel safe, secure, and comfortable.

Promoting Social Interaction

One of the core components of social studies is social interaction. Some social studies teachers do not promote social interaction because they prefer the "stand and deliver" method or the "read and answer the questions" method. ELLs need social interaction, and fostering an environment that encourages social interaction will allow ELLs to be more comfortable, thus increasing their chances of success. Social interaction promotes discussions among students. Discussion can increase students' interest in content and improve basic interpersonal communication skills (BICS) (Cruz et al., 2003). Oftentimes, English-dominant classrooms can subject ELL students to subtle segregation unless teachers are prepared to address their needs. Provide ELLs with opportunities to work with partners and/or in cooperative learning groups. Social interaction with peers can help ELLs with basic vocabulary, build BICS, increase self-esteem, and most of all prevent segregation.

Embracing the Culture

Another core component of social studies is culture. However, some social studies teachers often shy away from discussing the cultures of students. Embrace your ELLs' culture(s) by incorporating cultural information into the curriculum. Display photos, books, and images around the classroom. Have all students share artifacts, experiences, and/or stories about their culture. Utilize oral histories to have all students explore and learn more about their classmates' cultures. This will provide all students with an opportunity to highlight themselves and their culture without segregating the ELLs.

Delivering Content

Use a variety of instructional methods and present information in a variety of ways when teaching ELLs. Utilizing a variety of instructional methods can increase student achievement and understanding. ELLs will benefit from kinesthetic-related activities. Being hands-on allows ELLs an opportunity to complete a task and feel validated. Place new content terminology on the board and provide as many visual aids and demonstrations as possible. Using visual aids increases student understanding and comprehension of the material being presented. When delivering new content, give simple directions. Relate new information with students' everyday lives and help make connections to students' prior knowledge. Repeat and rephrase information frequently. List the lesson objectives and activities on the board and provide ELLs with step-by-step instructions. Allow students to interact. Be sure to check for comprehension. Have students demonstrate their learning to check for comprehension. Do not ask, "Do you understand?" Usually ELLs will reply "Yes" even if they do not understand.

FYI

It is important not to be overwhelmed or nervous about the idea of teaching ELL students. Many best practices for teaching ELL students are also wonderfully effective for all students in your class.

Visual Aids for ELLs

Teachers should utilize various visual aids to accommodate instruction. The utilization of visual aids is an essential feature of effective instruction because it provides the support needed to contextualize learning. Visual aids include real objects from the field, photos, images, drawings, charts, graphs, maps, music, video, and graphic organizers. Specifically, graphic organizers support ELLs' understanding of complex and difficult concepts and text (Weisman & Hansen, 2007).

Social Studies and Exceptional Education Students

Approximately 4 to 6 percent of students are considered exceptional education students because of a learning disability. Additionally, 1 percent of students have a diagnosed behavior disorder (Steele, 2008). Newman (2006) reported that approximately 70 percent of students with learning disabilities and/or behavioral disorders receive inclusive education. Inclusive education requires that exceptional students spend all or part of their time with non-exceptional/non-special education students (Minarik & Lintner, 2016). Social studies teachers often have students with exceptional needs in their classrooms; however, many teachers are uncertain what the label might imply regarding instruction. Most exceptional educators agree that students with learning disabilities have "normal" intelligence but do not process information in the same manner as students without learning disabilities. Students labeled exceptional can have difficulty with academic and daily living skills. A student with a behavior disorder may lack positive peer relationships, demonstrate non-age-appropriate behavior, lack academic abilities or achievement, and may appear unhappy or depressed. No single method can reach all learners. Thus, a teacher must approach the curriculum with a diverse set of instructional strategies.

Reading Adaptations

Selecting various reading materials including textbooks from lower grades can help accommodate students' individual learning needs. Provide students with instruction on the components of the textbook. Many students with learning disabilities require instruction regarding how to use the glossary, appendix, and table of contents as well as headings, boldface terms, and illustrations.

Study guides can promote comprehension of the text and encourage active learning. We recommend supplemental readings for students with learning disabilities. The supplemental readings component includes newspaper articles, historical fiction, and Internet sites (i.e., the Library of Congress, as well as magazines such as *Newsweek*). Supplemental materials associated with curricula are significant because the materials most often relate to the lives of those who lived in a certain time period. Historical fiction novels can be compared with factual text, engaging critical thinking and analysis of materials. Reading the newspaper builds community awareness and critical thinking skills and can be used to initiate cross-curricular relationships. Supplemental readings add depth to the content in the textbook and assist students with learning disabilities in clarifying themes, events, abstract ideas, and topics.

Writing Adaptations

Many students find writing difficult. Students with learning disabilities often need assistance, guidance, and modifications to writing requirements. Social studies teachers need to combine a variety of writing strategies like summarization, collaborative writing, specific product goals, word processing, sentence-combining, pre-writing, inquiry activities, process writing approach, study of models, and writing for content learning. Teachers should use mnemonic writing strategies to assist exceptional education students. Scholars (Graham & Perin, 2007; Mason & Graham, 2008) have developed various examples of mnemonic strategies, which are listed below:

PLAN (*P*ay attention to the prompt, *L*ist the main idea, *A*dd supporting ideas, *N*umber your ideas).

WRITE (*W*ork from your plan to develop your thesis statement, *R*emember your goals, *I*nclude transition words for each paragraph, *T*ry to use different kinds of sentences and *E*xciting, interesting, $10,000 words).

For paragraph-specific writing strategies, students can follow the SLOW CaPS mnemonic writing strategy listed below:

S = Show the type of paragraph in the first sentence.
L = List the type of details you plan to write about.
O = Order the details.
W = Write the details in complete sentences and cap off the paragraph with a
C = Concluding,
P = Passing, or
S = Summary sentence.

For sentence-specific writing strategies, students can follow the PENS mnemonic writing strategy listed below:

P = Pick a formula.
E = Explore words.
N = Note the words.
S = Search and check.

Teachers can use the COPS mnemonic strategy to help students proofread written work:

C = Capitalization: Have I capitalized the first word in the sentences and proper nouns?
O = Organization: Have I made any errors related to overall appearance such as handwriting, margin, messy?
P = Punctuation: Have I used end punctuation, commas, and semicolons correctly?
S = Spelling: Do the words look like they are spelled right? Can I sound them out, or should I use the dictionary?

Teachers can use the ANSWER mnemonic strategy to assist students in formulating answers to essay questions:

A = Analyze the action words in the question.
N = Notice the requirements of the quest.
S = Set up an outline.
W = Work in the detail.
E = Engineer your answer.
R = Review your answer.

Graphic Organizers

Graphic organizers facilitate comprehension by providing visual representations of materials for students. Graphic organizers are also known as knowledge maps, concept maps, story maps, cognitive organizers, advance organizers, and/or concept diagrams. Graphic organizers can be used to organize large amounts of material, creating timelines, cause and effect comparisons, and event relationships. Social studies teachers can use graphic organizers before, during, and/or after classroom activities such as assigned readings, direct instruction, discussions, and presentations. Graphic organizers help students create meaning of text, sort information, and promote easy and efficient information recall. Graphic organizers enable students to acquire information through their preferred learning style. For visual learning, it creates a visual representation of content. For auditory learners, graphic organizers can become the focus of discussion of materials with peers as the student explains the organizers. For tactile or kinesthetic learners, the activity requires creative thought processes, writing, and could involve bodily movements. When utilizing graphic organizers, teachers should use the following evaluation criteria for selecting suitable and appropriate graphic organizers:

> Analyze the learning task for words and concepts important for the students to understand.
> Arrange them to illustrate the interrelationships and pattern(s) of organization.
> Evaluate the clarity of relationships as well as the simplicity and effectiveness of the visual.
> Substitute empty slots for certain words in order to promote students' active reading.
> (Merkley & Jefferies, 2001, p. 351)

In addition to analyzing the usefulness of a graphic organizer, teachers should model the use of a graphic organizer and scaffold instruction from classroom, to small group, to independent utilization and writing. Teachers should have explicit instructions and model how to use the graphic organizer to ensure students' effective application of graphic organizers.

Looking Back

The ability to teach and accommodate the individual needs of all learners is a skill all teachers must acquire. As stated earlier, the techniques and strategies detailed in this chapter can be utilized and have been found to be effective with many, if not all, student populations. Social studies is as diverse a subject as the learning styles or the cultural make-up, spoken languages, and/or exceptionalities in your classroom. Teachers need to equip themselves with the tools, skills, and knowledge necessary to effectively teach and accommodate instruction to meet the diverse learning needs of all students.

No matter what the students' learning style, first language, exceptionality, and/or cultural background, social studies teachers will surely need to modify content and instruction. This chapter detailed Gardner's multiple intelligences, ideals of multicultural education, and what it means to be a culturally responsive teacher. In addition, this chapter shared numerous techniques and strategies for helping English Language Learners and exceptional education students learn social studies. One of the most significant changes to the world of education over the past 20 years is the increasing emphasis on diverse learners and meeting the needs of all students.

Extension Activity

Scenario

It is the Monday right after winter break at Yourtown High School (YHS). Your students arrive to school on time, well rested, and eager to learn. As you greet students at the door, students shower you with sweet and heartfelt comments about how they missed you and they hope you had a wonderful winter break. As you are about to greet the last student you realize that you do not recognize her. You say "Hi" and ask her "Where are you supposed to be?" She does not answer. Just then, the guidance counselor, Mrs. Benedict, comes from around the corner and explains: "You have a new student and her name is Carlota." You walk Carlota into the classroom and place her at an empty desk. Mrs. Benedict follows and explains: "Carlota has just moved here from Brazil. Her first language is Portuguese and she has a very limited understanding of English." Mrs. Benedict recognizes the look of concern on your face and asks: "Are you capable of effectively teaching English Language Learners?" You nod and say: "Yes." Pleased, she smiles and explains: "Be sure you accommodate your content and instruction to meet her learning needs."

Task

Imagine Carlota is in your class: how will you accommodate your social studies content and instruction to meet her learning needs? For this activity, select a social studies topic and grade level. Then, develop an engaging lesson plan that includes accommodations to meet the needs of all students, including Carlota. Share your lesson plan and accommodations with classmates.

Reflective Questions

1 What Howard Gardner's eight multiple intelligences?
2 What does it mean to be a culturally responsive teacher?
3 What are the ideals of multicultural education?
4 How can you accommodate instruction for exceptional education students?
5 How can you adapt instruction to meet the needs of English Language Learners?

Helpful Resources

Teaching Tolerance is a respected website and journal published by the Southern Poverty Law Center. *Teaching Tolerance* offers a free journal for educators interested in teaching tolerance. The journal highlights various teaching activities and practices for multicultural teaching.

www.teachingtolerance.org

Teachers of English to Speakers of Other Languages is a respected professional organization devoted to advancing expertise in English language teaching and learning for speakers of other languages worldwide. The association offers numerous publications, which include research and practice applicable to teachers.

www.tesol.org

Watch this video, which discusses the unique characteristics of ELLs and their learning needs. The National Council for the Social Studies created the video.

https://youtu.be/L9_cok-NYOE

Watch the following video in which students in a middle school classroom explore different cultures through art.

www.teachingchannel.org/videos/exploring-culture-through-art

This video shares how an experienced teacher teaches U.S. geography to ELL students.

https://youtu.be/-BEnlxdtzRM

Watch this video of an ELL student sharing his story and describing what his sees in a visual aid.

https://youtu.be/L44XW88fe5Y

The Council for Exceptional Children is a respected professional organization devoted to the teaching of students with exceptionalities. The website includes instructional strategies and lesson ideas for teachers. The association offers numerous publications, which include research and practice applicable to teachers.

www.cec.sped.org

Further Reading

Baum, S., Viens, J. & Slatin, B. (2005). *Multiple Intelligences in the Elementary Classroom*. New York, NY: Teachers College Press.

This book is a great resource for elementary educators interested in designing curriculum for students with diverse learning abilities.

Chandler, P. & Hawley, T. (Eds.). (2017). *Using Inquiry to Teach About Race in Social Studies*. Charlotte, NC: Information Age Publishing.

This book address teaching race in the classroom. It provides concrete lesson ideas for engaging learners in the social studies.

Hickey, G. & Clabough, J. (2017). *Digging Deeper: Activities for Enriching and Expanding Social Studies Instruction.* Charlotte, NC: Information Age Publishing.

This book showcases best practices and includes research-based lessons and activities that enrich and expand social studies instruction.

Lintner, T. & Schweder, W. (Eds.). (2011). *Practical Strategies for Teaching K–12 Social Studies in Inclusive Classrooms.* Charlottee, NC: Information Age Publishing.

This book blends best practices in social studies and special education instruction and details how to make social studies meaningful, relevant, and engaging for all students.

Minarik, D. & Lintner, T. (2016). *Social Studies and Exceptional Learners.* Washington, DC: NCSS.

The authors provide background information on categories of disability and laws driving disability services in schools and recommend best practices for educating exceptional students in an inclusive classroom setting. The book also offers carefully designed lesson plans for teaching economics, geography, history, and civics to exceptional learners.

NCSS. (1992). Guidelines on Multicultural Education. *Social Education*, 56(4), 274–293.

This article is a position statement of the National Council for the Social Studies detailing how multicultural education should be incorporated into social studies.

References

Cruz, B., Nutta, J., O'Brien, J., Feyton, C., & Govoni, J. (2003). *Passport to Learning: Teaching Social Studies to ESL Students.* Washington, DC: NCSS.

Cruz, B., & Thornton, S. (2009). Social studies for English language learners: Teaching social studies that matters. *Social Education*, 73(6), 270–273.

Educational Alliance at Brown University. (n.d.). Teaching Diverse Learners: Cultural Responsive Teaching. Available at: www.alliance.brown.edu/tdl/tl-strategies/crt-principles.shtml

Gardner, H. (1983). *Frames of Mind: The Theory of Multiple Intelligences.* New York, NY: Basic Books.

Gardner, H. (1999). *The Disciplined Mind: What All Students Should Understand.* New York, NY: Simon and Schuster.

Gay, G. (2000). *Culturally Responsive Teaching: Theory, Research, and Practice.* New York, NY: Teachers College Press.

Gorski, P. (2000). *Multicultural education.* McGraw Hill Supersite. Available at: www.mhne.com/socscience/education/multi/define.html.

Graham, S., & Perin, D. (2007). *Writing Next: Effective Strategies to Improve Writing of Adolescents in Middle and High Schools. A Report to Carnegie Corporation of New York.* Washington, DC: Alliance for Excellent Education.

Ladson-Billings, G. (1994). *The Dreamkeepers.* San Francisco, CA: Jossey-Bass Publishing Co.

Ladson-Billings, G. (1995). Toward a theory of culturally relevant pedagogy. *American Educational Research Journal*, 32(3), 465–491.

Mason, L.H., & Graham, S. (2008). Writing instruction for adolescents with learning disabilities: Programs of intervention research. *Learning Disabilities Research & Practice*, 23(2), 103–112.

Merkley, D.M., & Jefferies, D. (2001). Guidelines for implementing a graphic organizer. *The Reading Teacher*, 54(4), 350–357.

NAME (National Association of Multicultural Education). (2003). National Association of Multicultural Education: Definition of Multicultural Education Position Statement. Available at: http://nameorg.org/position-statements/

National Clearinghouse for English Language Acquisition. (2011). The Growing Number of English Learner Students 1998/99–2008/09. Available at: www.ncela.gwu.edu/

NCLB (No Child Left Behind). (2002). Act of 2001, Pub. L. No. 107–110, § 115, Stat. 1425 (2002). NCLB.

Newman, L. (2006). Facts Form NLTS2: General Education Participation and Academic Performance of Students with Learning Disabilities. U.S. Department of Education Institute of Education Sciences National Center for Special Education Research. Available at: www.nlts2.org.

Short, D.J., & Fitzsimmons, S. (2007). *Double the Work: Challenges and Solutions to Acquiring Language and Academic Literacy for Adolescent English Language Learners. A Report to Carnegie Corporation of New York.* New York, NY: Alliance for Excellent Education.

Steele, M.M. (2008). Teaching social studies to middle school students with learning problems. *Clearing House: A Journal of Educational Strategies, Issues and Ideas*, 81(5), 197–200.

Szpara, M., & Ahmad, I. (2007). Supporting English-language learners in social studies class: Results from a study of high school teachers. *Social Studies*, 98(5), 189–196.

Weisman, E., & Hansen, L. (2007). Strategies for teaching social studies to English-language learners at the elementary level. *Social Studies*, 98(5), 180–184.

7 Thinking, Problem Solving, and the Acquisition of Skills

Looking Ahead

In a democratic society, developing students' ability to think critically and solve problems are critical goals. The ultimate aim is to develop students into independent and self-motivated learners. Embodied in this goal is the notion that effective teachers allow, encourage, and challenge students to understand how to find, evaluate, and use information. If the development of independent learners is truly the goal of education, then it is important to teach students how to think, not what to think.

Thinking and problem-solving skills are the core purpose of social studies. The National Council for the Social Studies states that "the primary purpose of social studies is to help young people develop the ability to make informed and reasoned decisions for the public good as citizens of a culturally diverse, democratic society in an interdependent world" (NCSS, 2010).

Presentation-style social studies, where the teacher does most of the talking, is not likely to develop students' thinking skills. To ensure students become problem solvers, students must be involved and participate in the learning process. This means that discussion, teacher questioning, and carefully constructed assignments are critical.

Information is only important if it can be put to use. Students often feel that they are asked to learn information for which they have no use at all. As a result of this and other factors, students do not always learn in school the skills they need to use information.

If the teacher's goal is for students to become independent learners, and if the ability to solve problems is a major factor in that independence, then finding and analyzing information have to be viewed as critical skills. The focus of this chapter is on those skills that are needed to make the best use possible of information in every problems context. The chapter begins with general information skills, decision-making, and historical thinking skills before moving into two specific areas that have special importance to the social studies: map skills and economic skills.

Can You? Do You?

Can you …

- explain three ways to teach students to think logically?
- identify problem-solving tasks?
- identify several ways that you can stimulate curiosity in students?
- explain why map and globe skills are challenging for students?
- explain the three types of memory?

Do you …

- know how to help students to understand and retain information?
- know and understand the term *story map*?
- ever get the "Columbus urge" or have "Aha!" moments?
- know and understand the term *mnemonic device*?

DOI: 10.4324/9781003217060-7

Focus Activity

Before reading this chapter, try the focus activity below.

Think back about your education and life experiences. Can you recall an important decision you had to make in your life? How did you go about finding the ultimate solution? Share your decision-making experiences with classmates. Discuss the details of the decision-making experiences and compare. Does your decision-making process share common attributes with others? If so, what attributes?

Thinking Skills

Learning can be viewed in two different ways. The first we usually call rote learning. Rote learning means that information is memorized with little or no understanding of its meaning. For example, you may have learned a poem, speech, or song or learned to spell and pronounce words but had no idea of their meaning. Rote learning does not provide us with useful information because if we have no idea of the meaning of what we have learned, we cannot conceive how to put it to use.

The second way of learning begins with our understanding what we learn. The more sense we can make of something, the more it fits into patterns and stories in our minds, the more likely we are to retain it. Constructivism is the theory that explains that people come to understand new ideas and information by relating it to previous experiences. From a constructivist point of view, the way that new information is presented may be as important or even more important as the information itself because it will determine how we make sense of the information or how we give it meaning. The quest to develop students as problem solvers in social studies can be traced at least to the beginning of the twentieth century when a few innovative schools began to look at a life-centered problems approach as central to the curriculum. Beginning in the 1960s and 1970s, the notion of learning to learn became crucial to every social studies program as an approach called the inquiry method was widely advocated. The inquiry classroom differed from a traditional classroom. The students were to learn to ask questions, not just answer them. The teacher's role became less that of information provider and more that of coach, facilitator, and guide.

The term *thinking skills* refers to all of the mental processes that individuals use to obtain, make sense of, and retain information, as well as how they process and use that information as a basis for solving problems. The process of taking in the information likewise involves thinking skills, especially those related to observing, listening, and reading. Obtaining information and ideas is a sensory process, and all of the senses are used in information gathering. For many students, learning is easier through one sense than the others and thus teachers need to utilize multisensory learning materials wherever possible. Even so, learning to listen and observe are trainable skills acquired through directed and disciplined practice. Therefore, teachers need to help students acquire these important skills in a systematic and developmental way.

FYI

While teaching thinking skills is a fundamental objective of social studies instruction, it is important to remember that you are teaching the students how to think, not what to think.

Schema is a term used to describe relating new ideas to experiences (Driscoll, 2009). Schemata (the plural) are the various ways that we group ideas and knowledge in our minds. Our best chance at understanding new concepts is to tie features of those concepts to one or more of these schemata. To do this, we look for similarities, make assumptions, create analogies, and generally relate information to ourselves.

Another factor in comprehension is metacognition, a student's awareness of his or her own thinking processes and of the thinking processes of the people with whom he or she is communicating. The term has come to be used to describe a student's awareness and understanding of the organizational patterns of reading material and of speakers. Individuals who are able to form clear and accurate story maps of reading material or spoken material have a clearer overall understanding of that material. This, in turn, helps them to understand the meaning of specific parts of the communication as it relates to the organization and purposes.

To maximize student understanding, middle and secondary social studies teachers should provide story maps for students before they listen to, read, or view material. In effect, this means that teachers need to provide both sensitive and clear overviews of oral presentations, audiovisual programs, and reading material before students are exposed to them. A reflective review of material will also help students develop their metacognitive skills. Such reviews increase learning and retention in a clearly measurable way. These reviews generally involve teacher questioning, so that students become intellectually involved and, therefore, active in forming clearer cognitive maps of material covered.

Generally, teachers can help students understand and retain information by following a few principles:

- Associate new information with experiences that students have had in the past.
- Connect each piece of new information to other pieces of information using a pattern that students can follow (sensory or visualizable patterns are best).
- Repeat information and patterns often.
- Provide a shared purpose or use for the learning.
- Give opportunities for practice with feedback.

Logical Thinking and Analyzing Skills

In social studies, teachers help students gain logical thinking and analyzing skills in at least three ways: by modeling, through discussion, and through guided practice with feedback. Table 7.1 details thinking skills and possible activities.

Table 7.1 Thinking Skills and Activities

Thinking Skill	*Type of Activity*
Interpreting or explaining	Paraphrasing, rephrasing
Relating information	Advanced organizers for reading assignments
Applying previous knowledge	Charting, drawing parallels
Identifying implicit assumptions	Discussion of motives
Identifying key features and characteristics	Defining, describing, giving background
Summarizing and synthesizing	Writing summaries, reviewing, giving closure to lessons
Comparing and contrasting	Identifying attributes, pattern finding
Organizing information	Outlining, sequencing
Classifying and categorizing	Charting, sorting
Inferencing and concluding	Cause-and- effect exercises, following clues, guessing games, problem solving
Determining truth, accuracy, completeness, reliability	Cross-checking, maps of errors, peer evaluation

Critical and Creative Thinking

The chief dilemma of teaching is to show students where to look without telling them what to see. Helping students learn to think logically should lead them to critical and creative thought processes, not show them what to think. The teacher wants the student to be able to make informed decisions based on the information available and to have the ability and the mindset needed to come up with multiple and original ideas as solutions to problems.

Critical thinking can be defined as making evaluations or judgments of experience. When evaluation is based on analysis, then critical thinking involves often complex logical reasoning. Critical thinking requires comparing a personal set of experiences and values to current experiences, newly encountered data, and decision- and judgment-demanding situations. We think critically whenever we try to reason out decisions or judgments. Critical thinking relates to some very important functions of the mind. Those functions of the mind can be seen in Table 7.2.

Creative thinking also requires evaluative thinking as well as other abilities. Creative thinkers come up with new ideas, new ways of looking at things, and different ways of synthesizing or combining existing ideas. They see several logical possibilities in solving problems and also are open to illogical methods. They are not so much looking for the solution to a problem or answer to a question as they are trying to see various possibilities. Part of the creative mindset is a fluency and flexibility of thought. Creativity implies originality, the ability to come up with unique and unconventional approaches. However, creative thinkers follow through with the same openness, having the ability to develop and elaborate ideas in solving problems. Creative thinking is what we need when we try to find new and different ways of solving both new problems that we have never encountered before and older ones that have remained without satisfactory solutions.

It would be an oversimplification to say that creative thinking is the ability to solve problems; however, that ability is at least a focus of creative thinking. Creative thinking differs from most thought required in school chiefly because of its emphasis on alternative approaches and solutions and on multiple solutions.

Problem Solving and Inquiry

Problem solving most often begins with a situation that demands a solution or a response. A creative problem-solving experience is one where the individual has to figure out both what to do and how to do it. Creative problem solving, as it relates to social studies, can involve any one of the following thinking difficulties:

- Dealing with a negative or difficult situation
- Overcoming an obstacle
- Bringing about some desired outcome
- Bringing about change.

Table 7.2 Functions of the Mind

The Symbolic Process	*We allow words, numbers, and other symbols to stand for ideas.*
Visualization	We make mental pictures that represent our perceptions.
Characterization	We notice the qualities of things and that which we notice, in turn, builds our perceptions of similarities and differences.
Classification	We sort things into classes, types, families, and so on.
Structure Analysis	We notice how things are made and break classes into component parts.
Operations Analysis	We notice how things happen, successive stages, and so on.
Paralleling	We see how situations are alike.

In order to understand and use information, we must be able to put that information into a variety of logical structures. As this skill develops, it involves curious playfulness and a willingness to experiment with different ways of ordering and different ways of looking at information. As we learn to do this, we learn to identify relationships and patterns; to put information from different sources together; to make inferences and judgments; to recognize qualities such as relative importance, relevance, and usefulness; and to differentiate among degrees of partial, convincing, decisive, and conclusive evidence.

A critical issue in problem solving is the ability to recognize and identify the real problem(s). Once the real critical problem(s) are clearly and specifically identified, ways to find solutions are more easily determined.

FYI

Consider how the identification of problems directly relates to media literacy objectives in the current political and social climate of contentious news and information.

Inquiry teaching models use variations of the "scientific method." Most of us learned some version of this method in middle and/or high school science class. The scientific method is simply a sequence of the steps involved in any research. The following steps describe the basis of the scientific method:

1 Sense the problem (beginning with a doubt or uncertainty)
2 Define the problem
3 Come up with some hypotheses (possible solutions to the problems)
4 Gather evidence
5 Draw conclusions.

Inquiry has changed the way we look at teaching social studies and has provided problem-solving tools that continue to be useful in teaching students to become independent thinkers and problem solvers. One contribution of the inquiry approach has been the development of a variety of teachable, creative problem-solving strategies. These strategies were conceived with a problem that defies solution in mind, and they can be learned easily through experiences in which the teacher models them in discussion formats with specific problems. Successful strategies for approaching difficult problems are detailed in Table 7.3.

Table 7.3 Successful Strategies for Approaching Difficult Problems

Restate the Problem	Simply putting a problem into different words may make it more understandable and, therefore, more solvable. It gives the problem solver a fresh perspective.
Segment the Problem	Dividing the problem in some way, whether into identifiable components or simply into smaller pieces, is a useful strategy. Divided, the problem can be attacked as a cooperative learning task by a group or can be dealt with one piece at a time.
Tangential Problems	Try solving tangential problems. Look at the impact of the problem and identify side effects. Work on solving these relatively minor problems and they may provide a key to the central problem.
Analogies of the Problem	Look for analogies to the problem and try solving these analogous problems. For example, if we said that our polluted rivers are similar to clogged arteries and then looked at the solutions doctors suggest for clogged arteries, it may help us identify remedies for the rivers.
Reduce the Problem	If we try to say the problem in the minimum number of words and as simply as possible, then we may understand its essence more fully and be better able to solve it.

Table 7.4 Sample Guidelines for Problem-Solving Activities

1. The best way to get super ideas is to get lots of ideas and then discard ideas that are not so great.
2. Write down your ideas before you forget them (within 5 minutes).
3. Begin with the obvious and then look for more than one right answer.
4. Ask questions, even ones you may consider stupid.
5. Remember that nearly all words have several meanings.
6. Visualize the problem. See it backwards, forwards, inside out, and all mixed up.
7. Ask how nature would solve the problem.

The best way to get students to become active problem solvers is to give them lots of problems to solve. Real-life problems are most effective. The teacher needs to treat situations in the classroom as problem-solving activities. Give students a set of guidelines similar to those found in Table 7.4. When students encounter a problem, lead them through the list and ask students their thoughts about the problem in relation to each of the guidelines. Point out that every guideline does not have to apply to every problem.

Attempt to tolerate and encourage offbeat and unique but appropriate responses and comments. Also, keep the classroom atmosphere relaxed and welcoming. Help students realize that the true secret of problem solving is perseverance and that the process is often as valuable as the outcome.

FYI

It is best for teachers to begin the school year by building a culture of respect and openness to better facilitate meaningful and challenging discussions throughout the year.

Types of Problem-Solving Tasks

Once students learn to recognize and verbally describe problems, they need to learn to identify critical elements within these problems. Recognizing the presence of patterns and features in a problem may signal a possible way of solving it. A problem of a particular type can be approached in much the same way as other problems of that type. Knowing the elements of a problem will be of enormous help in identifying and using the most promising approach. Once the approach is identified, following a series of steps used in similar problems will often lead to a solution. Below are approaches that can be used as models for students. Each relates to problems of a particular type. Sample activities are given with each approach.

Identifying All Factors of a Problem

Identifying all factors of a problem requires looking at all related factors and issues involved. In these problem-solving strategies, the emphasis is on the nature of problems that have multiple possible answers. The approach is one that is effective for complex problems for which there is no perfect set of right answers. The actual number of possible answers will vary with such problems. However, the problem solver's task includes defining criteria for examining the appropriateness of answers. Examples of this approach follow.

1 *Example: Identifying All Factors of a Problem*
Pilgrims' Progress: If you were embarking with the early Puritans or Pilgrims who came to settle New England, what sort of supplies would you take with you? Make a list that includes

necessities as well as other things you might like to have. Remember that this is the 1600s. What kinds of supplies are going to be available, and what things simply do not exist yet? Think about the kind of place that you are going to and the kind of place you are coming from.

2 *Example: Identifying All Factors of a Problem*
Invention Brainstorm: Suppose we put the word *invention* in the middle of the board. Now let us think of other words that represent related ideas; we will place these words all around the board and connect the ones that are related to one another with lines.

Prioritizing a Problem

Prioritizing a problem requires setting priorities within the problem. Prioritizing is a lifelong problem. There are always too few resources, time, money, or goods for the demands. Individuals, communities, and nations continually have to decide which needs and wants to meet first. Prioritizing problems in social studies usually involves looking at lists of equipment or provisions as they relate to a particular problem or being faced with a series of problems in a given situation and having to decide in what order these problems need to be solved, based on immediacy, importance, or a combination of the two. Following is an example of a problem-solving task.

1 *Example: Prioritizing a Problem*
Shipwreck Rescue: You are the commander of a sailing ship bringing new colonists and supplies to the New World in the seventeenth century. Your ship has been caught in a terrible storm as you approach the coast. You have been unable to keep the ship from going aground on the rocky shore. The storm still is raging all about and may at any moment either wash you out to sea or break the ship into pieces. The water rushing all around is only about six feet deep, and you can see a solid beach perhaps a hundred yards away. Here are all the problems that you must handle. Number them according to the order in which you think they need to be handled. Suggest a solution for each:

- Sharp rocks can be seen dead ahead.
- There is a gaping hole in the hull and some water is rushing in.
- You fear that hostile natives may inhabit this area of the coast.
- The food supplies are in the hold, which is fast filling with water.
- The crew members are unhappy and are arguing among themselves.
- One of the ship's cannons has broken loose and is careening across the deck.
- A woman on board is about to give birth.
- A small fire has broken out in the ship's kitchen.
- One of the ship's masts has been broken by the storm and has fallen, pinning a crew member and perhaps breaking both of his legs.
- Some of the colonists are trying to break into the powder magazine containing all of the ship's weapons and gunpowder.
- A passenger is demanding that he and his scientific records be put ashore in the ship's boat.

Multiple Perspectives of a Problem

Multiple perspectives of a problem requires examining differing, conflicting, and opposing points of view. Understanding, accommodating, and relating to ideas and opinions of others is a problem of cooperation. It is also the foundation of understanding conflict of all kinds. Problem-solving exercises require students to identify the likely opinions of others. Examples of this type of exercise include the following:

1 *Example: Multiple Perspectives of a Problem*
The Telephone: Think about how people in the nineteenth century felt about the invention of the telephone. Think about the impact that the first telephones might have had on different people's lives. Just after the turn of the century there were only a few hundred telephones in use. Even then, people were beginning to see the change that a telephone network was going to bring. Write down a few sentences about the views of the people that follow. Then, we will assign roles in groups and discuss what our feelings would have been if we had lived at the turn of the century:
   - Opinion of the owner of the telegraph company
   - Opinion of a messenger boy whose job might be threatened
   - Opinion of a New York businessman
   - Opinion of a New York housewife
   - Opinion of a conservative, country minister.

2 *Example: Multiple Perspectives of a Problem*
Programming: Pretend that you are the programming director for a major television network. You are considering new programs for the 8 o'clock Monday night slot, where the program will be up against established shows that have had good ratings. You are considering: a long-running comedy program that has been revamped after being canceled by another network (as the ratings reached an all-time low); a new comedy with a star who once had a hit drama series but may not have comedic ability; a show aimed at preteen, teen, and young adult viewers and starring several young, unknown actors; a news program presenting controversial issues and public opinion; and a hard-hitting action show with an up-and-coming African American star and lots of violence. What would be the views of each of the following:
   - The conservative network president
   - The president of a fast-food chain that is a big sponsor
   - The head of an organization of concerned parents
   - An 11-year-old boy
   - A 12-year-old girl.

Problems with Alternative Solutions

Problems with alternative solutions begin with a problem that has several plausible solutions, none of which can ever be absolutely identified as the single correct solution. The basic question the problem solver must ask is, "What is the impact of each possible solution?" For example, the teacher might begin with a series of contemporary problems like drugs, gangs, pollution, prejudice, or terrorism and suggest, or have students suggest, several of the partial solutions that have been articulated by social scientists and politicians. Students would then try to think hypothetically about what positive and negative impacts each of these solutions would have if implemented.

> **FYI**
>
> Despite what many testing companies may have you believe, there is in fact more than one correct answer to some problems!

Identifying Purpose Problems

Identifying purpose problems involves identifying the aims, goals, and objectives of problems. The focus in this type of problem is on identifying the purposes that people might conceivably have.

It sometimes involves looking at our own aims as well. The basic strategy uses analogies, stories, and situational scenarios. The problem solver has to examine the wants, needs, and hopes of people involved in the particular setting. In each case the key problem is to identify the major aims, goals, and purposes that the individual or group is pursuing in the situation. This kind of problem focus should help students become more purpose-oriented and help them understand the reasons for the problem. Examples of problem tasks include the following.

1 *Example: Identifying Purpose Problems*
   - Identify the central aims, goals, and objectives of the main characters in a young adult novel or story (e.g., *Threads and Flames, Annexed*, or *Countdown*).
   - What are the main goals and objectives of al-Qaeda?
   - What are the main goals of the school rules?
   - What were the aims, goals, and purposes of African Americans during the civil rights movement?

Problems with Proposed Solutions

Problems with proposed solutions emphasize identifying advantages, disadvantages, unique, and interesting features. In this type of problem solving, the problem is an assertion or an idea to be examined. The purpose in the problem-solving process is for students to be able to see possible advantages and disadvantages that the implementation of that assertion would bring. A secondary purpose is to have them analyze the unique and interesting features of this assertion. The teacher might want to begin by having students show agreement by hand signals or standing up. A few examples of such assertions follow.

1 *Example: Problems with Proposed Solutions*
   Students should volunteer when they know the answer.
   - There should be a law that all containers and print materials be recyclable and that users recycle such containers.
   - Abraham Lincoln should have issued the Emancipation Proclamation immediately when the southern states seceded.
   - People need to be able to do whatever they want with property that they own.

Promoting Critical Thinking with Modules

Modules provide from one to a series of lessons, sometimes consisting of several activities centered on one or a series of closely related ideas, usually concept statements or generalizations. Modules may be used in isolation, as part of or in conjunction with a unit, or in clusters. Built into modular teaching is the notion of mastery. Mastery, in this case, means that the module teaches the idea to a point where some specified or at least defined level of understanding is reached. Evaluation and re-teaching, then, are necessary for module construction.

As the following examples of topics for modules might indicate, modules may aim at developing definitional understanding of concepts, helping students reach evaluation judgments, or providing experiences that cause students to arrive at a commonly shared generalization as a way of thinking. The following are examples of definitional topics:

- A map is a model representing some part of the surface of the earth or some other area and it is subject to various inaccuracies.
- A president is the head of a nation, organization, or business, having specific executive functions and powers for a defined length of time and under restricted conditions.
- Laws are rules recognized by a governing body as binding upon the members of the group.

Evaluation judgments include:

- A good country
- Responsibility
- Playing fair is more important than winning.

The following are examples of generalizations:

- Urban communities tend to change more rapidly than rural communities.
- Though all members of a community are consumers, only some are producers.
- A single event may have several causes and produce more than one outcome.

Once the topic is identified, the module consists of an array of activities, including examples and identified non-examples along with identifying experiences. The activities have the express purpose of bringing an understanding or mastery of the topic, requiring students to analyze and think critically about the topic.

Promoting Inquiry with Case Studies

The case study approach has become increasingly more viable with the development of computers and databases. The term *case study* implies a kind of intense examination of a particular event, person, or thing, or a grouping of these. One case is looked at as an example or model that can be studied in depth and even intently over time. In medicine a doctor might study the medical histories of a few patients. From these selected cases, it is hoped that insights about others who have similar medical histories may be derived. In law, a case study may be chosen because it represents a landmark decision or provides precedent in court procedure. Sociologists, historians, and psychologists may construct fictional cases to demonstrate typical behavior. In fact, the case study approach is used by almost all professions looking at human behavior simply because of the complexity of human thought and action.

> **FYI**
>
> Case studies can be very time-intensive in terms of planning, so make sure to give yourself ample time to effectively plan these learning experiences.

A case study is an intensive use of example(s). The example(s) provides a database for inquiry and concrete illustration(s) of principles, concepts, and ideas. Case studies used in social studies can help students see the personal and human aspects of a culture or of a time. Students look at one person, one family, one village rather than reading generalizations about a country, culture, or period of time. Human qualities seem less abstract. Below are some basic procedures for preparing a case study.

1. Identify the problem to be studied and the purpose to be accomplished.
2. Tentatively identify a research procedure for students to follow.
3. Select the appropriate example (or case).
4. Develop detailed procedural plans.
5. Collect resources related to the case. Examples of resources include:
   - Maps of varying sorts
   - Background information sheets

- Interviews on related topics
- Letters
- Descriptions of objects
- Diaries and journals
- Records and public documents
- Newspaper clippings.

6 Organize the materials and data related to the case. For example, one usable pattern of organization consists of:
- A single narrative or a series of narratives describing the facts of the case. These may include first-hand accounts, scholarly summations, and even slanted or biased descriptions;
- First-person (witness) interviews with principals in or witnesses to the case (transcripts or tapes of these);
- Pictures (photographs, drawings, etc.), films, and other media visualizations (including actual film coverage of an event) of the setting, the people, and the chain of events in the case across the time period involved;
- Exhibits (artifacts, realia);
- Maps, graphs, charts;
- Background information (including anecdotes).

7 Plan activities and materials structured to help or guide students as they examine the case or inquire into the evidence.
A few types of activities to use with case study material include:
- Research-based discussions and individual reports of controversies;
- Problem-solving situations calling upon data in the case;
- Role-plays involving the principals of the case;
- Developing reports or answering questions in which students draw from data;
- Debates involving controversies or points of view regarding the same or related cases;
- Creative writing to or about the principal characters in the case (e.g., letters, hypothetical diaries, fictional stories, etc.);
- Question-generating sessions;
- Data-generating sessions to build additional cases or to extend the data bank;
- Reenactments of events;
- Artistic endeavors (e.g., murals, models);
- Projective analysis (what are outcomes to be anticipated beyond the data?);
- Analysis sheets and questions to be answered by studying the data.

Incorporating Thinking and Learning Skills in Social Studies

Problem-solving and decision-making skills are the core of effective teaching. Only if students are mentally engaged in social studies are they going to learn. The major thrust of social studies is to develop the ability of students to think and learn for themselves. If they can do that, then they are ready for any social studies topic. If they cannot think, then each topic and each encounter with content requires the teacher to present and guide them through, and the student is always a dependent learner. Students who need such guidance will not fully develop into the ideal citizens that a democracy requires to survive.

Building the Desire to Master Study Skills

Students have to master some very complex and difficult information-processing skills. What makes learning more difficult is that students must master these skills during a period when they are going through physical and emotional changes and facing stressful social changes. Some of the students in the world today are in stressful home situations and that complicates the mix. A growing number are latchkey kids on their own for hours after school. Many are from single-parent homes. Many face physically or mentally abusive situations. Unemployment of parents, insufficient family income, or other major economic problems add to the insecurity.

There is an expression, "the urge gives you an edge." What it means is that the strong desire or want to do something well gives an individual a distinct advantage; it helps her or him to actually do well. Students often wonder about how they will ever use the learning that educators and parents are forcing upon them. It makes sense that the best opportunities that teachers have to help students acquire the kind of edge that the strong urge to learn will give them is when there are opportunities to put information to use. Learning to use knowledge is the heart of a problems approach. Once students learn that knowing information and how to get it is useful in solving real problems, it gives knowledge purpose.

Teachers have to convince students that knowledge really does empower because it can enable them to solve existing problems and anticipate and head off potential problems. If they believe this, students will learn because they need to know and want to learn, not because the teacher tells them they should.

Students have to deal with information that comes from an array of sources, an almost endless variety of print, electronic, and mobile-accessible materials. The textbook is not the most exciting of these materials or the easiest to handle. More exciting, but sometimes requiring more interpretation, is other information that comes from technology or print in audio or visual forms, from artifacts and other objects, and directly from other people. Reading, observation, and listening skills as well as technological competencies are needed as the basis for study.

Primarily, students need to be able to know where and how to find the information needed. As an accompanying processing skill, they have to be able to decide if information is true and accurate, relevant, important, and useful. Finally, they have to be able to remember, use, and present the information.

Finding Information

Locating information requires a kind of mindset, and teachers can help students acquire it. Mastery of accessing skills is needed, as are using various types of indexes and tables of contents, computer applications, and search engines. Students need to be taught skimming and scanning skills. However, all of these can be learned over time with effort if students develop the right mindset. We like to call that mindset the "Columbus urge." It is that irresistible desire to explore, to find out. Corny as the expression may sound, the "Columbus urge" causes students to seek the thrill of discovering and the sheer satisfaction of knowing that they know, transforming them into self-motivated students. If students can acquire this one quality, they will be driven to learn all of the necessary skills that it takes to gather information.

The "Columbus urge" can only be encouraged, never created, by the teacher. Key teaching elements that contribute to its growth include the teacher modeling an excitement about learning and developing a classroom that is a busy, exciting, stimulating place where provocative questions are constantly being asked and where tidbits of curious information of interest are constantly being unearthed and celebrated. Here are a few ideas to help students develop the "Columbus urge":

- Regularly give students things to find out that really catch their interest and stir their curiosity. Find out about their culture and what interests them. You are likely to find that things like "firsts", "longests", "shortests", and "mosts" work consistently.
- Leave questions dangling and unanswered and challenge them to find out.
- Model the excitement of researching and finding out.
- Celebrate when students discover solutions, making a big thing out of it.
- Challenge students to come up with questions and curiosities for you and for their classmates.

- Obtain and have students see and use as many interesting resources as possible.
- Give students opportunities to find information and then use it.
- Remember that "knowers" love to show off, so do not just let them; encourage them and even plan opportunities for them to do it.
- As a time filler, play the "I know something" game. In it the students try to discover what it is that the teacher, or someone else, knows. Students have to be trained to know that their first job is always to find out where the information can be found (e.g., dictionary, atlas, etc.).
- Have constantly changing displays and bulletin boards where students encounter people, actions, and things that are different and that create curiosity.

Last, yet far from least, among the classroom elements that the teacher can and must provide in order for students to develop their own "Columbus urge" is a structure that ensures the students' ownership of repeated successes. The greatest payoff that self-motivated problem solvers can experience is an "Aha!" moment. "Aha!" moments are those times when students feel the thrill of a breakthrough; a problem that they have worked on, that has eluded them, suddenly has a solution, the pieces of the puzzle fit together, the unexplainable makes sense. When a teacher can make these times of elation for students, then both have satisfaction.

Decision-Making

Give students lots of practice in decision-making. You can start with questions about how they distinguish things in popular culture. Here, they are the experts. What makes a particular video game or toy different from another? How do you tell the differences among cartoon characters? Play along as if you do not know the answers. Ask them about attributes of the video games, toys, or the characters that are not relevant but are, nonetheless, observable traits. All Dalmatian puppies are white and black and little. All cars have four wheels. These are characteristics all right, but they do not help us tell things apart. With students who are very ego-centered, go to the students themselves as examples. "Why do I like Penelope?" "Is it because she is wearing a pink shirt?" You can easily see where this questioning would go. The important thing is that through it students are learning that what may be important and relevant to one question has no merit or use with another.

You can also do a listing of traits. This can be transferred to unit study. For example, if you are teaching a country, a city, a state, or a geographic area, make a list of the characteristics of the area with students. Do this as part of a "Would you like to live there?" activity. That way, you can have two columns, one of traits that make a difference and one of traits that do not. You can do a similar listing with historical people or current candidates for political office. You are just deciding different things, whether they did their jobs well, whether they are suited for office, and so on.

Once they have the idea, move to some type of game activity. A favorite across grade levels is one called "mysteries." These are multi-clue riddle activities and they can even be done in groups cooperatively. The number of clues and the difficulty needs to meet the individual needs of your class. The idea is to reveal a series of clues one at a time, beginning with the hard clues that could apply to any number of possible answers and going to easier, more obvious ones. In some of these games, some clues may be irrelevant or unimportant.

Sorting activities also help students learn to distinguish relevance. A sorting activity that works very well is called a card sort. The activity begins with a deck of cards with facts or single words written on them. Have labeled category boxes ready and sort the cards into these. After you have done this sorting a few times as a group discussion activity, it may be assigned with multiple decks as a cooperative group activity as well. After the groups finish, they can explain their logic. It is good to include cards that do not fit any category in the deck. Using concrete materials is good for similar sorts that can be done with large amounts of information with the proper computer software.

Historical Thinking

For many years, the objective of history courses in schools was the mastery of specific content. Teachers would share stories, names, dates, and facts about past people and civilizations, while students were largely expected to remember and recall this information on assessments to prove mastery or understanding. Historical thinking is an approach to teaching history that challenges the aforementioned model of instruction and encourages teachers to allow students to actually be engaged in the process of "doing history." With historical thinking, teachers should include a variety of primary and secondary sources from multiple perspectives that push students to think critically and deeply about how historical narratives are constructed over time. While the content itself remains important, historical thinking puts more of the focus on students developing the critical skills necessary to understand the past, such as inquiry, analysis of sources, citing evidence to support conclusions, and constructing narratives. One common activity used by social studies teachers to engage students in historical thinking is using document-based questions.

Document-based questions, or DBQs for short, are a teaching strategy or assessment that asks students to utilize their own background knowledge and analysis of provided sources (documents) to construct a narrative demonstrating understanding using textual evidence. Most often, students are asked to construct a written response or short essay explaining their understanding of the historical issue, person, or trend using the provided documents to support their arguments. Document-based questions can be used to promote critical and historical thinking. Naturally, advanced reading levels of many primary and secondary sources coupled with varying reading and writing abilities of students means that teachers will need to take great care in planning and scaffolding DBQ instruction.

Retaining Information

In social studies, students are required to retain information for three reasons: (1) they have to understand and retain information just long enough to work through a single lesson or class; (2) they have to understand and retain information for a while longer, perhaps a few days, in order to do more extended, long-term assignments; and (3) there is information that teachers want students to retain over a long period of time. Driscoll (2009) refers to these as sensory memory, working memory, and long-term memory. It is important to realize that all three components of memory are important. A teacher's job is to help students learn how to decide what is important and how to retain the information.

Part of the secret of getting students to retain information and ideas is to present that information to them in memorable ways. That means it has to be interesting, even exciting if possible. If you do not think this is important, think about the fact that students can tell all about a movie they saw but remember nothing they read in a dull textbook. There are several ways that teachers can help their students learn and retain information:

- Work on a can-do attitude. This requires both encouragement and task control to keep the amount of information at a level that students can handle. Students need to feel confident that they can remember. (If they feel they cannot memorize something, their own prediction of failure will be one more hurdle to overcome.)
- Understanding precedes remembering. Yes, nonsense words can be memorized, but generally anyone is more likely to remember what they understand than what they do not understand.
- Talk with students about what they already know. If students can relate or associate information to their own experiences, it will make it easier for them to remember.
- Organize the information for them in a way that makes sense. Isolated pieces of information are often more difficult to remember than information that has patterns and structures that relate individual facts.

- Provide mnemonic devices for sets of information. Memory-jogging associations that are catchy and full of images really do work (e.g., Never Eat Soggy Waffles for remembering North, East, South, and West on a compass).
- Make memorizing work as much fun as possible. Play memory games and quick fun practices.

When it comes to reviewing for the purpose of remembering information of all types, the approach most often used is drill. Drill can be meaningless, boring, and totally useless as a learning activity. If students are tuning out mentally, they are not learning. This means that you must make it engaging and relevant. This can happen even if drill is the method. Even the rote learning drill can be so structured that it makes the fact that students are learning mean something. A good drill is going to help the learner put the information into logical and meaningful structures. It will put the stuff together in a way that makes sense and seems useful. Equally important, the drill has to be one that the student will participate in completely. If students find the drill uncomfortable or boring, they will start tuning out and/or daydreaming.

A drill is effective and more engaging when everybody is getting the answers quickly and correctly. Students are also more likely to learn if they repeatedly experience information with as many senses as possible. Picture flash cards, actual associated objects, actions or movements, even odors can be part of a drill.

One of the best ways to make drill effective is to turn it into a game. A drill game has to be one that students will enjoy and also one that covers the necessary information repeatedly. The best drill games are those that keep the majority of students mentally engaged. Games that give the information in written and oral form require more from students and increase participation.

Many commercial board games, card games, as well as television game shows and sports activities are adaptable to fact-learning activities. Games do not have to ask questions about the facts. They simply have to get the students to see, say, and hear the information repeatedly. "Monopoly" or "Candyland" types of games can be adapted so that the various board spaces and playing pieces are labeled to represent historic or geographic facts related to a topic being studied. This will enable students to encounter these words and images over and over. Similarly, many common games played with cards can be fact-learning games with specially made cards.

Maps and Globes

In today's society, with GPS and other mapping applications, students often complain that map reading is not an important skill to learn. However, despite the ease that technology provides, it is still important. Consider learning math. If schools and teachers eliminated mathematics from the curriculum once the calculator was invented, students and society would be in trouble. Why should map reading and other social studies skills be different?

The skills needed to use maps and globes depend on an extensive knowledge base regarding the types of maps and their purposes. Furthermore, they require the knowledge and understanding of map conventions, symbols, and of the nature of different land forms. To use these tools effectively, one must know something of the structure, functions, and terminology of different types of maps and globes. Maps and globes are sources of information about the geographic world. From them we can learn about the location, size, and names of particular places, about the economy, weather and climate, and natural features. Maps and globes provide important information that can help students understand their world and are tools for problem solving.

Choosing Maps and Globes to Use

We want to make students feel comfortable with maps and globes and to fascinate them with the kinds of information that they can find with them. We also want students to gain an understanding that different kinds of maps and globes can be used for different purposes. By the time they have reached the 4th or 5th grade, if not before, students should be able to use maps and globes to answer questions and solve problems.

We can define a globe as a three-dimensional representation of the earth's surface or the surface of another astronomical body. A map, however, is a two-dimensional representation of an area. Since maps are flat, maps depicting a very large area, such as the earth's surface, are going to be distorted from reality in some way.

It is important to choose maps and globes for classroom use wisely and carefully. Maps can be found in an atlas or on the Internet; additionally, interactive maps like Google Earth are excellent resources for exploring and examining the earth. To begin with, teachers need to keep in mind that the best globe or map (print or electronic) for a particular lesson will depend on several factors, including:

- The conditions under which it is going to be used;
- The number of students who will be looking at it (e.g., whole class, small group, individual);
- The ability, background, and skill levels of students;
- The purpose(s) for which it is going to be used (i.e., the type of information that the map will need to show);
- The types of tasks that students are going to have to complete;
- Available technology.

In purchasing and collecting classroom maps and globes (electronic or print) over time, teachers need to think about a number of things, especially the following:

- Relative cost
- Accuracy
- Readability
- Durability
- Writability (maps on which you can write, draw, and erase are very useful in the classroom)
- Storability (teachers have limited space)
- Usability (maps must be useful for a variety of teaching purposes)
- Technology requirements.

Maps and Globes in the Classroom

Students should be able to work with maps and globes containing differing amounts of information with increasing independence. As they spend more time learning about different cultures and regions, more and more information is presented to students in map form. By the time they have completed the early grades, students should be able to read, use, and make maps and globes in a way that shows mastery of the four basic map skills: (1) reading direction, (2) reading distance, (3) understanding map legends, and (4) orienting the map to the real world. They should be able to recognize and understand the purposes of the basic types of map projections and different thematic maps (rainfall, vegetation, product, etc.). Students at this level need to understand a number of terms related to maps and landforms. Teachers need to assign map activities carefully and often to develop map skills. Never assume previous knowledge and/or skills in using maps without verifying if students really do possess that knowledge or skill. Ask questions in discussion and writing that require students to get information from maps and globes. Have several easy-to-play map location and jigsaw map assembly games and activities available in the classroom and encourage their use during free time of any sort. Have plenty of activities such as treasure hunts and scavenger hunts and mapping of field trips that involve using or following maps as a means of reaching particular objectives.

Using Maps

One of the reasons students have trouble learning map skills is the majority of map work in school is too often just a series of questions and tasks for which students see no purpose. They really need to be exposed to maps in ways that seem meaningful and purposeful.

It seems amazing that we teach map skills without having students really use maps in the ways that adults do. Although GPS and other navigation systems are available, reading and understanding a map is still a much-needed skill for a variety of reasons: to find out where they are going or how to get there (GPS is not always accurate); to find alternate routes when there is some problem with the original; to help them decide about a new job; to locate a friend or relative; to find their way around some place they are visiting; to make business decisions that require a knowledge of distance and routes; to consider distance to supplies, equipment, or marketing; to determine the weather's effect on their travel; and to determine meeting places, etc. In short, maps can be used to plan, understand, solve problems, and dream about the world. Unfortunately, the teaching of map skills to students contains too little of this. Map skills are taught in a way that says to students that maps are to look at; to use to answer questions from worksheets; and sometimes to color, draw on, or mark. Students fail to discover that maps are useful items and that they can help in real-life activities.

This appears to cause any number of problems relating to sequential development of skills and concepts. One of these problems is that students tend to see map work as lacking in purpose. A second is that they never really learn to use maps to find specific information or to follow routes.

The following are map-using activities in which students can participate and from which they can learn how maps can be used. "Map-using activities" is a descriptive title for this type of exercise. It includes any method by which students experience relating maps to physical space or to problems involving that space. To be effective, such activities should be perceived by students as having sensible purposes and should involve short-term, specific tasks that are tightly structured.

Map-Reading Scavenger Hunt

A scavenger hunt taxes students' abilities to follow directions given on a map or in a set of written directions accompanying a map. It is an adaptation of the gaming sport of orienteering. Groups of students are asked to find a treasure by following a precise routine in the shortest possible time.

> **FYI**
>
> Remember to always get administrative approval for any activity that may take your students out of the classroom and around the school.

Each group is equipped with a compass, a meter stick, and a set of directions or a map showing the route to and location of one portion of the team's treasure map. Each group's route is different from others. The teacher will need to prepare in advance a treasure map or set of directions for each team. The treasure maps or directions are each cut or torn into sections and each section put into a separate capped plastic bottle or a can with a tight sealing lid. This enables the teacher to place the containers in advance without worry about weather damage. Of course, they cannot be set out too far ahead of time. Chance discovery and removal can happen too easily. The cans or bottles of all teams should be indistinguishable from one another. However, the maps inside might be color coded by team so as to be recognizable when discovered. The containers are then hidden in a pattern shown on the map or described in the directions. The sets of directions are written so that the discovery of one container gives a new set of directions leading to another. A team may, by following its own map, discover all of its own map pieces or directions. The activity should be monitored and any group that opens another team's container simply because it is discovered and not by following the map should be penalized by adding time (say, one minute). Teams are staggered in starting, but turns are recorded. The team completing the map in the shortest time wins.

Site Stakeout

For site stakeouts students are divided into groups of six to ten. If possible, work with one group at a time and keep accurate records of the time it takes a group to complete the task and any errors corrected or help needed. Each group is assigned a different site. Sites may be such things as castles, forts, museums, public buildings (e.g., city hall, the school, a jail or prison), typical small frontier towns, factories, or colonial farms. Groups are given sketch map drawings showing their own site in detail. Other information about activities on the site is also provided. The group's job is to "stake" its own site by outlining the perimeter and interior features as accurately as possible. Each group uses string and small wooden or plastic stakes (clothespins work well, too). Stakes are driven into the ground and string stretched between the stakes. All groups show such things as dimensions, relative size, and so on. All parts of the site are labeled corresponding to diagram labels. Upon completion, the staked-out sites are evaluated on the basis of their accuracy, the time elapsed in completing the stakeout, and the amount of adult assistance required.

Orienteering Scavenger Hunt

For the orienteering scavenger hunt some advance work will need to be done. Cooperation is needed among several people in the school and community. It is also recommended that an adult volunteer be recruited to accompany each team of students. The initial task is to identify places in the community, students' homes, places of business, offices, and so on, simply on the basis of the willingness of people in these places to participate in helping the students learn. A map of the community is drawn indicating by number each of the places where a cooperating person is to be found. No names of people or place titles are listed on the map.

Each team is given a copy of the map and an order in which they are to visit each place. The order is indicated only by the number (the order of the places is different for all teams). Teams are sent out at five-minute intervals. Their job is to use the map to find, in proper order, the places listed on their directions. At each stop, the team records the name of the person or the location and the time of arrival. The teams must get a verifying signature from the cooperating person at the site (they may wear badges or caps if there are several people about). The objective for each group is to finish all scheduled stops in the correct order on a timed schedule or in the shortest possible time.

Fantasy School Map

The fantasy school map activity is designed to help students understand the concepts of miniaturization or symbolism as they apply to maps. It is a map-making activity in which students try to translate a part of the world onto a map. Imagination and policing are needed, but it can be well worth the effort in terms of practical learning. The amount of space used may vary. A large area, such as a cafeteria, gymnasium, or playground, is best. Students imagine that the area used for the map is a part of some larger, distant geographic area. For example, it might be seen as an area of the gold fields of California, a township in the Northwest Territory, an area of land being opened for homesteading, a feudal manor, a Roman military encampment, or a contemporary community in any country.

It should be pointed out that the size of the actual area being imagined would be much larger than the actual space used. The first job of the group of students is to arrange and label the features of the area. Existing furnishings should be incorporated. A chair may be used to symbolize a building; a bookcase may be a mesa, and so on. But added features may be created simply by labeling sheets of paper. The students then map the area they have laid out.

Best Route

Best route involves studies in using maps to determine the best way to get from one place to another. For this activity students are put into small groups. Each group has a map of the local community around the school and a list of jobs to do. The tasks may simply be finding specific purchasable items (students need not buy, only locate where items may be purchased) or finding the best prices or set of items to deliver. But jobs could also include involvement in volunteer citizenship activities at several locations, community improvement, or helping elderly or disabled individuals, with students actually doing the work.

Each group is to determine the most efficient route for performing the tasks and the time it will take to complete those tasks. Groups go together and will need to use the map. They must anticipate delaying factors (such as hills or unmarked construction sites, heavily trafficked roads where crossing may be difficult, or even backtracking) and keep in mind the effort and time needed, including such factors as distances to carry heavy loads. A route plan and estimated time for each stop have to be submitted before the trip is taken. Afterwards, students can discuss alternative, better routes and factors influencing how well their plans worked.

Map Labeling

Provide students with an unlabeled map of a familiar area and have them fill in the labels. The location may be a place seen and traveled regularly, such as some part of a local neighborhood, or a place visited one or more times. If the latter is used, informing students before the actual trip can improve observation.

Where Does It Come From?

Divide students into groups. Each group is given a world map and a list of ten products, ten animals, or ten plants. Using reference books and the Internet, the group must determine locations where the items on their list may be found. They then must chart the shortest possible route for obtaining them.

Shortest Route to the Habitat

Give students a list of ten animals and ask them to pretend that they have been commissioned to return each animal to its natural environment. Have students discover the shortest distance that these animals may be taken by plane to a safe habitat that is similar to the one in which they are naturally found. The catch is that they cannot carry animals beyond a specified total weight or animals that are natural enemies on the same trip. The list of animals should include some relatively heavy ones, some that are prey, and some that are predators.

Mapping a School Activity

Have students make and use a map of the school and school grounds to set up plans for a school activity. These might be a school carnival (with specific locations for all attractions), a walking field trip (with specific places of interest noted), a class party, parents' night, or open house.

FYI

Inviting parents/guardians as chaperones to field-based learning experiences helps keep them involved and also is an efficient use of school resources.

Story Maps

Have students do story maps as book reports. A story map charts the geographic areas used as settings for the book. Inferences and direct statements of the author about relative distances, landmarks, and features are used by students; movements of protagonists and other characteristics can also be charted. Interior as well as exterior maps may be made. Fantasy and realistic stories set in fictitious places may be mapped almost as easily as those whose settings are real places.

A caution and guideline: Depending on school policy, these activities may be designed in such a way that they take students around the neighborhood for variety and interest. Local school policies, community cooperation, and the neighborhood will be determining factors in deciding if and how to use orientating approaches. Parent or other adult volunteers are essential precautions for many. However, simple adaptations may be all that is needed to use some such activities within school grounds.

Charts, Graphs, and Maps

In today's classrooms, teachers are encouraged and/or required to incorporate "tested subjects" (e.g., English, reading, math) into "non-tested subject areas" (e.g., social studies). However, it should be noted that many teachers already utilize many math-related concepts and skills within social studies curriculum. Mathematics-related skills are essential for learning about the world. It is important to help students learn to apply mathematical skills.

Begin with items that are relevant to students' everyday lives. The experience can begin as a class activity and then slowly move to group and individual practice. Charts and graphs can be used to show such information as:

- Students' attendance
- Completed work
- Teacher conferences
- Students' independent reading
- Class opinions
- How related ideas are alike and different
- Days remaining until some special event
- Competition among groups
- Numbers of different kinds of objects
- Work completed.

The use of measurement as well as charts and graphs can provide important, conceptually related experiences as students study other cultures and other times. They can measure areas equivalent to the sizes of the ships of explorers and colonists or of the log cabins of famous historical characters such as Abraham Lincoln. They can look to the contents and weight of backpacks soldiers carried in various eras. In fact, measuring is one of the most important ways of making verbal descriptions visual and tactile. Mathematics enables students to look comparatively at such things as personal income, shipping, manufacturing, mining, and farming in very concrete ways.

Economic Skills

Economic skills that students obtain have to do mostly with their roles as consumers. However, they also need to learn something about how producers and others operate. Among the economics concepts and skills that students need to learn to use are the following:

- Different types and values of money.
- How to manage their own money and time.
- How businesses and governments use money and time.
- What are needs and wants, and how do we tell the difference?
- What is meant by such concept terms as *value*, *cost*, and *price*?
- The relative costs/values of different goods and services.
- How to do comparative shopping.
- How and why exchange occurs.
- The skills needed for using bank accounts.
- What credit is and how it works (including what interest is).

Situational scenarios and hypothetical problems related to economics can be created and used at almost any level. Even in a kindergarten class, economic thinking can be part of many types of learning centers set up in the classroom: kitchen centers, post office centers, building construction centers, and so on. Students of all ages learn from trading and swapping activities, which can provide an experiential basis for discussion of relative merit and relative value. Many commercial games, perhaps the best known being "Monopoly" and "Pit," involve swapping activities and can be the basis for classroom activities.

- Teachers can make up card decks related to particular units. On each card, an item of property related to the unit can be listed. When cards are distributed, students can have a trading period. The follow-up should relate to issues such as scarcity and abundance, the costs of production and transportation at the place and time of the unit, and other factors relating to the trades.
- At a small cost to the teacher or perhaps with items from a school sponsor, the teacher may set up a "store." Students, over a period of time, can "work" for "store money," which they can exchange for items on a given day.
- Student groups can be set up as countries with sets of resources and needs. The game involves exchanging their resources for what they need.
- Card decks can be created with suits of cards based on items of values. Card games can involve exchange with the purpose of getting a monopoly by collecting a complete suit of one item.

Lots of commercial games deal with banking, budgeting, and using and conserving resources. The teacher needs to find out which of these the students are familiar with, extend their experiences with these games, and help them to understand what these games teach. Beyond the commercial games, numerous valuable classroom activities are possible. Class banks can be set up with accounts involving checks, balances, and other factors. Income and expenses can be assigned. The whole experience then can be used as the basis for discussion. Students can deal with pretend shopping lists for events like Thanksgiving or other holiday meals and make a visit to a grocery store to cost out their lists. Field trips to banks and businesses may be valuable. Students can be urged to ask questions to directors of zoos, hospitals, and other enterprises about their own expenses and budgets. Students can deal with hypothetical budgets for families in any period of history or in any culture being studied.

Activities that can build economic skills should be carefully planned to suit the level of ability and the interests of students. The following is a list of a few possible activity types:

- Planning dream vacations
- Exchanging play money representing different values or different currencies of countries
- Price-following activities and games (e.g., stock market, home prices, automobile prices, etc.) over time.

Looking Back

There is increasing concern over the development of thinking in social studies. If the major goal of teaching is to help students become independent learners, then there must be a real emphasis on the development of the ability to think and solve problems.

Obtaining, understanding, and retaining information are among the thinking skills that are important to social studies learning. Generally, students can learn to relate new information to previous knowledge, to identify the patterns and relationships of information and ideas, and to identify purposes for learning. They can be aided in learning to remember through planned repetitions of information accompanied by appropriate feedback. Thinking skills can be taught through modeling by the teacher, through carefully planned discussions, and through guided practice. Problem solving is the most essential thinking ability and is an important part of the inquiry process. The use of alternative problem-solving strategies can be taught directly through structured activities. Among these strategies, the following are useful as models:

- Identifying all the factors of a problem
- Prioritizing a problem
- Multiple perspectives of a problem
- Problems with alternative solutions
- Identifying purpose problems
- Problems with proposed solutions.

Well-developed study skills give students a winning advantage, an edge, when it comes to learning tasks or success in life. The most important study skills include knowing how to find necessary information, being able to make decisions about information, and being able to organize and retain information. Some study skills are specifically associated with the social studies because they relate to one or more of the social sciences. One of these is reading and using maps and globes. Students are more likely to develop map competency if they are exposed to many experiences interacting with maps, map problems, and problems that involve using maps. The maps used in these experiences need to be simple and purposeful. The experiences themselves should teach about distance, direction, scale, and map symbols at a developmentally appropriate level. Maps should be used purposefully in the classroom with a variety of applied map-reading and map-making activities. It should be stressed that maps can be engaging and there should be an abundance of map games and other activities that students enjoy doing. Time skills also require concrete hands-on activities with concrete materials that expand the students' awareness of the time relationships among events.

This is a society in which the development of economic skills is essential to survival. Students need experiences in dealing with money and exchange as well as a growing understanding of credit, banking, budgeting, and economic planning. These skills are important for students at a personal level as well as for communities up to the size of nations.

Extension Activity

Scenario

You are at the mid-point of the third nine weeks at YHS. The YHS principal, Dr. Russell, stops by your classroom to see if you are ready for spring break. During the conversation, Dr. Russell says "Your students enjoy your problem-solving-based classroom activities, and after spring break I would like you to share a new classroom activity with the superintendent, Dr. Turner, YHS assistant principal, Dr. Waters, and a local reporter. Have the new dynamic activity ready on the Monday after spring break." You agree to the challenge, and say "I am excited for the opportunity, thank you."

Task

For this activity, develop a new and innovative problem-solving-based classroom activity for the grade level and topic of your choice. The activity should be in written form and utilize the lesson/activity format required by your school/district/university. Share your response with peers and/or the instructor.

Reflective Questions

1 What are thinking skills and why are they important?
2 What does the term *critical thinking* mean?
3 Can you list five thinking skills and describe a class activity for meeting each thinking skill?
4 Can you identify and describe different types of problem-solving tasks?
5 What is a mnemonic device?

Helpful Resources

Watch this video created by C3 teachers detailing the importance of students asking questions.
https://youtu.be/GAzvec-cQpk
Watch the video of a master teacher teaching a model lesson from the C3 Framework.
https://youtu.be/tbWapv3m6y8
This website has an array of useful information, including sample critical thinking social studies lesson plans.
www.criticalthinking.org.
Watch this video of the creators of the Inquiry Design Model of the C3 Framework. They explore the model and how it can be utilized in the classroom.
https://youtu.be/FdypkpuKUy4
Watch this video about the DBQ project, an initiative focused on promoting the use of DBQs at all levels of education.
www.youtube.com/watch?v=y8MlNzi1s_k
Visit this web page for a list of several social studies games that could be utilized in the social studies classroom.
http://pbskids.org/games/social-studies/
Watch this video about the importance of map skills.
www.flocabulary.com/unit/map-skills/
Watch an example lesson showing a middle school teacher using maps to explore emigration and migration.
www.teachingchannel.org/videos/teaching-human-migration

Further Reading

Boostrom, R. (2005). *Thinking: The Foundation of Critical and Creative Learning in the Classroom.* New York, NY: Teachers College Press.

This engaging book encourages educators to think about the ways in which the practice of teaching unintentionally promotes non-thinking. The author makes suggestions and recommendations to promote a thinking environment.

Council for Economic Education. (2003). *The Great Economic Mysteries Book: A Guide to Teaching Economic Reasoning Grades 4–8.* New York, NY: Council for Economic Education.

This book introduces students in Grades 4 to 8 to an economics way of thinking by exploring the mysteries of everyday life. Students solve each mystery by responding to hints provided by simple true/false questions and by reference to a logical system of thinking.

Erickson, L. (2007). *Concept-Based Curriculum and Instruction for the Thinking Classroom.* Thousand Oaks, CA: Corwin Press.

This book details proven curriculum design with teaching methods that encourage students to learn concepts as well as content and skills for deep understanding across all subject areas.

Johnson, T. (2012). Exploring the options: Teaching economic decision-making with poetry. *The Social Studies, 103*(2), 61–66.

In this article, integrating instruction in poetry and economic decision-making is presented as one way to maximize the use of scarce instructional time. Following a brief introduction to the role of economics in children's lives and a rationale for using poetry to teach significant economic concepts, summaries of four appropriate poetry collections and a description of a recent experience teaching economics with poetry in a 5th-grade classroom are presented.

Kracl, C. (2012). Review or true? Using high-level thinking questions in social studies instruction. *The Social Studies, 103*(2), 57–60.

This article provides a foundation for K–12 teachers to begin the implementation of asking higher-level questions in their classrooms and engaging students in critical thinking activities. Using the work of Bloom (1956) and Kagan (1999), actual questions and ideas that can be used before, during, and after readings in the classroom will strengthen the ability of all students to think.

McIntyre, B. (2011). History scene investigations: From clues to conclusions. *The Social Studies, 23*(3), 17–21.

In this article, the author introduces a social studies lesson that allows students to learn history and practice reading skills, critical thinking, and writing. The activity is called History Scene Investigation (HSI), which derives its name from the popular television series based on crime scene investigations (CSI). HSI uses discovery learning and inductive reasoning. It requires students to use artifacts in a mock scene from history as clues for drawing conclusions about the scene. By selecting the appropriate types of artifacts to present to the students, the teacher can adjust the level of difficulty of an HSI lesson, making it appropriate for students.

Sewell, A.M., Fuller, S., Murphy, R.C. & Funnell, B.H. (2002). Creative problem solving: A means to authentic and purposeful social studies. *The Social Studies, 93*(4), 176–179.

This article argues that creative problem solving, CPS, has the potential to support the development of many citizenship skills, especially problem solving, communicating, critical thinking, and information skills. The authors describe how CPS was used to solve problems by students in Grades 2 and 6 of a primary school in a small New Zealand farming community. The case studies show how ordinary classrooms can be transformed so that learning is embedded in purposeful and authentic participation, which fosters a community of learners responsible for the direction of their learning.

Wineburg, S. (2001). *Historical Thinking and Other Unnatural Acts: Charting the Future of Teaching the Past.* Philadelphia, PA: Temple University Press.

For much more detailed information on historical thinking, consider this seminal book by Dr. Wineburg.

References

Bloom, B. (Ed.). (1956). *Taxonomy of Educational Objectives: The Classification of Educational Goals.* New York, NY: Longmans.

Driscoll, M. (2009). *Psychology of Learning for Instruction* (4th ed.). Needham Heights, MA: Allyn & Bacon.

NCSS. (2010). *National Curriculum Standards for Social Studies: A Framework for Teaching, Learning, and Assessment. Task Force on Standards for the Social Studies.* Washington, DC: NCSS.

8 Cooperative Learning in Social Studies

Looking Ahead

Since middle and high school students are so peer-centered, having them work in active learning groups offers particular advantages as a way of getting them involved. Though critics fear that the emphasis on teamwork may discourage brighter students (U.S. News and World Report, 1997), two specific types of approaches to grouping, cooperative learning and collaborative learning, have been found to work especially well at the secondary level because they also provide the structure and direction that many young adult learners need to succeed. The purpose of this chapter is to help develop some insights into cooperative learning and a variety of different group approaches. Information and ideas covered in this chapter will help secondary teachers effectively plan and implement cooperative learning activities in a meaningful way.

FYI

Do not assume that all students have the skills and dispositions required to work in a group. Make sure to spend time helping students develop these skills and understand what it means to work collaboratively and cooperatively.

Past research has shown that many teachers learn about cooperative learning incidentally, and that they often lack an accurate, complete, and specific understanding of the concept (Sparapani et al., 1997). Teachers need to understand what cooperative learning approaches actually involve and be able to distinguish between cooperative groups and other types of groups, as well as how to utilize these groups to create meaningful learning experiences for secondary students. To this end, educators in all fields of study have written entire books and countless articles dedicated to the incorporation of cooperative learning strategies into the K–12 classroom. This chapter is not meant to be an exhaustive look at cooperative learning activities. However, we will cover a great deal of the core concepts about this approach as an instructional method that will help teachers formulate a strong foundation for utilizing cooperative learning strategies in secondary social studies classrooms.

DOI: 10.4324/9781003217060-8

Can You? Do You?

Can you ...

- identify the differences and similarities between cooperative groups and collaborative groups?
- explain how cooperative and collaborative groups benefit student learning and enhance your instruction?
- describe how technology can be used to enhance cooperative and collaborative group projects?
- think of activities and assessments that utilize cooperative and collaborative groups in the secondary social studies classroom?

Do you ...

- know the social factors in cooperative learning groups?
- know different grouping strategies?
- know what is meant by the term *active learning*?
- understand different ways to implement cooperative and collaborative group activities in the social studies classroom?

Focus Activity

Before reading this chapter, try the thinking activity below.

Think back about your experiences in the classroom as a middle and high school student. What types of group activities did you complete? Do you have any memorable experiences? What were the positive and negative aspects of working with others? How might your experiences with cooperative group work as a student influence your perceptions of this method as a classroom teacher?

Social Factors in Cooperative Learning Groups

One component of cooperative learning approaches, which is usually considered a major strength, is that students understand that they cannot be successful unless other members of the group are successful. One term used for this quality is "positive interdependence" (Johnson & Johnson, 1995). Getting students to both understand and buy into positive interdependence is a pivotal factor for success in any cooperative learning activity. Why is this so important? The answer is that when students believe in positive interdependence it leads to individuals taking responsibility for their own work. That means, for those who do not normally take such responsibility, their peers may pressure them into doing so. This brings up a question that only you can answer: How does this seem both consistent and inconsistent with what you know about middle and high school students?

Positive interdependence is just one component of cooperative learning that speaks to the importance of social skills and the importance of group composition in highly structured group activities. Most of the literature related to cooperative learning advocates for "heterogeneous" groups. That heterogeneity usually refers to academics alone. But other factors in the social milieu and group dynamics of the class need to be taken into account. What other factors would you consider in forming cooperative learning groups in your classroom?

Different Approaches to Grouping

> **FYI**
>
> It is a long school year, and any teacher who routinely utilizes grouping activities may want to consider implementing these different strategies to keep the students engaged.

Before beginning any collaborative or cooperative learning activity in middle and high school classrooms, teachers need to spend time thinking about different ways of grouping students and which method gives all of the students the best opportunity to succeed. Teachers have always had recourse to several different approaches to grouping. All of these offer both advantages and disadvantages that teachers should consider purposefully before implementing into the classroom:

1. Students can be grouped by special interest or because they share common needs of some kind. In either case this creates topics-based groups, with the topic being set either by the interest or the need. Tasks for such groups follow logically in relation to the topic as either trying to meet the need or to follow the interest. In some cases, as in debate groups, the central job of the group may be to develop reasoning to support a point of view or "side." While this approach seems to offer built-in motivation, forming such groups has to be handled carefully or students may choose topics on the basis of social considerations, such as working with their friends, rather than what topics have their greatest interest.
2. Teachers often use ability as the basis for grouping. They may put together students of similar ability so that materials and instruction can be geared at the same level. However, most advocates of cooperative learning opt for heterogeneous groups. A group of four, for example, would have one of the very best students in the class, one less able student, and two from the middle level of the class. The resulting groups would each be a microcosm of the class, and no group would be very different from any other group. For all intents and purposes, this levels the playing field for the groups and expectations can be identical for all groups in the class.
3. Special-skill development groups are usually employed when some, but not the majority, of the students are lacking in some needed skill. The teacher identifies those who will profit from particular instruction and attempts to catch them up without making the rest of the class go through what they already know. Alternatives to special-skill grouping include peer tutoring and one-on-one work with volunteers, as well as cooperative groups, where the entire group is going to suffer if they do not get their teammate the help he or she needs.
4. Random groups are used for social purposes as a way of breaking up cliques and getting different students to work together. Random selection methods include counting off and drawing a group number by chance. The point is that with volunteer seating, you want a method that will separate those people who always sit together. It gives students a chance to develop group skills with no one having a great advantage.
5. Self-selected groups obviously allow students to work with whom they choose themselves. In secondary schools, this kind of group is not always the best option. Grouping in this way almost always results in making some students feel left out. It is a grouping procedure that only reinforces the "star" status of some students and the isolated status of others. However, some modified form of self-selection for project groups may be positive. The notion can give students the feeling of having some control and allow them the opportunity to work with people with whom they feel more positive and comfortable. We suggest some kind of "paper preference" process. For example, students may be asked to list four people with whom they would like to work, with the teacher guaranteeing that they will be with at least one person on their lists.

Use of groups in middle and high school social studies classes may vary in a number of other ways. Continuums include:

- Permanent groups to flexible changing groups
- Large groups to small groups
- Teacher-directed to student-directed groups.

Cooperative learning has always been associated with more or less permanent small groups. Though the overall direction of the group process is structured and teacher-controlled, the groups themselves are designed to be run by the students. Well-planned group tasks coupled with accountability measures make this ideally suitable for secondary students with their peer focus and emerging need for autonomy.

Cooperative Learning, Collaborative Learning, and Curricular Goals

Middle and high school students are doing an increasing amount of their work in small groups as the need for collaborative work skills continues to permeate throughout a variety of jobs once students enter the workforce. Students generally like working with others because they are at an age when social interaction is an important and valuable part of the school experience. In addition, middle and high school students enjoy working with others because it gets them away from purely passive learning activities, like listening to teachers lecture, completing worksheets, or reading textbooks. Cooperative and collaborative learning activities are undeniably much more active for students than traditional teaching methods utilized at the secondary level. The group work is generally task-oriented, making the assigned tasks seem more purposeful and important to the students. Both cooperative and collaborative group work give secondary students the feeling that they have a contribution to make and that what they contribute is important. They lean on, depend on, and support one another. Since peer orientation has been found to be positively related to achievement in cooperative learning settings (Onwuegbuzie, 2001), the approaches seem to be especially suited to peer-focused students in middle and high school. In these activities students develop social skills as well as leadership and responsibility, all of which are important goals of social studies instruction at the secondary level.

Some teachers will tell you that they have been doing cooperative learning for years. That may or may not be true because they may understand cooperative learning and group work to be the same thing. There are important distinctions. Traditional group work is, more often than not, very teacher-centered, teacher-paced, and teacher-controlled. The very essence of cooperative and collaborative groups is having the group itself take control and responsibility for getting those jobs done. The kinds of tasks teachers have students do in older forms of group work are either very loosely structured or engage students in tasks that required little or no decision-making. In cooperative and collaborative group activities, the groups themselves are highly structured. Solving problems and making decisions is part of the intrinsic design.

Two terms, cooperative groups and collaborative groups, are used here, because they seem to represent two similar, yet very different, approaches to organizing groups. These two approaches share a similar focus on task-centered groups that know their purpose. Advocates of both types of group tasks also recommend that relatively small groups, with around three or four students in them, are most effective in maximizing student involvement and participation. However, there are marked differences between the two approaches.

The term *collaborative learning* generally refers to temporary groups organized to complete single, often short-term tasks. The tasks involve the group cobbling together the work and ideas of all the individuals in it into a single cohesive whole. Collaborative learning is, more often than not, almost totally project-oriented. The outcome is a single work of some kind that includes the individual work of the group members, pretty much intact. The groups themselves, therefore, may begin and end with the single task.

To engage in cooperative learning groups, by contrast, generally requires a longer time commitment. Cooperative learning usually involves structuring the classroom into more permanent groups for learning purposes. Since the development of a substantial body of literature focused on cooperative learning, the term *cooperative learning* has generally come to refer only to the classroom use of purposeful, highly structured, small groups that complete specifically designed, highly structured tasks. A number of different models or ways of conducting cooperative learning have been developed and been supported by research. All these models stress certain key elements. The basic common traits, based on the work of Johnson and Johnson (1989), include:

1 Interdependence among group members with everyone in the group responsible for the work of everyone else;
2 Constant opportunities for the groups to interact face-to-face;
3 The accountability of the individual to complete his or her own share of the work;
4 The purposeful teaching of social skills needed to work in groups;
5 Groups discussing or "processing" how they are functioning and how well they are achieving their goals in order to make decisions to continue or change the way things are done.

FYI

Make sure that all students clearly understand their roles and how they will be held accountable for their work within the group.

Research has shown that cooperative learning promotes higher achievement. The group situation seems ideal for the development of thinking skills and gives students the opportunity to discover answers on their own. However, the affective results of cooperative learning are even more important to the aims of the middle and high schools. Cooperative learning has been found to positively influence motivation to learn, raise students' self-esteem, develop greater "liking" for school, increase student on-task time, and improve relationships among the students (Hertz-Lazarowitz et al., 1992; Martin, 1992).

Organizing Cooperative and Collaborative Learning Groups

Several cooperative and collaborative learning models, prescribing different ways of approaching group organization, have been developed. The secret of making any of them work is thorough planning and organization. Thompson and Taymans (1996) point out that teachers need to both have a clear system of managing student behavior and teach students the necessary interpersonal skills when they set up cooperative learning activities. Kagan (1992) has also found that some teachers lose control in cooperative learning because of the sheer amount of energy that is released by teaming students.

Some cooperative learning approaches are structured to set up competition among groups while promoting very strong cooperation within each group. Programs where groups study together and then take tests or quizzes more or less in a tournament style exemplify this concept. Average scores are computed for each total team and a running record is displayed showing how the various teams are doing. This means that a team with an exceptionally able student may not succeed unless the other members of that team, even the least able, also do their best. This mutual dependence can assist in encouraging all team members to help one another.

The whole strategy takes advantage of the exceptionally competitive nature of secondary students while causing them to pitch in and help others. Peer pressure prevents slower students from becoming intellectual dropouts. They keep trying, if only to please their friends and fellow group members. They feel much more as though others are depending on them. This kind of group cohesion and interdependence can also reduce the "geek" label in association with academic success that sometimes occurs in the middle and high school classrooms. The achiever has social status because the group needs him or her.

Other cooperative learning approaches avoid competition as completely as possible, stressing interdependence. As natural as competition is for secondary students, and as easy as it may be to take advantage of their competitiveness, Johnson and Johnson (1998) point out that competition reflects values that we really do not want to nurture in students. These are values like commitment to getting more than others; opposing, even obstructing, the success of others as a natural way of life; associating the pleasure of winning with others' disappointment in losing; and personal worth being based on "winning." The models of cooperative learning that Johnson and Johnson (1998) have developed are aimed at encouraging values that entail the importance of promoting the common good, success based on the joint effort of everyone, helping others to succeed as a natural way of life, and an unconditional belief in the worth of both one's self and others.

Cooperative groups can be especially useful when students are faced with a lot of new reading material or other work. Slavin (1995) has developed several generations of an approach called "jigsaw." If you are really interested in this approach you need to look into some of Slavin's books and materials. In simplified form, the "jigsaw" process generally begins by dividing the reading material and having each student responsible for learning in depth about his or her part and then teaching that part to the entire group. To give the presenters support and help in deciding what to teach and how to teach it, the class can be regrouped, with planning sessions held for all the presenters of each segment or part of the materials. This approach may be especially useful to students with low reading abilities who can be given responsibilities that are shorter or less difficult portions of the assignment to handle. The activity that follows shows how the "jigsaw" approach might work for a U.S. history class studying the first conflicts of the American Revolution.

> Begin by putting the students into groups of four or five. Have each group choose a number (one to four or five) then ask the class to regroup based on which number they picked. Once groups relocate, distribute primary and secondary sources (journal entries from American colonists and British soldiers, newspaper accounts, sworn court testimonies, textbook accounts, etc.) recalling the events of Lexington and Concord to each group, making sure all members of the newly formed groups have the same account. Explain to the class that each group will need to examine their document carefully to determine the strengths and weaknesses of the perspective being studied. Once all the groups have had ample time to examine and discuss their documents, have them return to their original groups and share what they think happened based on their document. After all group members share, have them discuss the various perspectives, strengths, and weaknesses of each account and decide on which source they believe to be the most reliable and why.

Collaborative and cooperative groups work well with projects and problem solving. In U.S. history, for example, groups can be given unfamiliar speeches or primary source documents with the lines out of order and asked to arrange them into an order that makes sense. Or perhaps in a world history course, the group may be asked to design a fort or castle that would be defensible against direct attack and against siege, or the group may be asked to develop a set of rules for a monastery, whether medieval Christian or Buddhist, so that the monks or nuns could live together in harmony. Box 8.1 illustrates how a cooperative learning activity might work in a secondary U.S. history classroom.

Box 8.1 Creating Civil War Newspapers: A Cooperative Learning Project

A high school U.S. History teacher has been discussing causes of the Civil War and all of the events that would eventually lead to this deadly conflict. Noticing the students' waning interest, the teacher decides to spice up the next section of the unit by dividing the class into cooperative learning groups. She organizes the class of 28 students into 7 cooperative learning teams. Each group will be assigned the task of publishing a newspaper covering major events of the war from 1863 to 1865, from the perspective of the Union or the Confederacy. The teacher brings in several examples of different newspapers prior to beginning this assignment in order to help the students understand the different components typically found in a newspaper. During this exploratory review, the teacher also initiates a discussion about media biases and writing for your readership. This review helps students better understand how newspapers during the civil war may want to slant their coverage to present events in the most positive light possible. To help students organize their thoughts, the teacher provides a brief list of topics that the students may want to consider as content for their paper, which include important battles and military strategies, social or economic conditions, biographies of important figures, major events during the time period, the role of women and slaves during the war, end of the war, cost of the war, Lincoln's assassination, etc.

For this activity, the main mission for each group is to come up with a thorough, accurate, persuasive, appealing, and creative newspaper that details events of the Civil War. The teacher has assigned each group to the Union or Confederacy perspective and has communicated a set of expectations for the newspaper project that includes a detailed rubric outlining responsibilities and assessment criteria. She is looking for unique and creative projects that are, nonetheless, well supported by reliable primary and secondary sources that the groups gathered and researched effectively. Each group has been provided with a set of resources and helpful websites to assist them in identifying important events and accurate information. Every group member has a different specific task and has a sheet of guiding questions and specifications for their role. However, each member of the group will be responsible for contributing at least one article to the finished paper, making every member a reporter in addition to other roles. Group member roles and tasks are as follows:

The Editor/reporter is to oversee the entire project and make sure the final product is up to the highest standard. Additionally, the editor will compose many of the additional articles and news pieces, to ensure all of the important information is covered. The editor will also need to coordinate with all other reporters (group members) to determine which news stories everyone will examine and write about for the paper. Are all aspects needed in the paper completed and of high quality? Is there anything missing from the paper that needs to be added in order to improve the reading experience?

The Designer/reporter is to organize the overall content of the paper, including where to publish articles (front page cover, back cover, and everything in between). The designer will also need to work closely with the artist and editor to coordinate the location of all images and articles to make sure information flows for the readers. What should be on the front and back page in order to draw in readers' attention? What headlines will you use to make articles more appealing? What materials will you use to construct your final product (computer software programs, construction paper, PowerPoint, poster boards, etc…)?

The Artist/Reporter must create and/or find all visual images to be used in the newspaper. What are the different topics in the paper being explored and what images can you use to support or enhance the writing? Where should images be placed to most effectively supplement the writing (beginning of the article? End?)? What captions will you use in order to explain photos to readers?

The Chief Researcher/reporter has to closely examine all of the material in the newspaper for accuracy (or purposeful slanting of coverage) and readability. Is the news story accurate and written in a way that will be positive for our cause (Union or Confederacy)? Is the length and vocabulary used in the article appropriate for the intended audience?

The activity is organized to take place over five days. The first day, the students will examine old or current newspapers for an idea of what components make up a paper and are placed in groups, introduced to the project, expectations and roles. The teacher gives an overview of the purpose for the assignment, and allows groups to meet to consider the roles. On the second day, groups rejoin and decide who will take on each role. If groups cannot reach an agreement on roles, the teacher informs them that she will assign roles to them randomly. Groups can then begin examining what events or people they want to cover and start researching information. The third and fourth days are devoted entirely to researching, writing articles, and constructing the groups' newspapers. The teacher will monitor progress and offer insight, direction, and advice as needed to make sure all groups are moving forward. The final day is devoted to the groups sharing their finished products with the rest of the class. Students will share what events/people they covered, why those topics are important, and the decision-making process associated with all aspects of their newspaper's construction. The teacher and students in the audience will pose questions as appropriate throughout the presentation. Once each group has presented, all papers will be displayed in different areas of the room for students to examine in further detail. The teacher asks questions, which lead students to compare and contrast ideas, events covered, and to look for the value in each group's finished product.

There are, in fact, many benefits that accrue through the use of cooperative groups in the middle and high school setting. Most important is the active learning style that is an intrinsic part of group work. Within groups, students can develop many qualities that are of practical importance for secondary students not only in the academic realm but also outside of the classroom. Based on the research of Johnson and Johnson (1998) and Slavin (1995), these include:

- Leadership
- Involvement
- Commitment
- Sense of community and shared purpose
- Sense of personal importance and worth
- Ability to work together
- Ability to follow
- Independence coupled with interdependence.

Student Roles in Cooperative Learning

Cooperative and collaborative learning bring about a change in the way students behave and a role shift from what they may experience in many traditional classrooms. Students move from being observers, listeners, and note-takers to active problem solvers, contributors, and discussants

(MacGregor, 1990). For example, in one type of cooperative learning activity, generally called team interview, two members of the four-member team interview the other two about the content that has been covered. The interviewers then summarize what they have heard. The roles are then reversed. At no point in this process is there anyone on the team who is inactive.

In fact, perhaps the most important part of both cooperative and collaborative learning groups is that all students have an active role and a personal responsibility. In cooperative groups, one indication of this is that every group member has a uniquely assigned, specific function within the group. A group of four, for example, might be organized with one individual as the group leader, another the group messenger and materials person, another the group note-taker, and another the group's self-evaluator. The specific roles and their titles vary greatly, but the basic principle is that everyone in the group has a personal and individual responsibility. Advocates of cooperative learning suggest that permanent cooperative base groups be united by a common goal or purpose. Base groups meet every day with one of their agenda items being the discussion of one another's progress toward that purpose. Members of the group are responsible for getting assignments to absent members, letting them know what went on in class, and helping them catch up. They feel the need to do this because the success of the absent members is necessary to the success of the group. Members help each other, encourage each other, and check to make sure that everyone is keeping up with assignments.

FYI

It may be beneficial to have descriptions of each position and its corresponding responsibilities available to students in each group.

"Minds-On" Learning Inquiry

A major benefit of cooperative and collaborative groups is that group members take ownership of their learning. Students are basically listeners in traditional teaching where the teacher presents lesson information. Therefore, students can, and often times do, tune out. At any given time when a teacher is talking, even the best students are drifting in and out. They may be thinking ahead to their next class, about what they are going to do after school, about what they think of someone or what someone thinks of them, about how they will talk to someone, or any of a million other things. The learning that occurs in this "listening" approach is basically passive. At best, the teacher keeps attention by interjecting questions and asking for responses from time to time.

When the group is gathering and sharing the information, though, the learning is active. Every group member's work counts and the weakest and the strongest members alike contribute to the group product. Everyone in the group has individual responsibility not to let the group down and to help his or her fellow group members. It is much more difficult to let your attention wander. Most of the time, in fact, neither the individual student nor the other group members will allow preoccupation and daydreaming.

The group's structure even promotes active learning. Everyone has a role, and no one is just a listener. Because they must participate, students cannot daydream or tune out. The whole group must function in completing every inquiry, completing every project, teaching and learning every new piece of information, and solving every problem. When the groups function as true inquiry groups they may do one or all of the following kinds of tasks:

- Define questions and problems and clarify their intent and purpose.
- Find, recall, and then assemble important information from past experiences as well as past solutions to similar problems.

- Identify and plan ways to attack and solve problems.
- Find, evaluate, and select new information.
- Organize and synthesize all related information.
- Interpret information and draw conclusions about it.
- Reflect on and then evaluate the whole process the group has gone through and the conclusions it has reached.

Cooperative and collaborative groups may engage in any array of information-gathering and synthesizing processes. To mention only a few, these may include: charting; collecting; constructing; demonstrating; drawing; drawing inferences; examining pictures; experimenting; graphing; listening to music; mapping; note-taking; observing; outlining; processing; reaching conclusions; reading; selecting information; questioning information; and writing for information.

Projects and Problem-Centered Group Activities

Middle and high school students are often very product-oriented. But they want the product to be concrete and sensory in some way, not just verbal. They want to do well with learning tasks that culminate with a product in which they can gain a sense of pride and accomplishment. For that reason, having groups show their learning with such products as creative posters, models, computer presentations, or recordings or digital videos suits the students academically while also increasing engagement and motivation for learning.

Problem-based learning offers another kind of project for group work with middle and high school students that situates itself nicely in the social studies curriculum. Not only do students learn more about working in groups by going through the process, they also learn to be problem solvers, a key objective in any social studies classroom. With problem-based learning, the learning is essentially about the problem-solving process and the products are satisfactory solutions to the problems. In groups, students are given what are described as ill-structured problems, meaning that there is limited or incomplete information provided. These problems are basically descriptions of open-ended situations that may have multiple solutions. Description material can be drawn from literature or real events either from history or current events. Teachers can even create hypothetical situations if necessary. If historical or social problems are used, teachers should be careful not to give the "desired" outcomes. Problems explored should have moral or ethical dimensions, and time restrictions may need to be put on the students at each phase of the process. The first job of the group is to determine what they think is the central difficulty and then do a concept map by brainstorming related issues. Ideally, this will lead to questions—some that teachers might anticipate and prepare materials for but others that teachers might not foresee. If the problems are engaging enough, this will lead students to additional research. For example, in a political science class, teachers could have students gather information about specific "hot topic" issues that may be coming up in political debates or that are causing a stir in the local community. Such problem-based learning may take several days, but the end result is often a learning experience that is quite meaningful for students.

The most difficult part of the problems approach for the teacher is withholding knowledge and expertise. The very nature of the process causes the learning to be integrated, involving many of the social science disciplines as well as other curricular areas. Students will undoubtedly pose continuous questions to the teacher in hopes of soliciting more information or to find out what you, as the teacher, "want." Teachers must remember that the problems approach is about the process and having students rationalize their own thoughts and opinions within their groups. While teachers can certainly guide wayward groups that may be going off topic a bit, the focus should always be on how the students analyze the problem at hand and how they justify their decisions or outcomes.

Though the problem description may often be much longer, here are several examples of problems that may be generated from several different social science disciplines. Even looking at them from a very superficial perspective, it is easy to see how other subjects are almost immediately involved. It is also apparent that one of the very valuable steps in the process is to ask questions about needed information.

- *U.S. History/Sociology*: In the middle of World War II, a group of scientists has been employed by the government to develop an atomic bomb. Such a weapon has only been theorized. Working under great secrecy, these scientists soon realize that they can actually produce such a powerful weapon but have concerns about the impact such a weapon may have on the global community. The group is to describe the moral dilemma of the scientists and to suggest what they would have done had they been in the place of those scientists.
- *World History*: The King of Crete has given a piece of gold to a goldsmith to fashion into a crown. The completed crown is beautiful and contains some beautiful jewels and some copper and brass decorations. The king suspects that the goldsmith has not put all of the gold into the crown. He asks the great mathematician Archimedes how he can know if he has been cheated or not, without destroying the crown. The group is to suggest ways that Archimedes might go about solving the problem and then research how the mathematician actually did find the solution.
- *Political Science/Government*: The group is given the text of a well-written essay or periodical article about a proposed tax increase. Each member is to identify four or five sentences or phrases within the piece that have essential ideas and are particularly appealing and/or alarming in the way they are stated. The group then puts together a "pros and cons" list for the proposed tax increase, with potential questions or concerns they may have from the sentences selected from the article.

FYI

This type of topic is always relevant and can lead to lively discussions about social justice issues, fairness, and equity.

- *Economics*: You are working at a job that you really hate. The working conditions are poor, and you think that there are some major safety issues. But you make a good wage, more than you could on any other job that you could get right now. You have been offered a job for less money that appears safer and that you think you would like a lot more. Would you quit and take the new job, or would you keep the job that you don't like? Why? What are the benefits and consequences of each decision, and what factor does the group feel is the most influential in making this choice?
- *All Subjects*: Each group is given a short series of statements, some true and some false. It is best if the false statements sound believable and the true statements appear at least a little preposterous. The group is to sort out the true from false statements and be able to give a reasonable explanation of their choices.

Cooperative Centers

Centers are places of specific activities located in different areas throughout the classroom. Though generally associated with lower grades, the center concept sometimes works even better with secondary grades because middle and high school students often need less direct supervision than their elementary counterparts. Centers are particularly useful for groups where there is a limited amount of equipment or materials. A group can do entirely different work with large maps and globes than can an entire class because students can gather around them. Since many classes have limited numbers of computers, the cooperative centers approach can allow students to still conduct valuable online research because access is granted on a rotation basis. Other factors may make centers the best option.

Some activities that groups do may generate necessary noise or mess that will be distractive to others in the class. Teachers may just want to contain the noise or mess to one area of the classroom. Cooperative centers can be very helpful for teachers wishing to conduct group work in an efficient and productive manner. If groups engaging in potentially disruptive tasks can be somewhat isolated, it can greatly help eliminate possible distractions and allow for the continual flow of learning taking place without interrupting the classroom momentum. Then too, project work sometimes needs to be done at or near the place where the projects are going to be displayed in an effort to minimize transportation damages or issues.

A center may also be appropriate for assessment activities in collaborative or cooperative groups. Different groups may reach the level of completion where assessment is to occur at different times. Teachers simply set up the assessment activities so that they are conducted at a center designed specifically for that purpose. The assessment itself may take one or more forms: doing a timed test; completing a questionnaire; doing a computer assessment activity; making an audio recording or a digital movie, etc. Since the assessment is being done in a center, you as the teacher can monitor it more closely, give more individual attention since the groups being assessed are relatively small, and stay more aware of the progress of students as a whole.

Cooperative Learning and Technology

Technology has the potential to change the entire concept of how we work in the classroom. That the technology itself is developing at what seems to be an accelerating rate makes it difficult to keep up with, especially for teachers who often receive less than adequate training with new resources. Teachers face constant retraining and a feeling of always being behind. That is one of the primary reasons that technology makes many teachers uncomfortable. They feel unable to cope with technological advances in an age when many students often possess greater knowledge of various hardware and software innovations. That discomfort is in itself a contributing factor to the absence, or at least to the shortage, of technology as a presence in many contemporary social studies classroom activities. What compounds the problem is that teacher training with technology is typically reactive instead of proactive. At best, teachers can hope for some type of in-service training at school; at worst, they are left to their own devices in order to determine how to incorporate new technologies. Even recently trained teachers who feel proficient with current technology can find themselves swept under the tide of constant technological innovations within the first several years of their careers. Finally, and not to be ignored, is the fact that getting and keeping up to date with technology is tremendously expensive, and most schools just do not have the resources they need to continually update and expand.

Even so, by the time this book is published, the great majority of secondary classrooms are going to have one or more computers and a growing array of mobile devices and other technological equipment available to them. A large number of these classrooms will contain such devices as interactive white boards, document cameras, digital cameras, tablets, iPads, and laptops. In addition to that, a large number of middle and high school students will have access to new devices and computers at home, not to mention the ability to access the Internet easily through nearly every mobile phone on the market. Because contemporary students are growing up with technology, many of them will be far more skilled and comfortable with technology than their teachers. It has been said that they are the first natives in the land of technology, while the adults who teach them are, for all the skills that they may develop, still foreign born.

Computer technology opens up any number of possibilities for cooperative and collaborative groups. Technology can not only change but also improve students' involvement, engagement, and effectiveness while participating in cooperative learning activities. There are at least four basic areas where technology can facilitate how teachers work with groups and make the group work even more appealing to secondary students in the social studies classroom. These areas are: research; record keeping and assessment; communication; and presentation. The brief sections that follow comment on each of these in turn.

Research

The widespread availability of the Internet has allowed the entire world access to more information than ever before. In classrooms where there are Internet connections, one or more computers set up for student use, and other equipment available, research can take on new dimensions. The Internet offers information on practically any topic imaginable. There are a lot of problems, dangers, and difficulties, of course, and educators are constantly trying to balance the positive uses of the Internet with the potential consequences. The major problems have to do with Internet safety issues and the inappropriate content that can be accessed during web browsing or searches. Students and adults have to learn how to find search engines, evaluate websites to determine what makes them credible, and decide if information uncovered is accurate and reliable. Then there is the problem of policing the web. Many firewalls have been created and are now implemented in school districts to restrict Internet access to websites deemed inappropriate for the school grounds. However, this means that some sites needed could be blocked, while others that are inappropriate for the educational setting will inevitably find their way through. The vastness of the Internet makes it nearly impossible for school systems to keep every inappropriate website off of school computers. Middle and high school students will certainly try to push their luck and access blocked sites regardless, particularly popular social networking sites like Facebook and Twitter. While efforts by technology experts are starting to reduce, if not solve this difficulty in student research, the ability of students to access inappropriate websites in the classroom is still a viable and prudent concern for contemporary teachers.

Internet information sources are important in two other ways: they are abundant and convenient. The Internet simply offers more readily accessible information and material to students than any group in history has had available. The problem is that it is not all "good" information. Sources do not always offer correct information. Inaccuracies, incomplete and false information about topics, and even unsupported opinion masquerading as fact are all part of what you find on the Internet. The plethora of information available on the web means teachers need to spend time helping students understand what makes websites reliable and how to distinguish between facts and opinions. But with all these problems, the web offers the potentiality to locate, read, download, copy, and share huge amounts of information on practically any topic, essentially expanding school libraries exponentially. And it is available to groups of students without their ever leaving the classroom itself. We simply have to teach them, often while we are learning ourselves, the skills needed to sort all the "stuff" out.

The Internet is also useful for quickly locating and ordering all kinds of materials from books to software to historical artifacts. Because of the ever-improving quality of Internet search engines, such resources can be found much more efficiently than ever before. This allows the teacher to be better prepared with materials for groups and to make cooperative learning experiences much more meaningful and engaging in the social studies classroom.

Technology also enables teachers to offer students access to more controlled materials and information at a relatively modest cost. Thousands of different reference materials, primary and secondary sources, and videos are now available in large digital collections, such as those found on the Library of Congress website. Literature and information books are also available in digital forms to supplement learning in and out of the classroom. In addition, hard-copy materials can be scanned in minutes to create resource banks around a topic of study.

Record Keeping

Another way in which technology can improve the effectiveness of cooperative and collaborative groups is by improving the capacity of teachers and group members themselves to record work and progress. Spreadsheets and databases can be set up by student groups to help them look at information that they collect in different and more insightful ways.

Records of the groups themselves can help both the groups and the teacher see progress and needs. New software is being developed every year that helps record and sort information related to work completed, individual contributions and progress, and assessment. Record keeping can be set up to allow each group access to information about their own group, but not about others. Sorting and statistical treatments of the data from the records can give teachers and students alike perspectives on what each group member is or is not accomplishing as well as comparative information about each group as a whole.

Communication

Perhaps the most important potential of technology for cooperative and collaborative groups in the secondary grades is in the area of communication. Technology can improve communication among group members and between groups, not to mention between teachers and parents.

Computers have taken classic middle and high school secretive communication efforts, like note passing, for example, to a whole new level. Networked computers in schools enable students to contact others, even if they are in different parts of the building, and have meaningful and useful conversations that can reduce the running back and forth we have been used to and also save a great deal of time. But even more important as communication tools are email, instant messaging, text messaging, and even video chatting. Email and instant messaging allow students to communicate with other group members or the teacher by sending messages. They can keep in contact with the members of their group when doing work at home, and they can send trial ideas and write-ups to other students and teachers for feedback. They can even send reminders and information to themselves. Instant messaging allows two or more people online at different locations to carry on instant conversations by typing notes back and forth. Video chatting allows members of groups to actually see what others are doing and working on and to show their own work.

If a website is available, discussion groups can be set up. These are more public than email, and that can have both positive and negative consequences. However, entire groups can have meetings and a shared discussion forum while members may not be on school grounds. Teacher-created websites and discussion forums can offer a safe environment for students to communicate virtually, with settings and interactions being monitored by the instructor. This will also provide an educational forum for groups to openly share and discuss topics rationally without resorting to popular social media sites. Teachers should view and present these online discussions and interactions as training the students on "netiquette," or how to conduct themselves responsibly while online.

FYI

How can social media applications be leveraged in this way to make learning meaningful?

Presentations

Technology also has expanded the possibilities for the kinds of projects and presentations that groups can develop. There are so many different options in this area that only a sampling of possibilities can even be mentioned. New software and hardware are appearing each year. Even something so traditional as group oral and written reports can now be augmented with downloaded visuals and audio clips as well as scanned material. Cut and paste with print programs allows incorporation of very sophisticated, data-rich materials. Pictures can be enlarged, doctored, and treated in many ways to make masks, collages, illustrated biographies, and a host of other visual aids for presentations and reports. Written reports can look like professional magazine and newspaper articles.

Presentation software, including the ever-prevalent PowerPoint, allows groups to develop interesting presentations, including audio and video clips, sound tracks, fades, and countless other professional components. These presentations can be used to enhance oral reports. They can also be made to stand alone by placing them into centers and allowing the students to have some control over the pacing.

New software and digital video cameras allow students to make well-edited movies. Digital movie making is a growing industry and a popular topic in the field of education. Since nearly all computers now come equipped with digital movie-making software, the process of making films has never been easier. Teachers could consider using this software to have groups create a public service announcement about global warming, a historical biography of Dr. Martin Luther King Jr., or an informational video introducing viewers to an important economic issue. The creation of digital films allows students to demonstrate their knowledge of a topic in a way that is unique and different from the traditional standardized tests. Groups engaging in this activity will have to consider a variety of factors, one of the most important being how to decide what images should be used in the film and how these images will support the message being conveyed. While there are certainly challenges to utilizing digital film software in cooperative group presentations (primarily finding the time needed to complete the activity), teachers should still consider this strategy as a powerful and alternative means of assessing student learning.

Looking Back

This chapter attempted to present a discussion of the use of grouping from several perspectives. Cooperative and collaborative learning groups are very different from traditional groups used by teachers in the past. The groups and the tasks that they do are much more highly structured, yet the groups themselves are student led rather than teacher led.

Collaborative and cooperative groups give the students ownership of the learning and require that students be active learners. In some cases groups allow all students to make better use of the facilities of the classroom; center-based activities may help that. Finally, technological advances have changed the complexion of group work in how research can be conducted, records can be kept, groups can communicate, and the ways that groups can assemble and present information.

While this chapter certainly does not cover every aspect of cooperative and collaborative learning, we hope readers have a better understanding of the foundations of group work and how this strategy can be extremely beneficial in the secondary social studies classrooms. For readers who would like to know more about cooperative and collaborative learning and see how other teachers have used these grouping approaches, please refer to the resources section at the end of this chapter for additional readings.

Extension Activity

Scenario

You are at the mid-point of the third nine weeks at YHS. Today is Friday and you have set up a class display of students' projects for parents, teachers, and administrators to view. During first period, Dr. Russell (the principal of YHS) and Dr. Waters (the assistant principal of YHS) stop in to see the projects. Pleased and impressed, they praise your efforts and explain that a local reporter will be coming to do a story about your dynamic teaching and the high-quality work YHS students are producing. They request that you provide them with written details of the activity by the end of the day. Thankful and excited, you agree.

Task

For this activity, develop an engaging cooperative learning activity that incorporates the use of primary sources and/or technology (6–12 grade level and topic of your choice). The activity should include a rationale for using cooperative learning, standards, detailed instructions for student roles within each group, and a method for assessing student learning (product, project, presentation, etc.). Share your products with peers and/or the instructor.

Reflective Questions

1 What social factors need to be considered in cooperative learning?
2 What are some of the different approaches to grouping?
3 What are the pros/cons to cooperative learning groups with secondary students?
4 How does cooperative grouping promote active learning?
5 What is a problem-centered group activity?
6 In what ways does technology enhance cooperative learning activities?

Helpful Resources

Visit the following website and view workshop #29 on how teachers design, implement, and assess group projects and presentations.

www.learner.org/resources/series166.html

Watch the following video for a discussion about cooperation and cooperative learning.

www.teachingchannel.org/videos/collaboration-vs-cooperative-learning-nea

Visit the following website and view workshop #20 for a middle school teacher's cooperative learning activity on landmark Supreme Court cases.

www.learner.org/resources/series166.html

Further Reading

Johnson, D. & Johnson, R. (1998). *Learning Together and Alone: Cooperation, Competition, and Individualism* (5th Edition). Boston, MA: Allyn and Bacon.

The authors of this book provide readers with valuable insights into the uses of cooperative learning in the classroom. With over 30 years of experience utilizing cooperative learning strategies, the authors provide readers with clearly organized materials that highlight the advantages and disadvantages of cooperative learning in order to help new or beginning teachers effectively implement this instructional method.

Morton, T. (1996). *Cooperative Learning and Social Studies: Towards Excellence and Equity*. San Juan Capistrano, CA: Kagan Cooperative Learning.

A former Teacher of the Year award-winner wrote this book, which serves as a practical guide for making social studies exciting and active with cooperative learning. There are a variety of cooperative activities provided for multiple social studies topics, subjects, and grade levels.

Schul, J. (2011). Revisiting an old friend: The practice and promise for cooperative learning in the twenty-first century. *The Social Studies, 102*, 88–93.

This article examines the similarities and differences between collaborative group work and cooperative learning, with examples of practical activities for each in the social studies classroom. Additionally, the article also provides insight about how cooperative learning can be even more impactful for democratic education in the twenty-first century.

Slavin, R. (1995). *Cooperative Learning: Theory, Research, and Practice* (2nd Edition). Boston, MA: Allyn and Bacon.

This book provides a tremendously detailed analysis on the theory and research that provide the foundation for cooperative learning in the classroom. Advances and developments in this method are described, as well as practical activities teachers can use to make cooperative learning meaningful and impactful for student learning.

Stahl, R., Vansickle, R. & Stahl, N. (2009). *Cooperative Learning in the Social Studies Classroom* (2nd Edition). Washington, DC: NCSS.

This edited book contains a great deal of practical and engaging strategies for teaching social studies through cooperative and collaborative learning. Edited contributions include a variety of detailed cooperative learning activities that social studies instructors will find easy to follow and implement in the classroom.

References

Hertz-Lazarowitz, R., Kirkus, V.B., & Miller, N. (1992). Implications of Current Research on Cooperative Interaction for Classroom Application. In R. Hertz-Lazarowitz, & N. Miller (Eds.), *Interaction in Cooperative Groups: Thee Theoretical Anatomy of Group Learning* (pp. 253–280). New York, NY: Cambridge University Press.

Johnson, D., & Johnson, R. (1989). *Cooperation and Competition: Theory and Research*. Edina, MN: Interaction Book Company.

Johnson, D., & Johnson, R. (1995). Goal structures. In L.W. Anderson (Ed.), *International Encyclopedia of Teaching and Teacher Education* (2nd ed., pp. 349–352). Tarrytown, NY: Elsevier Science.

Johnson, D., & Johnson, R. (1998). *Learning Together and Alone: Cooperation, Competition, and Individualism* (5th ed.). Boston, MA: Allyn and Bacon.

Kagan, S. (1992). *Cooperative Learning*. San Juan Capistrano, CA: Kagan Cooperative Learning.

MacGregor, J. (1990). Collaborative learning: Reframing the classroom. *Teaching Excellence*, 2(3), 51–56.

Martin, M. (1992). Cooperative learning. The Education Consumer Guide. ED/OER1 92–38. U.S. Department of Education. Washington, DC.

Onwuegbuzie, A. (2001). Relationship between peer orientation and achievement in cooperative learning-based research methodology courses. *The Journal of Educational Research*, 94(3), 164–183.

Slavin, R. (1995). *Cooperative Learning: Theory, Research, and Practice* (2nd ed.). Boston, MA: Allyn and Bacon.

Sparapani, E., Abel, F., Easton, S., Edwards, P., & Herbster, D. (1997). Cooperative learning: An investigation of the knowledge and classroom practice of middle grade teachers. *Social Education*, 118(2), 25–33.

Thompson, K.L., & Taymans, J. (1996) Taking the chaos out of cooperative learning: The three most important components. *The Clearing House*, 70(2), 8–11.

U.S. News and World Report. (1997). Pet teacher phrases. *U.S. News and World Report*, 123(9), 8–9.

9 Experiencing Social Studies

Looking Ahead

Teaching aims at "impact." We want to make the learning environment so powerful that students remember what goes on there as well as the information and skills. If students can *experience* social studies, it is more likely to be impactful. Several factors contribute to the impact of teaching, including: (1) the ability and interest of the learner; (2) previous background knowledge and experience; (3) how well particular teaching/learning experiences are understood; (4) the amount of practice or repetition; (5) student perceptions of the importance of learning; (6) the degree to which students feel or do not feel safe, secure, and accepted; and (7) the senses and intelligences involved in the learning experience.

Social studies teachers who think about meaningful learning experiences, the impact of the activities, and the pacing of the school day will more likely do high-impact teaching. If the way that we teach creates excitement, what we teach will be retained. School experiences that are truly educational will intellectually and emotionally involve students, commanding both interest and response. If they do not, they will have little or no positive impact on how students learn, think, and feel about people, places, and events. Utilizing teaching methods such as drama, role play, simulations, field trips, and service learning in the classroom will help teachers foster meaningful learning experiences.

The focus of this chapter is to discuss impactful learning experiences that social studies teachers can utilize. This chapter examines the utilization of drama, role playing, simulations, field trips, and service learning in the classroom. This chapter details how problem solving is a natural and intrinsic element of drama and how dramatic techniques can be a vitalizing and energizing force in social studies. This chapter offers explanations and examples of a wide variety of dramatic techniques. Furthermore, this chapter explores the utilization of field trips and service learning, along with mock trials and simulations.

Can You? Do You?

Can you ...

- explain how drama is a problem-solving activity?
- identify reasons for using dramatic activities?
- describe different forms of mock trials?
- organize a service learning project?
- plan an effective and meaningful field trip?

Do you ...

- understand the term *dramatic tension*?
- understand how to use a variety of dramatic techniques in social studies?
- know the forms of mock trials?
- know what steps to take to plan a field trip?

DOI: 10.4324/9781003217060-9

Focus Activity

Before reading this chapter, try the focus activity below.

In small groups, generate a list of powerful quotes from the speeches and writings of historic figures. Here are a few examples:

"I have a dream." Martin Luther King, Jr.
"A date which will live in infamy." Franklin Delano Roosevelt
"Ask not what your country can do for you." John F. Kennedy
"Ain't I a woman?" Sojourner Truth
"We hold these truths to be self-evident ..." Thomas Jefferson
"Four score and seven years ago, our forefathers set forth on this continent a new nation, conceived in liberty and dedicated to the proposition that all men are created equal." Abraham Lincoln
"Give me your tired, your poor, your huddled masses yearning to breathe free." Emma Lazarus

Repeat each quote several times, going around the group with each person trying to express the quote as dramatically and differently as possible. Discuss the meaning of each quote, and the nuances that the different ways of stating the quote add. What does this say about how we learn from dramatic and eloquent figures in history and what we can learn from using drama in teaching? Share responses with peers and the instructor.

The Importance of Drama in Social Studies

Every lesson in every classroom every school day should be a dramatic experience. If the teacher does well, the classroom experience is going to be interesting, exciting, and eventful. If the teacher has no flare for the dramatic, then the classroom is likely to be a somewhat lifeless and unexciting place where only routine learning occurs.

Drama is more than putting on a play, more than a category of techniques that teachers can use in social studies. Drama is a way of looking at the entire learning thrust of the classroom. That thrust is the product of the emotional atmosphere, the teaching style and range of the instructor, and the kinds of activities in which students are engaged. When dramatic tension is the focus of the classroom, there is a positively charged atmosphere that can be felt. This kind of tension is the distinguishing feature in the very best classrooms, regardless of the teacher's style. It is an almost visible glow of anticipation on students' faces. It is evidenced in the way students come into the room, what happens when class is begun, how small groups and large groups are handled, the things that contribute to order and management, the kinds of assignments that are made and how and when they are made, and when and how oral reading is done.

Positive dramatic tension in the classroom can be created by challenging students with little mysteries and surprises. To create the best kind of suspense, teachers need to see themselves as constant stage setters. A medieval helmet or a tricorn hat on the desk as the students enter, Luther's 95 Theses hung on the door, or a newspaper with a banner headline related to the Japanese attack on Pearl Harbor that is hawked by a "newsy" all can be productive bits of staging. Teachers also need to challenge students with provocative questions, problems to solve, and interesting anecdotal stories. What happened to the Roanoke colonists? Did Washington insiders aid Booth in his assassination of Lincoln? What happened to Amelia Earhart or to Meriwether Lewis? What can be done to preserve the ozone and the rain forests or to reverse global warming? What is being built in the construction site down the street and how will it change the neighborhood?

Teachers are always performers in the drama of the classroom, but their roles and the ways they play them vary. Some are wonderfully dramatic solo performers, good storytellers, and powerful mood setters. There are others who reveal their dramatic flair best while interacting with their students. Still others star at evoking passion and excitement and curiosity in a class while remaining quietly in the background. Many are talented organizers and catalysts to unleash the impassioned thoughts and feelings of the student. You can be a good teacher without being a ham, but not without enthusiasm and a flair for lighting the flame in others.

FYI

Teaching and learning can and should be fun for both teachers and students. It is a long school year, so have some fun out there!

Teachers need to be stage managers, providing students with a dramatic vision of history, culture, and human relationships. This allows students to experience and to become involved in the conflicts and controversies, the personalities and plottings—in effect, the drama—implicit in the very name "social studies." Teachers make students aware of the dramatic moments of the past and of the present; the elements of conflict, climax, comedy, and tragedy; the plot or story; suspense and resolution; setting, character, and dialogue. As stage managers, teachers can also utilize several dramatic techniques that get students involved, provoke curiosity and give reason for research, develop a sense of event sequence, develop skills of oral and written expression, and develop sensitivity to the feelings and ideas of others. The use of drama as a teaching approach makes social studies come alive. Most importantly, drama can stimulate interest and often give purpose and meaning to the content.

Only when the perspective of drama is understood is a teacher really going to be able to use the spectrum of dramatic techniques purposefully and effectively. Dramatic techniques are almost always involving. In almost every type, a variety of problem-solving opportunities occur. Fortunately for teachers, there are variations of drama that can be done with almost any ability level and require amounts of time, varying from a few minutes to a few weeks. The amount of teacher-centeredness and control also varies, and students can be moved slowly from dependence toward independence in planning and carrying out dramatic activities.

Drama through Reading

The dramatic power and eloquence of the printed word can be used to create images and suspense when read aloud. The following techniques have been found effective.

Guided Fantasies

Guided fantasies, also called visualizations, are dramas in which even the shy students can participate because no acting is required, only good listening, concentration, and sensory imagination. Students are asked to sit with their eyes closed and to envision as vividly as they can a scene as a reader describes it. If students are expressive readers, they can be involved in this capacity as well as being listeners. This is especially true in the upper grades.

A special kind of listening needs to occur when reading fantasy. The teacher wants students to get the feel of what it is like to be in another time and/or another place. The teacher wants students to be able to envision the scenes, smells, and sounds. What is wanted, in short, is a very imaginative sensory kind of listening, the kind that involves students and makes them want to interact with and know more about what is being described.

The readings need to be fairly short, certainly within the concentration span of students. They need to be very descriptive, sensory, and specifically detailed to the point of being graphic. The scenes that they describe should, of course, be relevant to the curriculum. They should help students envision the settings, the culture, and the sequence of events. You want them to smell the smoke of the battlefield, the stench of the prisons, the perfume of the flowers, and the aromas of the feast spread before the king. You want them to almost hear the royal court, the noises of battle and of the marketplace, and the voices and clatter that fill the city and the streets. In their mind's eye, you want students to see as clearly as they can the panorama and the detail of everything.

The scenes described can be historical or contemporary. The amount of imagery created in the story is an important process in getting students involved. Step out of the story to tell them to breathe in the smells and ask them what they smell. See if they can add detail to the vision. Re-read short segments of the description that are particularly strong in the images they create. Pictures and objects and things to touch, hear, and even smell can be examined to add to the intensity of the sensory experience and to increase input into the discussion from students.

Guided fantasies can describe a range of times from the distant past to the events in the news today. Newspaper and Internet accounts can be used. Since guided fantasies may be just too stressful and powerful, teachers should be careful what they choose to use with students. For example, you would not want to use the radio account of the destruction of the Hindenburg or the contemporary accounts of the killings at Columbine or the World Trade Center attack. But you could use descriptions of opening events at the Olympics, a World's Fair, or description of life in a historic mansion.

As a follow-up activity, the guided fantasy can be reenacted as a pantomime. Through pantomiming the event while the fantasy is read aloud, students can intensify the visualization and express the images they have seen in their minds.

Dramatic Example #1

The Tornado

Set-Up

Students are seated in a circle or perhaps on the floor so that there is a sense of closeness in the group. At its best, the technique allows the listener to be totally immersed in the images being created and suspend disbelief in their reality.

Teacher

Close your eyes and let your mind go blank for a minute. Form a picture in your mind. Try to make this picture as clear and as filled with vivid detail as you possibly can. This story is based on accounts of the destructive tornado that swept the Midwest on April 13, 1974.

Story

It has been an uneventful April day in the town of Xenia in central Ohio. It is a quiet kind of old-fashioned town most days. This part of Ohio is fairly flat and you can see from one end of town to the other. The carhops at the local drive-in root beer stand are taking orders. Along with other girls and boys, you are waiting for a ride in front of the school. The air seems strange, kind of heavy and oppressive, and there is a quietness in the air that does not seem normal even by the standards of a Midwestern American town. Though it is not raining, dark clouds are hanging low and daylight seems to be going early.

Something catches your eye. Off to the southwest, a huge darker cloud has formed and seems to be revolving. In minutes, it is funnel-shaped. You have been listening to radio weather, and you know that conditions are dangerous here in "tornado alley," so you have no doubt. That cloud is now a tornado! And this one looks like a bad one headed right into town.

You run back into the school screaming, "Tornado! Twister coming and coming fast!" Looking out the window of the school, you and other students and teachers can now see with horror a terrible fearsome twisting cloud only a few hundred yards away. Everyone hits the floor in terror as the tornado slams into the building with screaming force. Crashing, banging, and grating sounds fill the air along with the screams of terrified people. It is raining rocks, slabs of concrete, tree limbs, bricks, and great chunks of earth that have been ripped from the ground. Daggers of broken glass twirl through the air. The huge beams of the school are falling everywhere.

The tornado funnel moves across the town at 40 miles per hour, leaving a trail of destruction and rubble. Wood-frame houses are crushed or swept from their foundations. Huge old trees are torn from the earth and hurled in the air. The air is filled with objects, from furniture to cars and trucks, all now being hurled with monstrous force.

The black twisting tornado hits the rear of a train moving through town. Several train cars are thrown from the tracks across the main street where they crash into the red brick post office, a museum, and a restaurant.

Finally, the destructive tornado passes. Thirty-three people have been left dead and hundreds injured. Over 1,300 buildings have been destroyed. Of course, you do not find this out until later. For now, you can only see the awful damage everywhere. You and the rest are left dazed and unbelieving, but you feel lucky to have survived.

Class Action Dramas

A class action story is one that is read aloud. Students listen for particular words or phrases. When they hear them, they must quickly respond in a prescribed way. You may have done these little stories and called them by a different name or had no name for them at all. What they involve, more than anything else, is listening skills. Students should listen carefully to the story as it is read. The required words and actions usually involve only rudimentary drama, and generally even the shyest student will participate in most roles.

The stories themselves may include stereotypes and may even contain misinformation. The stories may also contain blatant exaggerations. Often the responses are made to look ridiculous. The stories can provoke solid discussion of issues and values.

FYI

This type of strategy is becoming increasingly important in contemporary society as the vast amount of information at people's disposal needs to be critically analyzed for responsible civic engagement.

For some words and phrases, a response may come from a single individual. For others, a group within the class may be asked to respond. In many cases though, the entire class may be required to react when a key word is read. Scripts can be adapted from historical events or from books and can even be written as class projects. The first job after writing the story and determining the key words and the responses is to assign the roles within the group. It is usually good to rehearse responses before doing the entire story. The story should be read with as much excitement and expression as possible, but the rate must be regulated to allow everyone to see, hear, and participate in the responses. Here is an example based on a familiar version of a series of historical incidents involving the famous Revolutionary War figure Paul Revere.

Dramatic Example #2

Paul Revere's Many Rides: A Class Action Story

This example involves whole class participation. Use the bold prompts to indicate when the class has to perform the relevant action.

When the Reader Says ...	*You Do and Say ...*
English	Shout, "The Regulars are coming!"
Paul Revere or Paul	Pretend to jump on a horse and ride.
Tea	Raise a pretend cup and pretend to drink while saying, "Mm, good!"
Taxes	Shout, "No taxation without representation!"
American(s)	Whistle the first line of "Yankee Doodle."
Horse	Shout, "Get your dogs, cats, and chickens off the road!"
Boston	Shout, "Is that where they invented baked beans?"
Philadelphia	Shout, "Is that where they invented cream cheese?"
Ride, Rode, Riding, or Ridden	Make the sound of a horse, "Neigh, Neigh."
Lexington/Concord	Shout, "BANG! BANG!"

The **English** wanted to tax everything in their **American** colonies, and **Paul Revere** and his friends in **Boston** didn't like it one bit. First the **English** put a **tax** on everything the **Americans** printed. Then the **English** wanted to **tax tea**, glass, and paper. The **Americans** protested so strongly that the **English** took back all the **taxes**, all, that is, but the **tax** on **tea**. The **Americans** liked their **tea** but they refused to pay the **English tax**. One night **Paul Revere** and some other **Americans** dressed up as Indians and boarded three **English tea** ships in **Boston** Harbor. They threw all the **tea** into **Boston** Harbor. Afterwards, **Paul** jumped on his horse and rode to tell other **Americans** in Massachusetts, Connecticut, and in **Philadelphia**, Pennsylvania. For the next year, **Paul Revere** kept an eye on the **English** soldiers who were now all over **Boston**. He **rode** his horse from **Boston** to **Philadelphia**, all the time carrying messages about what the **English** were doing. One night, a friend of **Paul Revere's** found out that the **English** soldiers were going to march to the towns of **Lexington and Concord** to capture guns and ammunition that the **Americans** had stored. The **English** also wanted to take two **American** leaders, Samuel Adams and John Hancock. **Paul Revere** and others were sent to warn the **Americans** in **Lexington and Concord**. So, off **rode Paul** on his **horse**. Before he even got to **Lexington** he was almost stopped by two **English** officers, but **Paul** got away and woke up Hancock and Adams. **Paul** and two others started out on their **horses, riding** toward **Concord**, warning farmers along the way. But the **Americans** were stopped by **English** soldiers who took their **horses**. **Paul** had to walk back to **Lexington**, where he met the **American** leaders, Adams and Hancock, just getting in their carriage to leave. **Paul rode** out with them but had to walk back to save a trunk full of secret papers that they had left behind. **Paul** walked back to **Lexington** to find it full of **American** farmers armed with muskets. In fact, **Paul** was just carrying the trunk out when the **English** troops arrived and he heard the sound of gunfire. So, **Paul Revere** actually heard what was later called, "The shot heard round the world."

Readers' Theater

Readers' theater involves turning a story that is written in narrative form into a play. A group of students read the story and then plan together how to alter it so that it can be read as a play. Young, Chase, and Rasinski (2009) found that the readers' theater enhanced reading fluency and comprehension. A critical benefit and dimension of readers' theater is that it focuses on the drama planning process. Students have to think out how they can change the way that the story is told. They have to develop a thorough understanding of the characters; a feel for the setting; and a mental map of the purpose, themes, and the plot line or sequence. They literally rewrite the story, putting in dialogue to cover narrative passages. They are made to think about what character would be most likely to relate the information and how it can be fitted in as conversation or as monologue. Of course, one of the natural tendencies is to fall back on the device of a narrator, but ideally the use of this voice should be minimized, if not prohibited.

FYI

All teachers are writing teachers. Take this responsibility seriously, but also remember to try to make the task interesting and engaging for students.

The focus of dialogue is human interaction. A monologue reveals inner thoughts, dreams, and concerns. Stories that place a lot of emphasis on character, are written in the first person, and/or are already rich in dialogue usually take less adaptation. For social studies content purposes, folk tales, biographical episodes (such as those in the books of Jean Fritz), historical fiction (such as *Nettie Goes South*), and stories that emphasize culture and human relationships (such as *Ming Lo Moves the Mountain* or *Frog and Toad Are Friends*) are most useful.

After the story is planned and usually rewritten, students can try reading through it different ways, running through it several times. This can allow different students to express themselves in the roles and can lead to rewriting and rethinking different parts of the story.

Dramatic Reading

There is a wealth of short dramatic material that students can read expressively. These can be funny and/or serious, depending on the material. The trick is finding and/or adapting. For adaptable material, popular descriptive histories and historical fiction are good sources. Good material can also be found in popular history and geography magazines such as *National Geographic*, *Smithsonian*, *Cobblestone*, and others. It is also productive for students to prepare their own readings as creative writing assignments and creative reporting exercises.

The teacher needs to set it up so that more than one student reads the material aloud. That way, students can begin to envision the range of expressive possibilities. Seven types of readings—brags, cliff-hangers, character monologues, in-role reports, first-person poems, expressive poems about human feelings, and historical poems—are detailed below.

Brags are comic devices. They are humorous partially because boasting is considered inappropriate behavior in mainstream society and partially because of the use of exaggeration that is implicit in all bragging. Most students' social interactions are filled with boasting claims from the stereotyped, "My father is stronger than your father!" to the "dares" that are so common in youth society and the name-dropping common among adults. Brags involve strength, ability, status, possessions, and relationships. Bragging has become and continues to be an art form in some societies (including that of frontier America).

Written brags make excellent oral reading devices. They invite competition and imitation. They make excellent models for creative writing, and they can incorporate a great deal of knowledge of a culture. Here are two brags, one from a fictitious inventor, the other from a real one. They might be used in a unit on invention and discovery or one dealing with a period of history where invention was a major theme. Have the students read these to see who can read most expressively. Then have them write their own brags.

Dramatic Example #3

Professor Ima Cheenius Brag

Of course, *I* am the greatest inventor of all time! *My* inventions will one day be household words. Why, *I* have inventions in process right now that will make life easier for everyone, save energy, repair the ozone, cure cancer, get us to other planets, make clothes and shoes and cars that will never wear out, and solve the energy shortage. And here is my little secret—*I* am inventing an engine that will run entirely on polluted air. Too much for you! Well, try this! *I* am going to invent instant water to save the world from water shortage. All you need to do is add water. Can you believe how clever *I* am? *I* just don't know what I'll come up with next, maybe chew-less gum or a math pill that helps children get their math homework done twice as quickly! Why, next to me, Edison was a bulb head, Newton was a fig cookie, and Bell was a ding-a-ling. And, just between you and me, *I* think Franklin flew a few too many kites in the lightning. *I* am just *so* clever!

Dramatic Example #4

George Washington Carver Brag

I am George Washington Carver. I am a modest man, so it is hard for me to brag. I worked my way through high school and was the first black student ever to attend Simpson College in Iowa. I worked as a janitor there until I got my degree in agricultural science, then I went back and got a master's degree. You think it is tough to do now; it was a thousand times tougher for a black man in the 1800s. But I was a worker and a man who looked, looked close at things. I once said that "When I talk to the little flower or the little peanut they will give up their secrets." And they did just that to me too.

Another thing I said was that "Ninety-nine percent of the failures come from people who are in the habit of making up excuses." And that I never did. In 1897, Booker T. Washington asked me to come to Tuskegee. I was there for 50 years. I invented 325 products from peanuts alone and 228 from sweet potatoes. My inventions would fill a large hall. I created synthetic rubber, synthetic marble, vanishing cream, wood filler, mucilage, rubbing oils, instant coffee, insulating board, linoleum, creosote, bleach—why it would be hard to name something that I could not create a version of. I even taught the black farmers to rotate their crops and restore the worn-out land.

Now this part you really are not going to believe. Most of my inventions I just gave away. I wanted people to benefit, not to make a lot of money for myself. I told people, "God gave my ideas to me, how can I sell them to somebody else?" In fact, in 1940, I gave my life savings to the establishment of a research foundation at Tuskegee.

But I did get my honors. Simpson College gave me an honorary doctorate in 1928. I became an honorary member of the Royal Society of Arts in London and received the Spingarn Medal from the NAACP. In 1939, President Roosevelt even gave me a medal for saving southern agriculture.

Cliff-hangers are readings in which the central characters are depicted in impossible situations—dire straits from which it may seem impossible that they can ever extract themselves. It is best to design these as problem-solving readings. After they have been read aloud a few times to try alternate expressions, have students try to suggest ways out of these truly solution-defying situations. Generally, the decisions do not involve moral dilemmas so much as insurmountable difficulties. They can really test students' problem-solving abilities. When faced with many impossible problems, one has to look at them individually *and* together, often beginning with the initial task of identifying the least impossible one to solve.

Dramatic Example #5

The Sea Captain Explorer

There I am. My ship has run aground in uncharted waters. There is a gaping hole in the hull, and even if it were fixed there seems to be no way to get this heavy ship back out into the water. Speaking of water, there isn't any, and thirst is a terrible killer at sea. The stores are in short supply and we've been eating wormy ship's biscuits for a week. The crew, which is made up of the worst cutthroats that ever-signed sailing papers, has been grumbling and refusing to take orders. The sailors are beginning to plan a mutiny, and some pretty nasty-looking types are starting to edge toward me with cutlasses and belaying pins in their hands. Out of the jungle-like growth just a few hundred yards away, a large group of hostile natives, wicked-looking spears at the ready, are moving toward the beached ship and me. Out to sea and moving toward us, I can see a fierce seasonal storm, the kind that can pick my poor ship up and break it entirely on the rocks. It is coming fast. The only path of retreat is the sea, which will soon be stormy. But that may not be the worst part. Out on the bay, I can see a half-dozen black fins slicing through the water. What am I going to do?

Dramatic Example #6

The New Country Explorer

I am climbing the mountain trail where no Englishman has gone before. The mountains tower all around me, and the only trails are those made by animals. I make a single misstep along a narrow ledge and I go crashing down through underbrush and scrub trees, hitting every rock as I go. Desperately grabbing at trees and rocks, I try to break my fall, finally sliding to a stop only inches from a 200-foot drop-off. Badly bruised and shaken, I try to struggle to my feet only to find one leg twisted grotesquely underneath my body. For a moment, there is no feeling at all in the leg. Then the pain hits me with a jolt and, in a cold sweat, I nearly pass out. Just then, I hear a snarling growling noise. The hair on my neck stands on end as a giant brown and gray grizzly bear rises on its hind legs not more than a hundred feet away. Pitifully, I struggle to drag myself away. Suddenly, there is a whizzing sound and an arrow thuds, quivering in a tree trunk a few feet away. I look up to see a party of dreaded Blackfeet warriors with bows drawn on the ledge above me. It is at that exact moment that I hear the warning rattle of the rattlesnake at my feet. What am I going to do?

Character monologues are readings that reveal the history, philosophy, or plans of an individual. Shakespeare's plays are filled with them—Caesar, Hamlet, and so on. Browning's poetry as well as the writings of people like Dickens, Poe, and Twain give other examples. Children's books, from Diane Stanley's book on Mozart (2009) to Margie Palatini's version of Aesop's "Fox and the Grapes" (2009) or Jean Fritz's treatment of the Jamestown colony (2010), are excellent sources. In addition, there are many usable primary source materials, particularly letters, diaries, and newspaper accounts. Generally, first-person writing is best, but individual examples should be judged on their own merits. Whatever the example, it should help students get a feel for the person and his or her cultural context and value system.

In-role reports represent one device that can be used to get students to write their own dramatic reading. In-role reports bring a refreshing change from standard student reports. It has been common practice for decades for students to copy reports directly out of an encyclopedia or some other reference and then read with little comprehension what they have copied. With in-role reports, students take a character role and give the report from the perspective of that character. Characters may be real or created. Students have to pick a point in time for the character and report as if they knew nothing from that point on. For example, someone taking the role of Lincoln on the 1st of April 1865, would know nothing about the assassination and might even end the report by describing plans to see *An American Cousin* when it plays at Ford's Theater. The point of these reports is to get into the feelings or perceptions of the characters involved.

First-person poems are one of the most personal forms of writing. Poetry is one of the most personal forms of writing. It expresses feelings in their most essential form. Poetry is also designed for oral display by its very nature. A number of kinds of poems are excellent material for dramatic and expressive reading. First-person poems are especially useful, especially when their subjects are historical and geographic characters. The poetry of Robert Service (2006) or Walt Whitman as well as more modern poem renditions help students get the "feel" of a place and time.

Role Plays and Other Structured Drama Techniques

Structured Role Play

Structured role plays are dramatic activities in which character information and a scenario are provided to students. Some device is used so that the teacher controls the sequence of the drama.

Dramatic Example #7

Structured Role Play

Set-Up

Create two groups of six to eight students each, the Roller-Coasters and the Merry-Go-Rounds. Other students can be observers, or activity participation can be doubled if space and control variables are favorable.

Scenario

The Roller-Coasters and the Merry-Go-Rounds live in neighboring villages, but their cultures are very different and neither knows much about the other. The Roller-Coasters have decided to invite the Merry-Go-Rounds to a big Getting-to-Know-You Party. The fact that no one in either village speaks the other's language causes some problems, but the invitation is finally sent and understood. There are some differences in culture, however, that may cause the people of the two villages to have different beliefs about what one can and cannot do. Only the Roller-Coasters know the following:

- You honor your people by always letting your guests eat first.
- The most honored people (your guests) are always served apples.
- Your teachers have taught you always to wear something blue.
- You must give a gift to a guest.
- During a meal, it is impolite to talk or stand, but just before and after the meal, everyone shouts, "Yeow!" very loudly several times.

Only the Merry-Go-Rounds know the following:

- It is impolite to start eating before your hosts take a bite.
- Apples are a forbidden and profane food. Any of your people who eat apples are thrown out of the tribe.
- Blue is a sacred color of the sky and sea, to be worn only by the most holy person in the village. When anyone else wears blue, it is a terrible, wicked thing.
- It is rude to take gifts from a host.
- When one is a guest, a good Merry-Go-Round does everything he or she can to please the hosts.
- One is silent before and after meals, but, while eating, a polite guest shouts, "Gooba!" and jumps up and turns around after every bite.

The role-play event involves the party. It can be played two ways, either with the two cultures able to speak to one another or with both ignorant of the other's language. The role play can be suspended at any moment with a "freeze" signal for discussion of questions about the nature or culture or about the culture clash that is occurring. This role play has children discuss the differences in how cultures resolve problems

Sociodramas

Sociodramas involve acting out the solutions to problems. The major difference between role play and sociodrama is that in sociodrama you are playing yourself. The essential problem situation begins, "If you were in this situation, what would you do and what would you say?" Quite often the problems are essentially of the sort that students encounter, such as someone wanting to copy their homework, seeing someone cheating or stealing, meeting someone new, relating to someone who is very old, getting directions when lost, giving "how to" directions, making a complaint in a store, or going to the principal about an unfair rule. However, students may be projected into a situation in which they are asked how they would act in parent or career situations if they were involved.

Children's Theater

Shotick and Walsko (1997) have described a structured approach they call children's theater, which they use to teach economic concepts. The term may be somewhat confusing since "children's theater" has long been the term to describe scripted dramas of any type done for a juvenile audience, but the idea itself is a useful one. A story is presented to the audience in play form with the audience being asked to interact with the actors, usually answering specific questions as the play develops. It is in some ways like the notion of interactional drama described later in this chapter. Morris (2009, 2001) and Morris and Hickey (2003) described a similar approach involving historical incidents and leading to writing activities for the students themselves.

Art- and Story-Related Dramatic Techniques

There are any number of techniques that specifically utilize art and literature. They not only develop cultural appreciation and expose students to exceptional examples but also show the relationship of the arts to culture and to history. The following two techniques have been found effective.

Picture Pantomimes

Picture pantomimes require prints of paintings showing historical or legendary events or people in action in cultural settings. Students look at the painting and isolate and focus on two or three motions they see that they can do in sequence. They then do these motions and each person's response is discussed, at the same time drawing out the meaning and explanations of the paintings.

Story Play

Story play is a technique in which stories are acted out without pre-written scripts. The story line, at least to begin with, is a familiar one. Students have a solid understanding of "how the story goes." This is either because the story is an extremely familiar one or because the teacher has taken them through the reading or the telling of the story enough times to give them a good sense of where in the story the characters are and where the plot line goes. Students then plan how to play the story and act it out based on their plan. The actual dialogue is improvised as they go. Students can do the story as it is written, experiment with different endings or different twists on the plot, or try putting the story in different contexts (doing parodies such as a modem version of "Cinderella" called "Successerella," based on economic problems, for example).

Usually these story plays are done not for an audience but for the experience of doing them. Students delight in having these videotaped or in doing a radio drama on audiotape. They also can profit from the opportunity these dramas afford for experimenting, redoing the same stories, using different students in the same roles, treating closed-ended stories as though they were open-ended, and so on.

One device that can be incorporated into these story plays is story cards. The teacher or students in the planning process create a storyboard of the story. Each story card on the storyboard represents an advancement of the plot, a different scene, or an event in the sequence of the story. For example, the first card from "The Brave Little Tailor" might read, "While working in his shop, the Little Tailor swats at some irritating flies, killing seven of them, and is so proud of his feat that he goes out to seek his fortune." All the story cards are then put in a stack on the chalk ledge and revealed one at a time as the story play is enacted. This gives students a better metacognitive map of the sequence of the story. It keeps the drama moving, and when students are in on the planning of these stories they learn about sequencing and writing a story. This enables them to develop a sense of the importance of sequence in any chain of events.

Story cards allow students to plan and create new endings as well. Most importantly, they give students an experience in drama that can be the basis of discussion. After students become familiar with using the story cards as a way of developing and pacing the drama, they can use them to develop entirely new story dramatizations. Students in a 6th-grade class created and dramatized the following story using their own story cards, creating various endings each time they played it out.

Story Card 1. The expedition was alert for any sign of danger as the horses moved at a slow trot along the dusty trail.
Story Card 2. The explorers were looking for a route that would lead them to the Pacific Ocean.
Story Card 3. From the dense undergrowth, the captain of the expedition felt hostile eyes watching his small party.
Story Card 4. In a small glen, a spring bubbled up out of the rocks and there the party stopped for a refreshing drink.
Story Card 5. The captain felt rather than heard the footsteps on the path behind them and turned to see a large party of armed natives moving toward him.
Story Card 6. The small party of explorers was helpless to do anything but follow the natives back through the undergrowth.
Story Card 7. The walls of the strange city loomed high in front of the party, catching the explorers by surprise.
Story Card 8. Where the explorers had been expecting primitive natives, they found a people who were far advanced in every way.
Story Card 9. The explorers were led into the magnificent halls of the king's palace.

Reenactment

FYI

As an extension of this type of activity, consider taking your students to visit a local reenactment as an experiential learning opportunity.

Reenactment groups across the country work at staging authentic Civil War and Revolutionary War battles. At various historic sites, local preservationists and employees go through the motions of living and working as early settlers as a part of the attempt to show visitors what life was like. Various plays and other performance pieces are staged at various times by theater groups. When teachers have students participate in any form of reenactment, they find that students can become very motivated to do the needed research. That purposeful research aimed at doing an authentic and accurate job in a reenactment role can be an invaluable experience.

The general guidelines for any reenactment begin with the selection of some event that will put students in touch with the historical and cultural world heritage. The event should be one that students can reproduce with some faithfulness to history, but it should also be one with an internal sequence that is simple enough for students to follow. Another consideration also might be that the event should be one that they can reenact without doing any violence to one another. (Battle scenes, so popular with reenactment hobbyists, are almost always excluded by this consideration.) The event should be one in which the sequence of actions by participants can be researched and reproduced.

Among the events that reenact well with young students are ceremonies and cultural rituals (greetings of two people, home entry rituals, tea ceremonies, a military group from a period setting up a camp, etc.), historic document development, exchanges and land sales (the Louisiana Purchase, the purchase of Manhattan, etc.), and parades and celebrations (women parade for the vote, labor movement picket lines, etc.). Once the event is selected, students need to do basic research, identify the sequence of events, and then plan how they are going to replay the event. If possible, go through the reenactment in the early stages of the research and then again after the research is complete. This gives the teacher and the students a better sense of what they know to begin with and what they have learned. It also gives some ideas about the kinds of questions that need to be answered in the research. During the planning period, the teacher needs to help discuss the meaning of what the students are doing as well as the things that they cannot accurately or fully portray.

Interactional Drama

Interactional drama involves an outsider or outsiders playing out a scenario from a historical context in front of students. The actors, usually in costume, play in such a way that they draw students into the dialogue, either by asking direct questions or asking students about what they think (in such a way that they solicit both opinions and viewpoints). The dramas are not scripted and are usually open-ended, leaving students to solve the problems and conflicts the actor/s brought.

Though interactional drama usually involves no role taking by students, the success of the technique depends on suspended disbelief, the ability of students to think and act as though what is happening is real instead of just pretend. Suspended disbelief is what enables anyone to enjoy a play, a movie, or a television program, thinking of the characters as real people instead of as actors playing people. To make this happen in interactional drama, older students especially may need to be coached beforehand. Finding convincing actors who stay in role and know their material is essential. It may be helpful but not essential to use actors who are not recognized by the class.

It may be best if the historical persons who visit the classroom for these dramas are not famous figures. In general, famous characters are more difficult for students to believe, especially if they already have an image of how the person looks. Ordinary people or less well-known historical personages are easier to impersonate. See Table 9.1 for several types of interactional drama that visitors can utilize.

The following sample scenarios indicate various types of interactional dramas.

Table 9.1 Types of Interactional Drama

Interview	The visitor gives an introduction of himself or herself and then answers questions. The actor really has to have a good background on the character to do this, and students will do better if prepared so that they can ask good questions.
Storytelling	The visitor, in-role, tells stories about his or her life.
Eavesdropping	The visitors have a conversation staged so that students seem to be overhearing something they were not meant to hear. There may be a "freeze" signal that causes the actors to seem to become statues while the teacher and the students talk about what has been said.
Recruitment	Different actors, taking different sides, try to get students to side with them.
Confrontation	The actors are set up to have a conflict. One of the characters wins the sympathy of students and gets them to help defend him or her against the adversary.

Scenario One

It is September 1776. Two revolutionary figures enter, arguing. One says that George Washington's situation is so hopeless that he ought to retreat from Long Island, burning New York City behind him so the British cannot quarter there for the winter. The other argues that this is too drastic because it would destroy a lot of American property and leave many people homeless. The other replies that two-thirds of the property in New York belongs to Tories anyhow. Both try to recruit students to their side.

Scenario Two

Two people dressed in turn-of-the-century garb enter, arguing. One thinks that women should be given the right to vote. The other is convinced that this is the wrong thing to do. The two (ideally both are women) try to recruit students to their view, limiting themselves to arguments of the period.

Scenario Three

A young man (or woman) dressed in ancient garb sneaks into the room looking frightened and wary. He claims that he is a Roman slave and that his master was killed in his home during the night. Because the murderer cannot be identified, Roman law says that all the slaves of the household can be jailed. He asks students to hide him. After he hides, a burly Roman enters looking for the runaway slave. He tries to get students to reveal the hiding place. When the young man is found, the teacher convinces the Roman officer that they should debate the law right there in the classroom before he is allowed to take the young man away. It is admitted in the debate that the circumstances of the death indicate that a much stronger man than this youth and probably an assassin from outside the house committed the crime.

Drama Units

Entire units can have a dramatic focus. One approach is what Fulwer and McGuire (1997) call "Storypath." It utilizes a story line as the effective organizer for a study. A story scenario is the point of departure, with students creating roles for themselves consistent with that scenario. Discussion and artwork allow students to elaborate the scenario. As events unfold in the scenario, students construct meaning for themselves. As stakeholders in the story line they have both character sympathy and a real need to solve the problems in the evolving plot line. Social interactions and involvement are natural. The technique is highly adaptable and may be used to create "neighborhoods" for stories set in any culture or period. One of the advantages of "Storypath" is that it can be used with students of all ages and abilities. McGuire has published multiple units (Cole & McGuire, 2011; McGuire, 2005) that teachers will find useful.

Storytelling in Social Studies

Storytelling is experiencing a worldwide revival. Throughout human history, storytellers have passed on their culture, created and preserved heroes, and passed on their history. Storytellers were often both the best historians and the foremost entertainers of bygone times.

Storytelling is included as a dramatic technique not because professional storytellers are consummate actors but because every good teacher is something of a storyteller. Story makes the past come alive and humanizes other people, no matter how different their culture or the geography of where they live.

Both social studies teachers and students learn and benefit from becoming better storytellers. Telling a story to an appreciative audience is extremely satisfying. More importantly, a story provides a context in which information is given meaning and may be remembered. There are only three steps in becoming a storyteller: learning to choose a story that is worth telling and fits your purposes; learning how to learn a story; and learning how to tell a story (Turner, 1994). Choosing a story may be as easy as contacting the school librarian. Simply find a story that you like; that teaches something important; and that is simple, suspenseful, exciting, and/or funny. Learning a story comes more easily once you learn how to "map" it out into a sequence of incidents and master a style of practice that fits you. Four suggestions for effective storytelling are listed below:

1 Know your story so well that you do not have to concentrate your attention on what comes next—so well, in fact, that you can change it and add material to it. If you do forget something, do not "double back." Either add what you lost later, make up stuff to cover, or forget it all.
2 Work on expression, putting a lot of emotion and change in your voice.
3 Involve your audience by asking questions during the story, getting them to do stuff, pretending that each one is a character, etc.
4 Keep the story simple and direct and human.

Process Drama in Social Studies

Process drama is an approach to drama that involves students deeply in the content that they are studying (Rosler, 2008; Baldwin & Waters, 2010). According to Baldwin (Baldwin & Waters, 2010), this approach has several key tools, including improvisation, teachers taking roles, meetings in which students talk about and plan the course of the dramatic action, thought tracking where individuals in role are asked to talk about their private thoughts about events, collective role play where multiple students play the same role simultaneously, and hot seating where students question the teacher in role about his or her character. The teacher's role is to guide the drama, stepping in and out of role as necessary and providing encouragement and motivation to students who are treated as experts. Narration and storytelling are used with the speaker directly addressing the audience (Hillyard, 2011). Process drama is rich in empathy and purposeful problem solving (Rijinbout, 2003). The following scenarios are examples of ones that can be used with the conventions of process drama:

- The class is told about the terrible conditions under which colonial prisoners of war are held by the British during the American Revolution. They are on a rotting decommissioned ship in leg irons and on short rations of mealy, spoiled gruel. They are treated with cruelty and threatened with hanging.
- The town is meeting to set up a volunteer fire department. The effort needs funding for equipment, vehicles, and training. Where do town leaders get the money, and how will they stop the growing number of fires in the meantime?
- The settlers in the new settlement are having trouble. Some of the people are lazy and do not want to work. Others are doing jobs that do not need to be done.
- One of the students in the class has lost his puppy. Everyone wants to help him find the young dog.

Effective Use of Drama in Social Studies

Drama in social studies can produce the kind of memorable Camelot moments that students will carry with them throughout their lives. It can help develop the research drive in lifetime students and make research purposeful and important to even marginal ones. It can make the classroom an exciting place to be and help students remember historical and cultural concepts and facts that they would otherwise forget. It can teach about social interactions and develop self-concepts in a way that traditional "lecture, read, and recite" social studies can never do. However, dramatic activities used without instructional purposefulness can be a waste of time. In fact, drama can even become disturbing. The difference lies in the way the teacher handles drama.

If drama is to be effective in social studies, the teacher has to first feel comfortable with it. He or she must be attracted to dramatic techniques and feel very positive about the potential to make the entire classroom a more exciting and interesting place. Teachers should avoid using techniques that make them feel uncomfortable or as if they are losing control of the classroom. Dramatic techniques require a high degree of student involvement and sometimes include student planning and student leadership in different directions. Teachers also need to feel that what they are doing with drama is solid and purposeful (McCaslin, 2006). Drama cannot be used as a mere time filler or entertainment. It must have curricular importance and value and the teacher has to effectively communicate that to students, parents, and administrators.

Drama requires preparation. If there is a first rule of the effective use of drama in the classroom, it is, "Be prepared!" The teacher has to know what he or she is about, find the right material, plan and structure the dramatic activity, and lead the students through planning and rehearsal up to the dramatic enactment moment. The plan and the material cannot be developed along the way. The teacher who shoots from the hip with drama is likely to fall flat or, worse, waste a lot of valuable learning time.

Drama only works in a positive, accepting atmosphere. That atmosphere is one that is open and experimental and charged with exciting stimuli. It also offers emotional security so that students feel safe psychologically. To take the kind of personal risks that drama demands, students should be sure that peers will not be ridiculing or demeaning them for their efforts. No student wants to appear to be foolish or ridiculous. Paradoxically, some students will act silly on purpose to avoid looking silly while trying to be serious. The safe conducive atmosphere for drama comes only with a series of positive experiences in which the teacher slowly edges the class toward dramatic expression that involves more risk taking.

Simulation Games

Perhaps the most familiar of social studies dramatic techniques is simulation gaming. Simulation games have become part of the culture. Fantasy simulations are played out recreationally by young people worldwide, and there are many well-known computer games (e.g., SimCity) that are simulations. Many popular board games, including the perennial favorite, "Monopoly," have elements of simulation gaming in them.

FYI

Always "proceed with caution" when implementing simulation activities. You never know how each student may handle a simulation emotionally or psychologically, so be purposeful and thoughtful.

Essentially, simulation games are structured decision-making activities in which students assume roles and then solve problems. Participants are given problem scenarios and additional information related to the problem and their roles. Their job is to come to the decision points in the simulation game and then make the best choice among the options available. Decisions and actions of students participating are limited by sets of restrictive rules. These rules make simulations more patterned than other role-play activities. The decisions often result in consequences and, often, at least some chance is involved in those consequences. The problem scenario itself, which serves as the beginning point, may be based on some very current or historical situation or on a hypothetical one.

Like any school activity, simulation games should be more than just fun. Both the choice of simulation games and the way that the activities are conducted are critical. There are several important considerations in choosing and playing such simulation games at any level. Perhaps the most critical of these is that the simulation should serve an important curricular purpose. Simply put, when students participate in simulations they should be learning social studies content and skills. The simulation should help them understand the concept and/or topic better. Once that is the prime consideration, other concerns follow logically. Students need to be aware of and understand what they are doing. The game should be one that students truly enjoy and one in which they will immerse themselves in the issues and the content. The best simulations provoke questions, reading, and research. These considerations should make teachers aware that how the teacher sets up the simulation and follows through after the dramatic playing is complete are critical to using simulation activities effectively. These are often referred to as briefing and debriefing, and few simulations have much meaning or learning value without them.

Simulation games can be simple. The amount of reading required to play the game is a factor that needs to be controlled to fit the abilities of the group of students. It is usually advantageous to use simulations that can be played in one day (from about 10 minutes to just under an hour), depending on the attention span and involvement level of the students. This reduces the possibility of students continuing the game in unsupervised settings. Another factor that the teacher may want to consider is the ability of students to work independently. Several different simulations are presented below. Each is a model that can be duplicated with similar information for many different units.

Simulation Example #1

The President's Cabinet

Type of Simulation: A Real Information Simulation

Mr. President, Whom Will You Choose?

The president's cabinet helps in decision-making and directs the day-to-day operations of the executive branch of the government. While the first president had only five members in the cabinet, more recent presidents have had far larger cabinets. The following is a list of some of the various cabinet offices held over the years. Which five of these do you think George Washington would have had on his first cabinet?

State	*Commerce*	*Housing and Urban Development*
Labor	Defense	Transportation
Energy	Justice	Attorney General
Education	War	Health and Human Services
Interior	Treasury	Health, Education, and Welfare
Navy	Agriculture	Postmaster General

President Washington had the same problem as every other president when it came to selecting the people to help him take on the job of chief executive. Who should he ask to serve on his cabinet, and in what jobs should he place them? Because his cabinet had only five members, the choices, even among the people Washington had known and worked with, were many. Washington's cabinet offices and brief descriptions of people who might have been considered are detailed in the potential cabinet members section.

Mr. President, Choose Who Will Serve!

Pretend that you are George Washington and make the choices and placements for your cabinet. Before you begin, you will need to answer one question. In choosing a cabinet, Mr.

President, which factors do you think are more important? To help you answer this question, nine of the factors Washington might have considered are identified on the following list. Rank order the factors (plus one factor of your own) to get the mindset for making your final selections among the ten finalists for your cabinet:

- Represent all regions of the country on the cabinet.
- Choose the people who are best qualified for the jobs.
- Represent the small states as well as the large states.
- Select friends who are loyal and true to you.
- Favor people who have great political influence.
- Have people with the most experience in government.
- Reward those who gave outstanding military service.
- Have people who have opinions and views like your own.
- Include people who have outstanding accomplishments.
- Other ______________________________.

Actual Offices of Washington's Cabinet

State	*War*
Treasury Attorney General	Postmaster General

Potential Cabinet Members

The teacher may want to assign to students each of the people under consideration for roles and let them try to make a case for themselves for a cabinet post.

1 Boston bookseller; forced to flee Boston in disguise in 1774; Revolutionary War general; served as an artillery officer with Washington's army; developed a reputation for being able to move equipment and supplies quickly; known as sound, solid, and dependable.
2 Revolutionary War general; served with distinction and bravery; considered a strong, brilliant leader in battle whom men would die for; fought guerilla-type warfare from the swamps of his native state for a considerable period of time while the British were in control of the area.
3 Strong-minded, clear-speaking champion of individual rights; opposed to a central government that is too strong; extensive experience in dealing with other nations; took a leadership role in Congress during the Revolution.
4 Supporter of a strong national government and a strong executive branch (may even want a king rather than a president); Revolutionary War officer on Washington's personal staff and strong supporter of Washington; good organizer and thorough planner; wants to establish a national bank and be sure that the new nation has a strong economic base.

5 Supporter of a strong central government; Southerner from a powerful state; lawyer by occupation; took a leadership role in the approval of the U.S. Constitution; keen observer and careful record keeper.
6 Elder statesman with ambassadorial experience; had a strong role in both the Declaration of Independence and the U.S. Constitution; extremely well liked; inventive and scientifically curious; writes extremely well and has many publications.
7 Outspoken critic of the U.S. Constitution and a defender of states' rights; spirited public speaker whose words caused many to support the Revolution; experienced as a state governor and a long-time member of a state legislature; has a real vision for the future.
8 Lawyer from a powerful northern state; took a key role in the effort to gain separation from Britain and helped in the writing of the Declaration of Independence; considered uncompromising, unyielding, but a man of principle; advocate of a strong central government.
9 Boston merchant; Harvard graduate; served in the Revolution, first as a captain and later as a colonel; strong supporter of the U.S. Constitution; first Commissioner of the U.S. Treasury, 1785–1789.
10 Virginia lawyer; aide-de-camp to Washington; governor of Virginia; member of Congress; attended Constitutional Convention but refused to sign; urged the ratification of the Constitution on the grounds that the union was necessary.

Students may want to compare their choices to Washington's and know the names of the people who were candidates. This is one case where it is not so important that their choices line up with the first president's. (The numbers below identify which of the descriptions correlate to the historical names.)

Actual Selections (First Term)

State	*Thomas Jefferson (3)*
Treasury	Alexander Hamilton (4)
War	Henry Knox (1)
Attorney General	Edmund Randolph (10)
Postmaster General	Samuel Osgood (9)

Not Chosen by Washington

Francis Marion (2)
James Madison (5)
Benjamin Franklin (6)
Patrick Henry (7)
John Adams (8)

Simulation Example #2

Who Will Go With the King's Envoy?

Type of Simulation: A Real and Hypothetical Information Simulation with One Decision

The people do not have to be real for simulations and the situations can be more general.

It is the fourteenth century. The English King is sending you as his envoy to the court of the King of France. You are to pick a party of five to go with you on the journey and to work with you at that court. Although there is currently peace between your country and France, it is an uneasy peace. There has been a series of wars spanning over half a century. Even recently, the two nations have been tottering on the brink of war. Your job is to make sure the peace continues so the King can fight wars in Scotland and Wales. You obviously want to pick the five people who can best help you. As ambassador, your task will be to keep things smoothed over, avoiding war if that is possible. You also are to find out as much about what France is planning as you can.

Sir William of Dobret speaks French fluently and has spent some time at the French court. He is a capable knight of 35 who rides well, has a reputation as a swordsman, and has battle experience. He is from a noble family of French descent and knows the people and the geography of the area well. He has never been disloyal to the King, but his loyalty has not really been put to the test and there is a widely held belief that he is more French than English.

Rowan of Logansby is a trusted friend and a seasoned fighter of unquestioned loyalty. He is a free man and a commoner, but his family has served your own for four generations. At 29, he is the best man with a longbow you have ever seen. He speaks a little French and has a good ear. Unusual for one of his class, he reads and writes. He is a blunt speaking, hot-tempered Englishman through and through.

Bertrand Dorsett is a clerk in the King's court. He is a source of knowledge about everyone and everything. He makes it his business to know. A young man in his early twenties, he is very ambitious, but he is loyal to no one but himself. As a clerk, he has mastered both Latin and French, and he speaks, reads, and writes fluently. He is an intriguer who will learn all of the ins and outs of the French court. He is very anxious for advancement.

The Count of Edwingham is an experienced diplomat of 50 who is somewhat resentful of you because he feels that he should have been selected as the ambassador. He is an old campaigner, still fit for battle. He has served in the French court in the past and knows many influential members of the French nobility. He speaks the language well and is totally loyal to your King.

Sir Geoffrey of Couran is not the type to love battle, loving the life at court and especially gifted as a minstrel. In his early thirties, he has managed to avoid serving in most of the constant wars. He has ability to charm men and women alike and he is especially adept at smoothing ruffled feathers and calming those who are angry. The King is particularly fond of him because of his wit, his charm, and his ability to sing and play the lute. Since he sings and speaks French as well as English, his skill as a minstrel will make him popular at the French court.

John Fitzhugh has been very helpful to the English King in identifying plots against the crown and helping identify agents of other kings. He is second to none in his skill at espionage, having a devious mind himself. He is a secretive, careful, and very thorough kind of man who likes to work behind the scenes. He can speak French with a variety of dialects and pass as a native. He is also a master of disguise. It is said that his father was a French knight and his mother the young widow of an English merchant.

Henry of Selfield is one of the most successful merchants in England. His ships have been trading at important ports in Europe for 20 years. He is neither a soldier nor a courtier and is not a member of the nobility, but he speaks several languages, including French, and knows the importance of commerce to the future of England. He has been of great help to the King in financing some of his military campaigns.

Lady Jane Selridge is a cousin of the Queen and highly thought of in the English court. She is witty, charming, an excellent hostess, and speaks flawless French. She knows all the intrigues of most of the royal courts of Europe and would offer the added advantage of having access to the talk of the ladies of the court.

Simulation Example #3

What Do We Need in Our Neighborhood?

Type of Simulation: A Speculative Information Simulation, With Many Decisions

Pretend that you are planning a new neighborhood with a shopping center. There is room for only ten businesses in the shopping center, but there are spots for four other businesses at other locations in the neighborhood. It is important to know that you and your family, as well as other people in the neighborhood, may have to travel a long way to get those services and goods not offered in your community. So, be very careful as you choose the 14 different types of goods and services you want. You also want to take care as to where the businesses are located within the community. Be very thoughtful as you place them on the map so that each business is at exactly the right spot. Here is a list of potential businesses:

Auto Supply Store	*Bakery*	*Bank*
Barber Shop	Beauty Salon	Bicycle Shop
Bookstore	Bowling Alley	Candy Store
China Shop	Clothing Store	Convenience Store
Craft Store	Delicatessen	Department Store
Dentist	Doctor's Office	Drug Store
Dry Cleaner	Eye Doctor	Fabric and Sewing Store
Fast-Food Restaurant	Flower Shop	Furniture Store
Garden Supply Store	Grocery Store	Hardware Store and Plant Nursery
Hospital	Ice Cream Store	Jewelry Store
Laundry	Library	Miniature Golf
Music Store	Pet Store	Post Office
Produce Market	Restaurant	Service Station
Shoe Store	Skating Rink	Souvenir Shop
Toy Store	Variety Store	Veterinarian
Video Store	Video Game Arcade	Zoo

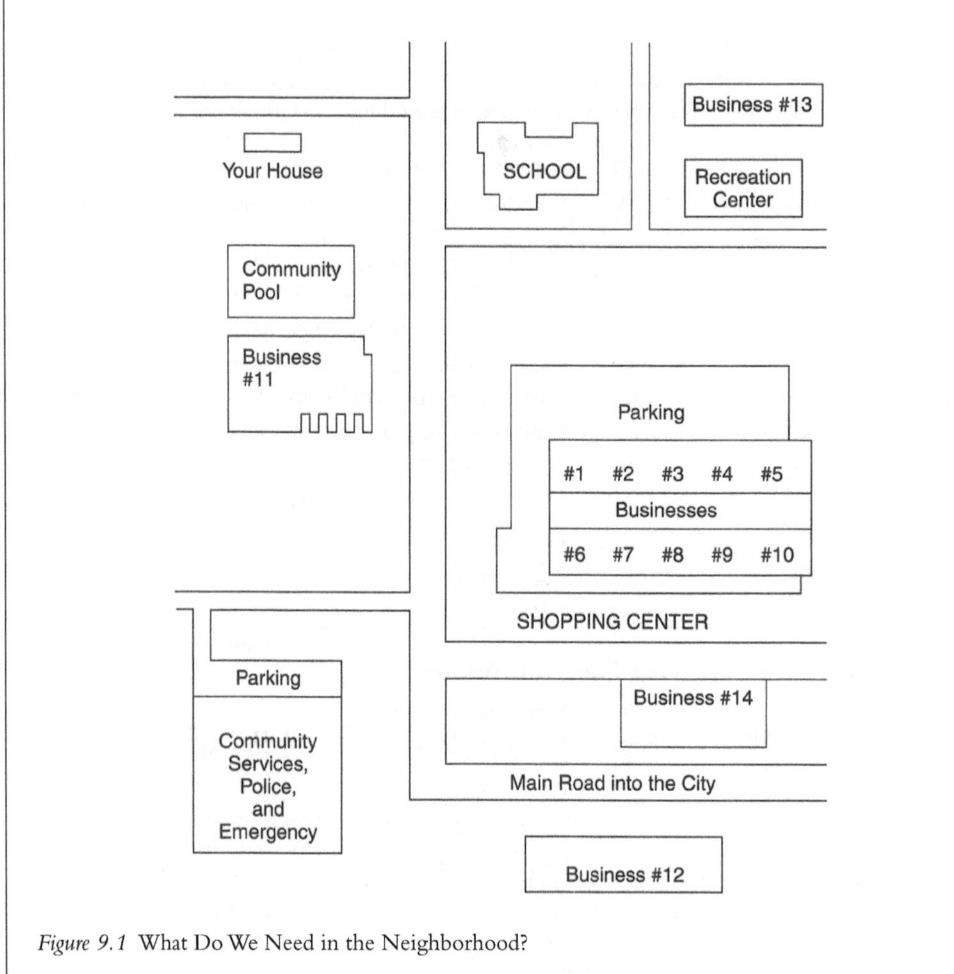

Figure 9.1 What Do We Need in the Neighborhood?

Simulation Example #4

Establishing a Colony

Type of Simulation: An In-Basket Simulation

In-basket simulation games are prioritizing activities. They are based on the notion that, quite often, life choices require us to decide what we must do first and what can be put off or done later. In-basket games begin with a list of activities or jobs that a single individual must do. The central question is, "In what order should these jobs be done?"

You are the leader of a group of colonists who have come to the New World during the seventeenth century. You have sighted the coast and sailed along it for several days, finally dropping anchor in a quiet cove. There is a likely area for a colony just ashore and a small river flows into the sea here. The area does not appear to have any permanent settlements, but you have seen natives peering at your ship from shore. You have no idea whether they are friendly or hostile.

You do not own your ship but have hired the ship along with the services of its crusty old sea captain, who wants to hurry you off his ship so that he can return home to take on other cargos. A number of tasks face you. The following is a list of some of them:

- Send scouting parties to explore the surrounding area to be sure that the best possible site for a colony is chosen.
- Find fresh water to replenish the ship's stores.
- Send a group to try to meet with the natives who have been seen looking out from the shore.
- Hold a meeting of all the colonists to decide on the rules of government for the new colony.
- Land all passengers from the ship.
- Pay the captain what is still owed him for the voyage.
- Draft a letter to the patrons of the colony telling of your safe arrival and suggesting what you will do now.
- Determine your exact location and how far your colony is from other colonies.
- Build a stockade for defense.
- Start building shelters for the colonists.
- Plant crops.
- Send out a hunting party to find fresh meat.
- Unload all supplies.
- Plant the flag of your country on the shore, claiming the land for your sovereign.
- Hold a Thanksgiving celebration.

Simulation Example #5

Nuclear Waste Disposal

Type of Simulation: A Single-Choice Decision Simulation Based on Vested Interest

Set-Up

For this game, you will need a large map of the United States and one of the world. The scenario is that there is a need to dispose of certain waste products from nuclear reactors and other sources. These waste products are radioactive. Students are divided into five groups, one representing the Congressional Committee that will be making the recommendation and the others representing various potential sites. The Congressional Committee and the four area groups meet as groups first to plan strategy. Then the Congressional Committee listens and asks questions while each group makes its case indicating why its area should not be chosen. Then the groups all meet separately again, the Congressional Committee to make its final decision and the area groups to come up with a contingency plan in case their area is the one chosen. This plan may include a set of safety recommendations, recommendations regarding specific site priorities, and some recommendations about how the amount of nuclear waste might be controlled (recycled, etc.).

Group 1: Congressional Committee

The committee is made up of seven members of Congress, one from each of the regions being considered and three from unspecified other areas of the country. A chairperson and a secretary are appointed. The chairperson should be an uncommitted individual. It is the job of the chairperson to keep the hearings flowing smoothly and to present the final recommendations of the Congressional Committee. The four options that the committee is considering are the following:

1. Burial of the waste in sealed containers in a southwestern state that has a small population.
2. Burial of the waste in sealed containers in a southeastern state relatively close to the majority of the facilities producing the waste. There is, of course, danger of spills and contamination whenever radioactive materials are moved.
3. Disposal of the nuclear waste by putting it in sealed waterproof containers that are then taken out to sea and placed on the ocean floor in a specified site, away from major shipping lanes or ocean currents.
4. Disposal in airtight sealed containers at a specific site in a mountainous area in a northwestern state with a low population.

Group 2: Representatives of a Southwestern State

They feel that their state does not get much, if any, benefit from the plants producing the nuclear waste. Neither does it profit from the products, which are largely military in nature. This state is one of the few areas of the country where pollution has not yet become a problem and they wish it to remain that way. They also point out that their state has many Native Americans in it and that putting the waste disposal site there would be yet another blow of oppression and discrimination against that population.

Group 3: Representatives of a Southeastern State

Their state has potential high population growth as part of the Sunbelt. They feel that as a producer of nuclear products for the nation their population is already exposed to enough danger. They also know that their population density already far exceeds that of the two western states.

Group 4: Representatives of a Coastal State

There is great fear in this state that no containers can be designed that can withstand the sea over time. If the waste is disposed of in this manner, it is believed that eventually leakages and seepage will bring about further damage to coastal plant and animal life and pollute the coasts themselves. This area already has one of the biggest pollution problems in the nation.

Group 5: Representatives of a Low-Population Northwestern State

The severe weather of the mountainous region and the difficulty of burying anything in the rocky area make the container problem a serious one. Falling rocks or cold weather could damage a container very quickly, and a nuclear leak problem would then exist. This is a nearly pollution-free area and the people are very independent and wish to stay that way. They also feel that the creation of this waste is not their problem and that the people who benefit from the nuclear energy produced should be the people who have the waste product disposal site.

Mock Trials

The activity of the courtroom offers many possibilities for drama. Because the justice system is so integrally important to understanding democracy and the democratic process, various kinds of dramatic activities can be built around the legal process. This can be useful in helping students understand the Constitution and the legal system as well as the various conflicts and controversies that have been and continue to be important issues. Understanding the legal system seems nearly as important as understanding the democratic process itself and developing the knowledge and attitudes needed to participate. Most people will be involved in the legal system several times in their lives, and the more students learn about the law and the courts and how they operate, the better prepared they will be to deal with these legal encounters throughout life.

By far the most used dramatic activity related to the legal process is the mock trial. Mock trials enable students to reexamine history and to look at questions of right and wrong as they relate to the law and the legal system. Mock trials can take numerous forms and be developed with varying thoroughness and detail, depending on such factors as the teaching purpose, the ability level of the students, and the time available. There are nine forms of mock trials detailed below.

1 *Re-creation of real trials from the past:* An attempt to reenact the trial as it took place. The more thoroughly the topic has been researched and the more preparation that has been done, the more completely this can be accomplished. Because of the court record-keeping system, almost exact reenactments are even possible if desired. Students giving the broad picture of what happened is more likely to be more comprehensible.
2 *Staging trials from the past with open verdicts:* This type of mock trial is like the first in all but one respect: the verdict can be changed. In fact, we want to see if a jury of students is going to come to the same decision that was reached at the original trial. When comparisons are made, the question is always going to be why the verdict was the same or different.
3 *Hypothetical trials of historical and contemporary figures who have never stood trial:* With this type of trial, the students' sense of justice and fairness or even their natural curiosity is served, as well as their biases. Trials of historical characters such as Oswald, Hitler, and Custer have been the subject of speculative movies and novels. The question is, what kind of evidence and testimony might have been given if the figure had gone to trial? Figures from centuries ago, such as Attila the Hun, Brutus, King John of England, Jack the Ripper, or Ivan the Terrible, might be tried. Trials of more recent figures, such as Richard Nixon or Harry Truman (and his decision to use the atom bomb), also give insight.
4 *Creating cases to retest a landmark decision of the Supreme Court:* The emphasis is on discussing the issues and the circumstances of the original case and then attempting through discussion to come up with a parallel case that might cause the Supreme Court to offer a modern opinion.
5 *Trials related to current controversies and issues:* The cases come right out of the newspapers and news broadcasts, and relatives and friends have information and opinions. The issues of current events become relevant and important to young learners as they try to make their own case.
6 *Reenactment of trials suggested in fictional books:* Trials are a popular subject in fiction. Having students develop the detail to enact one of these trials can help comprehension and test their creativity.
7 *Fantasy trials of story and book characters:* Moral themes are almost universal in children's fiction. Putting a fairy tale character like Jack or the Wolf on trial can be a delightful learning experience. The advantage is that students are very familiar with the story line and the characters. The trial gives them a new perspective on the events of the story.
8 *Creation of a new crime scenario and then staging the trial:* This is a creative experience in which students create a crime, a victim, witnesses and clues, and an accused perpetrator of the crime. The teacher can exercise some control by a discussion in which specifications regarding the nature of the crime are carefully drawn.

9 *Development of a classroom court to try discipline offenders:* Several systems, ranging from very simple to very elaborate, may be used to put members of the class on trial for breaking the classroom rules. The major benefit of the exercise is that students develop clearer, more meaningful ideas about such issues as reasonable doubt, the relationship of punishment to crime, and punishment as a deterrent to crime. The technique has been used successfully by teachers as part of their classroom management plan.

Trial-Related Activities

There are various activities that can help students learn about the legal system. Role playing a crime with various witnesses giving independent accounts of what they saw can teach students that people see and remember events differently. Visits to law school mock trials, to one of the mock trial competitive programs put on at the high school, or to an actual courtroom can be real learning experiences if carefully planned. Classroom visits by attorneys, judges, and police officers are also profitable if such guests can relate to students. Students can examine laws and go through the process of debate and enactment of a law. They can also go through structured writing exercises to write trial briefs.

FYI

Always remember to connect the purpose of the field trip to state standards and have an assessment plan for how you will assess student learning once students return from the field trip.

Field Trips

Many of us have participated in a variety of field trips throughout our educational experiences. The experiences and information learned during these adventures often make a meaningful and lasting impact on us (Kenna & Russell, 2015a). A field trip is an experiential activity that "consists of grasping an experience and then transforming it into an application or result" (Behrendt & Franklin, 2014, p. 236).

Whether you went to a local history museum for the day or on overnight field trip to Washington, DC, the experience was unique and often impactful (See Table 9.2 for a list of field trip ideas). Despite these memorable adventures, many educators tend to focus on field trips as rare learning experiences that are expensive and difficult to plan. These issues are compounded in many contemporary schools, where increased pressures to improve standardized test scores and teacher accountability measures have made both teachers and administrators more cautious about spending instructional time outside of the classroom (Kenna & Russell, 2015b). Now more than ever, teachers must purposefully and thoughtfully plan field trips that are engaging and fun but still align with instructional objectives and state standards. Despite these challenges, we maintain that field trips can be powerful and wonderful learning experiences for students, and teachers should spend the time necessary to plan learning experiences outside of the classroom setting. While types and scale of field trips certainly vary in terms of cost and planning (visiting a local history museum

Table 9.2 Possible Field Trip Ideas

Airport	Courthouse	Library
Aquarium	Farm	Memorial
Archeological Dig	Fire Station	Monument
Art Gallery	Harbor or Port	Museum
Battlefield	Health Clinic	Police Station
College or University	Historic Site	Post Office
Congressional Session	Hospital	State or National Park

is quite different from an overnight trip to Washington, DC), the important thing for teachers to remember is that the purpose of the field trip is student learning and it should align to local, state, or national standards.

As with any effective lesson, a successful field trip starts with a detailed plan. Teachers should adhere to the Russell's guide when conducting an effective field trip.

Russell's Guide to Planning and Implementing a Field Trip

Step 1: Instructional Planning

You need to have a clear plan. Establish the purpose and goals of the field trip. The following questions will help you get started.

a Where are you going?
b What is the purpose of the trip?
c What are your instructional goals?
d What subjects are you teaching?
e What standards are you meeting?
f Is this the best way to allow students to meet the standards?
g Are other teachers participating in the field trip?

Step 2: Organizing the Trip

Once you have the instructional component down, you will need to organize the field trip. You will need to do the following:

a Schedule with the site, museum, or location and obtain costs
b Plan transportation to and from the location and obtain costs
c How many chaperones will you need? What is the cost for chaperones?
d Plan for all meals, beverages, rest room breaks, and first aid emergencies

FYI

Will students buy lunch or bring lunch? What about students on free/reduced lunch? You will need to talk with the lunchroom staff. Will other meals than lunch be needed? What about snacks? What about drinks? You have a lot to organize and plan.

a Develop a backup plan. If you plan to eat lunch outside but it rains, you need to have a plan.
b Outline a detailed itinerary accounting for all educational time
c Outline a detailed budget of the field trip costs, along with how the trip will be funded (e.g., each student pays $6)

Step 3: Obtain Administration Permission

Once you have planned and organized the trip, you will need to submit a proposal to your administration for written permission. A typical proposal should include a detailed rationale for the field trip. It should include curriculum standards and academic goals. It should also include a detailed itinerary outlining a minute-by-minute schedule. Plus, you need to have a detailed budget of the field trip and how it will be funded if approved.

FYI

Every school/district has its own procedures and policies regarding field trips. We recommend talking with your administration about the specific protocol you should follow.

Step 4: Obtain Parent/Guardian Permission

Once you have approval from your administration, you are ready to obtain parent/guardian permission. Do not wait until the day/week before the field trip. Start early! Typically, parent/guardian permission will come in the form of a permission slip. Send home a letter to parents explaining the field trip and its value. Include your instructional goals, the purpose of the trip, and the standards you will be meeting. Also include the cost, what students need to provide (e.g., bag lunch or sun screen), and any special instructions. Also, this is the point in the process where you want to solicit parents to be chaperones. Be sure parents complete all required documentation to be considered as a chaperone. Be sure you have received all signed permission slips before you allow a student to go on a field trip.

Step 5: Conducting the Field Trip

This step is where you will go on the field trip. Make sure to account for all students before, during (multiple times), and after the field trip. Develop an accountability system. Whether every student stays with two friends or every student is assigned to a chaperone who constantly monitors a small group, you cannot be too cautious.

While on the field trip, make sure everyone has an itinerary, and try your best to stay on schedule. Be sure to assign certain tasks/duties to chaperones.

FYI

HELPFUL RESOURCES: Existing long-term programs like the American Red Cross (www.redcross.org); Boys and Girls Club of America (www.bgca.org); UNICEF (www.unicef.org).

You also want to clearly explain the students' responsibilities and what they should be doing. Sometimes, students will have a study guide or activity to complete during the field trip.

Assessing the Field Trip Experience

During the field trip, you can continually utilize informal assessment questions to obtain an understanding of the students' experience. If students complete a study guide or activity during the field trip, this can be one way to assess student learning. Additionally, at the end of the field trip or when you return to campus, you can often utilize more formal assessments to measure student learning. Ultimately, as the teacher, you will need to determine the best means to assess student learning. You know your students best; you decide what assessment strategies are needed to meet their individual learning needs.

Service Learning Experiences

Service learning allows students to truly demonstrate character and civic-mindedness. A service learning experience is simply having a student provide some type of service to an individual, group, or community. It is volunteering with the purpose of learning and obtaining something meaningful from the experience. One does not participate in a service learning project to have good karma. Instead, one participates to demonstrate and better understand your role as a citizen and your responsibility to your community and the world (Montgomery et al., 2017). For example, if your school has a problem with litter, maybe you can have your class organize a campus cleanup. This event can be spontaneous or a planned one-time event. These types of events are referred to as short-term service learning projects. However, you can also plan and organize service learning projects for longer terms. For example, you could work with your administration and plan an ongoing campus-wide beautification project. In such a project, each class adopts a section of the school and is responsible to keep it clean and improve the space throughout the school year. These types of events are referred to as long-term service learning projects. Long-term projects can also be more robust service learning projects and can include multiyear agreements or arrangements with an outside agency or partner. For example, you could forge a partnership with a local retirement home that allows your students opportunities to visit and spend time with the elderly multiple times throughout the year. Students can be assigned a resident and the students can build relationships with individuals and assist the residents with games, storytelling, memory keeping, and more.

All service learning projects require that students selflessly serve others in some capacity. The action students take to complete a service learning experience is often either social or political. Social action service learning experiences are projects to help the community or society without changing policy or laws. For example, if the beach or a local body of water is polluted with debris and trash, you may have your students help clean the polluted waters. If this was a political action service learning experience you may have students write letters to city/state officials seeking better enforcement of environmental laws or letters to the local business responsible for polluting the waters. These types of service learning experiences can be both social and political, but they all hope to make a difference, have an impact, and seek to make change. For a list of service learning ideas see Table 9.3.

Looking Back

Social studies teachers who have a strong sense of allowing students to experience social studies in the classroom are going to add suspense and excitement to their teaching. They create a dramatic atmosphere and meaningful experiences, and they give students visions of history, geography, culture, government, and society that are vivid, interesting, and memorable.

Among the many meaningful experiences, drama can help create in social studies instruction are dramatic reading, class action dramas, mock trials, story play, sociodrama, simulations, and role play. Drama can even be the focus of entire units. Even if other forms of drama are not used, certainly

Table 9.3 Possible Service Learning Ideas

- Food drive: This can be short- or long-term service learning experience. It most likely will be a social action project but could easily be adapted to political action if students seek to change policies. For example, students could seek to change the way a state or local government disburses food rations to those in need.
- Volunteer at a retirement home: This can be short- or long-term service learning experience. Most likely this will fall into the category of social action. Students will have the opportunity to learn from the retirees but also to teach them as well. (Fair & Delaplane, 2015).
- Assist at an animal shelter: Assisting at a local animal shelter would be a social action project and could be short- or a long-term service learning experience. However, you could adapt this project to political action if you had students seek to increase the funding for the shelter by contacting local representatives.
- Plan an international relief effort: Most likely this would be a short-term project, but there are existing programs available to teachers that would be considered long-term projects. If a hurricane devastates the coast and your class packs shoeboxes full of toiletries and food, this would be considered a social action service learning project. However, for political action service learning, you may have students write letters to the president of the United States pleading that the area be acknowledged as a disaster zone and federal aid provided.

all teachers and many students can become storytellers and, by doing so, make social studies more memorable and more involving. Dramatic activities of all types become memorable experiences themselves, and those experiences can provide the basis for learning new concepts and information.

Meaningful learning experiences like field trips provide students with unique experiences and memories. They can provide students with up-close and hands-on perspectives of places, people, and events. Like field trips, service learning is meant to provide students with memorable learning experiences. Service learning can provide students with an appreciation of volunteering and a better understanding of their role in the community and the world.

Extension Activity

Scenario

The fourth nine weeks at Yourtown High School (YHS) is off to a fabulous start. Dr. Russell, the YHS principal, stops by your classroom to inform you that he would like you to join his in-service training team. He explains that your role would be to develop and implement in-service training sessions for current teachers at YHS and other schools in the district. Realizing this is truly an honor, you accept. Appreciatively and enthusiastically, Dr. Russell explains that your first task is to share three different sample activities that have students experiencing social studies.

Task

For this activity, you will need to develop three separate original activities.

Activity 1: Develop a lesson that incorporates drama into the social studies classroom.
Activity 2: Plan and organize a field trip. Draft a field trip proposal for your principal. Be sure you plan for all aspects of the trip.
Activity 3: Plan and organize a service learning project.

All activities should be developed for social studies (6–12 grade level and topic of your choice). The activities should be engaging and informative. Share your products and all the required resources necessary to teach the activities with peers and/or the instructor.

Reflective Questions

1 What is a simulation game?
2 What are some basic components of a field trip?
3 What are the three types of mock trials?
4 What is readers' theater?
5 What is service learning?
6 How can service learning be used in the social studies classroom?
7 What are some ways in which a teacher or student can become a better storyteller?

Helpful Resources

Watch this experienced teacher discuss how she utilizes drama in the classroom.
www.youtube.com/watch?v=_c40Zpz0Ltk
Watch this video of how a teacher integrates drama with science and history instruction.
www.teachingchannel.org/videos/enhancing-learning-through-drama
Visit this website and you will find a useful collection of readers' theater scripts.
www.Teachervision.com
Watch this teacher implement a lesson that includes a small role-play experience.
https://youtu.be/Z0HXDYYJSSE?list=PLKrIs—7pqpiHq6kJB5ZIO9vG9V6tKQ8l
Watch an example of a mock trial titled "The State vs. Golden Locks."
https://youtu.be/qw7Z4dLkPko
Watch this video about how one school is utilizing service learning to promote meaningful learning experiences.
www.youtube.com/watch?v=7t30ZMX8uGw

Further Reading

Morris, R. (2010). *The Field Trip Book: Study Travel Experiences in Social Studies*. Charlotte, NC: Information Age Publishing.
This book provides educators with ideas for using field trips in the social studies classroom.

Pogrow, S. (2008). *Teaching Content Outrageously: How to Captivate All Students and Stimulate Learning*. New York, NY: Jossey-Bass.
This book explains how dramatic practices can serve as powerful tools for enlivening lessons and captivating students—even the most resistant learners.

References

Baldwin, P., & Waters, M. (2010). *School Improvement Through Drama: A Creative, Whole Class, Whole School Approach*. Bel Air, CA: Network Continuum Education.

Behrendt, M., & Franklin, T. (2014). A review of research on school field trips and their value in education. *International Journal of Environmental and Science Education*, 9(3), 235–245.

Cole, B., & McGuire, M. (2011). The challenge of a community park: Engaging young children in powerful lessons in democracy. *Social Studies and the Young Learner*, 24, 24–28.

Di Giacomo, R. (2008). *Short Role-Playing Simulations for U.S. History* (5th ed.). San Jose, CA: Magnifico Publications.

Di Giacomo, R. (2011). *Short Role Play Simulations for U.S. History Classrooms* (6th ed.). San Jose, CA: Magnifico Publications.

Fair, C., & Delaplane, E. (2015). It is good spend time with older adults. You can teach them, they can teach you: Second grade students reflect on intergenerational service. *Early Childhood Education Journal*, 43(1), 19–26.

Franklin, C.A. (2009). *Civic Literacy Through Classroom Drama*. Thousand Oaks, CA: Corwin Press.

Fritz, J. (2010). *Who's Saying What in Jamestown, Thomas Savage?* New York, NY: Puffin.

Fulwer, B. E., & McGuire, M. E. (1997). Storypath: Powerful social studies instruction in the primary grades. *Social Studies and the Young Learner*, 9, 4–7.

Hillyard, S. (2011). Introduction to Process Drama Conventions. Available at: https://tesoldrama.files.wordpress.com/2011/01/process-drama-conventions.pdf.

Janudom, R., & Wasanasomsithi, P. (2009). Drama and questioning techniques: Powerful tools for the enhancement of students' speaking abilities and positive attitudes towards EFL Learning. *ESP World Issues*, 8(5), 26.

Kenna, J., & Russell, W. (2015a). Tripping on the core: Utilizing field trips to enhance the common core. *Social Studies Research and Practice*, 10(2), 96–110.

Kenna, J., & Russell, W. (2015b). Elementary teacher's utilization of field trips in an era of accountability: A research study. *Curriculum and Teaching*, 30(1), 51–66.

McCaslin, N. (2006). *Creative Drama in the Classroom and Beyond* (8th ed.). Boston, MA: Allyn and Bacon.

McGuire, M., & Cole, B. (2005). Using storypath to give young learners a fair start. *Social Studies and the Young Learner*, 18(2), 20–23.

Montgomery, S., Miller, W., Foss, P., Tallakson, D., & Howard, M. (2017). Banners for books: "Mighty-hearted" kindergartners take action through arts-based service learning. *Early Childhood Education Journal*, 45(1), 1–14.

Morris, R.V. (2001). Drama and authentic assessment in a social studies classroom. *The Social Studies*, 92(1), 41–44.

Morris, R.V. (2009). *Bringing History to Life*. Lanham, MD: Rowman and Littlefield Education.

Morris, R.V., & Hickey, M.G. (2003). Writing plays for the middle school social studies classroom: A seventh grade case study. *International Journal of Social Education*, 18(1), 52–58.

Palatini, M. (2009). *Lousy, Rotten, Stinkin' Grapes*. New York, NY: Simon & Schuster.

Rice, J.W. (2007). Assessing higher order thinking in video games. *Journal of Technology and Teacher Education*, 15(1), 87–100.

Rijinbout, F. (2003). The unbearable lightness of process drama. *Stage Art*, 15(3), 6–11.

Rosler, B. (2008). Process drama in one fifth grade social studies class. *The Social Studies*, 99(6), 265–272.

Schneider, J.J., Crumpler, T.P., & Rogers, T. (2006). *Process Drama and Multiple Literacies: Addressing Social, Cultural, and Ethical Issues*. Portsmouth, NH: Heinemann.

Service, R., & Harrison, T. (illus.). (2006). *The Cremation of Sam McGee*. Tonawanda, NY: Kids Can Press.

Shotick, J.A., & Walsko, G. (1997). Using children's theater to teach economics. *Social Studies and the Young Learner*, 9(January/February), 11–13.

Stanley, D. (2009). *Mozart: The Wonder Child: A Play in Three Acts*. New York, NY: Collins.

Turner, T.N. (1994). Storytelling: It's never going to be easy. *Tennessee Education*, 24(Spring), 5–10.

Young, C., & Rasinski, T. (2009) Implementing readers theatre as an approach to classroom fluency instruction. *The Reading Teacher*, 63(1), 4–13.

10 Issues-Centered Learning and Decision-Making

Looking Ahead

Social studies helps develop students into effective citizens and helps students better understand the world and the various people in it. With this in mind, a focus of social studies has to be on understanding and discussing issues that cause conflicts in society, decision-making, values, and character development. This chapter focuses on the social studies teacher's role in issues-centered learning, the decision-making process, the development of values, and the cultivation of positive character development for the purposes of helping students become good citizens. While many of these topics, such as issues-centered learning, values education, and character education, will always be controversial, the necessity of effective democratic values and character education elements in the social studies program cannot be denied. Teachers want students to develop high moral character, and society expects teachers to be active agents in this process. We want children to grow in what is sometimes called "civic virtue," which is the central element of good citizenship. Both high moral character and civic virtue require strong positive values and attitudes. Civic virtue focuses on a commitment to democratic principles and values that manifest themselves in the everyday lives of citizens (NCSS, 1997).

Character education and values education are not quite the same. Character education is a broad, overreaching phenomena aimed at developing a personal code of behavior based on doing what is right rather than serving one's own self-interests. That code predisposes how an individual will act in any situation. Character education does involve developing a values system, though character is based on a values system.

FYI

Can someone be a "good citizen" without being a "good person"?

The word *value* may be defined in various ways. Value can be used to refer to the relative worth of a person, material goods, services, or ideas. Value education refers to what is important in life. Our values are the principles or standards of quality we use in making decisions. Our values shape our attitudes toward actions, people, and things. They also direct our aspirations and ambitions. Middle and secondary social studies teachers need an understanding of the ways that personal values are shaped during the middle and high school years. It is equally important that we think about our own roles and responsibilities in this process.

Character, values, and attitudes are critical attributes of school success or failure (Berkowitz & Bier, 2005). They influence whether students do their work and how well they do it, how students behave in any setting, and interpersonal relationships. Teachers deal with these values constantly. They want students to feel positive toward school; to strive to do their best work; to have certain

DOI: 10.4324/9781003217060-10

kinds of ambitions for themselves; to be fair and friendly in dealing with other students; and to be honest, industrious, loyal, and so on. However, there is a delicate balance between values and ways of teaching and dealing with values that are acceptable and appropriate and those that are not. In American public schools, for example, it is inappropriate to teach religious values or to advocate a religion, but religious values are not the only ones that are inappropriate. There is a point at which dealing with political situations or teaching about loving one's country becomes indoctrination. There is even a point when teaching what are thought of as family values may be in conflict with what is taught at home.

This chapter focuses on issues-centered learning, decision-making, values, and character education as a means to meet the "good citizen" requirement associated with middle and high school social studies. Additionally, this chapter will show how all of the aforementioned topics can be effectively utilized to actively engage students in meaningful discussions and reflections by examining controversial, values-laden issues to help students better understand the world and how to be responsible citizens in a democratic society.

Can You? Do You?

Can you ...

- explain why issues-centered learning is important for today's schools?
- describe your own values and tell how they were formed?
- identify or describe some specific decision-making skills?
- think of some activities in which students could have experiences in determining alternatives?

Do you ...

- know and understand the meaning of issues-centered learning?
- know what values to teach?
- understand why it may be necessary to deal with values related to living in a pluralistic society in school?
- understand different ways of teaching about values?

Focus Activity

Before reading this chapter, try the focus activity below.

Think back about your middle and high school experience. What were the controversial issues being discussed at that time? Did your teachers ever discuss these topics in class? Share experiences with classmates. Now consider your role as a future social studies teacher. What topics do you think are inappropriate to discuss with secondary students? What topics do you personally feel uncomfortable discussing with secondary students? Make a list of potential topics that fall under the two aforementioned categories. Share your lists with classmates and discuss why you believe certain topics to be inappropriate and/or uncomfortable to address with secondary students.

Issues-Centered Learning

Issues-centered learning is one of the oldest and most controversial topics in the field of social studies education. Based on the very important *1916 Report* discussed in Chapter 2, the goal of social studies as a course of study in public schools has long been the development of good citizens. While most social studies educators tend to agree with this goal, there has been and continues to be a great deal of debate regarding the best method for meeting the "good citizen" requirement. Issues-centered learning is one of the approaches developed to meet the "good citizen" goal that has demonstrated remarkable staying power in the field of social studies. Although never fully implemented into the curriculum for any extended period of time, issues-centered learning has historically been a very popular topic for social studies educators to revisit in an effort to make the classroom experience more authentic and democratic. Issues-centered learning can be considered both a pedagogical and curricular approach to teaching social studies. At its core, issues-centered learning focuses on important and meaningful social issues (poverty, injustice, discrimination, civil rights, equity, etc.) that students explore in an effort to better understand the world as well as their own roles and responsibilities as democratic citizens. The purpose of issues-centered education is not just to raise questions and expose students to them but also to teach students to offer defensible and intellectually well-grounded answers to those questions.

One of the most powerful arguments for the inclusion of issues-centered learning is its focus on active learning and student involvement, which is deeply grounded in constructivist learning theory. In the issues-centered learning approach, students are not simply trying to produce right answers; they are encouraged to explore complex problems from a variety of viewpoints and justify their positions or beliefs. Central to this approach is the notion that complex social issues often do not have simple right or wrong answers because we live in a multicultural, pluralistic society of many different values. The importance of issues-centered learning activities then becomes helping the students of today better understand and deal with the enduring problems of the adult world we are preparing them for as participatory democratic citizens. Evans et al. (1996) identified the following four essential principles of issues-centered learning:

1 The in-depth treatment of issues is more important than the broad, superficial exposure of topics.
2 Issues must somehow connect to one another through some historical or thematic structure.
3 The study of issues must draw upon challenging content that encourages students to engage in forms of reasoning and evidence-based decision-making.
4 Students are to experience some degree of control in the inquiry process.

FYI

Teachers can lose their jobs for handling these topics and activities inappropriately, so always prepare purposeful lessons and get parental and administrative approval if necessary.

For secondary teachers, the selection of appropriate social issues and the development of guiding discussion questions is often a major obstacle to classroom implementation. Teachers may question which topics are appropriate to discuss, at what length, and how such activities can be implemented into a contemporary social studies classroom that features significant time limitations and a focus on broad coverage of subject matter. First and foremost, we recommend that secondary teachers consider the following criteria carefully when selecting issues-centered content:

1 Relevance
   - Does the content relate to the students and the social context in which they find themselves?
   - Does the content relate to students in and out of school?

2 Reflection
   - Does the content trigger thinking?
   - Does the content engage the students in taking positions that can be explicitly grounded?
3 Action
   - Will the critical and systematic analysis of content produce action?
4 Practicality
   - Is the emerging content or program of studies usable?
5 Depth of understanding
   - Does the content promote or hinder reflection on perennial or persistent problems of humankind?

FYI

This is a fundamental step of effective teaching in the C3 Framework and the NCSS National Standards for the Preparation of Social Studies Teachers.

Another of the great aspects to issues-centered learning is the fact that it can be implemented in all social science content areas and addressed in an interdisciplinary effort. Meaning, to truly understand a historical or contemporary social issue, students will need to consider a multitude of political, social, economic, and cultural factors. The following list provides a few brief examples of the types of social questions that could be used to facilitate issues-centered learning activities. Consider how these topics could be relevant in different social science content areas.

- Human Rights
  - When, if ever, should one country enter into the internal affairs of another country?
  - What are the basic human rights and liberties that all people should have, and what happens when these rights are violated (or non-existent)?
  - Do we, as members of a global community, have a responsibility to fight injustice? How could this be done?
- Race and Ethnicity
  - What impact does race and ethnicity have on our lives?
  - Are quotas and affirmative action good ideas?
  - Are we responsible for the sins of the past?
- Gender and Sexuality in American Life
  - To what extent have we achieved gender equality?
  - How should we address heterosexism and homophobia in school and society?
  - How does the role of gender in our lives change over time?

FYI

Consider how the recent #Me Too movement can and should be addressed in the social studies classroom.

- Power in America
  - Who rules America? Is there a power elite? Can this change?
  - How and to what extent is power shared?
  - How could we alter and reform the power structure in the United States?

Approaches to Issues-Centered Instruction

After deciding what issues are relevant, engaging, and appropriate for classroom discussion and analysis, teachers will need to begin considering how exactly to implement issues-centered learning. To be sure, there are a variety of pedagogical approaches that teachers could utilize to address issues-centered learning. While there is no one "best" way to present this information, there are several approaches that we have found to be effective when planning and implementing issues-centered learning activities. The following list of instructional methods will be briefly explained and examples of how these approaches could be utilized for the purposes of issues-centered learning will be provided.

Case Studies

The use of case studies is probably one of the most popular approaches in any secondary classroom, but especially for social studies. A case study is generally a written (although it can be presented verbally or visually) account describing or explaining a particular event, person, or scenario. This account can be fiction or nonfiction and address historical or contemporary situations. The purpose of presenting students with a case study is to help them become active agents in their learning by requiring them to think critically and logically about a scenario that, typically, will have more than one possible outcome. Since a case study will not provide students with all of the necessary information to solve the problem being presented, students will have to begin developing skills that allow them to think clearly about unstructured, ambiguous situations. The lack of structure and clear-cut "right" answers inherent in case studies gives students an opportunity to grapple with important issues in a real-world context that pushes them to make their own decisions based on information provided or, sometimes more importantly, information not provided. While there are numerous types of case studies, the following are the most prominent types of case studies utilized in the social studies classroom:

- *Sequential Case Study*: narrative and background information is given out in installments so information cause change over time.
- *Research Case Study*: students are expected to research and gather information before making a decision.
- *Live/Current Case Study*: based on ongoing events; students are asked to make decisions while the real decision-makers are doing the same. The case could be a current court case in the local news or a national event.
- *Historical Case Study*: can be drawn from history and may or may not be disguised, depending on students' prior knowledge.
- *Social Issues Case Studies*: lend themselves to policy decisions and lawmaking cases. The issues that led to the implementation of mandatory sentences for criminals with multiple crimes (the "three strikes and you're out" policy) could be presented, and students could be asked to craft a policy other than mandatory sentencing to address the issue (General Procedures for Case Studies, n.d.).

After deciding on an issue and what type of case study will be most effective, teachers will need to consider what approach should be used to implement the case study. There are two main approaches to case studies that teachers often use: the open-ended approach and the closed-ended approach. An open-ended case study is one in which the teacher has not previously decided what knowledge or conclusion students are to gain. Teachers using this approach must be willing to entertain whatever conclusions or suggestions students provide. Obviously, the open-ended approach can be very risky since students will be given a tremendous amount of freedom to analyze the case study as they see fit. For that reason, teachers should always be extremely careful when utilizing an open-ended case study and consider the risks versus the rewards in doing so. The second, and more common, approach is the closed-ended case study. This approach is typically more practical because the teacher, with varying degrees of subtlety, will direct or prompt the students to reach a desired outcome or decision. While the closed-ended approach involves more teacher involvement, it does not call for the teacher to make decisions for the students. Rather, teachers should monitor the analysis process closely and offer questions when needed to help students stay on track and headed in the right direction. Typical procedures for implementing an open- or closed-ended case study will resemble something like the following:

1 *Introduction*: sets the case study in the context of what is being studied with a focus on students and establishing a purpose.
2 *Learning Experience (case study distributed)*: students examine the case study (either individually or in a group) with key questions being posed; involves active participation with students explaining and analyzing information.
3 *Comprehension Development*: students synthesize and evaluate the information with discussion between students and/or with the teacher.
4 *Reinforcement/Extension*: students transfer the learning to the topic in general with a teacher-led discussion (General Procedures for Lessons, n.d.).

Box 10.1 Issues-Centered Case Study Example

A high school history teacher is teaching a unit on WWII. Leading up to the end of the war, students begin posing a lot of questions about the atomic bomb and the devastation caused to Hiroshima and Nagasaki. There is much debate about this controversial decision that ignites some heated discussion. In an effort to build on this interest, the teacher decides to put students into cooperative groups and implement an open-ended historical case study to examine whether or not the United States should have in fact dropped an atomic bomb. Groups are provided with a variety of primary and secondary sources from multiple perspectives (U.S., Japanese, government officials, scientists, citizens, etc.) and they must analyze all of these sources and decide as a group if dropping an atomic bomb is the best plan of action. All groups must rationalize, explain, and justify their decision, while also refuting alternative plans of action based on evidence provided. After all groups have presented, discuss as a class the decisions made and what factors went into their final plan of action. How would this process be similar to what President Truman faced and why is it crucial to consider multiple perspectives and factors when making complex decisions?

Inquiry Learning

Inquiry-based learning is a type of instruction that transcends content area and grade level because it focuses on instilling an intrinsic desire to learn. The goal of inquiry teaching is to help students discover new knowledge and incorporate that knowledge into their daily lives. Inquiry learning is focused on the process in which one builds and constructs knowledge. This approach differs from many traditional methods because the focus is not on an end product or a "right answer," as often times there are not simple right or wrong answers. Rather, inquiry learning is about engaging with the decision-making process to practice developing realistic skills in analyzing information for the purpose of formulating rational and justifiable solutions to the problems at hand. When presenting material in this way, teachers need to play a supportive role and realize that the focus is on the students and their decision-making. Teachers should also remind students that there are often multiple solutions to problems, and justification of decision-making is key to helping others understand your perspective. The following are the typical procedures a teacher would use when implementing inquiry-based lessons for issues-centered learning.

Inductive Model
A question is raised and stated clearly.
A tentative answer is developed.
Evidence bearing on the tentative answer is gathered.
A conclusion is drawn from the evidence.
The conclusion is applied to the original questions and to subsequent similar questions.

Alternative Inductive Model
A question is raised.
Evidence is sought and evaluated.
A proposition, or general rule, is inferred from particular evidence.
The question is tested against the proposition or rule.
In future situations, the proposition or rule is tested against new evidence.

Deductive Model
A question is raised.
A known general rule is stated.
An answer is inferred from the general rule.
Evidence of the accuracy of the answer is sought.
Evidence is used to confirm the answer and the general rule.

Historical Model
Raising a question
Researching the source
Interpreting the evidence
Presenting the findings

Problem-Solving Model
Feeling of confusion or doubt
Recognizing and defining problems
Analyzing the problem and formulating hypotheses
Gathering evidence
Verifying and interpreting evidence
Formulating and accepting conclusions
Applying conclusions

Survey Model
Pose problem
Construct hypothesis
Construct sample pool, conduct survey
Draw conclusion/report conclusion

(General Procedures for Lessons, n.d.)

Moral Reasoning

Moral reasoning is based on research from Lawrence Kohlberg (1984, 1985). In this approach the goal is to advance the quality of student reasoning about ethical dilemmas. Moral reasoning proposes that students' reasoning becomes less self-centered and more attuned to the well-being of society as they age and mature. Kohlberg believed that students could advance through the different stages of moral development by examining various moral dilemmas to make tough decisions and then be able to rationalize or defend those choices. The five steps in this approach are:

FYI

If decision-making is the heart of social studies, then exploring morals, values, and belief systems must also be included in the curriculum.

Defining and clarifying the dilemma
Taking a tentative position on the dilemma
Dividing students into small groups to discuss the dilemma
Conducting a class discussion that defends, challenges, and probes for reasoning
Extending the reasoning to the larger moral question raised by the dilemma.

(General Procedures for Lessons, n.d.)

Public Issues

This methodology fits naturally and comfortably with issues-centered learning because the two are closely related. Analyzing public issues is a pedagogical method that focuses on the discussion processes by examining public issues that are often controversial because of the varying value systems present in a multicultural, pluralistic society. The overall objective of this approach is to train students to examine and analyze, through discussion and argument, the kinds of disputes that give birth to social conflict. Teachers will act as moderators and facilitators of classroom discussions, remembering that the emphasis is on continuing dialogue and expanding the students' perspectives. Since topics addressed will be controversial by nature, it is crucial that teachers remain non-judgmental of student responses, so long as the student can justify his or her opinions and beliefs (see Boxes 10.2 and 10.3).

Types of public issues questions include:

- Public Policy: a question involving a choice or a decision for action by citizens or officials in affairs that concern a government or community
  - Should Mr. Johnson be punished for his actions?
- Moral Value Issues: suggest that some object, person, or conduct is "good" or "bad"
  - Is racism wrong?
- Definitional Issues: revolve around the way important words or phrases are used in a discussion
  - What is the meaning of "racism," "personal rights," and "equal opportunity?"
- Factual Issues: disagreements about the descriptions or explanation of events
  - If Mr. Johnson were punished, would it prevent future problems?
  - Would a lighter punishment cause others to respect or disrespect Mr. Johnson and others more?

Box 10.2 Issues-Centered Moral Reasoning Example

You are an accountant at a large corporation and discover that someone is stealing from the company. Upon further investigation, you realize that the missing money has been taken by one of your coworkers, who happens to be your best friend. After approaching your friend about the situation, your friend immediately begins begging for your silence and offers to cut you in on the plan. Your friend tells you that the payday is worth millions and is nearly undetectable by the corporation's security software. What would you do? Would it make a difference if the company were a small struggling business with an owner who really cared about employees?

Box 10.3 Public Issues Scenario

The following is an example of a public issue scenario and the types of questions a secondary social studies teacher could use to facilitate a class discussion.

Mr. Johnson's Rooming House

Mr. Johnson is a retired war veteran living in a rural community in the South on the outskirts of a major city. Mr. Johnson has struggled to make a living since he came back from the war more than thirty years ago. While his pension provides some living expenses, Mr. Johnson relies mostly on the small rooming house he operates for money. Recently, the state passed a law that prohibited discrimination on the basis of race, religion or nationality in the renting of rooms. This upset Mr. Johnson because he was a firm believer that he should have the right to do whatever he pleases with his property and he really did not care much for members of minority groups.

Mr. Johnson felt that if he rented rooms to minorities that his regular boarders might get angry and move out. Additionally, he worried that if he allowed minorities into his boarding house that they may steal his personal belongings. "It's my property," he told his neighbors, "and no one has the right to tell me whom I must allow to sleep in my house."

One night, Mr. Johnson was disturbed at dinner by the ring of his doorbell. "An individual to occupy my vacant room," he thought happily. When he opened the door he saw a well-groomed Middle Eastern man. "My name is Mr. Patel. I've looked all over town and cannot find a reasonably price place to stay. Do you have a vacant room?' he asked. Mr. Johnson hesitated. "No, sorry we're full."

Adapted from the Harvard Social Studies Project, 1967

- Prescriptive Issues: things that should or ought to be done; in other words, judgments concerned with legitimacy and the rightness or wrongness of actions and policy. We could further classify prescriptive issues in such categories as:
  - Personal conviction and conscience (what should Mr. Johnson do or what would you do in his situation?)
  - Public policy (should the government do anything to regulate the renting practices of Mr. Johnson?)
  - Ethics (which value is more important: the owner's rights of "private property" or the tenant's right to "equal opportunity"?)
  - Law (is it "unconstitutional" to prohibit discrimination by law?)
- Descriptive Issues: focus on problems of fact, describing people's behavior in the past, present, or future; interpreting what the world is actually like; and explaining why circumstances occur
  - Were there other places for Mr. Patel to stay?
  - Was Mr. Johnson prejudiced?
  - Would refusing Mr. Patel a place to stay affect his future adversely or hurt him in any way?

Descriptive claims are generally used to explain why an event has happened or will happen. We could further classify descriptive issues in such categories as:

- Casual claims (Mr. Johnson is prejudiced because he is from the South)
- Associative claims (Southerners tend to be more racist than Northerners)
- Interpretive or speculative claims (it's against human nature to mix races; allowing people to stick with their own kind gives them a sense of security and belonging)

Values Clarification

In 1966, Louis E. Raths, Merrill Harmin, and Sydney B. Simon published their book entitled *Values and Teaching* (1966). The dominant premise of this book centered on an instructional method known as values clarification. Values clarification is a method that encourages students to formulate their own values through thoughtful analysis and reflection. However, this method has endured a fair amount of criticism over the years, mostly because values clarification assumes that all students are inherently "good" and that these morals would be revealed during well-planned scenarios and exercises. Opponents of values clarification consistently question how this method would account for negative values that may be justified by students during this process, such as lying, cheating, abuse of power, etc. Many of these claims are warranted, and proponents of the values clarification model have had difficulty addressing some of the fundamental flaws of this theory. Nevertheless, this method is still relevant and related to issues-centered learning because the focus is on creating an environment where students can openly and freely discuss value-related choices and alternatives. The following are two types of procedures secondary teachers should follow when utilizing values clarification instruction for issues-centered learning.

1 Value Integration:
   - Introduce the value (the activity)
   - Teacher explores and clarifies the value with the students (short discussion)
   - Students develop and explore the value in relation to themselves (usually done in small groups of three to four students)
   - Value is summarized (students present their findings and what the value/issue means to them)
2 Value Analysis (adapted from General Procedures for Lessons, n.d.):
   - Introduce the value (give an example, comment, etc. to gain students' attention)
   - Explore various value alternatives (brainstorm different ways to handle/solve the problem or value)
   - Brainstorm the positive and negative effects of each choice (can be done as group or individually)
   - Each student or group makes a value alternative choice
   - Students or groups defend their choices

Problems with Issues-Centered Learning

As with any approach to teaching and learning social studies, issues-centered learning does have some problems that make it difficult to implement in the classroom. First, schools are not generally innovative, proactive institutions. This is evident in the lack of curriculum change in many content areas, but especially social studies. The scope and sequence of most social studies courses has remained the same for almost a century, with the exploration of related topics coming in chronological order and a curriculum based largely on textbooks. Second, teachers are not always comfortable relinquishing the responsibility and control necessary for issues-centered learning to take place. This hesitation is completely understandable in the current educational climate with its heavy emphasis on classroom management and teacher accountability to content standards. Finally, an obstacle to issues-centered learning is high-stakes testing and the prominence of content facts being assessed as knowledge. Teachers are expected to produce good test scores, and many contemporary assessments place a premium on the memorization and recollection of various names, dates, events, and terms associated with a particular field. Testing students on this type of information certainly makes it more difficult for social studies educators to focus on more worldly skills such as reasoning, analyzing, evaluating, debating, and decision-making. However, as we mentioned earlier in this chapter, the goal of social studies has long been the development of good citizens. Therefore, we encourage secondary teachers to stay true to this objective and consider how issues-centered learning and decision-making activities can play a pivotal role in helping students understand their functions and responsibilities as democratic citizens.

Decision-Making Skills in Relation to Values

One goal of social studies education is to develop students' abilities to make decisions based on democratic principles and sound moral values. There is nothing new about this. It was implicit in the education of young Roman citizens in the ancient Roman Republic. In modern times, generations of social studies teachers have praised and quoted Shirley Engle's eloquent advocacy of the belief that decision-making is the heart of the social studies (Engle, 1960). Making decisions involves value judgment calls. Engle pointed out that evaluation skills are needed throughout life. People constantly have to decide not only what is the right thing to do, but also what is the best thing to do, what they want to do, and what they have to do. Evaluation skills are always difficult because of dilemmas and conflicts and because there is often doubt about evaluative criteria and questions such as relevance, truth and accuracy, suitability, importance, utility, greatness, potential, goodness, beauty, quality, effort, or even quantity.

We make judgments and decisions on the basis of what we hold to be important, sensible, good, and worthwhile. However, the essential evaluation skills that teachers need to develop in students build from awareness and reasoning. To develop this awareness, students need to be given frequent and significant opportunities to make decisions. They need to learn how and when to question what they see and hear. Teachers need to model how such decisions are made.

Students need to learn to determine when and how they should make decisions. They need to be able to distinguish between different kinds of situations requiring decisions. Although many secondary educators may consider these types of activities and procedures to be for younger learners, it is important to remember that not all middle and high school students have mastered the decision-making process. The middle and high school years are critically important for students because they begin to mature into young adults and the decisions and choices they make often have substantial influence on their futures. Social studies teachers have a responsibility to help students better understand their place in the world and how the decisions they make impact themselves as well as other people in society. Below are seven different situations a student may encounter that require decision-making:

1 Sometimes decisions have to be made on the basis of some single criterion, and sometimes it is necessary to weigh and consider several criteria.
2 Sometimes the difference between right and wrong is clear-cut, but more often the decision is not so clear.
3 Some decisions have to be made with only partial information.
4 Some judgment calls are easy and some are difficult because of conflicts in how we feel.
5 Often we have to make holistic judgments based on experience.
6 Some decisions are made on a purely personal basis, solely on what serves one's own ends, personal ambitions, or feelings and emotions.
7 Some decisions should be made altruistically with the good of one's self sacrificed for the good of others or of the group.

Values are involved in determining what alternatives are actually available (what the options actually are) in a given decision-making situation. Values also are the basis for making choices among the available alternatives:

- What course of action should be pursued?
- What solution is the best "fit" to existing conditions?
- What alternative offers the most advantages or fewest disadvantages?
- Which choice is most dangerous or most safe?

Values even influence how we deal with evidence (distinguishing fact from speculation, conclusion from opinion, fantasy from reality, truth from falsehood, etc.), determining relevance, determining adequacy of evidence, projecting a trend, and making personal decisions or a determination of ultimate courses to take (e.g., defining justice or morality in a particular situation). Helping students become more responsible as well as more effective problem solvers requires providing experience and practice that help develop evaluation skills. The following are evaluation skills and examples of each.

1 Determining Alternatives
   - On a map, have students determine alternative routes to a single location or alternative destinations that will fill a particular need for the crew of a ship (political safety during a war, water before the crew dies of thirst, etc.).
   - Have students hold class contests over topics such as a favorite historical character, favorite book, ideal vacation spot, best place to live, and so on. Have a nomination process and then choose advocates.
   - Have students nominate possible sites for real and hypothetical projects, field trips, and so on.
   - Have students suggest menus, ingredients, activities, etc., for social events and cultural celebrations.
   - Do brainstorming activities where students have a specific number of responses to something (e.g., ten best reasons for, ways to interpret music through movement, etc.).
   - Include nominating (favorite, best, etc.) as a regular part of daily activities.
   - As students read about people's actions, stop and ask what else these people could have done that would have demonstrated honesty, honor, caring, etc.

2 Choosing Among Alternatives
   - Give students alternatives from which to choose as a regular activity. These can be very real decisions that have an impact on them and what they do. Help them to understand the consequences and the implications of particular choices.
   - Talk about the reasonableness of different explanations and theories. Include the alternatives available to different people in history, the school, the home, and their possible reasoning in making the decision.
   - Give three or four alternative titles for stories or movies and let students choose among them and explain their reasoning.
   - Have students vote for favorites among short series stories, television shows, movies, and so on.
   - In studying history and geography, give students real or made-up biographies of several different people. Then have them choose the best person for such things as an Arctic expedition, a safari, a rescue mission, a delegation to take a particular message to the president, and so on.

3 Distinguishing Fact From Speculation, Conclusion From Opinion, Fantasy From Reality, and Truth From Falsehood
   - Give students a series of statements and let them try to identify which statements are fact and which are opinion.
   - Give students a series of untrue statements about a topic they have been studying, and have them tell why the statements are untrue.
   - Have students identify fantastic elements in stories, television shows, movies, and so on.
   - Show a picture and let the students make a series of statements about the picture. As each statement is made, have the other students determine if the statement is actually true or if it is speculation, conclusion, or opinion.

4 Determining Relevance
   - Give students a statement that makes an assertion or hypothesis. Then present them with a series of other statements of fact and opinion. With each of these, have the students decide if the statement is relevant.

- Write a question on the board. Have students scan a paragraph and volunteer to read any statements that are relevant to the question.
- Give students a proverb, truism, or superstition. Follow it with a collection of action statements and facts. Let the students classify the actions and facts as relevant or not. They should be able to reach the conclusion that a fact may be relevant and supportive without proving the original statement to be true.

5 Determining the Adequacy of Evidence
- Give students a series of arguments or reasons and then ask them to judge if a case has been made.
- Give students a series of "If A and B, then C" statements. Have them determine which ones they accept and which ones they do not.
- Give students a series of assertions. Ask them to tell what it would take by way of evidence for them to accept the truth of each one.
- Tell students a preposterous story about a well-known historical person. Make it so far-fetched that they cannot believe it. When they start expressing their disbelief, have them try to tell why they do not believe it. An example of a preposterous story could include the teacher explaining to students that it was not George Washington but an exact look-alike who turned up at Mount Vernon and the look-alike actually became the first president.

6 Projecting a Trend
- Give students a series of events and have them predict the event(s) that will follow.
- Describe a series of events and have students give the trend a name.
- Have students do a relevance web showing the connections among events that make the series of events a trend.

7 Defining Justice for Particular Instances
- Read stories with a moral purpose and let students verbalize their own views of the "moral of the story."
- Provide a series of open-ended scenarios and problems and ask students to tell what they think would be the right thing to do in these situations.
- Read some examples of actions of courts and governments and ask students to decide if the action taken was fair.

What Values Do You Teach?

The place of values in the classroom is controversial. Whether teachers should teach values is not really the point. Nearly everyone concedes that teachers have to deal with values in some form or capacity, whether it is implicitly or explicitly in the social studies curriculum. Opinions differ, though, about what values should be taught and how we should teach them. Teaching a particular religious or political viewpoint, how to vote in an election, or what constitutes acceptable reading or entertainment are certainly questionable. There are, however, at least three areas where it seems important that secondary schools take an active and effective role in developing students' beliefs. These are:

1 Values related to living in a democracy
2 Values implicit within a multicultural society
3 Values that relate to school success and to the functional classroom.

The main purpose of social studies is to help students develop as good citizens. To this end, there are a variety of different topics and subfields of social studies that propose a plethora of approaches. Democratic education, citizenship education, multicultural education, social justice education, and character education are a few examples of subfields associated with developing good citizens. However, character education is mandated as part of the K–12 school curriculum and continues to rise in discussions about middle and high school reforms. Character education programs are designed to be school-wide initiatives, but many states are going a step further and beginning to include character education initiatives into content standards. Social studies is a natural field for the combining of these goals. Character education is at least implied in the goal of civic virtue. While few would take issue with the importance of good citizenship or the development of character, there is controversy over what these terms mean and about the methods that can and should be used.

Emotional charges of indoctrination can be levied easily, and words such as *nationalism* can be intoned with either positive or negative meanings. Though a broad spectrum of viewpoints exists, there seem to be at least six areas of values where teachers need to work in order for democracy to continue to exist:

1 The need for participation
2 The worth of and rights of the individual
3 The rule of the majority and the rights of the minority
4 Personal responsibility
5 Respect for law and authority and for other people
6 Equality and justice.

The goals of character education in relation to these values can be developed in a number of ways. Developing classrooms that are moral communities, where fairness, trust, caring, and taking responsibility are both expectations and norms for all students.

History is an important part of the development of these values and intrinsic to character education. Classrooms that are themselves moral communities should promote greater awareness in students of what has happened in the past and what is happening now related to their own country and others. Knowledge of the reasons that governments exist, the principles and purposes upon which they were founded, and the events leading up to their present state is essential for understanding the present and preparing for the future. Looking at the founding of this country and others and studying history in general, of course, are part of an established educational tradition. However, to build democratic values, an active learning approach is needed. Students can be given responsibility, make decisions, and develop their own views in relation to what has happened in the past. Teachers can hold mock elections and mock trials, and they can use opinionnaires and polls in the classroom. They can set up classroom governments and look at questions of human rights and individual and corporate responsibility in current events. Even playing games and sports can become occasions to talk about the importance of rules, personal responsibility, and concern for the rights of others. Things that teachers do to help individuals gain acceptance, success, and confidence are all an important part of citizenship education in a democracy.

Values Implicit Within a Multicultural Society

Multicultural education is a definitive attempt to make students more aware of the distinguishing differences and unifying similarities among various cultures and ethnic groups in the world. It is not simply education of a particular nature designed for minority groups. Part of its outcome should be helping students to value themselves and others. Multicultural education is directly tied to our democratic values, the principle of equality, the pluralistic nature of our society, and the concept of the global village. Multicultural education is aimed at the eradication of racism, classism, discrimination, sexism, prejudice, and ethnocentrism.

FYI

It is much easier to teach about values than it is to teach values.

There are many reasons for moving to greater emphasis on multicultural education in social studies. Among them are the following ideas:

- We live in a pluralistic society, a global village.
- Almost without exception, cultural groups have a history of prejudice and discrimination.
- There is a natural tendency among human beings to distrust people who are different and to hold them at arm's length.
- It is generally believed that the more people know about another culture, the more positive they will feel about it.
- Women, ethnic groups, racial groups, and numerous cultures have been largely ignored or misrepresented in curriculum materials in the past and present.

Multicultural education works on several basic assumptions and beliefs. For example, there are some generally held beliefs about the nature of various cultural, ethnic, and racial groups in the world. One of them is that members of every cultural and ethnic group have been and are productive and resourceful and, therefore, have made substantial contributions to world civilizations. Another is that no sex and no race or cultural or ethnic group is innately superior or inferior to any other. Such assumptions become important teachings in multicultural education, as do assumptions about people. The latter include the belief that historic injustices and discrimination are not reasons for present personal guilt or retribution and neither are they cause for the continuation of prejudice into the future. An important realization that is part of this assumption system is that everyone has prejudices and biases.

Finally, multicultural education is based on some major educational assumptions. The chief among these is that ethnocentrism, racism, and provincialism are going to continue to thrive without the kind of strong positive effort of multicultural education. These assumptions have led to the development of a variety of goals for multicultural education. Typical of such goals is the following set. Students will develop:

- understanding of cultural diversity within our society and diversity within culture groups;
- the ability to communicate with other culture groups both to resolve conflict and to improve relationships;
- attitudes, values, and behaviors that are supportive of ethnic and cultural diversity;
- pride in their cultural heritage;
- knowledge, appreciation, and understanding of other cultures both in this country and throughout the world;
- a sense of the history of both their own culture and those of others.

The most significant tool of multicultural education is knowledge. Knowing about one's own and other cultures, viewing others through undistorted pictures of their strengths and accomplishments, is essential to appreciation. Naturally, it follows that increased positive, mutually beneficial contact with people of other groups (e.g., other cultures, races, religions, sex) is going to promote mutual understanding and appreciation.

Values That Relate to School Success and to the Functional Classroom

Values relating to being good students have implications for both the present and future lives of students. The success of the school experience is based on a student's doing his/her own work, giving effort, staying on task, completing work on time, getting along with others, participating, not bothering others, obeying the rules, doing what the teacher says, and other related behaviors. These, in turn, are based on values such as: integrity and honesty; the work ethic, the view that success ought to come from work and indeed will result if you work hard; the high value of achievement;

the importance of honest effort; the importance of and belief in the essential codes of fairness, justice, and equality governing individuals and, to an acceptable extent, societal behavior; concern for others; and complying with and having respect for authority.

The fact is that secondary schools function on such values. The classroom can only "work" if most of these values are, at least in some measure, broadly accepted. The same is true of most workplaces and of the entire society. Secondary social studies teachers need to help students make connections between how these values, and the decision-making processes associated with them, affect their lives and futures beyond the classroom walls.

Essentially, many of the previously mentioned values are taught in a number of ways, not the least of which are traditional expectations that students bring to the first day of school. Students come to school expecting to have to behave in certain ways and with a set of preformed notions about what teachers are and how they are supposed to be treated. Schools continue this development through the classroom expectations of teachers, through the development of patterns and habits of behavior, through constant and consistent practice, and through setting and making clear sets of school and classroom rules.

Developing Values

Those who attempt to develop and/or alter values and beliefs, including character educators, use a number of different approaches. Some of these approaches utilize questionable propaganda techniques, even to the point that they appear to be nothing less than types of indoctrination. A teacher should have ethical concerns about such approaches, even when motivated by unselfish caring and concern. Other approaches, at first glance, seem unlikely to have any influence at all. However, the teacher should realize that any single approach could be used ineffectively as well as effectively. Ryan (2000) has explained that talking about character education is easier than doing it. He outlines six methods that he calls the six "Es" of character education: example, explanation, exhortation (praise and pep talks), ethos (ethical environment), experience, and expectation of excellence. The six "Es" are one way of conceptualizing how we go about teaching value-laden material. However, we have found the following five basic categories of methodology to be more useful.

Teaching Values Through Pronouncements, Rules, and Warnings

Many times adults simply tell young people what to believe. This may occur very openly, or it may be much more subtle. In school, for example, it is common to begin by giving students a set of classroom rules. There may or may not be discussion of these rules, but the fact is that students are told that these rules have to be obeyed. The rules tell them what is right, what is wrong, what is good, what to admire, and so on. Values are also taught very directly when certain behaviors are expected in students. Teachers, parents, and other adults imply what is good and bad by the behaviors that they demand or expect. Values are taught directly through home and school rules, requirements, and individual and group orders and statements. The teacher says, "Sit up in your chair!" "Do your homework!" "Arrive to class on time and prepared!" The teacher wants and expects work to be complete, correct, and turned in by the due date. The headings have to all be alike. Paper and writing utensils have to meet certain standards. Students are to be quiet except when the teacher wants them to talk. All of these actions imply compliance with authority, responsibility, taking pride in work, and other attributes that constitute at least part of being good. The pronouncements are often supported with consequences.

Middle and high school students vary in the extent to which they may be influenced by this way of teaching. They are not as likely to believe something that contradicts values they have learned earlier, especially strongly entrenched beliefs. Nonetheless, a constant and unvarying repetition of the same message or of the same expectations has a conditioning effect. For instance, when students are quieted whenever they speak out in class, when they are required to sit in the same seat every day, or when at the same hour and on the same cue they are required to get out a particular book and turn to a prearranged page, they grow to believe that this is the way things are supposed to be. When behavioral expectations are accompanied by a consistently applied punishment and reward system, over time behavior and beliefs fall into line. Some systems of classroom management are based on this approach.

Teaching Values Through Examples and Models

Middle and high school students have idols—heroes and role models they strive to be like. These include people they know, people they see on television and in movies, and people they read about or hear about. Famous athletes and celebrities (for better or worse) serve as models of ideals for many secondary students because of the money, power, or fame associated with their profession. When used in school, the modeling approach involves getting students to look at figures in stories and history as the kinds of people they should aspire to be like. As a way of teaching values, modeling involves making students more aware of people, accomplishments, and principles and makes students consider more carefully the types of people they look to as role models.

Teachers often model values unconsciously. They show who and what they think highly of or, conversely, do not think highly of, by their emotional reactions. They share personal role models, preferences among activities, approval and disapproval of the actions of people, and other qualities with emotional signals that communicate in infectious ways to students. We also should not ignore the fact that teachers become models themselves. Over the course of a school year, students grow to like and admire different qualities that they see in their teachers. Teachers are often models of fairness, caring, intelligence, dress, and so on for students. Teachers also unconsciously or consciously begin using a modeling approach when they hold students up for praise or when they display students' work. They are saying to students, "this is the way I want you to be."

The most obvious use of modeling in social studies involves identifying role models in history, the present day, fiction, radio, motion pictures, or television. Secondary teachers do this by examining current events and contemporary leaders, encouraging discussion, and by having students read biographies of historical figures. Teachers who use this approach most effectively present desirable role models in exciting ways and bring out the most admirable qualities of these individuals. For example, students could do character presentations of role models, dressing and acting as the individual for an oral report in the classroom.

This approach can make school more interesting and positive and may even make the teacher seem more aware of the real world in which the students live. Schools tend to ignore the many positive characters in television shows and in movies, and this is one place where this set of experiences can be brought to good use. In addition, folk tales are rich in heroes and can provide a way of helping students to see qualities that are admirable while examining cultural values and beliefs. Most books involve protagonists who represent good versus the antagonists who are perceived as bad.

A major issue of the modeling approach with real-life role models is that real people have weaknesses, shortcomings, and even vices. Whenever we deal with real role models we risk later disillusionment. Students find out that some of the stories that they learned as "truth," stories that even their teachers thought were true, are merely legends and are probably not true at all. The story of George Washington chopping down the cherry tree is a prime example. Even worse, students may discover that the role models they thought were perfect have made bad mistakes, shown prejudice or other very negative emotions, or been unfair or even dishonest. It is often difficult to maintain admiration for what role models have stood for when their imperfections and humanity are revealed. Disillusionment with a hero or role model may also mean rejection of the positive values she or he represents.

The problem is that there are no infallible role models. This may be an argument for reliance on mythical and fictional heroes. These kinds of models have a distinct advantage. Their lives are limited to the stories in which they appear. Hidden flaws cannot be discovered outside that context. But the advantage is also a limitation. Most story heroes lack depth, and because of this they do not always seem real enough to serve as models. The best solution seems to be to continue with a combination of historical and fictional heroes, teaching students to admire the positive aspects of their role models while recognizing shortcomings and weaknesses.

Teaching Values Through Stories with Morals or Lessons

Another way of approaching morals, values, and worldviews is through stories and examples that speak directly to particular values. A story is told with a lesson embedded in it. Typically, the stories show how to behave or act in situations where a decision has to be made. Often in these stories acceptable behaviors and actions are rewarded and, of course, unacceptable behaviors bring undesirable consequences.

Fables and parables have been used to teach right and wrong for thousands of years. This approach is most effective when the listener or reader is provoked to think and discuss the story, leading to the discovery of the embedded moral or lesson. This approach is not very successful if a lesson runs contrary to the existing worldview of the audience or when the story seems to be an attempt to force a belief that they do not want to accept. The story approach offers a lot of possibilities for the teacher. Most importantly, stories have plots, characters, and settings, which are all factors that make them both interesting and memorable.

Nonfiction or fiction stories provide a way to look at different cultures, different times, and different beliefs. Every folk story tells a great deal about the culture from which it came. It shows what the people believed and, more importantly, what they thought was worth teaching or passing along to the younger generation.

Stories offer opportunities for discussion and thinking, for questions, for focusing on alternatives, and for comparison both with other stories and with personal experiences. Students can learn through dramatizing experiences with stories, looking at character motivation, examining alternative outcomes and beginnings, and looking at the author's viewpoint, for example.

Teaching Values Through Examining Personal Actions of Self and Others

Secondary teachers can help students to develop their values by giving them experiences where they can become more reflective and analytical about what they do and what they see. Teachers need to have students examine the occurrences of everyday life, how they have acted and felt in particular situations, and the reasons behind those feelings. This kind of values analysis involves looking carefully and sequentially at the details of what happened, making special note of behavior, then looking at the causes or reasons contributing to that behavior as well as the outcomes of it. The analysis does not end there. The next step is to speculate about alternative possible behaviors and consider what might have been more reasonable, moral, acceptable, and effective in the situation. There must be constant reminders of what the principal people involved did and did not know at the time.

One of the outcomes of this approach is that it gets students to look at their own lives instead of just two-dimensional characters in media, storybooks, and history. The teacher may begin with autobiographical anecdotes or descriptions of events in the classroom that students have experienced. The autobiographical stories serve as models to provoke examples from students and as one way of communicating the real humanity of the teacher. Often the stories point out times when the teacher did not act in the best way. If the teacher can share an embarrassing moment, it may have a releasing effect on students. The shared class experiences need to be carefully selected, however, and developed as a group effort. The teacher should not be using the approach as a way of criticizing or scolding students. Rather, it should be an honest joint exploration of an event that was not exactly satisfactory in its outcome. Used well, the approach also has a bonding effect for the class.

Usually, the approach goes through a series of definitive steps beginning with a narrative description of the situation, which is then discussed from the standpoint of identifying the central issue, concern, or problem. This method may require considerable time because it is critical to get a clear vision of the heart of the matter. The next step is to look at all sides of the matter, examining minute details and looking for things that may appear trivial but, upon examination, are critical. This is essentially an information-gathering stage. That information is then examined and sifted to remove the clutter of irrelevant or unimportant observations that are not needed for judgment. The final stages take the students through tentative judgments that are evaluated and appraised before final assessments are made.

Teaching Values Through Problem Solving

Many of the approaches to effective teaching that have been developed involve problem solving. They begin with dilemmas or conflicts where decisions are demanded and ask the learner to make a judgment and then explain it. Both the moral reasoning approach, which involves moral dilemmas, and clarification approach are essentially of this type. Moral reasoning approaches, popularized by Lawrence Kohlberg (1984, 1985), involve the development of a sense of justice through a series of progressive stages. The basis of Kohlberg's approach is that individuals can be guided and accelerated in these stages, developing their reasoning ability by thinking about a series of dilemmas in which there are no clear-cut right and good actions to take. In essence, the individual has to choose between alternatives where it is a matter of determining the "lesser of evils." Box 10.4 is an example of such a dilemma.

If they are shown dilemmas such as the one described here, students can soon develop the ability to create their own in a guided discussion format. The dilemmas themselves, which can be designed to fit any age level and relate to the content being studied, should create involving points of departure for discussions of moral values. The essential position of the Kohlbergian research is that the development of moral reasoning occurs through exposure to such dilemmas and that growth is both irreversible and important in influencing moral behavior.

Values analysis approaches are designed to help students become clearer about why they act and think as they do. The essential view is that people should reflect their values in the way they act, but they do not always do so. The reason they do not is that they do not see what implications their belief systems have for their lives. The approach confronts students with decisions that simply have to be reasoned out or clarified. Teacher questions that probe the reasons for feelings and decisions are at the heart of this technique. The student is often confronted with open-ended situations

Box 10.4 Dilemma Example

In the 1840s, a boy who was traveling by wagon train to Oregon becomes the head of his family when his parents sicken and die. Other families in the wagon train are too much occupied with their own survival problems to try to take all these children under their wings, so the boy is pretty much on his own. Soon, the boy and his brothers and sisters are the last wagon in the train, struggling just to keep up. Because the wagon train has been slowed by a series of difficulties, the food supply for the boy's family soon begins to run out. One day, the boy sights a herd of deer crossing the trail in back of the wagon train. If he stops to hunt, the wagon train will move on without his family and the winter may close down on them in the mountains. If he does not hunt, he and his brothers and sisters may starve. Should he have his own family make camp while he goes after the deer or simply try to keep up with the rest of the wagons?

where the question of what the meaning is becomes most important. Students may be asked to set priorities, choose from among alternatives, and examine choices.

Problem-related approaches could be adapted for use with practically any topic or theme under study. They allow the students to examine questions of right and wrong as well as other values in the past, in other cultures, in hypothetical and fictional settings, in current events, and in their own lives.

Character Development and Citizenship

Over the last decade there has been increasing support for programs and approaches in school that will develop students' characters in an effort to produce better people and citizens. In November of 1996, the NCSS approved a report by its Task Force on Character Education. The thunderous message of that report, "Fostering Civic Virtue: Character Education in the Social Studies" (NCSS, 1997), was that social studies teachers have a "clear responsibility and duty to refocus their classrooms on the teaching of character and civic virtue." The report made strong statements about fostering moral and civic virtue in school environments, which are themselves models of the core values and principles being taught to young people. Teachers are reminded that they have a responsibility to be role models. The report also points out the need for schools to have dialogue with community members over the values that schools will teach. Similar statements have been issued by the organization of state social studies supervisors (CS4, 2000) and the organization of secondary school principals (Harned, 1999).

Character and Values: A Worldview Perspective

The goals of character education include establishing life patterns and personal codes of behavior that include qualities such as integrity, belief in self and others, responsibility, and honor. Character itself has a strong relationship to how individuals view the world and their values. What individuals feel to be important or even worthwhile has impact upon character too, as does how they view the importance of themselves and others.

During adolescence and young adulthood, an individual's values and worldview are developing and changing. The family and school, as well as other formal and informal social structures, help shape and form the individual's worldview and his or her interwoven values, attitudes, and appreciations. In a democratic society, we want students to grow in their reasoned commitment to such democratic principles as majority rule, equal opportunity, individual rights, the rule of law, freedom of speech, and religious freedom.

Every society tries to shape the values of young people. Those who personally care about an individual student (and hopefully this includes parents, teachers, and a lot of others) want that student to grow up with the very best set of values possible and mature into a responsible adult. But not everyone agrees about just what that set is or about how it needs to be developed.

Parents and other family members present young people with their perspective, often a complex one. Various social groups attempt to exert pressure as well, having what is termed a "conserving influence." Conserving influences in any culture are those that transmit, maintain, and preserve that culture as it is. Religious, political, and social groups pressure young people to accept and believe in the values upon which the groups themselves are based. Schools also exert their own conserving influence. It should go almost without saying that the influence of any of these forces is not always unified (nor is it always positive).

Social Justice Issues, Decision-Making, and Values

If one of the main goals of social studies is civic engagement and being a good citizen, then certainly social justice issues will need to be addressed in the secondary social studies curriculum.

While topics such as racism, discrimination, poverty, etc. can be controversial, that does not mean teachers can simply ignore these topics to preserve their own comfort. Teachers have a responsibility to engage students in these important discussions from historical and contemporary perspectives. Given the current social and political climate in the United States, it is evident that teachers need to spend more time guiding students to a more nuanced understanding of the complexities in the world. Obviously, secondary social studies teachers have a major responsibility in regards to curricular and instructional choices in related to social issues. What issues can/should you discuss with middle and high school students? What is age-appropriate? How much details do you provide? How should you introduce or frame discussions surrounding social justice issues?

We believe decision-making, values, and character education can be used as a catalyst for meaningful instruction surrounding social issues. For that reason, all of the aforementioned examples and instructional approaches in this chapter could be used to develop social justice lessons by focusing on controversial topics. Moral dilemma discussions, for example, could easily be geared to focus on important social justice issues like gender equality, rights of the LGBTQ community, racial discrimination, and climate change (just to name a few!) We present these topics as intertwined because we have found this to be an effective method to introduce social issues to young learners in a systematic way that is less threatening to parents that might have strong values, opinions, and viewpoints. Anyone that has taught in public schools will likely tell you that parents (and even some administrators) are not always keen on teachers discussing social issues in the classroom setting. Whether they think the topic is inappropriate, the students are too young, or they do not trust the teacher to responsibly and objectively handle such important topics, parents certainly do have rights and legitimate concerns that should not be overlooked. However, when these social issues are introduced and framed within the decision-making, values, and character education context, there is always a solid foundation of standards and instructional precedent to introduce controversial topics in scaffolded ways. Utilizing children's and young adult's literature is an excellent resource for secondary social studies teachers that want to tackle social issues through the decision-making process. For a list of appropriate and relevant children's and young adult's literature, we strongly recommend the National Council for the Social Studies (NCSS) Notable Trade Books for Young People annual list found at https://www.socialstudies.org/notable-social-studies-trade-books. These lists are updated yearly and organized by grade levels, themes, topics, and reading levels. While obviously not exhaustive, these lists do provide secondary social studies teachers with a good starting point of appropriate children's books that could be used to address social issues and the decision making process.

Looking Back

In the social studies, teachers need to be most concerned with helping students become good citizens. This complex process requires a variety of approaches, materials, and skills to help students of today become the participatory democratic citizens of tomorrow. Issues-centered learning is one approach that secondary teachers should consider when addressing the "good citizen" objective because it forces students to actively engage and discuss controversial issues that are important in society. Building off of these discussions, teachers should also address the decision-making process and provide students with ample opportunities to explore various decisions, their alternatives, and consequences both in the classroom and beyond. Additional work in preparing students to be good citizens focuses on the exploration of values, particularly values related to living in a democracy, values implicit within a multicultural society, and values related to school success and the successful functioning of the classroom. Teachers develop values through a variety of approaches, including direct teaching, modeling, moral stories and lessons, and examination of personal actions and the actions of others.

Character education is also an important component of the "good citizen" goal associated with social studies classrooms. As a mandated part of the school curriculum, character education involves the development of moral and civic virtue. This means that teachers need to be involved in developing the value systems of their students. Values have a close relationship to our personal worldview. They have an impact on decision-making ability and especially on every aspect of evaluation. Teachers should expose students to many types of values-based, decision-making activities, including those in which students determine alternatives; those in which they choose alternatives; those in which they are required to distinguish fact from speculation, conclusion from opinion, fantasy from reality, and truth from falsehood; those in which they determine relevance or adequacy of evidence; and those in which they project trends.

Extension Activity

Scenario

You are at the mid-point of the fourth nine weeks at YHS. Dr. Russell, the principal of YHS, drops by your classroom to schedule a meeting after school. As the day passes, the anticipation overwhelms you and you are so nervous you find yourself gnawing on your fingernails throughout the day. The meeting finally arrives and you are pleasantly surprised to hear the news. Dr. Russell informs you that your contract has been renewed for the upcoming school year. Dr. Russell acknowledges your hard work, dynamic teaching, and your ability to "get students to think." He follows his praises with a request. Dr. Russell asks that you provide a sample activity that "gets students to think" to share with the other faculty. Giddy with excitement, you agree and promise to bring an activity next Monday.

Task

For this activity, locate a current news article or story (no more than two years old) that deals with a public issue relating to the lives of middle or high school students. After reading the article, create a series of ten discussion questions you could use to facilitate a dialogue with secondary students about the article/topic being addressed. Keep in mind that these questions are meant to provoke students to think critically and rationally about difficult issues and utilize the decision-making process to develop informed opinions.

Reflective Questions

1 What is the purpose of issues-centered learning?
2 What are the benefits of engaging students in discussions about social issues?
3 Why are values both controversial and necessary to social studies instruction?
4 What are some different ways of modeling values?
5 How are issues-centered learning, decision making, values, and character education all related?

Helpful Resources

In this video, a school principal shares how character education is implemented in her school and the role students play.

https://youtu.be/zofsiFm8Eto

Watch workshop video #27 for a Grade 12 lesson on gender-based distinctions.

www.learner.org/resources/series166.html

Watch this video for a Grade 8 lesson on the Holocaust.

www.teachingchannel.org/videos/holocaust-history-lesson-plan

Watch this Boston University TED talk about the importance and need for character education in a multicultural society.

https://youtu.be/AWtK0oUNsls

Watch this video about Character Counts and the importance of developing life skills in students through character education programs.

https://youtu.be/cmHf7qTxtR0

Watch this video by Character First Media that argues for character first education.

https://youtu.be/AWtK0oUNsls

Character Counts is a useful program. Visit the website to explore more information about the program. www.charactercounts.org.

Further Reading

Berkowitz, M. & Bier, M. (2005). *What Works in Character Education: A Research-Driven Guide for Educators.* Washington, DC: Report from the Character Education Partnership.

This comprehensive report contains a detailed synthesis and analysis of research on many character education programs being implemented in U.S. schools. The purpose of the report is to examine more closely and critically the effects that character education programs have on student achievement to determine what is, or is not, working in schools.

Engle, S. & Ochoa, A. (1988). *Education for Democratic Citizenship: Decision Making in the Social Studies.* New York, NY: Teachers College Press.

This book is expertly written by two educators renowned for their work in the field of social studies and decision-making. The book focuses on the importance of the decision-making process and why it is an essential part of social studies and educating students to become democratic citizens.

Evans, R. & Saxe, D. (Eds.). (2007). *Handbook on Teaching Social Issues: NCSS Bulletin No. 93.* Charlotte, NC: Information Age Publishing.

This comprehensive edited volume features the work of more than 40 experts in the field of issues-centered teaching. The book examines the rationale, objectives, methods, assessments, and challenges to implementing issues-centered learning into the social studies curriculum. There is also a good selection of teaching ideas and resources for secondary teachers.

Kohlberg, L. (1966). Moral education in the school. *School Review, 74*, 1–30.

This article is a must-read for moral education because it marks the first time that famed educational psychologist Lawrence Kohlberg connected his research on moral reasoning to the practice of moral education in schools. This article provides educators with a framework for Kohlberg's interpretation of appropriate moral education, known as the moral development approach.

McClellan, B.E. (1999). *Moral Education in America: Schools and the Shaping of Character From Colonial Times to the Present.* New York, NY: Teachers College Press.

This book provides an extensive and complete history of moral education in America. The author provides excellent documentation and evidence explaining how the practice of educating students in the moral domain has changed and evolved throughout the history of the United States.

Raths, L., Harmin, M. & Simon, S. (1966). *Values and Teaching: Working With Values in the Classroom.* Columbus, OH: Charles E. Merrill.

This book outlined the foundation of the controversial "values clarification" approach to moral development during the turbulent 1960s. The book explains how teachers should approach the task of values education in the classroom.

References

Berkowitz, M. & Bier, M. (2005). *What Works in Character Education: A Research-Driven Guide for Educators.* Washington, DC: Report from the Character Education Partnership.

CS4. (2000). Character Education and the Social Studies: A Position Statement for the Council for State Social Studies Specialists. Available at: www.cssss.org/character_education_position_paper.html

Engle, S.H. (1960). Decision making: The heart of the social studies. *Social Education*, 24(November), 301.

Evans, R., Newmann, F. & Saxe, D. (1996). Defining issues-centered education. In R. Evans & D. Saxe (Eds.), *Handbook on Teaching Social Issues* (pp. 2–5). Washington, DC: National Council for the Social Studies.

General Procedures for Case Studies (n.d.).

General Procedures for Lessons (n.d.).

Harned, P. (1999). Leading the effort to teach character in the schools. *NAASP Bulletin*, 83(October), 25–32.

Harvard Social Studies Project. (1967). *Cases and Controversy: Guide to Teaching*. Middletown, CT: Xerox Corporation.

Kohlberg, L. (1985). *The Meaning and Measurement of Moral Development*. Worcester, MA: Clark University.

NCSS Task Force on Character Education. (1997). Fostering civic virtue: Character education in the social studies. *Social Education*, 61(April/May), 225–227.

Raths, L., Harmin, M. & Simon, S. (1966). *Values and Teaching: Working With Values in the Classroom*. Columbus, OH: Charles E. Merrill.

Ryan, K. (2000). The Six e's of Character Education: Practical Ways to Bring Moral Instruction to Life for Your Students. Available at: www.sed-mac66.bu.edu/CharacterEd/6Es.html

11 Technology and Media in Social Studies

Looking Ahead

What is technology? This seemingly simple question will undoubtedly produce a wide variety of responses from teachers as well as members of the general public. For many people, technology today is simply a synonym for computers. To be sure, technology covers a wide range of devices, such as televisions, DVD players, LCD projectors, CD players, overhead projectors, smart boards, document cameras, and a variety of other equipment that can and should be used to enhance classroom instruction.

Technology advancements of the late twentieth and early twenty-first centuries have greatly altered the world, changing how people interact and access information. As society becomes more accustomed and dependent on new technologies, the need for the presence of technology in schools increases greatly. Many jobs of the twenty-first century now require an understanding of technological hardware and software in order to function. Skills such as word processing, web browsing, and sending electronic mail are now considered very basic abilities required in a variety of workplaces.

This chapter focuses on various types of technologies and the ways that teachers can effectively utilize these valuable resources to enhance social studies instruction in secondary classrooms. Since students in secondary schools will likely bring with them a variety of different prerequisite skills and knowledge regarding technology, the authors will discuss everything from the uses of basic software and hardware in the middle grades to more advanced uses of contemporary technology resources for more proficient high school students. It is important to remember that technology serves as a tool for instruction and should be utilized only to supplement or enrich the curriculum.

Can You? Do You?

Can you ...

- explain how technology benefits students' learning and enhances your instruction?
- describe your own skills and abilities in utilizing technology?
- identify or describe specific technology skills that are important for your students to master?
- think of activities in which students could have experiences in utilizing classroom technology?

Do you ...

- know where to find valuable resources using the Internet?
- know what technologies are typically found in schools and how they should be used?
- know the definitions of *media literacy* and *visual literacy*?
- understand different ways of using technology to enhance classroom instruction?

DOI: 10.4324/9781003217060-11

Focus Activity

Before reading this chapter, try the focus activity below.

Think back about your experiences in the classroom as a student. What types of technology did your teachers use in the classroom? Consider how technology from your experiences as a student has evolved over the years. What technology do you expect to see in contemporary classrooms? What resources and technologies do you feel comfortable working with, and which technologies might you need more support utilizing?

Rank the following technologies based on how important you think they are for classroom instruction (1 being most important, 10 being least important). Use this list as a basis for discussion. Why are some resources more valuable to you than others? How do you envision technology being used in your classroom? You might also like to generate additional resources not listed in this overview.

- Television
- Internet Access
- Document Camera
- Video Recorder
- DVD/VCR
- iPads (for student use)
- Computer (for teacher use only)
- Interactive White Board (smart board, Promethean, etc.)
- LCD Projector
- Computers (for student use)

Getting Started: Technology as a Productive Tool

Before any advanced discussion can take place about the use of technology as an educational tool, we must first consider the basic skills expected of twenty-first century teachers. The rapid development of new and emergent technologies has drastically changed the way people live and, in turn, these developments have also changed the perception of what it means to be a technologically proficient teacher. Teachers are now expected to bring with them certain prerequisite skills regarding the use of technology. For example, when was the last time you heard of a school offering professional development for teachers about composing type-written documents or sending email?

As schools continue to place increased emphasis (and funds) on classroom technologies, it is important to consider the expectations placed on teachers. Many contemporary classrooms now come equipped with a great deal of technology. Resources such as classroom computers, televisions, LCD projectors, document cameras, Internet access, and interactive white boards are becoming increasingly present in modern classrooms. However, the mere presence of technology does not ensure a better education for the students. Teachers must continually work to gain proficiency and knowledge about technological innovations, specifically focusing on how these devices can enhance instruction and/or student learning. Learning about the best applications of classroom technology is a process critical to the success of new and experienced teachers alike. Rapid innovations and developments in the technology realm mean that nearly every teacher will need some support or training about the emerging uses of new devices.

Luckily, teachers often have several options for acquiring skills operating new technologies. The most common and accessible form of training typically comes from professional development offered by schools or districts. Nearly every public school in the country has "teacher training" days that provide some form of professional development to classroom teachers. While many schools frequently use this time to help train teachers, it is safe to say that this may not always be the case. Classroom teachers interested in more training should always discuss the issue with school administrators. Whether the training is offered during in-service days or sometime outside of school hours (before class, after class, weekends), teachers need to actively seek support in the use of instructional technology. Other options outside of school offering professional development could include taking courses at a college or university focusing on instructional technology or attending professional conferences designed to improve the teaching profession.

Technology and Standards

Like all areas of education in the era of accountability, advocates for the inclusion and increased presence of technology in the classroom have created specific standards and benchmarks to guide instruction. These standards are significant for teachers to be aware of because they are the indicators of what is deemed "important" in curriculum and pedagogy at national and state levels.

The International Society for Technology in Education (ISTE) has created a set of National Educational Technology Standards (NETS) for students, teachers, and administrators. ISTE lists five main standards for teachers (listed below) and contends that effective teachers should model and apply the NETS as they "design, implement, and assess learning experiences to engage students and improve learning; enrich professional practice; and provide positive models for students, colleagues, and the community" (ISTE, 2008).

1 Facilitate and Inspire Student Learning and Creativity
2 Design and Develop Digital Age Learning Experiences and Assessments
3 Model Digital Age Work and Learning
4 Promote and Model Digital Citizenship and Responsibility
5 Engage in Professional Growth and Leadership

NCSS, the largest organization dedicated to social studies in the U.S., has also issued standards, bulletins, and position statements that specifically highlight the importance of integrating technology into the social studies curriculum. One aspect that makes the NCSS positions unique from those of other organizations is that they go beyond advocating for inclusion of instructional technology by also promoting the exploration of technological developments on society to provide context for students about the social, economic, and political impact technology has on society. The eighth strand of the NCSS themes is titled, "Science, Technology, and the World." NCSS states under this theme that "social studies programs should include experiences that provide for the study of relationships among science, technology, and society" (NCSS, 2012). The following are a few examples of key questions that NCSS believes social studies educators should address under the technology theme:

1 What can we learn from the past about how new technologies result in broader social change?
2 Is new technology always a good thing for society?
3 How should society cope with rapid changes and potential inequities caused by technological innovations?
4 How can we manage technology so that the greatest numbers of people benefit? How can we preserve fundamental values and beliefs in a world that is rapidly becoming one technology-linked village?
5 How do science and technology affect our sense of self and morality?
6 How can technology advances help alleviate global issues such as poverty, human rights violations, etc.?

In addition to the overview of national standards provided here, teachers should also be aware of state standards. Many states have recognized the importance of technology in the classroom and have incorporated this significance into state standards at all grade levels. State standards should always be closely monitored when planning lessons not just for content, but also for skills that are deemed a valuable part of students' education.

Online and Virtual Teaching

2020 was a year that brought forth many changes around the world due to the rise of the Covid-19 pandemic. The impact of this virus spread across all aspects of society, and schools were no different. As schools began to close, many also explored the prospect of pivoting to online/virtual learning environments. To be sure, online and virtual teaching have been around for many years. However, schools and teachers have never seen anything quite like the shift that took place in 2020. Seemingly overnight, teachers were required to create online learning materials, Google classrooms, digital resource libraries, and become "Zoom" teachers all at the same time. These issues were exasperated in middle and high schools, as teachers, students, and parents struggled with the shifting role of learning in a virtual setting and the disruptions to traditional school experiences such as the cancellation of team sports, school dances, graduations, etc. Aside from the normal technical issues associated with virtual learning (lacking technology, internet, at home supports, etc.), secondary social studies teachers also found themselves teaching in new and unfamiliar ways. Designing lessons dependent on technology, rather than using technology as a supplement to normal classroom instruction.

As most teachers are not trained specifically for teaching in virtual environments, it is safe to say that this year has been a learning experience for everyone. Fortunately, teachers and students have been using much of the technology and resources used in virtual learning for many years. For example, teachers routinely utilize the internet for supplemental readings, videos, and materials to enrich student learning. Students increasingly are using mobile and technology devices at home for personnel and educational purposes. While an extensive discussion around teaching secondary social studies in the virtual setting would be outside the scope of this book, we do believe the resources and approaches covered throughout this chapter (and all the chapters really) can be scaffolded to support the teaching and learning of secondary social studies in online and virtual environments. Additionally, for teachers interested in more general supports about designing online instruction, we highly recommend the Teaching Channel's website on distance learning (https://www.teachingchannel.com/).

Enhancing Instruction with the Internet

The Internet might arguably be one of the most revolutionary innovations in the history of education. Access to the web allows people all over the world to share information, experiences, knowledge, and ideas faster than ever before. In addition, the Internet also contains a vast amount of resources that enable teachers to do their jobs in a more effective, efficient, and engaging way. In fact, the popularity of web resources has increased so much that teachers and students probably need more practice narrowing down search results and determining what is actually a reliable resource than they do about the process of finding websites. For contemporary students, the importance of understanding what makes a website valuable and relevant is an essential process in education during the digital age. Before ever bringing any websites into the classroom, it is the teacher's responsibility to thoroughly examine the website to determine how appropriate the resource is and look for any potential problems with using the site to enhance instruction. The following section will discuss how teachers could go about evaluating websites for their classroom instruction or to help students understand how to critically analyze web resources.

Evaluating Websites

> **FYI**
>
> Evaluating web content for accuracy and biases is increasingly important in today's world. Consider relating to the current political climate and the rise of the term *fake news*.

The evaluation of websites for classroom use is a task that should first be completed by the teacher. Before utilizing any website in the classroom, make sure to thoroughly examine the site for things like accuracy of content, information about the author of the site, the date the site was last updated, and security of the site (i.e., can the website be accessed at school, which might have Internet restrictions). After analyzing the site and determining its appropriateness, consider going through a similar process with the students. Middle and high school students in today's classroom will almost certainly bring with them some knowledge and understanding of the Internet. However, this exposure to the Internet does not necessarily translate to understanding regarding the educational quality of particular websites. Secondary teachers need to spend time helping students understand what makes a website reliable, how to correctly and safely conduct online research, and methods of citing online work to prevent plagiarism issues. The following list provides some quality example questions that secondary teachers should consider covering with students while evaluating the usefulness and relevance of a website:

- What is the title of the website being evaluated?
- What is the URL of the website being evaluated?
- What is your research topic?
- Who is the author of the website?
- Is there contact information for the author? If so, what is it?
- What is the purpose of this website?
- Is the website published by a webmaster or by the author?
- Is the person qualified? How do you know? Does the person list qualifications?
- How detailed is the information?
- Does the information express any bias? If so, what is it?
- When was the website created?
- When was the website last updated?
- Did an organization, institution, government agency, or foundation publish the website? If so, what is the name of the agency?
- Is the information on the website outdated?
- Overall, what are the strengths and weaknesses of the web page?

While the aforementioned list of questions is certainly not exhaustive, it will provide teachers and students with a strong enough foundation to proceed with the utilization of websites for educational purposes both at home and in the classroom. Teachers should always remember that student safety is the most important component of online exploration. Helping students to better understand the complexities of the Internet, with all of its glories and pitfalls, is an essential part of education during the digital age.

Media Literacy

Media literacy is particularly important for secondary students in today's schools because it revolves around trying to understand the intentions and motives implanted within the media. Media literacy can be defined as having the necessary skills to access, analyze, evaluate, and create media in a variety of forms (Center for Media Literacy, 2012). Students in the digital era face an onslaught of media. Television programs, commercials, films, billboards, and countless other forms of advertising all attempt to deliver an assortment of messages to students about an even wider range of topics. Today's society is one infatuated with the media culture, which is the primary reason why billions of dollars are spent every year in the advertising industry. Every day students see commercials, billboards, and advertisements encouraging them to buy products and/or look a specific way. The proliferation of images facing students in the media becomes even more problematic when considering the widespread use of software programs (like Photoshop) to manipulate and alter digital images, blurring the lines of reality and making critical analysis of media messages more important than ever.

Some people may consider media literacy as the ability to effectively navigate and utilize the Internet. To be sure, true media literacy skills involve much more than operational web browsing. Teaching students to be media literate is about teaching them to think critically and learn to ask the right questions about what they are reading, watching, or hearing in the media. While finding reliable and quality resources on the Internet is certainly a starting point for instruction, students still face the challenge of media influence in other forms such as television advertisements, commercials, popular films, billboards, and various other outlets. Since all of these sources attempt to exercise influence over students and the social studies is concerned with developing good decision-makers and citizens, it becomes necessary for teachers to help students become critical viewers of media and not passive consumers. For example, secondary teachers could show students commercials or advertisements related to popular clothing lines, shoes, restaurants, or other products. Then have students analyze and discuss what the advertisement is trying to accomplish and who are the intended audiences. Teachers could then allow students to compare popular products with substantial advertisements (such as Nike, for example) to similar or comparable products. What are the major differences between these products? Do these differences justify the disparity in costs? This is just one brief example of how media literacy skills can be explored through economic concepts and principles using technology. As contemporary media continues to use advertisements in an effort to influence society, educators should strongly consider making time to explain and instruct in this unique discourse to help the students of today become responsible consumers of tomorrow.

Visual Literacy

Visual literacy is a field similar to media literacy, but it does contain some prominent differences that make it worth addressing as a separate topic. The purpose of visual literacy is to help students understand, evaluate, and create meaning from images. Braden and Hortin (1982) defined visual literacy as "the ability to understand and use images, including the ability to think, learn and express oneself in terms of images." This definition works well when considering the implications of visual literacy for secondary students because it goes beyond simple recognition of images, symbols, people, places, or things by also focusing on the creation of visuals to communicate meaning to diverse audiences.

Traditionally, education in the U.S. has placed very little emphasis or value on visual communication (Felten, 2008). While the primary grades tend to be more liberal in the use of visuals to learn and communicate, this emphasis tends to fade as students begin to develop traditional literacy skills in the reading and writing domain. As Kress (1997) has duly noted, "The visual representations, which children produce as a matter of course in the early years of schooling, are not developed and built on as a means for future communication use." The lack of focus given to visual literacy in schools becomes more problematic when considering the technological advancements associated with the digital era. More and more in professional and commercial occupations people are asked to communicate and present information utilizing the visual arts. Consider the regularity in which Microsoft PowerPoint appears in conference boardrooms and presentations all across the country.

The problem for society, and especially for educators, continues to be the false assumption that students in today's classrooms already have an understanding of visual communication because of the predominantly visual culture in which they live. However, as Felten (2008) has accurately noted, "living in an image-rich world, however, does not mean students (or faculty and administrators) naturally possess sophisticated visual literacy skills, just as continually listening to an iPod does not teach a person to critically analyze or create music."

The good news for secondary teachers is that many visual literacy strategies are already quite popular tools for social studies instruction. Resources such as graphic organizers, historic photographs, charts, maps, monuments, and films are among some of the more prominent resources that can be easily woven into the middle and high school classrooms. Social studies textbooks have also begun including more images and supplemental materials over the past 20 years (many of which now include interactive CD-ROMs, vocabulary guides, and student workbooks). The purposeful inclusion of images in the classroom and supporting resources directly reflects a shift in how educators are beginning to view the importance of visuals in knowledge comprehension and retention.

The multimodal principle of learning, as discussed in James Paul Gee's, *What Video Games Have to Teach Us About Learning and Literacy* (2003), addresses how "meaning and knowledge are built up through various modalities (images, texts, symbols, interactions, abstract design, sound, etc.), not just words." With the knowledge that students learn much more when information is presented in a variety of ways, secondary teachers should more actively pursue instructional methods that place an emphasis on multimodal learning in the social studies. Since many secondary students are at a variety of different reading and writing levels, teachers should consider giving students the opportunity to demonstrate learning in other, more non-traditional forms. For example, many students that struggle with traditional text-based assignments can routinely recite quotes from movies or the lyrics to their favorite songs. Also, allowing students to demonstrate their learning in visual forms, such as drawing a picture, creating a photo collage, or constructing a digital presentation or video, can greatly increase engagement and critical thinking when dealing with abstract concepts. Consider the prospect of trying to examine a topic such as global warming with secondary students. If students were asked to demonstrate their knowledge of this concept in the traditional form of writing a research paper, they would spend time collecting information and preparing a paper with citations. However, say students were given the same topic of global warming but with an alternative assignment like creating a public service announcement video. Students working on a public service announcement video would go through the same research process but would be required to truly think critically about the topic because they would not be able to restate (or worse, plagiarize) information they have read. Students creating this public service announcement video would have to consider not only how to communicate their ideas orally but also what images to use in an effort to connect the audience with the message they wish to convey. This brief example is one way that secondary teachers can implement multimodal learning. By having students examine information in one form (text) and then create and convey meaning from that information in a different form (visual/video), teachers provide students with an authentic assessment that allows for the simultaneous expansion of content knowledge and visual literacy skills.

Digital History

The term *digital history* is one that has gained a tremendous amount of attention in the fields of history and social studies since the web became available for widespread public use during the late 1990s. John Lee (2002) defines digital history as, "the study of the past using a variety of electronically reproduced primary source texts, images, and artifacts as well as the constructed historical narratives, accounts, or presentations that result from digital historical inquiry." As the Internet became faster, cheaper, and more easily accessible during the first part of the twenty-first century, historians, librarians, and teachers began to realize the potential of information sharing via the web. As a result, countless websites all over the world began uploading millions of primary and secondary resource materials in order to place these valuable sources of information at the fingertips of anyone with an Internet connection. Teachers and students in contemporary classrooms now have access to more primary and secondary resources than any group in the history of public school education. These resources, when utilized correctly, have the opportunity to turn social studies instruction into a dynamic experience. Instead of simply reading about social studies content in the typical classroom textbook, teachers can engage students with thousands of photos, video clips, interviews, and historical documents in an effort to bring historical content to life.

The following list provides a few examples of popular digital history websites that secondary social studies teachers might find useful. Teachers should find the vast collection of resources available on these digital sites to be quite helpful while also considering how students could use the sites for various research projects or activities. A brief description of each website is provided along with the web address. Teachers should spend time carefully examining all that these sites have to offer and consider activities or teaching opportunities that could be implemented while browsing through the collections.

- *Library of Congress.* The Library of Congress website is one of the largest and most useful digital collections of historical resources available to classroom teachers. This free website allows teachers to explore documents, photos, video clips, and a variety of other materials covering historical content. Web address: www.loc.gov
- *University of Houston.* This website was designed and developed to support the teaching of American history in K–12 schools and colleges and is supported by the Department of History and the College of Education at the University of Houston. Web address: www.digitalhistory.uh.edu/
- *Virginia Center for Digital History.* The Virginia Center for Digital History (VCDH) at the University of Virginia promotes the teaching and learning of history using digital technologies. Research projects from this website are useful to a wide range of educators (teachers, librarians, professors, historians, etc.) at all levels of instruction. Web address: www.vcdh.virginia.edu/index.php?page=VCDH

Virtual Field Trips

Virtual field trips are becoming one of the more popular and practical uses of the Internet in social studies instruction. A virtual field trip can be defined as an activity that allows students to visit historic sites, monuments, museums, or other locations via the Internet. These trips allow teachers to guide students on a journey to faraway places in order to examine both the content and context of materials being studied. Consider the Egyptian pyramids or the Taj Mahal. These are historic structures that students may never get to actually visit in person but now have the ability to explore online. Many websites now offer virtual tours that are easy to navigate and offer very detailed, high-resolution images. However, as is the case with any instructional activity, teachers do need to carefully consider a few things before engaging in a virtual field trip.

1 Always visit and carefully examine the site first before introducing it to the class.
2 Make sure you have developed a clear educational purpose for the virtual field trip as well as a way to assess student learning from the activity.
3 If students are going to explore the site on their own, make sure to thoroughly explain and model instructions for navigating the site, highlighting key aspects of the trip that students should inspect.
4 Once the trip is complete, a discussion or debriefing activity is necessary to help clarify any questions the students may have and also to initially check for students' understanding of the virtual field trip objectives.

It should also be noted that virtual field trips are not designed to replace real-life field trips as an instructional tool. Taking students on trips to local historic sites is something that always should be included in the curriculum because it allows students to connect content with real-world experiences in a personal way. Virtual field trips should be considered a valuable option for teachers with a desire to expose secondary students to distant locations and cultures that normally would be out of reach, helping to expand the traditional classroom by making the world more accessible.

WebQuests

A WebQuest can be defined as any inquiry-based activity that requires students to navigate through the Internet for part or all of the assignment. WebQuest activities began during the mid-1990s and have steadily evolved over the years as advances in technology have increased accessibility to the Internet while simultaneously making websites more inclusive and user-friendly. The premise behind WebQuest activities is to allow students to explore various social studies topics by conducting online research and interacting with a variety of primary and secondary sources such as photos, news stories, film clips, etc. While these activities can be time-consuming for teachers to create, as much effort is spent finding appropriate websites for the activity, there are some websites that contain large collections of WebQuest activities for interested teachers. QuestGarden (http://questgarden.com/) contains a large collection of WebQuest activities for a variety of subject areas and for teachers at all grade levels. Secondary teachers should carefully consider the pros and cons of utilizing WebQuest activities in the classroom and always preview any websites being used to make sure the site is up to date and there are no inappropriate materials for students.

Mobile Technologies and Apps

The use of mobile technologies could be the most popular movement in contemporary classroom instruction. All across the U.S. and the entire world, schools and educators are investing a great deal of time and money into the use of mobile devices in the classroom. Laptops, tablets (iPads, Chromebooks, etc.), and even cell phones are beginning to become the norm in K–12 schools. Unfortunately, schools often do not provide the level of professional development and in-service training necessary to maximize learning opportunities with these devices. This can be extremely frustrating to classroom teachers as school administrators push for teachers to not only use the technology that cost so much for the school but also demonstrate a connection between mobile devices and student learning gains. To be sure, the use of mobile devices certainly has the potential to improve teaching and learning. In many ways, these devices have already transformed how classrooms operate and how teachers and students access information. However, it is important to remember that these devices are simply tools, and teachers need to constantly seek out training and professional development opportunities to find the best ways to utilize mobile devices to support classroom learning. As technology and its various resources are constantly evolving and being updated, it would be well beyond the scope of this chapter to attempt to cover all of the tools available to teachers and students. However, we would like to provide a few selected apps that we have found to be particularly useful in teaching and learning secondary social studies. For more detailed information on teaching and learning with mobile devices, see *Learning with Mobile and Handheld Technologies* (Galloway et al., 2015).

Selected Apps to Consider:

Today in History: True to the name, this app provides teachers and students with insights into relevant historical events that occurred on given days throughout human history. The app provides text, images, primary and secondary sources, and other resources about global events in human history to help students and teachers make learning connections in the classroom.

Padlet: Teachers often utilize this free app as a digital bulletin board to help organize content. Additionally, users can work on projects simultaneously, which makes it a favorite for activities like building interactive maps or timelines.

Socrative: This assessment tool allows teachers to quickly and efficiently assess student understanding through quizzes and "exit ticket" types of features. Students can respond to these teacher-designed assessments with their mobile devices and a report is sent to the teacher's device instantly.

Kahoot: Similar to Socrative, this assessment app allows teachers to generate interactive quizzes with time limits for each question, offering a playful "game show" feel for students. Students respond to the questions on their phones or mobile devices, and their answers are instantly sent to the teacher. If every student in the class does not have a smartphone or mobile device, consider having the students work in small groups or with a partner.

Educreations: Teachers can use this app as a presentation tool or method for allowing students to explain their thinking. The app allows you to record your voice and draw or import pictures. Teachers could have students upload a primary source document and then have students circle "key words" and record their analysis of the document.

Nearpod: Mostly for use in one-to-one classrooms, this app allows teachers to control how and when screens advance for students. This is an especially effective resource for teachers when working with younger students, who often want to click or swipe on the screens during activities.

Aurasma: This augmented reality app allows users to bring content to life. Devices can be held over selected images or objects (known as triggers), bringing forth some form of 3D video or animation. Teachers can create their own triggers as well, making it especially useful for field trips to local historic sites and/or museums.

Explain Everything: Teachers can use this app to transform their phones or tablets into an interactive white board. Images and files can be uploaded, manipulated, and shared with students. Additionally, teachers could use this as an assessment tool, uploading student work to the app, recording audio and written feedback directly on the assignment, then sending the video recording of the feedback directly to students and/or their parents.

Interactive White Boards

Interactive white boards are among the most popular technology devices found in contemporary classrooms. While there are many different brands and variations (Smart board, Promethean board, etc.), the basic functions of these devices is to increase student learning and engagement by combining the features of a traditional dry erase board with an LCD projector. Teachers can use these boards for a plethora of activities such as showing video clips, completing graphic organizers, playing games, completing interactive maps or timelines, along with thousands of other things. Students also enjoy coming up to interactive white boards and engaging directly with the technology and content, bringing a certain level of excitement to the learning experience. This continues to be an important feature when teaching social studies content that is not always the most interesting for many students. Like all other technology resources, interactive white boards require a great deal of training in order for classroom teachers to truly maximize all of the potential offered through both the hardware and software available with these devices.

Flipped Classrooms and One-to-One Instruction

In addition to investing time and money into classroom technologies, many schools are also embarking on initiatives to provide laptops and/or tablets to all students school-wide. Often referred to as "one-to-one" schools or instruction, the idea behind this initiative is to increase student engagement, learning, and technological skills and address issues of equity and access. One of the rising trends in many areas of the country incorporating "one-to-one" technology is the flipped classroom. While the definition of a flipped classroom model contains many variations, the basic premise is that students will complete traditional classroom activities (like note taking, readings, listening to lectures, etc.) at home via videos and other online resources, which then would allow students to engage in more meaningful classroom projects, discussions, and activities that might traditionally be assigned for homework. Obviously, this approach to teaching and learning requires technology access and skills, which teachers cannot assume that all students will have. For example, even if the school provides students with laptops or tablets, there is no guarantee that all students will have Internet access at home in order to complete many activities or assignments. While flipped classrooms could certainly be a meaningful way of teaching and learning moving forward, we encourage teachers to conduct additional research in order to better understand the strengths and limitations of this practice. For more information, we recommend the *Handbook of Research on Active Learning and the Flipped Classroom Model in the Digital Age* (Keengwe & Onchwari, 2015).

Teaching with Film

The use of film as an instructional tool is not a new concept in the field of education. Every day teachers in secondary classrooms all over the country utilize this powerful tool to motivate, engage, and inform students about a variety of topics and concepts. Teaching with film is considered a best practice in classrooms during the digital age and an effective way to teach secondary social studies content (Russell & Waters, 2010; Russell, 2009; Holmes et al., 2007). Since numerous popular films are based on historical events, many social studies teachers view films as a reliable resource to engage students. However, as most social studies teachers know, not all films are historically accurate. While some may argue that films should not be included in the curriculum for this very reason, teachers could utilize the historical discrepancies depicted in Hollywood films to encourage students to view films critically. In addition to popular Hollywood films, there are countless documentaries, television series, political advertisements, commercials, and digital videos that can be utilized to actively engage secondary students in social studies content.

One major concern for advocates of using film in the classroom is the lack of formal training that teachers receive in how to effectively use film. Teachers often show films as a "time filler" or simply show historical films as a way to supplement texts, without any serious critical thinking, or analysis of what they are viewing. Historical films, much like texts, are examples of how history is constructed and should always be open to interpretation. As Rosenstone (2006) writes, "the past told in moving images, doesn't do away with the old forms of history—it adds to the language which the past can speak." Teachers should spend time explaining the nature of the film industry and how the primary goal of most films is to make money, not to accurately portray people, places, or events. Since films about historical events can often be misleading, or, worse, blatantly incorrect, students need practice in analyzing not only the characters and plots of films but also how the information presented relates to content from different sources, such as the textbook, newspapers, and various other primary/secondary resources.

Film is an effective and powerful tool for teaching social studies. For film to be effective it must be used appropriately. To ensure appropriate film use, teachers should adhere to the Russell model (2004, 2007):

- *Step 1: Preparation.* The preparation step includes creating lesson plans that incorporate film while still meeting instructional goals/objectives, state standards, and national standards and adhering to all legal requirements.
- *Step 2: Previewing.* The previewing step is done prior to students viewing the film. The previewing step should include an introduction of the film and the purpose for viewing the film.

FYI

Never assume that a film is appropriate to show in class based on rating alone. Always preview a film before showing it in class, even if you have already seen it!

- *Step 3: Watching the film.* During this step the teacher will show students the film (in its entirety or in clips). Teachers need to ensure that students are aware of what they should be doing (taking notes, jotting down questions, etc.) and looking for while watching the film.
- *Step 4: Assessment.* The assessment step is done after students have watched the film. The assessment step includes assessing student learning in some fashion.

There are a number of ways film can be used in the classroom. The methodologies described below are effective pedagogical practices for using film in the secondary classroom (Russell, 2004, 2012):

- *Film as a visual textbook.* Using film as a visual textbook is the most common method used by teachers. Teachers often will use a film as a visual record to convey "what happened."
- *Film as a depicter of atmosphere.* Using film to depict a time period or setting allows teachers to display architecture, living conditions, clothes, weapons, etc. Thus, conveying the atmosphere to the students only requires short film clips, which saves instructional time.
- *Film as an analogy.* Using film as an analogy includes using films that are similar to events, people, places, etc. but otherwise different. There are many films that can be utilized as an analogy for various issues, events, and/or people.
- *Film as a historiography.* Artifacts (like films) created during a time period can be a valuable resource. Many older films, as well as contemporary films, portray the relevant issues of society. The film is used to demonstrate important societal issues and topics relevant to the time period.
- *Film as a springboard.* This often is done with short film clips to provoke interest and discussion, but entire movies can be used. The film is used as a motivator to jump start or springboard into the material.

Beyond dealing with historically based or themed films, secondary social studies teachers could find several other types of films useful in the classroom. Consider the fact that character education is mandated in over 30 states as part of the secondary curriculum. Middle and high school social studies teachers could use a variety of films related to social studies concepts that also help build on the decision-making skills associated with character education goals. Decision-making is a skill that transcends content of school curriculum and finds itself at the core of all education. When showing films or clips from films, teachers can help provoke meaningful inquiry regarding social issues, personal values, and moral dilemmas, thus allowing students to personally reflect and make insightful decisions, which is a key characteristic of being a good citizen in a global society. Oftentimes, films are very effective in presenting the complexity of character choices and decision-making by providing students with situational context and scenarios to see how character-based decisions have influenced historical and contemporary events. Take, for instance, the concepts of responsibility and citizenship as explored in the film *Gandhi* (1982). In this film, Mohandas Gandhi becomes disillusioned with discriminatory and biased laws against Indians living under the control of the British Empire. He initiated non-violent protests and campaigns to urge the British government to change these discriminatory laws. In spite of facing constant harassment and imprisonment, Gandhi eventually succeeds in helping India win its freedom, only to see violence erupt within his country between Hindus and Muslims.

Questions to consider in this film include: What does it mean to be a good citizen? Do good citizens always obey the laws? Can being a responsible citizen sometimes mean breaking the law?

What does it mean to be a good citizen in a country with conflicting definitions of this term? It is also worth noting that this film was an international collaboration between production companies in India and the United Kingdom in an effort to be culturally sensitive to both sides during this project. This is just one brief example of how films can introduce and encourage discussion about value conflicts and help students examine the complexity of character-driven decision-making in the context of the global world. By critically viewing films in this way, students have the opportunity to reflect on their own values, decision-making, and civic responsibilities. For a more detailed look at using film to teach character education, see *Reel Character Education: A Cinematic Approach to Character Development* (Russell & Waters, 2010).

Selected strategies for using film include:

1 *Films to entertain*. Have a discussion with your students about the nature of the filmmaking industry. Explain to them the different types of films and how most films are made with the explicit purpose of entertaining to make money. Have students examine popular Hollywood films that are based on historical events, such as *All the President's Men* (1976), to identify the historical inaccuracies or exaggerations in the film. Teachers could also have students reenact or rewrite specific scenes in the film that were particularly misleading about the true nature of the events being covered.

2 *Exploring social issues with film*. Many controversial and important contemporary issues are depicted in the film industry. Issues such as teenage pregnancy, violence, drug use, bullying, discrimination, and poverty all routinely appear in many Hollywood films. Allowing students to examine social issues with film will provide them with insight into the complex dynamics of these topics while also building an emotional connection through relationship building with characters. This type of activity can be done at all grade levels with all types of students, but teachers must be sure the topic and film being explored is age-appropriate. For a more complete look at teaching social issues with film, see Russell (2009).

3 *Using film to examine civic and character concepts*. Similar to social issues, the film industry also has a certain level of influence on public perception regarding civic and moral behaviors. Students should be given the opportunity to analyze films to see what messages they are attempting to convey or promote through characters in the story.

   Teachers could show students films created during different time periods to critique, analyze, and compare cultural norms and how the film industry perpetuated these beliefs. For example, show students selected scenes from films created during the 1950s and 1960s. What character traits are valued in these films? Are there any negative character beliefs that are commonly found (discrimination, stereotypes, racism, etc.)? Then show students selected scenes from films created during the 1990s and 2000s, repeating the aforementioned tasks. Once completed, students can compare how films from different decades depicted controversial topics relevant to the development of good character and examine how the film industry influenced or perpetuated popular character traits at different times in our country's history. For a more complete look at teaching character education with film, see Russell and Waters (2010).

4 *Creating films*. Having students create films is an exciting and engaging way to assess student learning and comprehension. This type of activity will allow students to not only demonstrate what they know but also build a skillset in media production that is becoming more and more important in the twenty-first century. Students can use popular programs like Microsoft Movie Maker or iMovie to create short films about nearly any topic. For example, teachers could have students make a documentary video about a historical figure, create a public service announcement drawing attention to important issues, or develop an informational film about social studies concepts. These types of assignments will give students another way to exhibit learning while simultaneously giving them valuable experience in the increasingly popular and diverse realm of media production.

5 *Oral history videos.* The creation of oral history videos will allow students to become historians by capturing the unique perspectives of individuals who have experienced certain events. Combining this classical form of historical research with contemporary technology will give students the chance to integrate history skills with popular digital media skills. Oral history projects can be used with a variety of topics, ranging from the Vietnam War to the more recent War on Terror in Iraq. By giving students the opportunity to interview and carry on a discussion with individuals in the community about relevant social studies topics, learning is given a new sense of significance as students see how many events resonate in the lives of citizens and how new technology can be utilized to share these stories with others.

Social Media

Of all the technological developments of the twenty-first century, there are few that have experienced the growth and influence of social media websites. Social media sites such as Facebook and Twitter are now dominant fixtures in mainstream culture that have drastically altered the way information is shared and people connect. Consider Facebook, a social networking service started in 2004 by a group of college students and led by Mark Zuckerberg. Fast-forward to today, where Facebook now boasts over 1 billion active users worldwide and Mark Zuckerberg is a multibillionaire. The quick rise of social media websites like Facebook presents several unique opportunities and challenges for educators. Teachers need to carefully consider all of the positive and negative outcomes that can come from social media sites, not only for their students but also for themselves.

There is much debate about the educational value and appropriateness of social media sites in the field of education. First and foremost, secondary teachers need to be extremely careful about the use and implementation of these sites in the classroom. The popularity of social media sites such as Facebook and Twitter makes them ubiquitous and, in turn, very intriguing to students and young adults. Consider how many celebrities, professional athletes, famous political figures, and even businesses and corporations say things such as, "Follow us on Twitter" or "Like us on Facebook." Students are bound to be influenced by these requests, so teachers should discuss the purpose of these sites and how to use them responsibly, if at all. Teachers will certainly need to play a role in helping students understand the potential dangers of social media sites by addressing how information shared on the sites can be open to the public and how that information can be used against them.

A final element of consideration regarding social media sites is the impact information shared on these sites by teachers, or future teachers, might have on their careers. There has been a great deal of controversy about how information shared on sites such as Facebook can adversely affect people in the field of education. Teachers who share or "post" information about students, administrators, or other school personnel have been increasingly scrutinized over the past several years, with some cases ending in the termination of the teacher's contract. In addition, many schools looking into hiring new teachers are beginning to pay more attention to what potential applicants are sharing on social media sites as a means to gather more information about candidates. Everyone in the field of public education must approach social media interactions with extreme caution.

Challenges to Technology Integration

As is the case with any instructional strategy or resource, there are always challenges to classroom implementation that need to be carefully considered. Teachers must always keep in mind the inherent responsibility to try and maximize the learning opportunities presented to every student in the class. Since the student population can vary tremendously based on learning styles, capabilities, etc., teachers should always ask themselves the following questions before planning any activity using technology:

1 Does the use of technology contribute to student learning?
2 Does the technology improve the learning opportunities of students?

3 If the activity involves student interaction with technology, do all students have the necessary skills to complete the activity? What modifications/accommodations might need to be made for students needing additional support?
4 Is the activity or lesson dependent on the technology, and how would you respond if the technology failed (power outage, Internet down, etc.)?

Access at Home: Addressing the Digital Divide

Although technology continues to spread and widely influence the way people work and live in society, it is naive to think that all regions have equal access to technology. Students from impoverished communities often have far less home access to resources such as the Internet or computers. Teachers need to gain an understanding of the student population and the community in order to address any potential issues that might occur from the incorporation of technology. Much like any other skillset, it is likely that students will bring with them into the secondary classroom a great deal of variability regarding technological proficiency. For that reason, teachers will need to scaffold the use of technology resources and instruction based on the individual needs of the students. Teachers should also never assume that any technology resource will be available to students at home and make sure to plan assignments and homework accordingly.

Cyberbullying

As we mentioned earlier, social media sites and Internet communications are changing the way that people interact. This is especially true for children growing up in the age of instant messaging, text messaging, and virtual social networks. One potentially negative outcome of all of these methods of communication is the possibility of abuse by the students. Cyberbullying refers to any attempt to harass or bully someone using the Internet or any other types of electronic devices. Bullying in general is a major concern for secondary school teachers and is considered part of most character education programs. Teachers should help students realize the consequences of their actions online, as many students may simply think it is a joke and not understand how hurtful these activities may be to others. Since social studies is concerned with the citizenship development of students, addressing cyber etiquette and behaviors in the classroom will certainly continue to develop as a critical need in the secondary social studies curriculum.

Copyright

A great deal of attention has been given to copyright issues during the digital age. The Internet has made more information available and accessible than ever before, leading to a blurred interpretation of what constitutes copyrighted materials on the web. Teachers should help students understand that not everything on the Internet is reliable, free, or acceptable for educational purposes. In addition, teachers need to address the importance of citing works from the Internet or giving credit to the creator of products online. This foundational information is crucial to address in secondary schools to help students avoid potential problems of plagiarism as projects and activities utilizing online instruction and resources continue to grow.

Internet Safety

One of the primary goals of secondary school teachers utilizing the Internet should be to ensure the safe and educational use of the Internet by students. Although many secondary students are transitioning from childhood into young adulthood, they are still quite impressionable and, perhaps at times, even a little naive. Helping secondary students understand the joys, benefits, challenges, and dangers of the Internet is becoming an increasingly necessary part of the teaching profession. While some students may have parents or guardians at home to assist in explaining the vast possibilities associated with web browsing, other students might not be as fortunate. Secondary teachers can help establish a foundation for safe Internet use in the lives of students by directly discussing and implementing activities that encourage responsible web browsing. Showing students how to effectively evaluate websites is a great starting point for secondary school teachers because these activities will teach students to ask the right questions about Internet resources.

Looking Back

Technology innovations continually change the way people communicate, socialize, interact, and learn. This means that teachers will also need to constantly evaluate and develop new teaching strategies to incorporate instructional technology into the curriculum. Teaching social studies is about much more than the transmission of content knowledge. Social studies is about preparing students to be good decision-makers and citizens in an increasingly global society. As technology becomes more and more connected to daily life and the business world, skills for understanding these devices and their implications become a critical aspect of being an effective citizen in the digital era. Some of the skills necessary for students include the ability to understand the nature of media and visuals in our society and how to safely utilize the web.

Social media sites and online etiquette are areas that need more direct attention in the educational environment. If teachers consistently ignore these issues simply because they are controversial or difficult to discuss, students will be far more likely to fall victim to dangers of the digital age such as cyberbullying or cyber predators. This chapter has examined several of the challenges and opportunities that are presented by incorporating instructional technology into the secondary classroom. To be sure, the vast field of technology in education surely indicates that not all aspects of this crucial area have been covered in this chapter. However, we have provided a solid foundation of essential information needed to effectively utilize technology to enhance social studies instruction in the secondary classroom. As technology will continue to develop and change over time, it is crucial for teachers to continually grow as life-long learners and explore all of the exciting educational opportunities that come with new technological innovations.

Extension Activity

Scenario

You are at the end of the fourth nine weeks at YHS. The end of your first year of teaching is quickly approaching and your excitement can hardly be contained. At a faculty meeting the principal of YHS, Dr. Russell, explains that the district has allotted YHS some additional funding for technology for the enhancement of social studies instruction. Excited, the entire faculty starts clamoring about what they will buy. Before the meeting can get off task, Dr. Russell explains that he has selected a committee to determine what technologies are important for enhancing the teaching and learning of social studies. As Dr. Russell is finishing, he concludes by identifying the faculty members chosen to serve on the committee. You hear your name called. Shocked, a little embarrassed, and secretly proud, you willingly accept the appointment.

Task

1. Dr. Russell has charged you with chairing a technology committee to determine what technologies are needed to enhance the teaching and learning of social studies. What are the advantages to having a committee like this in a school? Are there any disadvantages?
2. Do you think having teacher input on technology purchases will produce better social studies instruction for students? Why or why not?

Reflective Questions

1 What is meant by the term *media literacy*?
2 Why is there a need for helping students understand how to use technology?
3 What makes the Internet considered both a positive and negative resource?
4 What are some ways to enhance instruction utilizing technology?
5 What areas of instructional technology are you comfortable using, and in what areas might you need more development?
6 When is it appropriate to use technology?

Helpful Resources

Visit the ISTE website for a variety of helpful tools and resources.
www.iste.org
Watch this video discussing tips for new teachers to consider when planning technology-enhanced lessons.
www.teachingchannel.org/videos/technology-in-the-classroom
Watch this short video about the evolving world of technology and its impact on twenty-first century teachers.
www.youtube.com/watch?v=Ax5cNlutAys&list=PLvzOwE5lWqhSgJVgg7VfRkBisbmm-BFUL&index=2
For more information on media literacy, visit the Center for Media Literacy website below.
www.medialit.org
For more information on visual literacy, visit the International Visual Litearcy Association website below.
http://ivla.org/new/
View the following video for an overview of Promethean ActivBoard possibilities in your classroom instruction.
www.youtube.com/watch?v=_y_kS9d_Vgs
Watch this video of a middle school teacher teaching a lesson on immigration using a documentary film.
www.teachingchannel.org/videos/teaching-cultural-identity
Visit the Carnegie Corporation Oral History Project website for examples of oral history videos.
www.columbia.edu/cu/lweb/digital/collections/oral_hist/carnegie/video-interviews/
Visit the Common Sense Education website for a list and overview of different social media websites and apps that could be used by teachers or students.
www.commonsense.org/education/top-picks/social-networks-for-students-and-teachers

Further Reading

Berson, M.J., Cruz, B.C., Duplass, J.A. & Johnston, J.H. (2007). *Social Studies on the Internet* (3rd Edition). Upper Saddle River, NJ: Merrill/Prentice Hall.

This book is professionally written by well-respected educators in the field of social studies education with a significant background in technology incorporation for effective classroom instruction. This book is a great resource for identifying quality Internet sites and activities for maximizing social studies instruction using new technology.

Cohen, D. & Rosenzweig, R. (2005). *Digital History: A Guide to Gathering, Preserving, and Presenting the Past on the Web*. Philadelphia, PA: University of Pennsylvania.

This introductory textbook goes step by step in explaining to teachers, historians, and other educators how to navigate the vast amount of material found on the Internet and how to utilize these resources for classroom instruction. It also offers information on how to set up learning projects using historical documents found on the web.

Diem, R. & Berson, M. (Eds.). (2010). *Technology in Retrospect: Social Studies in the Information Age, 1984–2009*. Charlotte, NC: Information Age Publishing.

This edited book compiles the work of social studies professionals to examine how technology has changed the nature of instruction in social studies classrooms. This book will prove to be a valuable resource for teachers or researchers interested in the nature of social studies instruction during the information age.

Galloway, J., John, M. & McTaggart, M. (2015). *Learning with Mobile and Handheld Technologies*. New York, NY: Routledge Publishing.

This book explores the possibilities and pitfalls of teaching and learning with mobile devices as well as of e-learning in general. Resources and teaching project ideas utilizing mobile devices are provided.

Lee, J. & Friedman, A. (Eds.). (2009). *Research on Technology in Social Studies Education.* Charlotte, NC: Information Age Publishing.

This edited book focuses on empirical research on the effectiveness of technology on the teaching and learning of social studies. Included in this book are numerous works that discuss what is being done in the social studies field in relation to the use of technology and how these important studies can guide the research of future educators.

Prensky, M. (2010). *Teaching Digital Natives: Partnering for Real Learning.* Thousand Oaks, CA: Corwin.

This book examines the promising practices of educating students during the twenty-first century. The author discusses how technology and new teaching methods should be combined to create a unique form of learning that is extremely beneficial to students in today's society.

References

Braden, R.A. & Hortin, J.A. (1982). Identifying the theoretical foundations of visual literacy. *Journal of Visual/Verbal Languaging*, 2(2), 37–42.

Center for Media Literacy. (2012). Empowerment Through Education. Available at: www.medialit.org/

Felten, P. (2008). *Visual literacy*. Change: The Magazine of Higher Education (November/December), 60–64.

Gee, J.P. (2003). *What Video Games Have to Teach Us About Literacy and Learning.* New York, NY: Palgrave Macmillan.

Holmes, K., Russell, W. & Movitz, A. (2007). Reading in the social studies: Using subtitled films. *Social Education*, 71(6), 326–330.

ISTE (International Society for Technology in Education). (2008). National Educational Technology Standards. Available at: www.iste.org/docs/pdfs/nets-t-standards.pdf?sfvrsn=2

Keengwe, J. & Onchwari, G. (2015). *Handbook of Research on Active Learning and the Flipped Classroom Model in the Digital Age.* Hershey, PA: IGI Global.

Kress, G. (1997). *Before Writing: Rethinking the Paths to Literacy*. London, UK: Routledge.

Lee, J.K. (2002). Digital history in the history/social studies classroom. *The History Teacher*, 35(4), 503–518.

NCSS. (2012). Chapter 2: The Themes of Social Studies. Available at: www.socialstudies.org/standards/strands.

Rosenstone, R.A. (2006). *History on Film/Film on History*. London, UK: Pearson Education Limited.

Russell, W. (2004). Teaching with Film: A Guide for Social Studies Teachers. ERIC Document Reproduction Service No. ED 530820.

Russell, W.B. (2007). *Using Film in the Social Studies*. Lanham, MD: University Press of America, Inc.

Russell, W. (2009). *Teaching Social Issues with Film*. Charlotte, NC: Information Age Publishing.

Russell, W. (2012). The art of teaching social studies with film. *The Clearing House: A Journal of Educational Strategies, Issues, and Ideas*, 85(4), 1–8.

Russell, W. & Waters, S. (2010). *Reel Character Education: A Cinematic Approach to Character Development.* Charlotte, NC: Information Age Publishing.

12 Lesson Plans for Secondary Social Studies

Looking Ahead

No matter what grade level or subject area one teaches, there is a universal need for effective planning. Planning lessons in the secondary classroom is becoming increasingly important as the emphasis on standardized test scores continues to place unprecedented restrictions on instructional time. In addition, the heavy reliance on textbooks when planning social studies curriculum causes many teachers to focus much more on breadth than depth of content. Many state standards for social studies also perpetuate the breadth over depth approach, making it difficult for teachers to plan meaningful activities that may take up too much class time. For this reason, efficient and purposeful planning needs to be considered by all social studies teachers in order to make sure that as a content area, social studies is considered engaging, purposeful, meaningful, and challenging and pushes students to think critically about issues of historical and contemporary importance.

As you may recall from Chapter 3, there are a variety of ways to develop and plan excellent social studies instruction. Teachers in schools all over the country routinely create lesson plans based on state, district, school, or administrative requirements. Some school administrators may require teachers to submit detailed, narrative-based lesson plans weeks in advance, while others may only require a brief outline of activities. Whatever the policy may be, it is crucial that teachers understand the lesson plan requirements and expectations of their school. The great diversity of lesson plan structures and requirements in middle and high schools is demonstrated in the following section of classroom-tested social studies activities, written by secondary social studies teachers for secondary social studies teachers.

The lesson plans provided in this chapter were created by middle and high school social studies teachers with various years of teaching experience from Grades 6 to 12. There are two lesson plans for each prominent social science field in the 6–12 social studies curriculum (U.S. history, world history, geography, U.S. government, economics, psychology, and sociology) for a total of 14 lesson plans. All of these teachers come from different schools with a variety of different lesson plan requirements and writing styles. To provide some commonalities, we suggested categories that might be included in the lesson plans but allowed classroom teachers the freedom and creativity warranted by professional educators to complete the lesson plans however they saw fit. Readers will find that some lessons are described in great detail using narrative explanations, while others contain bulleted points or outlines of procedures to follow. It is also important to note that the authors of this textbook did not solicit any specific social studies topics from the classroom teachers who composed these lesson plans. Teachers were simply encouraged to submit lesson plans that worked well for them while teaching social studies in the secondary classroom.

DOI: 10.4324/9781003217060-12

We offer these lessons to you as examples of engaging classroom strategies and also as examples of the different ways that lessons can be written. It is important for the reader to determine which style of lesson plan writing best meets school requirements and your own method of effectively planning.

FYI

We highly recommend that pre-service and beginning teachers start out with more detailed, narrative lesson plans. While this may take a bit more time, it is essential that you gain experience working through the details of a lesson plan, including pacing, transitions, etc.

Can You? Do You?

Can you ...

- explain how effective planning benefits classroom instruction and learning?
- describe what a "good" lesson plan looks like?
- identify or describe supplemental resources that improve lesson plans?
- think of social studies activities that are engaging and encourage critical thinking at various grade levels?

Do you ...

- know where to find lesson plan resources using the Internet?
- know what lesson plan formats are typically expected of teachers working in your local school district?
- understand how to engage multiple learning styles in your lesson plans?
- understand different ways to plan for the needs of diverse learners?

Focus Activity

Before reading this chapter, try the focus activity below.

Think back about your experiences during your pre-service education. What types of social studies lessons did you typically see in the classroom (if any) or read about in professional journals? Can you remember any really engaging activities? What made these lessons exciting? Share and discuss your experiences with classmates. After a brief discussion, create a list of components you consider essential in a good lesson plan.

Economics

Lesson Plan One

Teacher: Jordan Webster and Kelsey Evans
Subject/Content Area: Economics
Unit Topic: Personal Finance
Lesson Title: Budget Project

OBJECTIVES — Clear, Specific, and Measurable. NOT ACTIVITIES

Student-Friendly

- The student will be able to analyse the cost of daily living.
- The student will be able to explain how to properly budget.

STANDARDS — **Identify what you will be teaching**. Reference only NCSS standards and/or Common Core standards.

NCSS Standard 7: Production, Distribution, and Consumption: *Social studies programs should include experiences that provide for the study of how people organize for the production, distribution, and consumption of goods and services.*

DAILY PLANNER — **Summary** of the activities with suggested time allotments for each step included in this lesson.

Introduction and explanation of common advertising strategies: 10 minutes

Budget activity: 1st day
Budget activity: 2nd day
Presentation: 3rd day

ACTIVATING STRATEGY — Motivator/Hook

An Essential Question encourages students to put forth more effort when faced with complex, open-ended, challenging, meaningful, and authentic questions.

How do you create a proper budget?

Instruction

1 Ask students what they think their average salary will be once they enter the workforce. Have students volunteer their answers, then show them what the average American salary is.
2 Explain three-day budget project instructions.

Overview and Purpose

According to the Washington Journal, the average salary of a student just graduating from college with a liberal arts degree is $33,540. To most students, this is a lot of money. That being said, with daily expenses as well as rent, insurance, food, gas, and fun—the money that we assume we have can quickly disappear. It is our goal to teach the students money managerial skills as well as the value of a dollar—all without the possibility of failure (unless you do not do this assignment, of course). All students will assume they have received a job offering at the Amway Center, located at 400 W. Church St. Orlando, FL 32801. They will also assume their hourly rate will be $10 + 10% of their year to date grade before taxes, for example a person with a 75% year to date would make $17.50. Students should assume they will want to live alone, live in an area they feel safe/comfortable, will have at least the Internet and a cell/home phone, will eat three full meals a day, will follow all laws (not stealing anything or failing to pay bills), will want a social life of some sort, and will definitely want to be with that super special boyfriend/girlfriend they will most assuredly have in the future.

Year to date grade: ______________________________

Hourly wage (10 + 10% of YTD): ______________________ x 40 hours a week = $__________________.

Weekly Gross Pay

Student's salary will be based on their grade in the class.

GUIDED AND INDEPENDENT PRACTICE	"We Do", "You Do" Encourage Higher-Order Thinking and Problem Solving Relevance Differentiated Strategies for Practice to Provide Intervention and Extension

Students will be required to do personal research based on their salary cap and given life situation. It depends on the resources of the school, but if there is one student to one computer, students will be able to do personal research in the classroom or may be required to use the computer lab for two days. Students will be required to research how to live and budget on a monthly income.

Table 12.1 Handout A

STUDENT NAMES: ______________________
DATE: _______________

Item	*Country*	*Region/Continent*
1		
2		
3		
4		
5		
6		
7		
8		
9		
10		
11		
12		
13		
14		
15		
16		
17		
18		
19		
20		

Table 12.2 Budget Expenses

Field	*Contributions*
Trade and Economy	
Education	
Math	
Science	
Medicine	
Writing and Literature	

CLOSURE	Reflection/Wrap-Up Summarizing, Reminding, Reflecting, Restating, Connecting

After students have completed all the questions and filled out their charts, students will do a presentation on the third day detailing their life and their budget choices.

ASSESSMENT/EVALUATION	Students show evidence of proficiency through a variety of assessments. Aligned with the Lesson Objective Formative/Summative Performance-Based/Rubric Formal/Informal

The students will be assessed via their culminating presentation.

MATERIALS/TECHNOLOGY	What materials are utilized for this lesson? What types of technology are utilized to enhance learning and engagement? What primary and secondary sources are present to meet the learning objectives?

- Technology for Research
- Budget Handouts

MEETING INDIVIDUAL NEEDS OF DIVERSE LEARNERS	How does the lesson meet the needs of students with different learning styles (multiple intelligences) and what accommodations are made for diverse learners?

The teacher will be monitoring and roaming the class continually throughout the class period to ensure individualized instruction.

CHARACTER EDUCATION CONNECTION	What character and value-related issues are present in your lesson?

Students will develop the ability to make wiser financial choices through the development of financial literacy.

Lesson Plan Two

Teacher: John Pagnotti
Subject/Content Area: Economics
Unit Topic: Globalization
Lesson Title: Comparative Advantage: "Where are you wearing?"

OBJECTIVES	Clear, Specific, and Measurable. NOT ACTIVITIES

Student Friendly

- Students will understand the interwoven nature of the global economic system, their role as a consumer and change agent within it.
- Students will understand that certain areas have a competitive advantage in manufacturing different types of goods and the reasons why.

STANDARDS — Identify what you will be teaching. Reference only NCSS standards and/or Common Core standards.

CCSS.ELA-Literacy.RH.11–12.2: Determine the central ideas or information of a primary or secondary source; provide an accurate summary that makes clear the relationships among the key details and ideas.

CCSS.ELA-Literacy.RH.11–12.3: Evaluate various explanations for actions or events and determine which explanation best accords with textual evidence, acknowledging where the text leaves matters uncertain.
NCSS Standard 3: People, Places, and Environments
NCSS Standard 7: Production, Distribution, and Consumption
NCSS Standard 9: Global Connections

DAILY PLANNER — **Summary** of the activities with suggested time allotments for each step included in this lesson.

- This is a one-day activity designed for a single 120-minute block or three 50-minute periods.
- The warm-up activity and introduction will take 30 minutes.
- Independent Group Work and Guided Practice will take 55–70 minutes.
- The Debrief tying concept to real world ramifications will take the last 20 minutes.

ACTIVATING STRATEGY — Motivator/Hook
An Essential Question encourages students to put forth more effort when faced with complex, open-ended, challenging, meaningful, and authentic questions.

INSTRUCTION	Step-by-Step Procedures Sequence Discover/Explain, Direct Instruction Modeling Expectations: "I Do" Questioning/Encourages Higher Order Thinking Grouping Strategies Differentiated Instructional Strategies to Provide Intervention and Extension

1 As students come in, begin the class with the "quick write" prompt: "What country makes most of the stuff we own and how do you know it?": 1 minute.
2 After students have had a few minutes to write their responses, ask them to share which countries they chose and why. In a chart, all students can see a record of each student response to see which countries have the most "votes." Follow by asking the question, "I see the class has made the argument that countries X, Y, and Z are the countries that produce most of our stuff. Let's figure out why": 5–10 minutes.
3 After students have had a chance to respond, let them know that in the free market-based global economy in which we live, goods and services are produced by manufacturers in countries that usually offer the best combination of quality and price to make sure consumers are satisfied. These countries offer the manufacturer a comparative advantage, or the ability to produce a good or service at a reduced opportunity cost. The comparative advantage offered can be because of a greater rate of production efficiency (lower cost per unit), access to resources (specialized or cheap human capital and/or plentiful or less expensive natural resources), or customized manufacturing processes (regulatory environmental oversight or specialized machinery). As it is the purpose of any corporation to make a profit, companies that manufacture "stuff" will almost certainly do so in the country that offers the greatest comparative advantage. Examples of this to offer students would be, "Why much of the farming in the United States occurs in the Mid-West region" (access to resources, human capital); "Oil refinement in Louisiana and Texas" (specialized machinery, natural resources, and human capital); and "Precious metal mining in the Rocky Mountain Region" (human capital, access to resources): 10–20 minutes.

GUIDED AND INDEPENDENT PRACTICE	"We Do", "You Do" Encourage Higher Order Thinking and Problem Solving Relevance Differentiated Strategies for Practice to Provide Intervention and Extension

1 Let students know that they will be using the "stuff" they have with them to draw conclusions about which countries and regions of the world offer comparative advantages on certain types of manufactured goods. Divide students into groups of four to five and ask them to take all of the "stuff" they have on their person (clothes, personal items, notebooks, backpacks, any consumer electronics, supplies, jackets, or lunch boxes) with them. Provide each group with Handout A, making sure that one student has been assigned as the record keeper. Students should be instructed to generally describe each product (e.g., T-Shirt), the country of origin listed on a label on the product (e.g., Guatemala), and the region of the country (e.g., Central America) for at least 20 items in their group. Provide students with a World Almanac or allow access to computers to ensure students are able to record the region: 15–20 minutes.

2 Ask groups to share their lists with the class. Be sure to record each entry into a chart for all students to see. With students, group all the items into general categories so trends in industries can be inferred. These general groups can also be thought of as "industries." For example, T-Shirts, shorts, gloves, and hats could fall into a general category labeled "clothing," while iPods, cell phones, tablets, and e-book readers could fall into a category labeled "personal electronics." Wallets, belts, and straps that are leather can be labeled "leather." As each response is regrouped and tallied, please be sure to keep track of which country it came from. So if ten pieces of "clothing" are recorded and five pieces are from Nicaragua, two are from China, and three are from India, you need to put a little tally mark by each country: 10–15 minutes.

3 For Example:

General Category	*Country of Origin*	*Region*
Clothes	China II	Asia
	India III	Asia
	Nicaragua IIIII	Central America

4 After all the items have been recorded and regrouped in general categories on the board, remind students they are to make inferences about which countries or regions of the world offer a comparative advantage on the types of goods that made up the "stuff" the classroom had based upon the information in the chart. Assign each member of the group at least one general category; the student is responsible for leading a discussion in the group regarding which region(s) offer comparative advantages to the assigned "industry." During this part of the activity, be sure to circulate to informally conduct a formative assessment to ensure students understand the concept of comparative advantage: 10–15 minutes.

5 As students finish up their discussions, facilitate a whole group discussion with students about what the information the class compiled during the activity can infer about the comparative advantage of the different regions relative to the industries identified. Be sure to ask why certain regions offer comparative advantages to certain industries and give real-world examples to students (lower cost per unit, specialized or cheap human capital and/or plentiful or less expensive natural resources, regulatory environmental oversight or specialized machinery). Some examples might be: how the lax environmental policies of China allow for cheap manufacturing; cheap labor in India because the country has too many people and not enough jobs; the absence of African comparative advantage due to longstanding political, social, and economic crisis: 15–20 minutes.

CLOSURE	Reflection/Wrap-Up Summarizing, Reminding, Reflecting, Restating, Connecting

For closure, remind students that the concept of comparative advantage is based upon the premise that certain countries and regions offer reduced opportunity costs for the production of certain goods. Based upon the information that was offered from the stuff in the room, it's easy to see that certain areas offer a "better deal" for different industries than others. In our free-market global economy, manufacturers look for that "sweet spot" where the price and quality of a good intersect to maximize profits because that's what their customers expect. Unfortunately, many of the regions that produce much of the world's goods (China, South-East Asia, and Central America) do so at a terrible human rights cost. Let students know that many of the people who manufacture their iPhones, clothes, and accessories make an extremely low wage and that has a lot to do with why those goods are so cheap. Remind students that in many cities in China, the air is not breathable many days out of the year because factories manufacture goods without any environmental oversight. This keeps cost low so profits can be sustained.

If everything were made in countries that were ethical and using clean manufacturing practices, the cost of those goods would be much higher. Ask students to take a moment to reflect on their role as consumers in this global economy. Can consumers affect how things are made? Ask students to conclude the lesson by answering the following question in a paragraph as their "Exit Ticket": 20 minutes.

"Do consumers have the power to move the comparative advantage to produce a good from a region or country that exploits human capital and resources to one that is more ethical in their perspective? Would it always be a good thing to do so if they could?"

ASSESSMENT/ EVALUATION	Students will demonstrate mastery of the concept of comparative advantage through informal formative discussion and through a formal written exercise at the conclusion of the lesson connecting the concept to personal action.
MATERIALS/ TECHNOLOGY	What materials are utilized for this lesson? What types of technology are utilized to enhance learning and engagement? What primary and secondary sources are present to meet the learning objectives?

Materials:

Handout A (1 per group)

World Maps (1 per group)

Primary Source:

The country of origin label from many personal items in the students' possession.

Technology:

Smart Board (optional)

Projector (optional)

MEETING INDIVIDUAL NEEDS OF DIVERSE LEARNERS	How does the lesson meet the needs of students with different learning styles (multiple intelligences) and what accommodations are made for diverse learners?

- Auditory learners through discussions, open-ended questioning and responses, lectures.
- Kinesthetic learners through group work, hunting through personal effects to find country of origin labels.
- Visual learners through working with maps, written assignments, and extended written response.

CHARACTER EDUCATION CONNECTION	What character and value-related issues are present in your lesson?

This lesson focuses learners' attention on their actions as consumers and the effects of those actions.

Table 12.3 Economics Lesson Plan Two: Handout A

Achievements	**Impact**	**Visual**
At least three achievements are presented. (4 points)	Impact of achievement(s) is explicitly addressed, and relevance to modern day is at least mentioned. (4 points)	Visual representation of how achievement(s) is (are) used in modern day. (2 points)
Two or less achievements are presented. (2 points)	Impact of achievement(s) is somewhat addressed, but neglects the relationship to modern day. (2 points)	Visual representation is present, but does not apply to modern use. (1 points)
0 Points	0 Points	0 Points

Geography

Lesson Plan One

Teacher: Mary Duddles
Subject/Content Area: Geography
Unit Topic: Industrialization and Economic Development
Lesson Title: Human Development Index

OBJECTIVES	Clear, Specific, and Measurable. NOT ACTIVITIES Student-Friendly

Enduring Understanding (B):

students will understand that measures of development are used to understand patterns of social and economic differences at a variety of scales.

Learning Objective: students are able to explain social and economic measures of development:

- define development and Human Development Index (HDI)
- identify the four indicators use to calculate HDI

- analyze data (comprised of several indicators of development) to determine the level of development of various "mystery countries"
- identify typical data patterns for the three levels of development according to Wallerstein's World-Systems Analysis.

Essential knowledge:

1 students will know that measures of social and economic development include Gross National Income (GNI) per capita, sectoral structure of an economy (primary, secondary, tertiary jobs), income distribution, fertility rates, infant mortality rates, access to health care, and literacy rates.

2 students will know that measures of gender inequality include reproductive health, indices of empowerment, and labor-market participation.

3 students will know that the HDI is a composite measure used to show spatial variation in levels of development.

STANDARDS	Identify what you will be teaching. Reference only NCSS standards and/or Common Core standards.

NCSS Themes: III: People, Places, and Environments

National Geography Standards: Standard 14: How human actions modify the physical environment

CCSS Reading History/Social Studies: 10: Read and comprehend complex literary and informational texts independently and proficiently

---

DAILY PLANNER	**Summary** of the activities with suggested time allotments for each step included in this lesson.

LESSON TIMELINE Duration: 3 days, 45 minute periods

(1) Build Background Knowledge
(2) Provide Accountability for Student Ownership of Learning
(3) Hook/Intro to Lesson
(4) Mini-Lesson/Instruction
(5) Guided Practice
(6) Independent Practice
(7) Review/Formative Assessment
(8) Extended Learning

ACTIVATING STRATEGY	Motivator/Hook An Essential Question encourages students to put forth more effort when faced with complex, open-ended, challenging, meaningful, and authentic questions.

Students view random images, discuss them with their partner, and look for clues as to the level of development of each of the countries the images represent (allow 2-minute partner discussion). Then teacher chooses a few students, each to share their thoughts about one image: their observations and reasons for their analysis (more developed countries or less developed countries).

INSTRUCTION	Step-by-Step Procedures Sequence Discover/Explain, Direct Instruction Modeling Expectations: "I Do" Questioning/Encourages Higher-Order Thinking Grouping Strategies Differentiated Instructional Strategies to Provide Intervention and Extension

Teacher will go over the RCQ with students and provide clarification on content. There are excellent YouTube videos that you could use: www.youtube.com/watch?v=HbZMXdADBWM and www.youtube.com/watch?v=7vOnhtFedKg

GUIDED AND INDEPENDENT PRACTICE	"We Do", "You Do" Encourage Higher Order Thinking and Problem Solving Relevance Differentiated Strategies for Practice to Provide Intervention and Extension

Teacher asks student volunteers to explain each of the indicators of development. For each indicator, teacher asks how it can be used to indicate whether a country is more or less developed. For example, a high life expectancy would indicate that the country has a good healthcare system, people have good nutrition and are knowledgeable of healthy living practices. This is review for students; they should know what a more developed country (MDC) and less developed country (LDC) is.

The teacher goes through each of the indicators. When she gets to crude birth rate (CBR), crude death rate (CDR), and natural increase rate (NIR), she will remind students how to calculate NIR (CBR – CDR) and review how NIR can be used to determine the Demographic Transition Stage (NIR of 2+% is stage 2, NIR of 1–2% is stage 3, NIR of 0–1% is stage 4, NIR of <0% is stage 5).

The Gini coefficient is the only indicator the students will not be familiar with since it was not in their background reading. Teacher should explain what it is and why. There are maps available that show where income inequality it high. Latin America is notoriously high. See article for reference. www.weforum.org/agenda/2016/01/inequality-is-getting-worse-in-latin-america-here-s-how-to-fix-it/

Teacher can allow students to read the direction and have them complete the worksheet with or without guidance. See lesson documents for answers.

CLOSURE	Reflection/Wrap-Up Summarizing, Reminding, Reflecting, Restating, Connecting

- Teacher will have students complete exit tickets at the end of each day to examine where students are in their learning and comprehension of the material.

ASSESSMENT/ EVALUATION	Students show evidence of proficiency through a variety of assessments. Aligned with the Lesson Objective Formative/Summative Performance-Based/Rubric Formal/Informal

After students have had 2½ days to work on the analysis, at the end of day three, teacher has student volunteers share out (whole class setting) which level of development they think each "mystery country" is: very high, high, medium, and low. Have students justify why (use an indicator and explain why this number caused them to hypothesize the level) and then also have them guess what world region the mystery country is from and have them speculate why (as they did at the end of their assignment).

MATERIALS/TECHNOLOGY	What materials are utilized for this lesson? What types of technology are utilized to enhance learning and engagement? What primary and secondary sources are present to meet the learning objectives?

- Computer and Projector
- Videos
- Handouts

MEETING INDIVIDUAL NEEDS OF DIVERSE LEARNERS	How does the lesson meet the needs of students with different learning styles (multiple intelligences) and what accommodations are made for diverse learners?

- Low-level students will benefit from being in groups and should experience extra scaffolding
- High-achieving students will be encouraged to document three extra inferences from the maps.
- Visuals will be used to aid ESOL students (i.e., when telling students to get a piece of paper out I will literally pull out a piece of paper as I give the directions). Also the teacher should try to translate the key vocabulary words in students' native tongue if possible.

CHARACTER EDUCATION CONNECTION	What character and value-related issues are present in your lesson?

- Responsibility
- Citizenship

Lesson Documents

Human Development Index (HDI) ACTIVITY

The Human Development Index (HDI) was created by the United Nations during the latter part of the twentieth century to act as a measurement of development for any given country. The HDI number is between 0–1, 1 being the highest level of development. Four indicators are used to **calculate HDI: life expectancy, expected years of schooling, mean years of schooling, and GNI per capita**.

For this activity, use the most up-to-date HDI data provided to you. The data sheet intentionally leaves out the country name; it is only identified by a letter. The purpose is so that you will develop the skill of analyzing data without knowledge of the country, which might skew your analysis. It is more important that you practice this skill than get the correct answers.

WORKSHEET 1:
Categorize all the indicators on the HDI Data Sheet (i.e., life expectancy, expected years of schooling …) into these three categories: social, demographic, and economic.

Economic: A decent standard of living
Demographic: A long and healthy life
Social: Access to knowledge

Discuss which category you think each country belongs to and list the countries by letter in their prospective categories: core (very high HDI), semi-periphery (high and medium HDI), periphery (low HDI). Use the descriptions to help.

Wallerstein's World-Systems Analysis (levels of development, separated into the following categories) Country letters that correspond to each category	*Core* is made up of highly developed countries that are centers of wealth and power. They are powerful and influential economically, politically, and culturally at a global scale.	*Semi-Periphery* is made up of countries that are in the middle regarding their process of development. They have moved out of the periphery, but are not quite up to the powerful influence of core countries.	*Periphery* is made up of developing countries that are the least developed: have LESS access to world centers of consumption (stuff to buy), communications, wealth and power and are LESS economically, politically and culturally influential.

Now look at your analysis and indicate below what seems to be TYPICAL DATA for each of the categories. You can use a range of data if you like.

Indicators of development	*Core*	*Semi-Periphery*	*Periphery*
life expectancy			
mean years of schooling			
(GNI) per capita			
% youth vs elderly pop.			
NIR (%)			
IMR (Infant Mortality Rate)			
literacy rate (M/F)			
labor force (primary, secondary, tertiary)			
GII (Gender Inequality)			

Now, use what you know about different regions of the world and try to match four mystery countries (only known by their letters) with the following four regions. Indicate the country by its letter and write your justification for this match using at least one bit of data (use a different indicator for each hypothesis. See example.

Lesson Plan Two

Teacher: Jennifer Johnson
Subject/Content Area: Cultural Geography/World History
Unit Topic: Islam
Lesson Title: Contributions of Islamic Civilization

> **FYI**
>
> Consider the importance of discussing positive contributions of groups, religions, and countries that may have complicated relationships with the U.S. today.

Objectives	Clear, Specific, and Measurable. NOT ACTIVITIES Student-Friendly

At the end of the lesson, the student will be able to distinguish and explain several contributions of Islamic civilization and how they influence the modern world.

STANDARDS — Identify what you will be teaching.
Reference only NCSS standards and/or Common Core standards.

- I. Culture
- II. Time, Continuity, and Change
- IV. Individual Development and Identity
- VIII. Science, Technology, and Society
- IX. Global Connections

DAILY PLANNER — Summary of the activities with suggested time allotments for each step included in this lesson.

- Warm-up: Review questions about expansion and achievements of the Muslim Empire: 10 minutes
- Direct Instruction: Video *(Islam: Empire of Faith)* with note guide: 20 minutes
- Guided Practice: Short reading ("Expansion and Achievements of the Muslim Empire") and creation of a thank you card to the Abbasids, based on one of six different topics, thanking them for the cultural and scientific achievements developed during the Golden Age of the Abbasid Empire: 30 minutes
- Assessment: Students will complete charts outlining all six topics of contributions and achievements of Islamic civilizations by trading cards with one another before submitting thank you cards: 30 minutes

---

ACTIVATING STRATEGY — Motivator/Hook
An Essential Question encourages students to put forth more effort when faced with complex, open-ended, challenging, meaningful, and authentic questions.

What were some cultural and scientific contributions and achievements of Islamic civilization?

INSTRUCTION — Step-by-Step Procedures Sequence
Discover/Explain, Direct Instruction
Modeling Expectations: "I Do"
Questioning/Encourages Higher Order Thinking
Grouping Strategies
Differentiated Instructional Strategies to Provide Intervention and Extension

---

1 In order to activate student learning and engage prior knowledge, the teacher will have students complete the first two questions on the "Expansion and Achievements of the Muslim Empire" handout. This will help students review Islamic Empires that came before the Abbasid Empire. This will not only serve as review, but it will also set the stage for the Golden Age of the Abbasids, which is the focus of the lesson. In order to differentiate this warm-up, the teacher could group students together to work through the questions.

2 Direct instruction will start with a short video, *Islam: Empire of Faith*. This video will review concepts from the previous lessons about Islamic Empires and add to the knowledge of Islamic contributions to civilization; namely, in the fields of science, math, art and architecture, education, trade and economy, and writing and literature. Students will complete a video note guide, which will gauge their level of attention during the documentary. In order to differentiate this instruction, the teacher could pause the video in between questions to discuss the answers as a class. Additionally, the teacher could ask students to make predictions about the video questions.

GUIDED AND INDEPENDENT PRACTICE	"We Do," "You Do" Encourage Higher Order Thinking and Problem Solving Relevance Differentiated Strategies for Practice to Provide Intervention and Extension

---

1 For guided practice, students will continue to read their "Expansion and Achievements of the Muslim Empire" handout. This will introduce their major assignment for the day. Students will create a thank you card to the Abbasids, thanking them for the cultural and scientific achievements developed during the Golden Age of the Abbasid Empire. Student will be given a sheet of colored cardstock. There will be six different colors of cardstock, and the colors will be distributed at random. Each color represents a different topic of contributions and achievements during the Muslim Empire (Green = Trade and Economy; Gray = Science; Pink = Education; Coral = Medicine; Blue = Math; and Yellow = Writing and Literature). In order to differentiate this lesson, students could have a bank of contributions from which to choose. Additionally, students could be required to include how the contributions/achievements were applied during the Golden Age of the Abbasids.

2 Once students complete their thank you cards, they will get together in groups of six, with each group having each color of cardstock represented in order to ensure that all topics will be covered in each group. Students' cards will be assessed on achievements in the topic, their impact on the modern world, and a visual representation of the innovation if used today. Students will also be required to complete a chart listing the six different topics. In their small groups, students will have to complete their charts by trading cards and discovering the things for which each group member thanked the Abbasids.

CLOSURE	Reflection/Wrap-Up Summarizing, Reminding, Reflecting, Restating, Connecting

---

In order to close the lesson, students will be asked to answer the following prompt in a "Think-Pair-Share" format:

What do you think is the most influential category and/or specific contribution/achievement of Islamic civilization and why?

ASSESSMENT/ EVALUATION	Students show evidence of proficiency through a variety of assessments. Aligned with the Lesson Objective Formative/Summative Performance-Based/Rubric Formal/Informal

---

- Formative: The warm-up activity will assess the knowledge retained from readings and previous lessons about the spread of Islam and different Islamic empires that emerged over the course of the time period in focus (i.e., about A.D./C.E. 600 to 1000).

- Formative: The "Islam: Empire of Faith Video Notes" handout will assess student ability to interpret and analyze information about the cultural and scientific contributions and achievements of the Muslim empires. It will also serve as an assessment of student ability to comprehend information delivered through a different electronic medium (e.g., video).
- Lesson Summative and Aligned with the Lesson Objective: The thank you cards to the Abbasids and the chart categorizing contributions of the Golden Age of the Abbasids both assess student understanding of the most important and influential scientific and cultural achievements and contributions of the Muslim empires. The thank you cards also assess student ability to synthesize something new given a set of information. The chart assesses student ability to analyze and evaluate information in specific classifications.

MATERIALS/TECHNOLOGY	What materials are utilized for this lesson? What types of technology are utilized to enhance learning and engagement? What primary and secondary sources are present to meet the learning objectives?

The materials that are used for this lesson are:

- Student textbook: *Ancient World History: Patterns of Interaction* (McDougal Littell)
- Video: *Islam: Empire of Faith* (PBS Documentary)
- Colored cardstock
- Markers, pens, colored pencils, glue sticks, and other necessary craft supplies for making thank you cards
- Appendix A: "Islam: Empire of Faith Video Notes" Handout
- Appendix B: "Expansion and Achievements of the Muslim Empire" Handout
- Appendix C: "Contributions of the Golden Age of the Abbasids" Chart
- Appendix D: "Achievements of the Muslim Empire: Thank You Card Rubric"

Meeting Individual Needs of Diverse Learners	How does the lesson meet the needs of students with different learning styles (multiple intelligences) and what accommodations are made for diverse learners?

In order to accommodate different learners, video is included for auditory and visual learners. A group activity gives students the option to move around the classroom for kinesthetic learners. The creative card-making activity gives creative and spatial learners a chance to excel. Read-write learners are accommodated through the use of text and the writing assignments of both the card and the chart.

The adaptations that could be made for individual learners might be one-on-one work with the teacher, teacher-assigned group work, or perhaps discussion to enhance learning. The teacher could also pause during the video to stop and assess class understanding of the material. If necessary, students could have small group discussions to compare answers.

Character Education Connection	What character and value-related issues are present in your lesson?

The character and value-related issues present in this lesson include students' ability to deal with diversity of religion, which can be a sensitive topic for instruction. Students will gain tolerance and understanding through education. By learning about Islam and the contributions and achievements of Islamic civilization, students are exposed to material about which they may have prior misconceptions.

Notes/Additional Resources

Appendix A

Islam: Empire of Faith Video Notes

- What does the Arabic word for "conquest" mean?
____
____
- What is the sacred pilgrimage to Mecca called?
____
____
- What does the Hajj symbolize?
____
____
- What were some direct results of the Hajj?
____
____
- What is the geographic significance of the Islamic world?
____
____
- What was the extent of the Islamic Empire?
____
____
- What made Baghdad the greatest city of its time?
____
____
- What was sought after in the first international scientific venture in history?
____
____
- What are **three** scientific and/or cultural contributions of the Islamic Empire?
____
____
- What is considered the language of learning?
____
____
- What is considered the most important contribution of the Islamic Empire?
____
____
- Where did Islamic culture spread to Europeans? How did this place compare to Paris?
____
____
- Describe the architecture of the Great Mosque of Córdoba in the south of Spain.
____
____

- What is the Alhambra? Describe it.

  ____

  ____

- Describe privileged life for medieval Muslims.

  ____

  ____

Appendix B

Expansion and Achievements of the Muslim Empire

Overview: After the death of the Prophet Muhammad, Islam expanded very rapidly. Muslim armies conquered territories once held by the Persian Empire and the Byzantine Empire. Within 120 years of Muhammad's death, the Muslim Empire stretched from the Indus River to Spain. The empire was ruled by a caliph, which means "successor to the prophet."

Directions: Read the text on page 269–271, and then answer the questions below:

- We were the first group of caliphs. We ruled from 632 to 661 and brought southwest Asia and northern Africa under our control.
- Who are we? ____________________________
- Our family of caliphs expanded the empire from the Indus River in the east to Spain in the west. By the time we were done, our empire was twice the size of Rome's. We ruled from 661 to 750.
- Who are we? ____________________________

By 750, expansion had slowed and the Muslim Empire began focusing more on trade, discovery, science, and the arts. A new family of caliphs emerged in 750, and members of this family would rule until 1258. This new family of rulers was called the **Abbasid Dynasty**. The Abbasids moved their capital from the ancient city of Damascus to the newly built city of **Baghdad**. During the Abbasid period, a great period of peace, prosperity, and advancement in learning took place. This time period is also known as the **"Golden Age of the Abbasids"** because of all the new learning and discovery that took place. Many of those discoveries have a modern impact.

Your Job: You will be assigned a topic in which the Abbasids made great discoveries. You can find out more about your topic by reading pages 273–279. As you read, think about the importance of the discovery(ies) made in your field. How did they improve life? How have they impacted our world today? Are they things we now take for granted? What would life be like if we didn't have that knowledge? Then, as a show of appreciation, write a thank you card to the people of that time. Show them the impact that their hard work so long ago has had on us today. Your card should include the following things:

- Achievement(s) in your topic.
- Its impact on our world today.
- A visual representation (cartoon, picture) of how we use that discovery in our world today.

Circle Your Assigned Topic

Trade and Economy	*Education*	*Math*
Science	Medicine	Writing and Literature

Appendix C

Contributions of the Golden Age of the Abbasids

Directions: *Get together with five other students who have different topics than you. Each group should have a letter from each of the six topics. Exchange letters and fill out the chart below.*

Table 12.4 Geography Lesson Plan Two: Appendix C

	Latin American Cultural Trunks			
	Everyday Dress	*Celebratory Events*	*Music*	*Cultural Symbols*
Mexico	Name and describe the artifact. What does it tell you about the culture?			
Cuba and the Caribbean				
Mayan People of Guatemala				
Central America				
Costa Rica				

Appendix D

Achievements of the Muslim Empire: Thank You Card Rubric

Table 12.5 Geography Lesson Plan Two: Appendix D

Congress: What Can It Do? **Article 1 Section 8**
Clause 1: Clause 2: Clause 3: Clause 4: Clause 5: Clause 6: Clause 7: Clause 8: Clause 9: Clause 10: Clause 11: Clause 12: Clause 13: Clause 14: Clause 15: Clause 16: Clause 18: The Necessary and Proper Clause *McCulloch v Maryland, 1819* What standards should be used to decide whether an act of Congress is or is not "necessary and proper"? Did the decision in *McCulloch v Maryland* strengthen or weaken the federal system?

Psychology

Lesson Plan One

Teacher: Kelsey Evans
Subject/Content Area: Psychology
Unit Topic: Sensation
Lesson Title: Sensation and Mindfulness

Objectives	Clear, Specific, and Measurable. NOT ACTIVITIES Student-Friendly

Students will: explain the auditory process, including the stimulus input and the structure and function of the ear; describe the interaction of visual and auditory processes and their impact on interpretation (McGurk effect); experience the interaction of the chemical senses (smell and taste); experience their blind spot reviewing the location of their optic nerve; experience the accuracy of their sense of touch; experience how sensation affects perception.

Standards — Identify what you will be teaching. Reference only NCSS standards and/or Common Core standards.

Content Standard 1: The processes of sensation and perception
- Discuss the process of sensation and perception and how they interact
- Explain the concept of threshold and adaptation

Content Standard 2: The capabilities and limitations of sensory processes
- Describe the visual sensory system
- Describe the auditory sensory system
- Describe the other sensory systems, such as olfaction and gustation

---

Daily Planner — **Summary** of the activities with suggested time allotments for each step included in this lesson.

Bellwork, Instruction, and Guided Mindfulness Activities.

Activating Strategy — Motivator/Hook

An Essential Question encourages students to put forth more effort when faced with complex, open-ended, challenging, meaningful, and authentic questions.

What techniques do you use to decrease stress and anxiety? Have students discuss amongst themselves and then together as a class.

Instruction — Step-by-Step Procedures Sequence
- Discover/Explain, Direct Instruction
- Modeling Expectations: "I Do"
- Questioning/Encourages Higher Order Thinking
- Grouping Strategies
- Differentiated Instructional Strategies to Provide Intervention and Extension

---

Discussion of how mindfulness affects the senses and the brain.

Guided and Independent Practice — "We Do," "You Do"
- Encourage Higher Order Thinking and Problem Solving
- Relevance
- Differentiated Strategies for Practice to Provide Intervention and Extension

---

Techniques for Sensory Meditation

Grounding:

- Sit in a chair with your feet on the ground to begin. Choose a quiet place without disturbances. As you practice this exercise, you can perform it anywhere.
- Notice your breathing. Clench your stomach, tighten your muscles and breathe up high in your chest. How does that make you feel? People often say, "anxious," "tense," "panicky." Chest breathing is not deep breathing, and it is often an unconscious reaction to stress or trouble.
- Relax your stomach and let your breath down into your belly. Imagine it flowing down into your toes as your belly expands. Do you start to feel different? Some people find this sort of deep breathing unnatural. To learn it, put your hand on your belly and breathe so that your belly pushes your hand out. Practice regularly, so that it becomes easy and natural.
- Stretch your arms out to your sides as you move, as far as they'll go, until you can't see your hands if you look straight ahead. Now wiggle your thumbs, and slowly bring your arms in until your thumbs are just visible on the edge of your peripheral vision. Notice how wide your field of vision can be. As you walk, breathing deep, grounded, activate that peripheral vision. Know that you can be aware of what's going on around you.

The chocolate meditation:

Choose some chocolate—either a type that you've never tried before or one that you have not eaten recently. It might be dark and flavorsome, organic or fair-trade, or, perhaps, cheap and flavorless. The important thing is to choose a type you wouldn't normally eat or that you consume only rarely. Here goes:

- Open the packet. Inhale the smell.
- Break off a piece and look at it. Really let your eyes drink in what it looks like, examining every nook and cranny.
- Pop it in your mouth. See if it's possible to hold it on your tongue and let it melt, noticing any tendency to suck at it.
- If you notice your mind wandering while you do this, simply notice where it went, then gently escort it back to the present moment.
- After the chocolate has completely melted, swallow it very slowly and deliberately.
- Repeat this with one other piece.

How do you feel? Is it different from normal? Did the chocolate taste better than if you'd just eaten it at a normal breakneck pace? Do you feel fuller that normal, more satisfied?
Abdominal Breathing Technique:

- How it's done: With one hand on the chest and the other on the belly, take a deep breath in through the nose, ensuring the diaphragm (not the chest) inflates with enough air to create a stretch in the lungs. The goal: Six to 10 deep, slow breaths per minute for 10 minutes each day to experience immediate reductions to heart rate and blood pressure

Closure	Reflection/Wrap-Up Summarizing, Reminding, Reflecting, Restating, Connecting

Have students describe how they feel before and after the introduction of a variety of mindfulness techniques that require all the senses of the body.

Assessment/Evaluation	Students show evidence of proficiency through a variety of assessments. Aligned with the Lesson Objective Formative/Summative Performance-Based/Rubric Formal/Informal

Teacher observation, reviewing of student feedback.

Materials/Technology	What materials are utilized for this lesson? What types of technology are utilized to enhance learning and engagement? What primary and secondary sources are present to meet the learning objectives?

PowerPoint, chocolate.

Meeting Individual Needs of Diverse Learners	How does the lesson meet the needs of students with different learning styles (multiple intelligences) and what accommodations are made for diverse learners?

Activity accommodates visual, auditory, and kinesthetic learners. It also allows the teacher to monitor and refocus instruction in a positive non-threatening way.

Character Education Connection	What character and value-related issues are present in your lesson?

Cooperation and awareness.

Lesson Plan Two

Teacher: Cyndi Mottola Poole
Subject/Content Area: Psychology
Unit Topic: Learning
Lesson Title: Classical Conditioning

Objectives	Clear, Specific, and Measurable. NOT ACTIVITIES Student-Friendly

The student will be able to describe the process of classical conditioning.

The student will be able to identify the neutral stimulus, conditioned stimulus, unconditioned response, and conditioned response in a classical conditioning scenario.

The student will be able to design a classical conditioning experiment.

The student will be able to evaluate the ethicality of a proposed psychological experiment.

Standards	Identify what you will be teaching. Reference only NCSS standards and/or Common Core standards.

APA Psychology Standard Learning 1.1 Describe the principles of classical conditioning.

APA Psychology Standard Learning 1.2 Describe clinical and experimental examples of classical conditioning.

APA Psychology Standard Learning 1.3 Apply classical conditioning to everyday life.

APA Psychology Standard Scientific Inquiry 2.1 Identify ethical standards scientists must address regarding research with human subjects.

NCSS Standard 4: Individual Development and Identity

NCSS Standard 5: Individuals, Groups, and Institutions

Daily Planner	**Summary** of the activities with suggested time allotments for each step included in this lesson.

1 Explain the concept of classical conditioning to the class.
2 Have students read information on Pavlov's dog experiments.
3 Guide students through the experiment and help them to identify the unconditioned stimulus (US), unconditioned response (UR), conditioned stimulus (CS), and conditioned response (CR).
4 Present students with several brief summaries of classical conditioning scenarios and have them identify the US, UR, CS, and CR in each scenario.
5 Ask groups of students to design their own classical conditioning experiment.
6 Ask groups to switch papers and act as the Institutional Review Board (IRB) to evaluate each other's experiments according to ethical guidelines.

Activating Strategy	Motivator/Hook An Essential Question encourages students to put forth more effort when faced with complex, open-ended, challenging, meaningful, and authentic questions.

Are there any smells that make you feel nauseated? Can you explain why?

Instruction	Step-by-Step Procedures Sequence Discover/Explain, Direct Instruction Modeling Expectations: "I Do" Questioning/Encourages Higher Order Thinking Grouping Strategies Differentiated Instructional Strategies to Provide Intervention and Extension

1. The teacher will present the concepts of classical conditioning, stimulus, and response to the class through mini-lecture or other similar presentation style.
2. The teacher will distribute to the students a description of Pavlov's dog experiments. The students will read the information provided, and then as a whole class group, they will decide what the US, UR, CS, and CR are in each experiment.
3. After the teacher feels comfortable that students can accurately identify the different types of stimuli and responses, the teacher will provide students with a sheet of brief summaries of other possible classical conditioning experiments. The students will work independently or in pairs to identify the US, UR, CS, and CR in each experiment.
4. The teacher will lead a discussion of the short assignment and check to make sure students have been successful in their analysis of the experiments.
5. The students will then work in groups to design their own hypothetical classical conditioning experiments. They will create a brief written proposal explaining their purpose and methodology.
6. After each group has completed a proposal, groups will switch papers and will act like an Institutional Review Board (IRB) by examining other groups' proposals for ethical concerns.
7. IRB groups will respond in writing to approve or deny the proposals based on ethical considerations.
8. The teacher will lead the whole class in discussing each proposed experiment, whether it was a true example of classical conditioning, and why it was approved or denied by the mock IRB committee.

Guided and Independent Practice	"We Do," "You Do" Encourage Higher Order Thinking and Problem Solving Relevance Differentiated Strategies for Practice to Provide Intervention and Extension

The teacher will model analyzing classical conditioning experiments before asking students to analyze them independently.

After analyzing several examples of classical conditioning scenarios, students will be asked to create their own proposed classical conditioning experiment.

Closure	Reflection/Wrap-Up Summarizing, Reminding, Reflecting, Restating, Connecting

The teacher will lead the whole class in discussing each proposed experiment, whether it was a true example of classical conditioning, and why it was approved or denied by the mock IRB committee.

Assessment/Evaluation	Students show evidence of proficiency through a variety of assessments. Aligned with the Lesson Objective Formative/Summative Performance-Based/Rubric Formal/Informal

Students' knowledge will be assessed informally by their ability to analyze classical conditioning experiments as demonstrated through the independent or pair work practice sheet.

The teacher can collect the proposals and IRB responses to use as a formal assessment of students' abilities to design a classical conditioning experiment and to analyze an experiment from an ethical point of view.

Materials/Technology	What materials are utilized for this lesson? What types of technology are utilized to enhance learning and engagement? What primary and secondary sources are present to meet the learning objectives?

The teacher will need information about Pavlov's experiments and other simple examples of classical conditioning experiments. A PowerPoint presentation can be used if desired.

Meeting Individual Needs of Diverse Learners	How does the lesson meet the needs of students with different learning styles (multiple intelligences) and what accommodations are made for diverse learners?

Students of diverse learning styles can play different roles within their experiment design and IRB committee groups. Group work can assist ESE and ELL students since other students can support them as necessary during the assignment.

Character Education Connection	What character and value-related issues are present in your lesson?

Students will practice working successfully in groups. Students will consider the ethical implications of psychological research.

Sociology

Lesson Plan One

Teacher: Samantha Sanders
Subject/Content Area: Sociology/U.S. History
Unit Topic: Imperialism
Lesson Title: Imperialism and American Society

Objectives — Clear, Specific, and Measurable. NOT ACTIVITIES Student-Friendly

---

Students will: be able to analyze the causes of America's emergence as a world power and understand how those causes impacted American society.

Standards — Identify what you will be teaching. Reference only NCSS standards and/or Common Core standards.

NCSS Standard 5: Individuals, Groups, and Institutions
NCSS Standard 6: Power, Authority, and Governance

DAILY PLANNER — **Summary** of the activities with suggested time allotments for each step included in this lesson.

DAILY PLANNER Summary of the activities with suggested time allotments for each step included in this lesson.

1. In their groups, students will develop a definition for the term "imperialism," based on what they remember from world history. Each group will share out and the best definition will be written on a poster board to be displayed. (5 mins)
2. Students will complete a Google Slides Notes template, based on a teacher version of the Slides Presentation and a direct instruction lecture. Throughout the presentation:
   a. Students will analyze political cartoons and primary source documents using the HIPPY (Historical Context, Intended Audience, Purpose, Point of View, and Y is this Important?) model.
   b. Students will respond to Higher Order Thinking questions about the content.
   c. Students will use the Cornell Way to edit/revise their notes both throughout the lesson and on their own time for homework. (40 mins)
3. Students will complete a Comparison Matrix about the various countries the U.S. imperialized, using the textbook and provided web links. They will work in trios, each person doing research for one country. Once the information has been gathered, students will share out in Jigsaw style with their group-mates and everyone will complete their own Google Docs. After the Comparison Matrix is complete, students will answer a Reflection Question: Which country was the most significant or had the biggest impact for the U.S.? Explain WHY.
   a. Plan/Prep Time: 5 mins
   b. Individual Research: 20 mins
   c. Presentation: 5 mins each = 15 mins
   d. Reflection Question: 5 mins

Activating Strategy	Motivator/Hook An Essential Question encourages students to put forth more effort when faced with complex, open-ended, challenging, meaningful, and authentic questions.

Imperialism Definition Brainstorm

Instruction	Step-by-Step Procedures Sequence Discover/Explain, Direct Instruction Modeling Expectations: "I Do" Questioning/Encourages Higher Order Thinking Grouping Strategies Differentiated Instructional Strategies to Provide Intervention and Extension

1 The teacher will begin the lesson by asking the groups to discuss and share what they think the word "imperialism" means. As a group, students will draft one definition to share out. The teacher will select the best definition, modify it if necessary, and then write it out on a poster to be displayed in the classroom.
2 The students will be a given a student version of the Google Slides notes template—this is where they will fill in their notes from the lesson. The teacher will display the teacher version of the presentation and present a lecture about imperialism.
3 Throughout the notes, students will be expected both independently and in their groups to interact with the content they are learning. On every other slide or so, there will be a Thinking Question students must respond to. There are also primary source documents, such as political cartoons, embedded throughout the slides presentation. Students will HIPPY each document and then discuss as a class the main idea or significance of the docs.
4 On their own time, students will be expected to go back and edit/revise their notes, add annotations, develop HOT Questions, and create summaries based on the content (Cornell Way).
5 The next day, the students will complete a Comparison Matrix, working in trios. They will be researching, using the textbook and provided web links, when and how we imperialized each country; why we imperialized each country (what did we want?); and how it impacted the U.S. Each student will research one country and fill in that part of the Matrix. Once the info has been compiled, the trios will present what they have found to each other and be able to fill in the rest of their Matrix. They will each individually respond to a reflection question.

GUIDED AND INDEPENDENT PRACTICE	"We Do," "You Do" Encourage Higher Order Thinking and Problem Solving Relevance Differentiated Strategies for Practice to Provide Intervention and Extension

Embedding primary source document analysis and thinking questions into the lecture presentation.

Incorporating the Cornell Way to encourage students to go back and review their notes.

Monitoring each group and rotating around the room to ask clarifying questions and to check for understanding.

CLOSURE	Reflection/Wrap-Up Summarizing, Reminding, Reflecting, Restating, Connecting

Cornell Notes Summary for the notes presentation,

Reflection Question for the Comparison Matrix activity.

ASSESSMENT/ EVALUATION	Students show evidence of proficiency through a variety of assessments. Aligned with the Lesson Objective Formative/Summative Performance-Based/Rubric Formal/Informal

At the end of the Imperialism mini-unit, students will complete a checkpoint quiz to check for understanding of key content and get a data-based evaluation.

MATERIALS/ TECHNOLOGY	What materials are utilized for this lesson? What types of technology are utilized to enhance learning and engagement? What primary and secondary sources are present to meet the learning objectives?

The teacher will provide the students with a student version of the lecture presentation and with the Comparison Matrix.

Students all have laptops to use to complete the classwork and do the research.

Notes Presentation:
https://docs.google.com/presentation/d/18sc3oyv-W96DtiEJKKuaQk2vrxtHr-2Gei5KzsALW494/edit?usp=sharing

Comparison Matrix:
https://docs.google.com/document/d/1cHluWEnw7u_nS8-1h0gD9K1p9uJ0oZrNbv-mOYdxBBV8/edit?usp=sharing

---

MEETING INDIVIDUAL NEEDS OF DIVERSE LEARNERS	How does the lesson meet the needs of students with different learning styles (multiple intelligences) and what accommodations are made for diverse learners?

Students with lower English writing skills can draw pictures to represent their understandings.

ELL students can be given a completed version of the lecture presentation and be tasked with adding annotations during the lecture.

The use of the Comparison Matrix graphic organizer will help ESE and ESOL students to organize their thoughts.

ELL students will be paired with peer tutors who speak their first language when applicable.

ELL students can use Google translate.

CHARACTER EDUCATION CONNECTION	What character and value-related issues are present in your lesson?

This lesson delves into a dark chapter in U.S. history—racism and white superiority. Working in groups and with partners, respecting other people's points of view, gathering evidence on which to base one's arguments.

Lesson Plan Two

Teacher: Stewart Waters
Subject/Content Area: Sociology
Unit Topic: Social Conformity and Behavioral Controls

FYI

How could this type of lesson be modified and adapted to discuss current issues of #fakenews, Russian interference with the presidential election, and social media influences on societal perceptions of major events.

Lesson Title: Red Scare

OBJECTIVES	Clear, Specific, and Measurable. NOT ACTIVITIES Student-Friendly

Students will understand the amount of pressure and stress facing American citizens during a period of communist paranoia known as the Red Scare. By studying the case study of Ruth Goldberg, students will know and understand how collective societal suspicion led many citizens to become unjustly critical of and fearful toward people accused of being communists.

STANDARDS	Identify what you will be teaching. Reference only NCSS standards and/or Common Core standards.

I Culture
II Time, Continuity, and Change
III People, Places, and Environments
IV Individual Development and Identity
V Individuals, Groups, and Institutions

DAILY PLANNER

Summary of the activities with suggested time allotments for each step included in this lesson.

(10 min.) Activating Strategy
(10 min.) Playing Mafia Cards Game, illustration
(20 min.) Case Study
(10 min.) Classroom Reflection

ACTIVATING STRATEGY

Motivator/Hook
An Essential Question encourages students to put forth more effort when faced with complex, open-ended, challenging, meaningful, and authentic questions.

Ask students to reflect on a time in their life when someone was suspicious or accused them of doing something that they did not do. Why did the person or persons think you were guilty? How did the accusation make you feel? How did you go about trying to convince the accusers of your innocence?

INSTRUCTION

Step-by-Step Procedures Sequence
Discover/Explain, Direct Instruction
Modeling Expectations: "I Do"
Questioning/Encourages Higher Order Thinking
Grouping Strategies
Differentiated Instructional Strategies to Provide Intervention and Extension

1 Provide students with time to respond to the activating strategy, discuss students' thoughts with the class. Ask what factors go into accusations and if all of these factors are, in fact, credible and reliable.
2 After discussing the activating strategy question, place students in large groups of 10–13 students (depending on the number of students in the class). You will need a deck of cards for each group. See directions for Mafia card came in the resources section.
3 Once the Mafia card game is complete, ask students to discuss how they felt during the activity. Were they confused? Angry? What types of questions did they ask to try and find out who was responsible for the kidnapping?
4 Following the discussion, place students into smaller cooperative learning groups of three to four students. Distribute a copy of the case study about Ruth Goldberg.

GUIDED AND INDEPENDENT PRACTICE	"We Do," "You Do" Encourage Higher Order Thinking and Problem Solving Relevance Differentiated Strategies for Practice to Provide Intervention and Extension

1 Each group should read the case study (provided in the resource section) about Ruth Goldberg. Have students discuss their thoughts on this situation and formulate answers to the key questions at the end of the case study.
2 After students discuss the case study, have a class discussion about social paranoia and conformity. Are there any current groups of people in the U.S. that face unjust scrutiny and skepticism in the public eye (racial groups, political groups, immigrants, religious groups, etc.)?

CLOSURE	Reflection/Wrap-Up Summarizing, Reminding, Reflecting, Restating, Connecting

Have students think of someone they know who may have been adversely affected by harmful gossip, rumors, or stereotypes. Why is it important to speak up and help others who may be facing unjust criticism?

ASSESSMENT/ EVALUATION	Students show evidence of proficiency through a variety of assessments. Aligned with the Lesson Objective Formative/Summative Performance-Based/Rubric Formal/Informal

1 Case study response questions
2 For homework, have students find a current event news article that discusses or perpetuates social stereotypes, rumors, or paranoia. Students should bring a copy of their article to class for discussion the next day.

MATERIALS/TECHNOLOGY	What materials are utilized for this lesson? What types of technology are utilized to enhance learning and engagement? What primary and secondary sources are present to meet the learning objectives?

Two or three decks of playing cards.
Copies of the case study.

MEETING INDIVIDUAL NEEDS OF DIVERSE LEARNERS	How does the lesson meet the needs of students with different learning styles (multiple intelligences) and what accommodations are made for diverse learners?

This activity meets various learning styles by having kinesthetic activities and simulations. Any ELL students will be provided materials in their native language and have the opportunity to practice language acquisition and development during group discussions.

CHARACTER EDUCATION CONNECTION	What character and value-related issues are present in your lesson?

Responsibility
Fairness
Justice
Equality

Notes/Additional Resources

Mafia Card Game

You need regular table cards. Only up to 12 people can play. This is just an illustration for students to understand the Red Scare situation. The teacher (facilitator) will pass out 10 to 13 cards from the deck. Out of those 12 cards, 2 must be Kings, 2 must be Queens, and 1 must be a Jack. The rest of the 7 cards can be any from Aces to 10. Kings represent the mafia, Queens represent the town sheriffs, and the Jack represents the nurse. Deal these cards out randomly to students and inform them to keep their cards secret and not share with classmates.

In each round the 12 students must close their eyes, the facilitator will say "Mafia, wake up." *Only the two students who have the Kings* will wake up and both agree to "kidnap" somebody in the group and quietly point them out. Then, those two will close their eyes.

Right after that, only the two sheriffs (Queen cards) will open their eyes (when the facilitator says), then they will randomly point to somebody in the group and ask the facilitator whether they are Mafia, Nurse, or regular citizens.

Right after that, the facilitator will call out the nurse, *only the Jack card* and the nurse can get to pick who she/he would save. Once the nurse makes the decision, everybody is awake. At this point nobody, except for five people, knows anything. The facilitator will announce who got kidnapped and who got saved. It is up to the group to find out who is in the Mafia and responsible for the kidnapping. The point is that regular citizens will be judging who is in the Mafia based on actions, words, facial expressions, attitudes, etc. Students must figure out who is responsible for the kidnapping without showing their cards, and if everybody agrees that person is out.

Case Study

In the 1940s, Ruth Goldberg belonged to the Parent-Teacher Association in Queens, N.Y. In 1947 she agreed to run for PTA president, but the campaign turned nasty. Because Goldberg had associated with people of left-wing, liberal interests, a rumor spread through the neighborhood that she was a communist. Suddenly Goldberg's quiet life became terrifying. Callers threatened her, and the local priest denounced her in his sermons. One afternoon, Goldberg's eight-year-old son came home in tears. A playmate had told him, "You know, your mother's a Red. She should be put up against a wall and shot."

Looking back much later, Goldberg saw the PTA campaign as part of a bigger and more complex pattern of distrust and hatred. "It was a small thing, but it was an indication of what had happened with the Cold War, with this Red specter, that somebody like me could be considered a danger to a community."

Key Questions:

1 What does it mean to stereotype? Where do stereotypes come from, and what purpose do they serve?
2 If you were Ms. Goldberg, how would you go about defending yourself and responding to these accusations?
3 If you were Ms. Goldberg, would you drop out of the race? Why or why not?
4 Why are rumors and gossip potentially harmful? Can you think of a time that rumors or gossip adversely affected you or someone you care about? Explain.

World History

Lesson Plan One

Teacher: Paul Howard, Stephanie Hall, Nick Kraly, Taylor Smith, Tina Ellsworth, and Joe O'Brien
Subject/Content Area: World History
Unit Topic: Latin American Cultures
Lesson Title: Culture Cubed

OBJECTIVES — Clear, Specific, and Measurable. NOT ACTIVITIES
Student-Friendly

Students will be able to:

- identify cultural elements for five different cultures in Latin America;
- categorize cultural artifacts into the categories of Music, Celebration, Dress, and Symbols;
- analyze Latin American artifacts to determine what they tell us about the different cultures and aspects of them;
- compare and contrast Latin American artifacts from different cultures.

STANDARDS — Identify what you will be teaching.
Reference only NCSS standards and/or Common Core standards.

NCSS Standard(s):

I Culture: Social studies programs should include experiences that provide for the study of culture and cultural diversity, so that the learner can:

- explore and describe similarities and differences in the ways groups, societies, and cultures address similar human needs and concerns;
- give examples of how experiences may be interpreted differently by people from diverse cultural perspectives and frames of reference;
- describe ways in which language, stories, folktales, music, and artistic creations serve as expressions of culture and influence behavior of people living in a particular culture;
- compare ways in which people from different cultures think about and deal with their physical environment and social conditions;
- give examples and describe the importance of cultural unity and diversity within and across groups.

DAILY PLANNER	**Summary** of the activities with suggested time allotments for each step included in this lesson.

Activating Strategy: 10 minutes
Instruction

- Start: 10 minutes
- Lesson: 50 minutes

Closure: 5 minutes

ACTIVATING STRATEGY	Motivator/Hook An Essential Question encourages students to put forth more effort when faced with complex, open-ended, challenging, meaningful, and authentic questions.

Essential Questions:

- What are ways in which people express their culture?
- How are cultures alike and different?
- How does learning about other cultures help us to better understand our own culture?

Hook:

- The teacher will ask students what an outsider could learn about them if s/he looked through their cell phone, book bag, purse, bedroom, etc. Students may mention sports, family, friends, religion, etc. The teacher will discuss the "evidence/artifacts" students had that would draw those types of conclusions.
- Then, the teacher will have students classify those evidences into categories of their own choosing.

INSTRUCTION	Step-by-Step Procedures Sequence Discover/Explain, Direct Instruction Modeling Expectations: "I Do" Questioning/Encourages Higher Order Thinking Grouping Strategies Differentiated Instructional Strategies to Provide Intervention and Extension

Start:

- The teacher will then define "culture" and explain four categories of culture.
- The teacher will take some of the artifacts students mentioned in the opening activity and explain in which category of culture they belong.
- The teacher will explain that today we are going to look at digital trunks full of these same types of evidences/artifacts that represent several facets of a people's culture: music, dress, celebratory events, and cultural symbols. During this activity, students will categorize these artifacts onto a graphic organizer. Then, students will analyze those artifacts to determine what they tell us about these nations.

Lesson:

- Prior to the start of class, the instructor will set up five stations with a laptop already logged onto a different digital trunk from the Latin American Studies Department at the University of Kansas: http://latamst.ku.edu/resources/lending-library/trunks.shtml. If technology is not readily available, the physical versions of the digital trunks can be sent to your Kansas school free of charge. Contact the LAS Dept for more information.
- The instructor will divide the class into five equal-sized groups and hand out the graphic organizer to each student.
- The teacher will model how to fill out the chart using a trunk that is not listed on the organizer.

Example: the Andean trunk. (Click on the artifact for additional information, or read the informational card that accompanies the physical trunk.)

Music: Cinturon Cacho de Semillas—a rhythm instrument

Dress: Muneca Peruana wearing "polleras" and "mantillas"—everyday dress for a woman in the region

www.threadsofperu.com/ (colors indicate where they are from; embellishments show social class; during celebrations, multiple skirts are worn)

Celebratory Events: Palo de Lluvia (aka: Rainstick)—used in religious celebrations to end the drought and call in rain

Symbols: Llama (on the fabric)—native to the region and important to the area's economy

- Then, each group will explore its culture trunk for 8 minutes and classify the artifacts onto their graphic organizer.
- Students will then rotate to the next station and repeat this process until every trunk has been explored.
- Once all stations are complete, the teacher will redirect the students to share their graphic organizers with the class. Students will justify why they put which artifact in which category. Teachers should ask students what the artifact tells us.
- Once the trunks have been discussed, the teacher should have students compare and contrast artifacts between trunks.

GUIDED AND INDEPENDENT PRACTICE	"We Do," "You Do" Encourage Higher Order Thinking and Problem Solving Relevance Differentiated Strategies for Practice to Provide Intervention and Extension

Guided/Independent Practice:

- Students will be working together to classify artifacts on the graphic organizer.
- Students will inevitably justify the classification of their artifacts.

Differentiated Strategies:

- Teacher will explain culture.
- Teacher will show how culture is explained through artifacts.
- Students will work together to dissect other trunks with artifacts.
- Students can choose which artifact they want to demonstrate that category of culture.
- When students create their own trunk, they will be able to use pictures, audio clips, video clips, or whatever they would like to demonstrate the culture.

To meet the needs of individual learners, the teachers can:

- provide pictures of the artifacts with the accompanying text for reference. Text can be rewritten for students who may need it.
- create audio files to read the information cards from the artifacts to students.

CLOSURE	Reflection/Wrap-Up Summarizing, Reminding, Reflecting, Restating, Connecting

The teacher will restate the objectives of today's lesson and will recap the discussion regarding the cultural trunks. The teacher will then connect the trunk activity with the opening activity about what we can learn from exploring our own surroundings. Then explain that the students will be creating their own trunk for another Latin American culture using Internet research and resources.

ASSESSMENT/EVALUATION	Students show evidence of proficiency through a variety of assessments. Aligned with the Lesson Objective Formative/Summative Performance-Based/Rubric Formal/Informal

Formative/Summative: The teacher will be able to gauge student understanding by:

- Having each student turn in his/her graphic organizer at the end of the class period.

Formal/Informal: The teacher will be able to gauge student understanding by:

- traveling around the room during the exploration of trunks;
- ensuring students participate in the class discussion and activities.

Performance-Based/Rubric

- Students will then create their own cultural trunk for a country not covered in this activity.

MATERIALS/ TECHNOLOGY	What materials are utilized for this lesson? What types of technology are utilized to enhance learning and engagement? What primary and secondary sources are present to meet the learning objectives?

- At least five laptops with Internet access
- Graphic organizer
- Writing utensil
- Free "Prezi" account: www.prezi.com

MEETING INDIVIDUAL NEEDS OF DIVERSE LEARNERS	How does the lesson meet the needs of students with different learning styles (multiple intelligences) and what accommodations are made for diverse learners?

To meet the needs of individual learners, the teachers can:

- provide pictures of the artifacts with the accompanying text for reference. Text can be rewritten for students who may need it;
- create audio files to read the information cards from the artifacts to students.

CHARACTER EDUCATION CONNECTION	What character and value-related issues are present in your lesson?

- Cooperation and collaboration among students are emphasized over competition.
- Values such as fairness, respect, and honesty are part of everyday lessons in and out of the classroom.

Notes/Additional Resources

This graphic organizer will allow students to compare multiple countries by various types of cultural expression.

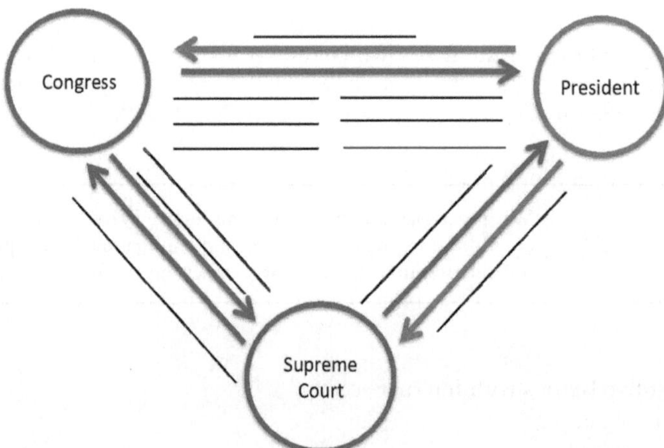

Figure 12.1 World History Lesson Plan One: Graphic Organizer.

Lesson Plan Two

Teacher: Zoe Park
Subject/Content Area: World History
Unit Topic: Early Globalization
Lesson Title: The Silk Road

OBJECTIVES — Clear, Specific, and Measurable. NOT ACTIVITIES
Student-Friendly

- Students will be able to recognize that people traveled bringing trade goods and ideas on land and water in Asia, East Africa, and the Mediterranean Basin.
- Students will be able to identify how physical characteristics, natural resources, and location influenced the economies and trade along the Silk Road.
- Students will be able to identify the various forms of exchange used when trading along the Silk Road.
- Students will be able to identify products that were traded among Asia, East Africa, and the Mediterranean and at least one trade barrier that existed.
- Students will be able to use the information gained to later explain the significance of the Silk Road in relation to its impact on cultural diffusion.

STANDARDS — Identify what you will be teaching.
Reference only NCSS standards and/or Common Core standards.

I Culture
II Time, Continuity, and Change
III People, Places, and Environments
IV Individual Development and Identity
V Individuals, Groups, and Institutions

DAILY PLANNER — **Summary** of the activities with suggested time allotments for each step included in this lesson.

1 Students will listen and read along with the story told by the teacher in order to answer a few questions upon reading.
2 The teacher will ask the students in pairs to determine, based on their current knowledge, what they think was the purpose of the Silk Road.
3 The teacher will lead the class in a textual reading in order to determine the purpose of the Silk Road. Students will highlight key information.
4 Using the maps, the teacher will model how the students are to annotate the maps, starting with physical characteristics and then routes. Once the maps are annotated, the students will discuss in pairs how the physical climate impacted the Silk Road routes.

5 The teacher will make a list on the board of students' thoughts. This will be used to help bring up the question regarding how goods were transported along the Silk Road.
6 The class will discuss the role of supply and demand in trade and how one good was traded for another good
7 Students will use the maps to then categorize the goods and ideas that were transported along the Silk Road. The teacher will first model how this is done. Students will categorize the items based on category (goods, technology, and religion) and location (region) using a list of items provided.
8 The class will come up with a list of key people who participated in the silk trade and then define each role.
9 The teacher will lead the class into examining how the movement of goods and ideas might have led to the exchange of culture, resulting in cultural diffusion.

ACTIVATING STRATEGY	Motivator/Hook An Essential Question encourages students to put forth more effort when faced with complex, open-ended, challenging, meaningful, and authentic questions.

- Bellwork: Have students, as they are entering the classroom, log onto NearPod and enter the class. Instruct students that their username must be their actual name.
- Read "A Single Pebble: A Story of the Silk Road" to the class and have students pay attention to the types of people in transporting the pebble, the types of goods added along the way, the forms of travel used, and how long/far it took for the pebble to reach the end of the road
- Questions related to story:
  - What types of people played a role in transporting the pebble from the East to the West?
    - Merchants/Traders
    - Monk
    - Acrobats
    - Pirates/Nomads
  - What types of goods were added to the gift along the way?
    - Pebble
    - Flute
    - Box
    - Ivory elephant
    - Cinnamon
  - What forms of travel were used?
    - Horse
    - Boat
  - How long did it take for the pebble to reach the end of the road?
    - Two years
  - How far is it from one end of the road to the other?
    - Over 4,000 miles

INSTRUCTION	Step-by-Step Procedures-Sequence Discover/Explain, Direct Instruction Modeling Expectations: "I Do" Questioning/Encourages Higher Order Thinking Grouping Strategies Differentiated Instructional Strategies to Provide Intervention and Extension

1 The teacher will begin the lesson by asking the students what they think was the purpose of the Silk Road based on the story they just heard. Have students answer on NearPod. Once students have shared their opinions, see if anyone can explain the reasoning behind some of their answers.
2 Give an overview of what is going to be covered in the lesson. Tell students that today they are going to find out the purpose of the Silk Road, in addition to gaining an understanding of how the physical geography impacted the routes travelled, how and what goods were exchanged along the Silk Road, and those who used the Silk Road.

GUIDED AND INDEPENDENT PRACTICE	"We Do," "You Do" Encourage Higher Order Thinking and Problem Solving Relevance Differentiated Strategies for Practice to Provide Intervention and Extension

1 Together have the class examine a paragraph on the purpose of the Silk Road to determine if students had correct inquiries. Have students highlight the key information in the text.
2 Point to the map in the storybook and explain that Mei's pebble traveled from Chang'an, China to Torcello, Italy, two cities that are from very different parts of the world and each impacted by different physical characteristics.
3 Hand out a map to each student. Explain that the students are going to identify the key physical characteristics that impacted the Silk Road by coloring each aspect a different color (deserts = yellow, grasslands = green, mountains = orange, rivers = dark blue, and oceans = light blue). Remind students that their coloring does not need to be perfect or neat but should simply allow them to get an idea of where each characteristic is located. Students will also have a chart provided to them that indicates which names need to be colored which color.
4 Tell students that within the story there were three different ways people traveled along the Silk Road: camel, horse, and boat. Based on this information, invite students to share what they think were two types of routes people used for traveling.
5 Have students draw the land and sea routes used by travellers on their maps. Explain to the students that the Silk Road is not just one road but is the name given to the vast network of routes between the Mediterranean Sea and East Asia that covers 4,600 miles.

6 Have students examine how they believe the physical characteristics just examined impacted the location of the Silk Road routes.
7 Now that the students have an understanding of the Silk Road routes and how the geographic landscape impacts them, have the students examine what goods were transported and how they were transported along the Silk Road.
8 Within the story various items were added to the "gift" along the journey, each slightly different as the travellers moved farther West (jade pebble, flute, box, ivory elephant, cinnamon). Explain that the Silk Road was used to move goods and ideas from one region and culture to the next. Students in pairs will categorize goods and ideas transported along the Silk Road based on type of item (goods, technology, and religion) and location (region).
9 Students will identify the methods of exchange used along the Silk Road by recognizing that often the movement of goods and ideas was not conducted by a single individual but a group. Remind students that within the story the pebble does not travel the whole distance with Mei's father; rather, several different individuals helped transport the pebble along the Silk Road. Students will discuss how trade along the Silk Road involved the exchange of one good for another good.
10 Have students do a group brainstorm on the types of people they remember hearing about in the story. Using the brainstorm list, add a few additional individuals who travelled along the Silk Road. The list should consist of: merchants/traders, caravan leader, nomads/pirates, officials, soldiers, monks/missionary, and performers. Provide this to the students with the names and definitions of the various travellers and have them in pairs match the traveller to the correct definition.

CLOSURE	Reflection/Wrap-Up Summarizing, Reminding, Reflecting, Restating, Connecting

1 Summarize key points and introduce cultural diffusion. Define cultural diffusion and explain to the students that the Silk Road played a key role in the spread of ideas since the movement of goods and ideas allowed for a cultural exchange to occur.
2 Preview to the students what is to come. Tell students that over the next few lessons you will use various documents to create five journal entries, written from the perspective of the individual they discussed yesterday.

ASSESSMENT/ EVALUATION	Students show evidence of proficiency through a variety of assessments. Aligned with the Lesson Objective Formative/Summative Performance-Based/Rubric Formal/Informal

1. Formative Assessment
   a. Questions and Tracking
   b. Notes created throughout the lesson
2. Summarize Assessment
   a. DBQ Journal Entries, due at the end of the Unit

MATERIALS/TECHNOLOGY	What materials are utilized for this lesson? What types of technology are utilized to enhance learning and engagement? What primary and secondary sources are present to meet the learning objectives?

- *A Single Pebble: A Story of the Silk Road* by Bonnie Christensen
- Document camera
- Map of Silk Road www.washburn.edu/cas/history/stucker/EurasiaOutMap.html
- Colored pencils
- The teacher will need a computer and a projector
- Students will need computer access.

MEETING INDIVIDUAL NEEDS OF DIVERSE LEARNERS	How does the lesson meet the needs of students with different learning styles (multiple intelligences) and what accommodations are made for diverse learners?

- All of the text covered will be read aloud and each student will be provided with a copy of the text in order to help ESOL students.
- Intentional pairing of students to meet learning needs
- Visual aids used to help support ESE and ESOL (used to represent each good, technology, and religion and to show each type of traveller)

CHARACTER EDUCATION CONNECTION	What character and value-related issues are present in your lesson?

- Working with partners and responding to the other person's ideas
- Listening to instructions in order to complete a task

U.S. Government

Lesson Plan One

Teacher: Kristen Braun
Subject/Content Area: U.S. Government
Unit Topic: Foundations of Government
Lesson Title: Declaration of Independence

OBJECTIVES — Clear, Specific, and Measurable. NOT ACTIVITIES Student-Friendly

STANDARDS — **Identify what you will be teaching**. Reference only NCSS standards and/or Common Core standards.

NCSS Standards:

- Theme 2: Time, Continuity, and Change
- Theme 5: Individuals, Groups, and Institutions
- Theme 6: Power, Authority, and Governance

DAILY PLANNER — **Summary** of the activities with suggested time allotments for each step included in this lesson.

Summary of Learning Activities

1. Warm-Up (5 minutes)
2. PowerPoint Lecture and discussion (20 minutes)
3. Break Up DOI assignment (25 minutes)

ACTIVATING STRATEGY — Motivator/Hook

An Essential Question encourages students to put forth more effort when faced with complex, open-ended, challenging, meaningful and authentic questions.

Bellwork: How would you react to a relationship that was no longer "working"? Would you try to fix it? Or would you break up?

5 minutes: Sharing and Discussion

INSTRUCTION — Step-by-Step Procedures Sequence

Discover/Explain, Direct Instruction
Modeling Expectations: "I Do"
Questioning/Encourages Higher Order Thinking
Grouping Strategies
Differentiated Instructional Strategies to Provide Intervention and Extension

Procedures for Learning Activities

1 Bellwork (5 minutes):
   a Students will discuss analogy of break-up.
2 Hand out Declaration of Independence and Modern Translation of DOI; have students read through (10 minutes)
3 PPT (15 minutes):

Slide 1: Major Events of the Time

   a England banned all forms of self-government
   b "No taxation without representation" (all the acts)
   c *Common Sense* is pamphlet published January 1776

Slide 2: Main Points of DOI

   a All men are created equal (not completely correct).
   b Men are given by God certain unalienable rights.
   c Colonies have the natural right (by God) to declare independence from England.

Slide 3: 3 Parts of the DOI

   a Basic ideas about people and government
   b Reasons the Founders thought they had the right to be free from British rule
   c Complaints against the British King

4 In Class Group Assignment (20 minutes):
   Choose one of the following:

   a Break-up letter (at least a page/3–4 paragraphs)
   b Break-up text convo (that's low …) between TJ and King George III (at least a page)
   c Break-up song from TJ's point of view

   Must include (at least) 4 reasons for the break up, explain each reason fully, be creative. Students will present the following day.
5 Use exit slip questions for students to summarize their understanding of the Declaration of Independence.

GUIDED AND INDEPENDENT PRACTICE	"We Do," "You Do" Encourage Higher Order Thinking and Problem Solving Relevance Differentiated Strategies for Practice to Provide Intervention and Extension

1. Model a break-up letter, students then work in groups to create their own.
2. Grouping of students of similar ability levels to evaluate scenarios and assignment of scenarios to enable success.
3. Students will be provided both the primary resource document of the DOI and a modern translation.
4. PowerPoint
   a. Project ppt on screen;
   b. Model underlining/highlighting words that may cause confusion, write explanations in margins

---

CLOSURE — Reflection/Wrap-Up
Summarizing, Reminding, Reflecting, Restating, Connecting

Use exit slip questions for students to summarize their understanding of the Declaration of Independence.

ASSESSMENT/EVALUATION — Students show evidence of proficiency through a variety of assessments.
Aligned with the Lesson Objective
Formative/Summative
Performance-Based/Rubric
Formal/Informal

---

1. Formative: monitoring student participation in learning activities:
   a. Monitor understanding during ppt presentation
   b. Monitor students' reading of the DOI
   c. Monitor group work for DOI assignment.
2. Formative: completion of exit slip summarizing and applying key concepts.
3. Summative: completed group assignment of the DOI.

MATERIALS/TECHNOLOGY — What materials are utilized for this lesson? What types of technology are utilized to enhance learning and engagement? What primary and secondary sources are present to meet the learning objectives?

Materials Utilized:

1. PowerPoint presentation
2. Grade-level textbook
3. Support textbook
4. Assignment sheet
5. Exit slips

Technology Component:

- Smart board technology used to project ppt for class discussion and assignment.

Primary Sources Utilized:

- Primary:
- The DOI

MEETING INDIVIDUAL NEEDS OF DIVERSE LEARNERS	How does the lesson meet the needs of students with different learning styles (multiple intelligences) and what accommodations are made for diverse learners?

Multiple Intelligences:
The reading and writing components of the lesson primarily address linguistic intelligence.
Evaluating the Declaration of Independence is not easy, and dictionaries will be provided to help with the difficulty.
Working in groups with classmates to evaluate and solve a problem addresses interpersonal intelligence.

Accommodations for Diverse Learners:
Use of grade-level and support textbooks helps students of varying ability levels access the information.
Group activity allows students to support each other in learning activities and allows students of all ability levels to participate in creating knowledge.

CHARACTER EDUCATION CONNECTION	What character and value-related issues are present in your lesson?

This lesson plan relates to the citizenship component of character education. The Declaration of Independence provides a foundational understanding for citizenship and what it means to be a "good citizen." The content of the DOI is explicit in its description of citizenship and character.

Lesson Plan Two

Teacher: Brian Furgione
Subject/Content Area: U.S. Government
Unit Topic: Rights of the People
Lesson Title: Evolution of Voting Rights in America

OBJECTIVES	Clear, Specific, and Measurable. NOT ACTIVITIES Student-Friendly

- I will be able to examine and evaluate the impact of various legislative actions relating to voting in America (15th Amendment, 19th Amendment, 23rd Amendment, 24th Amendment, Voting's Rights Act, 26th Amendment, etc.).
- I will understand and be able to explain the importance of voting in a democratic nation.
- I will be able to analyze current events and hypothesize the potential impact of government action.

STANDARDS

Identify what you will be teaching. Reference only NCSS standards and/or Common Core standards.

- Common Core CCSS.ELA-LITERACY.CCRA.SL.1: Prepare for and participate effectively in a range of conversations and collaborations with diverse partners, building on others' ideas and expressing their own clearly and persuasively.
- Common Core CCSS.ELA-LITERACY.CCRA.SL.2: Integrate and evaluate information presented in diverse media and formats, including visually, quantitatively, and orally.
- NCSS Standard 2: TIME, CONTINUITY, AND CHANGE
- NCSS Standard 3: PEOPLE, PLACES, AND ENVIRONMENTS
- NCSS Standard 5: INDIVIDUALS, GROUPS, AND INSTITUTIONS
- NCSS Standard 6: POWER, AUTHORITY, AND GOVERNANCE
- NCSS Standard 10: CIVIC IDEALS AND PRACTICES

DAILY PLANNER

Summary of the activities with suggested time allotments for each step included in this lesson.

~ 90-minute lesson ~

- Opening: Who Can Vote in America? (5–10 minutes)
- Introduction: Evolution of Voting in America (10 minutes)
- Activities
  - Primary Sources Carousel (40 minutes)
  - Current Events: Article Study (15 minutes)
  - Question Generation (5 minutes)
  - Class Discussion, Paired Discussion (10 minutes)
  - Reflection/Feedback (10 minutes)
  - Closing (5 minutes)

ACTIVATING STRATEGY	Motivator/Hook An Essential Question encourages students to put forth more effort when faced with complex, open-ended, challenging, meaningful, and authentic questions.

- Teacher will post a slide of images of citizens voting. These images can be either positive or negative in nature, as long as they are school-appropriate. (Great resources can be found through the Library of Congress: www.loc.gov/.) Above the images post the following question for the students: "Who can vote in America?"
- Give the students enough time to discuss the question with their peers and briefly analyze the images provided. Using a timer helps facilitate the conversation and keeps students on task.
- Once time has expired, randomly select students to stand and share their responses with the rest of the class. Most likely, the students will try to say "everyone" or go into extreme details. This will provide the foundation and purpose of the lesson.

INSTRUCTION	Step-by-Step Procedures Sequence Discover/Explain, Direct Instruction Modeling Expectations: "I Do" Questioning/Encourages Higher Order Thinking Grouping Strategies Differentiated Instructional Strategies to Provide Intervention and Extension

Getting Prepped: Introduction
Introduction: Evolution of Voting in America (10 minutes)

- Following the share out, introduce the topic for the day: "The Evolution of Voting Rights in America."
- Ask the students if they have any glaring questions about the topic. Proceed by explaining to students there were times throughout U.S. history that not every citizen had the right to vote and the activity will help to create a timeline of the evolution of voting rights.
- Explain to the students that the carousel, or stations activity, will facilitate the exploration of this topic and provide the foundation for the second part of the day's lesson.

GUIDED AND INDEPENDENT PRACTICE	"We Do," "You Do" Encourage Higher Order Thinking and Problem Solving Relevance Differentiated Strategies for Practice to Provide Intervention and Extension

Activity 1: Primary Sources Carousel
Stations Activity detailing the history of voting rights in America.

- Students should be separated into groups of four prior to starting the activity. Once they are separated, explain to the students the task at hand.
- At each station, you will find various primary and secondary sources regarding voting in America. Students will create a living timeline within their groups that details who was able to vote at different time periods, why things changed, and how they would feel about the voting rights in that time period.
- It is suggested that you use a timer and allow for 6 to 8 minutes at each station, with a 30-second buffer to allow for transition time.
- Students should analyze each document at the stations fully and discuss the impact with their group members. Classroom teacher should facilitate the transitions and monitor student groups, offering support when necessary.

Suggested Stations

- 15th Amendment
- 19th Amendment
- 23rd Amendment
- 24th Amendment
- Voting Rights Act
- 26th Amendment
- Following the station rotations, teacher should review the "proper" timeline with students and discuss any questions students may have regarding the stations. Providing feedback and probing questions will help students progress through their discussions.

Activity 2: Current Events Connection
Article Study: Who CAN'T Vote

- Provide students with an article that explores modern issues relating to voting rights in America. Articles can be about voting rights for felons, voter ID laws, areas of the country that cannot vote in certain elections (Guam, Puerto Rico, etc.). The article is intended to push the students thinking past the traditional "All Americans can vote."
- Have students read through the article, annotating key concepts and ideas relating back to the evolution of voting rights. A few sample articles can be found below, but personalizing the story to your students' and local community will help garner greater buy-in:
  - More than 4 million Americans don't have anyone to vote for them in Congress: https://goo.gl/Vagh6X
  - Why 10% of Florida Adults Can't Vote: How Felony Convictions Affect Access to the Ballot: https://goo.gl/XTHg5p
  - What Does the Constitution Actually Say About Voting Rights?: https://goo.gl/QxmtrS
- Allow students enough time to fully review the article and generate questions regarding the content (this will vary depending on the article selected).
- Providing multiple articles to different groups of students will help to differentiate.
- Following the article reading, have students discuss their findings and questions with their "neighbor," using any number of cooperative learning structures that may help bolster the conversation.

CLOSURE	Reflection/Wrap-Up Summarizing, Reminding, Reflecting, Restating, Connecting

Closing: Classroom Wrap-Up!

- Close out the lesson by collecting all necessary materials. Have students return to their seats and post the question, "Who can vote in America?" with the original intro slide on the board. Have students summarize what they have learned, clarify any issues/misconceptions they may have, and discuss the potential future of voting rights in the United States.

ASSESSMENT/EVALUATION	Students show evidence of proficiency through a variety of assessments. Aligned with the Lesson Objective Formative/Summative Performance-Based/Rubric Formal/Informal

Use a note card to have students record their responses as an "exit ticket" prior to leaving the classroom.

MATERIALS/TECHNOLOGY	What materials are utilized for this lesson? What types of technology are utilized to enhance learning and engagement? What primary and secondary sources are present to meet the learning objectives?

Materials

- Primary/secondary sources of citizens voting (or not voting)
- Current events/news article
- Station labels
- Timeline template
- Highlighters
- Index cards

Technology

- Projector
- Desktop/Laptop

MEETING INDIVIDUAL NEEDS OF DIVERSE LEARNERS	How does the lesson meet the needs of students with different learning styles (multiple intelligences) and what accommodations are made for diverse learners?

- ELLs: Visuals aides are embedded throughout the lesson. The teacher should translate the key vocabulary words in a student's native language, as well as provide a translated copy of the article.
- If articles are pulled from sites like https://newsela.com/, the teacher can scale the lesson based on Lexile level.
- Partnering students with peers can scaffold the learning process and ensure students are held accountable while having someone to support their learning throughout the lesson.

CHARACTER EDUCATION CONNECTION	What character and value-related issues are present in your lesson?

- Working collaboratively with others.
- Discussing current events and moral dilemmas.
- Understanding how citizens contribute to their communities.
- Problem solving and critical thinking.

U.S. History

Lesson Plan One

Teacher: Katie Pertschi
Subject/Content Area: U.S. History
Unit Topic: Introduction to Research
Lesson Title: Play Ball

OBJECTIVES	Clear, Specific, and Measurable. NOT ACTIVITIES Student-Friendly

Students in a group research and provide evidence and background for sports teams within the United States.

FYI

How could a lesson like this generate dialogue and debate settler colonialism and contemporary debates about sports teams like the Washington Redskins or Cleveland Indians?

Students will be able to analyze and understand the history behind the names of their favorite sports teams.

STANDARDS	**Identify what you will be teaching**. Reference only NCSS standards and/or Common Core standards.

Use questions generated about multiple historical sources to identify further areas of inquiry and additional sources.

What's in a name? Have you ever wondered why your favorite sports teams chose their mascots? Here's your chance to find out. Many sports teams chose their names based on the history or the geography of the area in which they are located. For example, the New England Patriots are named after the citizens of Boston who fought for American independence during the Revolutionary War. Some teams have moved from the area they were named for, like the Los Angeles Lakers. Originally the Lakers were located in Minnesota, the "land of 10,000 lakes," and were named for the state's nickname.

DAILY PLANNER	**Summary** of the activities with suggested time allotments for each step included in this lesson.
ACTIVATING STRATEGY	Motivator/Hook An Essential Question encourages students to put forth more effort when faced with complex, open-ended, challenging, meaningful, and authentic questions.

How do you think like a historian? (Students work in small groups to answer this question, which is used to focus their attention on the lesson's central question: what's in a name?) Students work in groups to answer the question.

INSTRUCTION	Step-by-Step Procedures Sequence Discover/Explain, Direct Instruction Modeling Expectations: "I Do" Questioning/Encourages Higher Order Thinking Grouping Strategies Differentiated Instructional Strategies to Provide Intervention and Extension

1. Activating strategy: Teacher presents students with the opening question: "Who is your favorite sports team and why?" Students are to provide a one-sentence answer and two reasons for their answer with supporting examples in writing.
2. Class discussion/Transition: Small groups report results of their work. Teacher then asks if they know anything about their favorite team's history.
3. Explanation of project/Modeling expectations: Teacher shows how to research and uses the example of the Los Angeles Lakers. Students receive information about the project specifications.
4. Identification and categorization: Working in groups, 1. Your first task is to make a list of 20 U.S. sports teams and explain how they got their names, using 2 to 3 sentences for each team.
5. Online research: The groups of students use the graphic organizer and start with the recommended sites to research teams.
6. Your second task is to create a new sports team for a place of your choosing in the United States. The team mascot must reflect something about the history of the area. You must explain why you chose the mascot for your team in a paragraph (5 sentences) and design a logo (hand drawn or computer generated) for your team.
7. Closure: Refer below.

GUIDED AND INDEPENDENT PRACTICE	"We Do," "You Do" Encourage Higher Order Thinking and Problem Solving Relevance Differentiated Strategies for Practice to Provide Intervention and Extension

See Instruction section

CLOSURE	Reflection/Wrap-Up Summarizing, Reminding, Reflecting, Restating, Connecting

Debrief the results of their research. Remind students of the importance of research and the need to know more background. Explain how during the next class they will use the results of their research to prepare information to explain change over time.

ASSESSMENT/EVALUATION	Students show evidence of proficiency through a variety of assessments. Aligned with the Lesson Objective Formative/Summative Performance-Based/Rubric Formal/Informal

Summative assessment: each pair of students turns in a completed PowerPoint. The teacher checks the accuracy and clarity of each team's work. The teacher also checks for the reasoning of each explanation and accuracy and appropriateness of each team. This assessment also serves a formative purpose since the next day in class the teacher is to provide students with feedback on their research.

MATERIALS/TECHNOLOGY	What materials are utilized for this lesson? What types of technology are utilized to enhance learning and engagement? What primary and secondary sources are present to meet the learning objectives?

Sites for researching: http://sportsteamhistory.com/; http://ftw.usatoday.com/2015/02/how-nfl-teams-got-nickname-mlb-nba-nhl-origin

One to One: Computers provided to every student; or request computer lab or laptop cart

MEETING INDIVIDUAL NEEDS OF DIVERSE LEARNERS	How does the lesson meet the needs of students with different learning styles (multiple intelligences) and what accommodations are made for diverse learners?

The lesson occurs toward the beginning of the school year and is intended to enable students to understand how to properly research and the change over time/cause and effect present in American history.

The teacher will group students accordingly dependent on any accommodations present in class.

CHARACTER EDUCATION CONNECTION	What character and value-related issues are present in your lesson?

Students learn how to work together in groups, which is vital to building class character at the beginning of the year.

Notes/Additional Resources

Rubric

- A (90–100) 20 teams identified and explained in detail. New team created, complete with explanation and logo. Neat, organized, effort shown.
- B (80–89) 15–19 teams identified, missing some details. New team created, missing a few details. Some effort shown.
- C (70–79) 13–15 teams identified, lacking many details. New team created, missing elements (logo or explanation). Little effort, sloppy.
- D (60–69) 11–13 teams identified, hardly any details. New team created, hardly any details. Little effort, sloppy.
- E (59 & below) Fewer than 10 teams identified, no details. No new team. No effort/time.

Lesson Plan Two

Author: Courtney Sanders
Grade Level: U.S. History
Unit Topic: WWII
Lesson Title: American Involvement and Battles Chart

FYI

How could a lesson like this generate dialogue and debate about settler colonialism and contemporary debates about sports teams like the Washington Redskins or Cleveland Indians?

OBJECTIVES — Clear, Specific, and Measurable. NOT ACTIVITIES Student-Friendly

I can examine the causes, course, and effects of the global and U.S. involvement in WWII; I can examine and identify key Florida connections to WWII.

STANDARDS — **Identify what you will be teaching**. Reference National and/or Common Core standards.

NCHS Historical Thinking Standard 2I. Draw upon the visual data presented in photographs, paintings, cartoons, and architectural drawings.

NCHS Historical Thinking Standard 4A. Formulate historical questions.

NCHS Historical Thinking Standard 4C. Interrogate historical data.

CCSS.ELA-Literacy.RH.6–8.1 Cite specific textual evidence to support analysis of primary and secondary sources.

CCSS.ELA-Literacy.RH.6–8.2 Determine the central ideas or information of a primary or secondary source; provide an accurate summary of the source distinct from prior knowledge or opinions.

DAILY PLANNER — **Summary** of the activities with suggested time allotments for each step included in this lesson.

1. Students will complete a TACOS (Time, Actions, Caption, Objects, Significance/Summary) for two political cartoons having to do with WWII.
2. Students will be given a Google Slides presentation to fill in notes about America's involvement in the war. They will follow along with a direct instruction lecture that includes:
   a. Thinking Questions
   b. Videos
   c. Checkpoint Quizzes
   d. Document Analysis (Maps)
   e. Summary
3. Battles Experts Charts: Using the notes from the previous day and the textbook, each group will create a poster about a specific battle, including key content. Then, each poster will be displayed around the classroom and students will walk around, Gallery Walk-style, using the posters their classmates created to complete a Comparison Matrix that includes all significant battles. After they have completed the chart, they will respond to Reflection Questions.

ACTIVATING STRATEGY	Motivator/Hook An Essential Question encourages students to put forth more effort when faced with complex, open-ended, challenging, meaningful, and authentic questions.

TACOS: Political Cartoon Analysis

INSTRUCTION	Step-by-Step Procedures Sequence Discover/Explain, Direct Instruction Modeling Expectations: "I Do" Questioning/Encourages Higher Order Thinking Grouping Strategies Differentiated Instructional Strategies to Provide Intervention and Extension

1 The teacher will begin the lesson by displaying a WWII political cartoon. Students will complete a TACOS chart for the document, identifying the Time, Actions, Captions, Objects, and Summary for the doc. Students will complete two TACOS for bellwork.
2 The students will be a given a student version of the Google Slides notes template—this is where they will fill in their notes from the lesson. The teacher will display the teacher version of the presentation and present a lecture about America's involvement in WWII.
3 Embedded in the presentation are THINK! Slides, where students pause to answer thinking questions about the content they are learning. These questions are Level 2/3 questions. There are also Checkpoint Quizzes throughout the lecture, to ensure understanding of key content. There are video links with THINK! Questions, as well as document and map analysis questions.
4 Throughout the lecture, the teacher helps the students add annotations and identifies key content for them. On their own time, students are expected to go back, review the notes, and create a summary paragraph.
5 Once the notes/lecture is complete, the students will create Battles Experts Posters to be used in a Gallery Walk. Each group will be assigned a specific battle and tasked with creating a poster that includes certain key information. They will use their notes from the previous lesson and their textbooks to gather the information and must include a visual.
6 Gallery Walk: Once the posters are complete, they will be posted around the classroom. Individually, students will rotate around the classroom, using the information on each poster to complete a Comparison Matrix worksheet for the battles. Once their worksheet is complete, students will respond to a couple Reflection Questions.

GUIDED AND INDEPENDENT PRACTICE	"We Do," "You Do" Encourage Higher Order Thinking and Problem Solving Relevance Differentiated Strategies for Practice to Provide Intervention and Extension

The lecture is direct instruction, with guiding THINK! Questions throughout to encourage higher-level thinking and interaction with the content.

The Battles Poster and Gallery Walk activity is a good extension activity and gives kids with more kinesthetic abilities a chance to shine.

CLOSURE	Reflection/Wrap-Up Summarizing, Reminding, Reflecting, Restating, Connecting

Summary for the notes presentation.
Reflection Questions for the Comparison Matrix activity.

ASSESSMENT/ EVALUATION	Students show evidence of proficiency through a variety of assessments. Aligned with the Lesson Objective Formative/Summative Performance-Based/Rubric Formal/Informal

Checkpoint Quizzes throughout the lecture/presentation
Embedded THINK! Questions
WWII Exam

MATERIALS/ TECHNOLOGY	What materials are utilized for this lesson? What types of technology are utilized to enhance learning and engagement? What primary and secondary sources are present to meet the learning objectives?

The teacher will provide the students with a student version of the lecture presentation and with the Comparison Matrix.

Students all have laptops to use to complete the classwork and do the research.

Notes Presentation:

https://docs.google.com/presentation/d/1AAgzzEL77kVsmLKTyhKMUV-8BRV0om-IKykCUI8_k0fs/edit?usp=sharing

WWII Battles Chart:

https://docs.google.com/document/d/1q5Gzfr6nf3eYB-pk47sLfbdEJe8g9aDyq-aSl-5jhwsA/edit?usp=sharing

MEETING INDIVIDUAL NEEDS OF DIVERSE LEARNERS	How does the lesson meet the needs of students with different learning styles (multiple intelligences) and what accommodations are made for diverse learners (e.g., English Language Learners and Special Education)?

ELL students are given dictionaries, access to Google Translate, and seated with peer tutors in their groups.

ELL/ESE students are given the completed teacher version of the notes presentation, so they can focus on listening and adding in annotations.

ELL/ESE students can write their summaries/reflections in their home language or deliver oral summaries and responses to Reflection Questions.

ELL/ESE students may be assigned a peer tutor to help with completing the Comparison Matrix.

CHARACTER EDUCATION CONNECTION	What character and value-related issues are present in your lesson?

Working in groups and with partners, respecting other people's points of view, gathering evidence on which to base one's arguments

Looking Back

Effective planning is one of the most important factors in becoming a successful classroom teacher. Planning engaging social studies activities in the secondary classroom is even more important considering the vast amount of content expected to be covered in most subjects, on top of all the pressure to increase test scores on standardized performance assessments. One of the easiest ways to create meaningful social studies activities in middle and high school classrooms is to relate the content covered to the students' daily lives and to vary instruction to meet multiple learning styles. The lessons provided in this chapter deal with a variety of social studies topics for each of the most popular social science content courses. While constructed somewhat differently (narrative form, outline form, etc.), the reader may notice some common elements in the lesson planning process. All lessons need to consider students in the classroom of different ability levels and learning styles. Teachers must always work and strive to help each and every student be successful in the classroom, and if an activity may prove to be difficult for certain students, modifications or accommodations can be made to support learning. Also, it is imperative that teachers become aware of some Internet resources that can help when planning lessons. In the Helpful Resources section, you will find a list of various websites that contain lesson plans, activity ideas, and valuable resources that can be used/modified to create dynamic learning opportunities. While this list is in no way comprehensive, it will provide secondary social studies teachers with a good starting point for finding out more information about the types of lessons that are already available and potentially serve as a catalyst to your own creative lesson ideas!

Extension Activity

Scenario

It is the last day of school at YHS and you are getting excited about the summer break. As the school day comes to a close, you begin cleaning up your classroom when in walks the principal of YHS, Dr. Russell. He greets you with a pleasant smile and congratulates you on a great year of classroom instruction. Dr. Russell continues by informing you that the district has asked him for examples of outstanding lesson plans created by teachers to place on the district website. He explains that these lessons should not only be engaging but also show productive use of school technology, address multiple learning styles, and accommodate for diverse learners. Since Dr. Russell has witnessed your wonderful and engaging social studies activities, he asks you to submit one of your best lessons for this project.

Task

For this activity, you will need to create and design a dynamic social studies activity that utilizes available technology and is engaging/challenging to all learners. Your lesson plan should have measurable learning objectives, include standards addressed, have multiple forms of assessment, and be detailed enough that other teachers in the district could implement the lesson in their classrooms. All supported resources should be cited and any original materials needed to implement the lesson provided as attachments.

Reflective Questions

1 Why is effective planning critical to quality classroom instruction and learning?
2 What would you describe as the characteristics of a "good" lesson plan?
3 Why are supplemental resources an important part of lesson plans?
4 What are the lesson plan expectations and guidelines in your local school district?
5 Why is it important to specifically plan for accommodations of diverse learners in your lessons?

Helpful Resources

American Memory Learning Page website compiles many lessons and activities relating to the Library of Congress' American Memory collections. It is an excellent place to visit for primary resource documents and photos to supplement social studies lessons.

www.loc.gov/teachers/index.html

PBS Teacher Source. The Public Broadcasting Service website contains a teacher-friendly section with over 1,400 lessons and activities in five broad areas, including arts and literature, health and fitness, math, science and technology, and social studies.

www.pbs.org/teachers

Smithsonian Education page. This website contains links to teacher resources (including lesson plans) as well as information about professional development sponsored by the Smithsonian, a calendar of important events, and information about current and future Smithsonian exhibits.

http://smithsonianeducation.org/

This website provides a series of free lesson plans to incorporate into social studies instruction for all secondary grade levels. There is also an interactive discussion board by state to help educators stay in touch with the most relevant issues to their classrooms.

https://teachers.net/lessonplans/subjects/social_studies/

Further Reading

Chandler, P. & Hawley, T. (Eds.). (2017). *Using Inquiry to Teach About Race in Social Studies*. Charlotte, NC: Information Age Publishing.

This book addresses teaching race in the classroom. It provides concrete lesson ideas for engaging learners in the social studies.

Clabough, J., Turner, T., Russell, W. & Waters, S. (2015). *Unpuzzling History With Primary Sources*. Charlotte, NC: Information Age Publishing.

This book addresses teaching with primary sources. It provides concrete lesson ideas for engaging learners in the social studies.

Hickey, G. & Clabough, J. (2017). *Digging Deeper: Activities for Enriching and Expanding Social Studies Instruction*. Charlotte, NC: Information Age Publishing.

This book showcases best practices and includes research-based lessons and activities that enrich and expand social studies instruction.

Nganga, L., Kambutu, J. & Russell, W. (Eds.). (2013). *Exploring Globalization Opportunities and Challenges in Social Studies: Effective Instructional Approaches*. New York, NY: Peter Lang Publishing.

This book addresses instructional approaches to global education in social studies.

Turner, T., Clabough, J. & Coles, W. (Eds.). *Getting at the Core of Common Core Standards With Social Studies*. Charlotte, NC: Information Age Publishing.

This book addresses lesson planning and instructional strategies in the age of Common Core Standards.

About the Authors

William B. Russell III is Professor of Social Science Education at The University of Central Florida, Orlando. He teaches social studies-related courses and serves as the Social Science Education PhD coordinator. Dr. Russell serves as the Director for The International Society for the Social Studies and is the Editor-in-Chief of the preeminent journal in the field of social studies education, *The Journal of Social Studies Research*. His research interests include alternative methods for teaching social studies, pre-service teacher education, and teaching with film. Dr. Russell has published numerous books and peer-reviewed journal articles related to social studies education.

Stewart Waters is Associate Professor of Social Science Education in the Department of Theory and Practice in Teacher Education at the University of Tennessee, Knoxville. His research interests include alternative methods for teaching social studies, character education, visual literacy, social studies curriculum, and teaching with film. Dr. Waters is the Conference Coordinator for The International Society for the Social Studies and is the Associate Editor for *The Journal of Social Studies Research*. Dr. Waters has authored numerous books and peer-reviewed journal articles related to social studies education.

Index

Page numbers in *Italics* refer to figures; **bold** refer to tables

Abbasid Empire 250–251, 254
abdominal breathing technique 257–258
ability, basis for grouping 145
accountability 147, 219
active learning 206
Adams, John 179
Addams, Jane 92
advertising **41**, 222
advocacy 6, **7**, 31, 79, 111, 120, 144–146, 151, 179, 194, 203–204, 219, 227
Africa **21**, 243
African Americans 18, 126–127
age-appropriateness 114, 213, 229
agriculture 167, 177, 242
Alleman, J. 68
All President's Men (1976) 229
alternatives: choice among 204; determination 204
ambitions 193–194
American Federation of Teachers 11
American Historical Association 17
American Memory Learning Page website 296
American Red Cross 188
American Revolution **22**, 112, 148, 165, 172, 174–175, 178–179, 289
American society 262–265
Amway Center 238
analogy 16, 24, 228, 281
analytical assessment 76–78
analyzing skills 121
Ancient World History: Patterns of Interaction (McDougal Littell) 252
anecdotal material 79
animal shelter **190**
anthropology **7**, 14, 27–28, 31
APA standards 259
apps 225–226
archaeology 14, 27, 99
Archimedes 153
assessment: errors 68–69; and evaluation 66–81; plans 80; principles 68–69; procedures 71; purpose 68; role in social studies 67–68; tests 72–75
assessment guidelines 69–71; problems 70
assessor error 69
Association for Middle Level Education **7**, **9**; AMLE Annual Conference **10**
Association for Supervision and Curriculum Development 36, 55
Association of American Geographers 29
attention span 74, 177; concentration span 163
Attila the Hun 104
auditory learners 245, 252, 258
Aurasma (app) 226
authentic assessment 66, 68, 71–72, 79–80; significance of "authentic" 71
awareness 15, 19, 25, 30, 37, 114, 121, 140, 203, 206, 258

Baghdad 254
Baldwin, P. 175
Barth, J.L. 15
Barton, Clara 104
basic interpersonal communication skills (BICS) 113
basis of comparison 24, 67, 80
Baum, S. 117
bayou 88, **88**
behavioral controls 265–269
behavioral objectives 46, **47**
Berkowitz, M. 215
Berson, M.J. 233
bias 29–30, 85, 110–111, 129, 149, 185, 207, 221, 228
Bier, M. 215
biography 97, **97**, 204
Bloom, B. 142
Bloom's Taxonomy 64
boldface 85, 95, 114
book format and purpose xv
Boostrom, R. 142
Boys and Girls Club of America 188
Braden, R.A. 222
brags (comic devices) 166–167
brainstorming 47, 58, 60, 125, 152, 202, 204, 263, 278
Brophy, J. 68
Bruner, Jerome 24
Brunner, L. 85
budget project 237–240

California 112, 136
canal 88, **88**
Carnegie Corporation Oral History Project 233
Carnegie Foundation 17
Carver, George Washington 33, 167
case studies: approaches (close-ended versus open-ended) 197–198; example 198; issues-centered learning 197–198; procedures 198; promoting inquiry with 128; types 197
case study approach 128–129; activities 129
castles **21**, 26
cause and effect **21**, 30, 85, 100, 103, 115, **121**, 291
celebratory events 271–272
Center for Media Literacy website 233
Central America 243–244, **255**
Chandler, P. 64, 117, 296
character concepts 229
Character Counts 215
character development 193, 212, 229
character education 62, 194, 205–206, 213–215, 228–229, 231; definition 193; developing values 208–212; goals 212; lesson plans 240, 245, 252, 258, 261, 265, 268, 274, 279, 283, 288, 291, 295; six "Es" (Ryan) 212
Character First Media 215
character monologues 166, 169
character and values, worldview perspective 212
checklist assessment 76, 78–79; third-grade reporting activity **77**
Cheenius, Professor Ima (brag) 167
Children's Book Council (CBC) 97
children's theater 171
China **21–22**, 243–244
chocolate meditation 257
Christensen, Bonnie: *Single Pebble: Story of Silk Road* 276–277, 279
citizenship 13–18 *passim*, **21**, 212; character development and 212; *see also* good citizenship
civic ideas and practices (NCSS theme) **20**
civic virtue 13, 206, 214
Civil Rights Movement **22**
Civil War **21**, 104, 172; cooperative learning project (creating newspapers) 149–150
Clabough, J. 64, 118, 296
class action dramas 164–165, 189
class divide-ups 93
classical conditioning 259–261
classroom, dramatic climate 37, 48
classroom episodes, reading and writing in social studies 104–105
classroom excitement 175–176
Clearing House: Journal of Educational Strategies **9**, 55
Cleopatra 104
cliff-hangers 168
clothing 26, 89, 181, 222, 243
Cobblestone (magazine) 166
code of conduct 10; Florida 3–5
code of ethics 10–11; Florida 3, 5
Cohen, D. 233
Coles, W. 296
collaborative learning 143; definition 146–147
collaborative learning groups 157; organizing 147–150
collaborative units 42–43, 63
colony, establishment 182–183
Columbus urge (mindset) 130–131
comic books 25, 99, 101
Commission to Reorganize Secondary Education (CRSE) Committee on Social Studies: *1916 Report* 17, 194
Common Core Initiative (2012) 22
Common Core Standards 20–23, 33, 61, 106, 296; economics 237, 241; geography 250; history 246; psychology 256; U.S. government 284; World War Two 292
Common Core State Standards website 32
communication 38, 69, 82, 156
communism 31, 265, 269
comparative advantage 240–245
Comparison Matrix 262–265, 294
computers 36, 48, 50, 91, 128, 130–131, 149–157 *passim*, 176, 217–218, 231, 238, 243, 248, 279, 290–291
conclusion (versus "speculation" and "opinion") 204
conditioned response (CR) 259–260
conditioned stimulus (CS) 259–260
conferences 8, **10**, 55
conformity 265–269
confrontation, type of interactional drama **173**
Congressional Committee 183–184
conserving influences 212
Constitution **22**, **40**, 179, 185
Constitutional Amendments 286
constructivism 24, 120, 195
contemporary social studies 13–33; classroom episode (#1) 25–26; college, career, civil life framework 22–23; Common Core Standards 20–22; constructivism 24; controversy 16–19; curricula 16–20, **21–22**; definition (NCSS) 14; goals 14–17; NCSS national standards for preparation of teachers (2018) 23–24; place in school curriculum 13; priorities 15; problems approach 24–25; purpose 14; social science disciplines 27–31; thematic units for each grade level **21**
contextual locating 90
cooperative centers 153–154
cooperative learning 143–159; definition 147; permanent base groups 151; student roles 150–151; technology 154–157
cooperative learning groups 75, 157; organizing 147–150; social factors 144
copying 75–76, 102–103, 169–170
copyright 231
Cornell Way 262–264
Council for Economic Education **7**, 33, 142; CEE National Conference **10**
Council for Exceptional Children 117
Council of Chief State School Officers (CCSSO) 20
Couran, Sir Geoffrey of 180
Covid-19 pandemic 220
creating context 90

creative writing 103–104
creativity 43, 54, 73, 76, 106, 122, 185, 219, 235
criterion-based assessment 67, 76
critical thinking 114, 119, 197, 222–223; definition 122; incorporation in social studies 129; promoting with modules 127–128
cross-curricular connections 61, 96, 114
crude birth rate (CBR) 247
crude death rate (CDR) 247
Cruz, B.C. 233
C3 Framework, Inquiry Design Model 141
C3 Framework (NCSS College, Career, Civic Life Framework, 2013–) 15, 22–23, 30, 196; authentic assessment 71; dimensions **23**, 23; objective 23
cultural change 16, 27
culturally-responsive teaching 111–112
culture **20**, 27–28, 113; definition 27
culture clash 170
Culture Cubed 269–274
current case study 197
curriculum maps 39, 42, 63–64; "foundations of government" example **40**; "political behavior" example **41**
cyberbullying 231

daily planner 58, 64, 237, 241, 246, 250, 256, 259, 262, 266, 270, 275, 280, 284, 289, 292
Damascus 254
decision-making 13, 129, 131, 150, 176; issues-centered 193–215; selective 72; situations requiring 203
decision-making process 198–199, 215
decision-making skills 228; in relation to values 203–205
Declaration of Independence (DOI) 280–283; main points 281; parts 283
deduction 199
definitional issues 200
definitional topics 127
democracy 15, **22**, 89, 185, 205–206, 212–213
Demographic Transition Stage 247
descriptive issues, classification 201
descriptive paragraph 90, **90**
Dewey, John 24, 78
dialogue 162, 166, 171, 173, 200, 212, 214, 289
diamonte (diamond-shaped poem) 90, **90**
dictatorship 87, **88**
Diem, R. 233
digital divide 231
digital history 223–224; definition 223
dilemmas, example 211
disability 62, 137
discrimination 4, **22**, 184, 195, 201, 206–207, 213, 229
diverse learners 62, 109–118; lesson plans 240, 244–245, 248, 252, 258, 261, 264–265, 268, 274, 279, 283, 288, 291, 294–295
Dobret, Sir William of 180
document-based questions (DBQs) 132, 141
document cameras 61, 154, 217–218, 279
Dorsett, Bertrand 180
drama 190–191; art-and story-related techniques 171–172; effective use in social studies 175–176; importance in social studies 161–162
drama through reading 162–166; class action dramas 164–165; example (1974 tornado) 163–164; example (Revere's many rides) 165; guided fantasies 162–163; readers' theater 166
dramatic reading 166–169, 189
dramatic tension 160–161
drama units 174
dress 26, 165, 174, 209, **255**, 269, 272
drill 133
Driscoll, M. 132
Duplass, J.A. 233

Early Globalization 275–279
eavesdropping, type of interactional drama **173**
economics 18, 28, 153, 171, 237–245; skills 139–140; reports 99
economics lesson plan #1 (Budget Project) 237–240; activating strategy 237; assessment 239–240; character education 240; closure 239; daily planner 237; diverse learners 240; guided and independent practice 238; materials and technology 240; objectives 237; overview and purpose 238; standards 237
economics lesson plan #2 (Where are you wearing?) 240–245; activating strategy 241; assessment 244; character education 245; closure 244; consumer ethics 244; daily planner 241; diverse learners 244–245; guided and independent practice 242–243; instruction 242; materials and technology 244; objectives 240; standards 241
education, years of schooling (expected) 248; years of schooling (mean) 248
Educreations (app) 226
Edwingham, Count of 180
elderly people 137, 189, 249
Emancipation Proclamation 127
Emerson, R.W. 83
Engle, S.H. 203, 215
English as Second Language (ESL) students 112
English Language Learners (ELLs) 62, 109, 112–114, 116, 261, 265, 268, 288, 294; classroom management 112–113; communicating with 112; delivering content 113; embracing the culture 113; social interaction 113; visual aids 113–114
English Speakers of Other Languages (ESOLs) 112, 248, 265, 279
Erickson, L. 142
ESE students 261, 265, 279, 294
essay tests 73; criticisms 73–74; thinking required 74
ethics 3, 5, 10–11, 201
Ethics of Teaching (Strike and Soltis, 2009 edition) 11
ethnocentrism 28, 207–208
evaluation: always comparative 66; judgments 128; purpose 67; role of students 71; should be different in problems approach 66; tools 68–69
evaluation skills 203; examples 204–205
Evans, R. 195, 215

evidence, determination of adequacy 205
examples and models 209–210
exceptional education students 114–116; graphic organizers 115–116; reading adaptations 114; writing adaptations 114–115
expanded textbook units 41–43
Expanding Communities Model 17–18
Expanding Environments curriculum 17–18, **18**
experiences 2, 36; classification 88
experiencing social studies 160–191; art-and story-related dramatic techniques 171–172; dramatic reading 166–169; drama through reading 162–166; drama units 174; effective use of drama 175; field trips 186–189; importance of drama 161–162; interactional drama 173–174; mock trials 185–186; process drama 175; reenactment 172–173; role plays and other structured techniques 169–171; service learning experiences 189; simulation games 176–184; storytelling 174–175
Explain Everything (app) 226
extended teacher definitions 89
extension activity: assessment and evaluation 80; becoming social studies teacher 11; contemporary social studies 32; cooperative learning 158; diverse learners 116; experiencing social studies 190; issues-centered learning and decision-making 214; lesson plans 295; planning social studies instruction 63; problem-solving 141; reading and writing in social studies 106–107; technology and media 232

Facebook 155, 230
fact 200, 204
fake news 221
falsehood 204, 214
Federalist **40**
Federal Resources for Educational Excellence (FREE) 64
feedback 67, 75–76, 78
Felten, P. 223
fiction and poetry 98–99
field trips 186–190; Russell's guide 187–189; virtual 224–225
film 227–230; effective pedagogical practices 228; Russell's model 227–228; strategies for using 229–230
finding information 130
First Days of School (Wong and Wong, 2005) 11
first-person poem 169
Fitzhugh, John 180–181
flipped classrooms 226–227
Florida 5, **8**, 53, 112, 286, 292, 297
Florida Teacher Certification Examination 3
folk tales 209–210
food drive 190
Foundations of Government 280–283
Franklin, Benjamin 38, 179
Frayer Model 86–87, **87–88**
freedom of religion 31, **40**
Friedman, A. 234
Frog and Toad Are Friends 166
frontier 89
Fuller, S. 142
Fulwer, B.E. 174
fun 162
functional classroom 207–208
Funnell, B.H. 142

Gallery Walk 293
Galloway, J. 225, 233–234
Gandhi (1982) 228–229
Gardner, H.: multiple intelligences 110, **110**, 116
Gateway to 21st Century Skills 64
Gee, J.P.: *What Video Games have to Teach Us* (2003) 223
gender 24, 112, 196, 213–214, 246
Gender Inequality Index (GII) 249
generalizations 128
geographic education, themes 29
geography 18; circle your assigned topic 254–255; lesson plans 245–255; notes and additional resources 253–254; social science discipline 28–29
geography lesson plan #1 (Human Development Index) 245–249; activating strategy 246; assessment 247–248; character education 248; closure 247; daily planner 246; diverse learners 248; documents 248; guided and independent practice 247; instruction 247; materials and technology 248; objectives 245–246; standards 246
geography lesson plan #2 (Islamic Civilization) 249–255; activating strategy 250; assessment 251–252; character education 252; closure 251; daily planner 250; diverse learners 252; guided and independent practice 251; instruction 250–251; materials and technology 252; objectives 249–250; standards 250; think-pair-share format 251
Geography Teacher (journal) **9**
Gini coefficient 247
global connections (NCSS theme) **20**
globalization **21**, 240–245, 275
global warming 157, 161, 223
globes 133–134, 140, 154; definition 134
goal-centered assessment 68
Goldberg, Ruth 265–269
Golden Age of Abbasids 254–255
good citizenship 17, 193–195, 202, 205–206, 213, 222, 283
Google 55, 220; Google Docs 262; Google Earth 134; Google Slides 262–264, 293; Google Translate 265
Gorski, P. 111
government (school subject) 18; curriculum map **40**
GPS 134–135
grade-level teams 42
grades 68, 70; emphasized in schools 66; "indicators of student progress" 67; mix 70
graphic organizers 115–116
Great Books Foundation 107
Griffin, Susan 32

Gross National Income (GNI) per capita 246, 248–249
group activities, problem-centered 152–153
grouping, approaches 145–146
guardians 138, 188, 231
guided and independent practice 60
guided discussion format 211

Haiku 100, 104
Hamilton, Alexander 178–179
handouts **40–41**, **239**, 243–244, **245**, 250–252
Hanna, Paul 17–18
Harmin, M. 202, 215
Hartoonan, M. 15
Hawley, T. 64, 117, 296
helpful resources 141; contemporary social studies 32
Henry, Patrick 179
Herczog, Michelle 32
Hickey, G. 64, 118, 296
Hickey, M.G. 171
high-impact teaching, factors 160
HIPPY model 262–263
Hiroshima and Nagasaki 198
historical case study 197
history 18, 100, 114, 132, 153, 199, 206, 227; classroom episode #1 25–26; social science discipline 29–30
History Scene Investigation (HSI) 142
History Teacher (journal) **9**, 55
Hollywood films 227, 229
Holocaust 214–215
Hortin, J.A. 222
human capital 242–243
Human Development Index 245–249
human interaction 166
human rights 196, 244
Hunter lesson sequence (1990–1991) 57, 63

iMovie 229
imperialism **22**, 262–265
in-basket simulation games 182–183
inclusive education 114
independence (economic) 13
independent learner 68, 140
independent working 177
India 229, 243
individual development and identity (NCSS theme) **20**
individual instruction 61
individual needs (diverse learners) 62
individual rights **40**
individuals, groups, institutions (NCSS theme) **20**
indoctrination 194, 206, 208
induction 199
industrialization and economic development 245–249
industries 92, 243–244
infant mortality rate 249
information 68, 82, 132
information-finding 130–131, 140
information-retention 132–133, 140
inquiry learning 198–202; goal 198; moral reasoning 199–200; procedures 199; public issues 200–201; values clarification 202
in-role reports 169
in-role writing 104
in-service training 190, 225
Institutional Review Board (IRB) 259–261
interactional drama 171, 173–174; types **173**
interdependence 14, 17, **20**, 119, 144, 147–148, 150
interdisciplinary aspects **7**, **9**, 27–28, 65, 196
interest groups 16
international relief effort **190**
International Society for Social Studies (ISSS) **7**, **9**; Annual Conference **10**
International Society for Technology in Education (ISTE) 219; website 233
internet 36, **41**, 106, 114, 134, 137, 154, 163, 218, 231, 295; enhancing instruction 220–227; safety 231–232; safety and reliability issues 155; search engines 155
Internet 4 Classrooms website 80
interview, type of interactional drama **173**
Introduction to Research 288–291
Islam 249–255
Islam: Empire of Faith (video) 250–254
issues-centered learning 194–198; approaches 197; case studies 197–198; content-selection 195–196; inquiry learning 198–202; principles 195; problems 202–203

Japan **22**
Japanese American Internment Camps 56–62
Jefferies, D. 116
Jefferson, Thomas **40**, 52–54, 104, 161, 178–179, 281
John, M. 233–234
Johnson, D. 147–148, 150, 158
Johnson, R. 147–148, 150, 158
Johnson, T. 142
Johnston, J.H. 233
Journal of Social Studies Research (JSSR) **9**
journals 6, **9**, 36

Kagan, S. 147
Kahoot (app) 226
Kambutu, J. 296
Keengwe, J. 227
Kellough, R. 65
Kent, A.M. 84
kinesthetics 59–60, 62, **110**, 113, 115–116, 245, 252, 258, 268, 294
King, Dr. Martin Luther, Jr. 157, 161
Klemp, R. 107–108
Knox, Henry 178–179
Kohlberg, L. 199, 211, 215
Kracl, C. 142
Kress, G. 222

Lakein, Alan 37
language abilities 75
Latin America 247, 269–274
LCD projector 218, 226

leadership 37
learning 110; active versus passive 51–152; disability 114; goals 69; issues-centered 194–198; to learn 68; multi-modal principle 223; objectives 64, 80; theory 24
learning inquiry, "mind-on" 151–152
learning outcomes 67–68, 70, 73; desired (clear picture) 46
learning skills, incorporation in social studies 129
leather 243
Lee, J. 234
Lee, J.K. 223
less developed country (LDC) 247
lesson plans 235–296
Lewis and Clark expedition 51–55
Lexile level 288
Library of Congress 114, 155, 224, 285, 296
life expectancy 248–249
Limited English Proficient (LEP) students 112
Lincoln, Abraham 127, 138, 149, 169
Lintner, T. 64, 118
listening skills 164
literacy rate 249
live case study 197
Logansby, Rowan of 180
Longfellow, Henry W.: *Paul Revere's Ride* 98
long-term memory 132
Los Angeles Lakers 289–290
Louisiana 50–53, 55, 173, 242

MacArthur Foundation 17
Madison, James 179
Mafia card game 266, 268
Manhattan 173
mapping school activities 137–138
maps 133–138, 140, 153, 183; definition 134; skills 141
map-using activities 135–137; best route 137; fantasy school map 136–137; map labeling 137; orienteering scavenger hunt 136; scavenger hunt 135–136; shortest route to habitat 137; site stakeout 136
Marion, Francis 178–179
mascots 289–290
materials **9**, 24, 33, 41–42, 45, 50, 55, 61, 82–98 *passim*, 114–115, 120, 127, 129–131, 140, 145–158 *passim*, 169, 207, 213, 220, 223–225, 231; lesson plans 240, 244, 248, 252, 258, 261, 264, 267–268, 273, 279, 282, 287, 291, 294–295
mathematics 14, 16, 22, 28, 72, **110**, 133, 138, 153, 167, **239**, 251, 254, 296
McBride, B. 107–108
McClellan, B.E. 215
McGuire, M.E. 174
McGurk effect 256
McIntyre, B. 142
McLaughlin, M. 84
McTaggart, M. 233–234
media **41**, 149
media literacy 221–222, 233
memory 132–133
Merkley, D.M. 116
Me Too movement 196
Microsoft Movie Maker 229
Middle East 44–45
Middle Ground (journal) **9**
Middle Level Learning (MLL; journal) **9**, 55
Middle School Journal **9**
Mid-West region 242
mindfulness 256
mind, functions **122**
"minds-on" learning inquiry 151–152
Ming Lo Moves the Mountain 166
misinformation 164
mnemonic devices 114–115, 133
mobile technologies 225–226
mock trials 185–186, 189; related activities 186
monitoring 5, 45, 57, 94, 101, 136, 150, 154, 156, 188, 198, 220; lesson plans 240, 258, 264, 282, 286
monologue 166, 169
moral reasoning 199–200, 215; example 200
moral value issues 200
more developed country (MDC) 247
Morris, R. 191
Morris, R.V. 171
Morton, T. 159
Mraz, M.E. 108
multicultural education 111–112, 206–207; knowledge "most significant tool" 208
multiculturalism 200, 213
multiple intelligences (Gardner) 62, 110, **110**, 116, 283
Murphy, R.C. 142
museum reports 99
music 271
mysteries (game) 131

narrative historians (humanist historians) 29
National Assessment of Educational Progress 112
National Association for Gifted Children 64
National Clearinghouse for English Language Acquisition 112
National Council for Geographic Education **7**, **9**, 29, 33; NCGE Annual Conference **10**
National Council for History Education **7**; National Conference **10**
National Council for Social Studies *see* NCSS
National Educational Technology Standards (NETS) 219
National Education Association (NEA) 11, 17, 36
National Geographic 166
National Geographic Society 17
National Governors Association for Best Practice (NGA Center) 20
nationalism 206
National Middle School Association **7**
Native Americans 54; concept web *48*
natural increase rate (NIR) 247, 249
NCHS standards, World War Two 292
NCSS College, Career, Civic Life Framework *see* C3 Framework

NCSS (National Council for Social Studies, 1921–) 6, **7**, **9**, 33, 36, 64, 81, 117–119, 219; Annual Conference **10**; definition of "social studies" 14–15; "Fostering Civic Virtue" (1997) 212; *Notable Trade Books for Young Readers* 96–97, 107, 213; purpose of social studies 14–15; ten themes **20**; website 11, 23–24
NCSS National Standards for Preparation of Social Studies Teachers 30, 71, 196; website 32
NCSS standards: economics 231, 237; geography 246, 250; psychology 256, 259; sociology 262, 265; U.S. Government 280, 284; world history 270, 275
NCSS Task Force on Character Education 212
NCSS Task Force on Creating Effective Citizens (2001) 17
NCSS Task Force on Standards for Social Studies: *Charting A Course* (1989) 17–18; *Expectations of Excellence* (1994) 18; *National Curriculum Standards* (2010) 19, **20**
NearPod 226, 276–277
netiquette 157, 232
Nettie Goes South 166
new country explorer 168
New Social Studies (1960s, 1970s) 18–19
newspapers 114, 163
Newsweek 114
New York 174
Nganga, L. 296
Nicaragua 243
No Child Left Behind (NCLB) Act 2, 112
nonfiction books 97
nuclear waste 183–184
nuclear weapons 153, 198

objective and subjective tests, strengths and weaknesses 66
objective measures 72–73; criticisms 73
objectives 16–17, 23, 33, 39, **40–41**, 42–58 *passim*, 68, 73, 79; definition 67
observational checklists **79**; types 79
Ochoa, A. 215
Ogle, D. 107–108
Ohio tornado (1974) 163–164
Onchwari, G. 227
one-to-one instruction 226–227
online and virtual teaching 220
opinion 204
oral history videos 230
originality 75
Osgood, Samuel 179

Padlet (app) 226
Paine, Thomas: *Common Sense* (1776) 281
parables 210
parallel structure 96
parents 5–6, **7**, **9**, 38, 48, 67–69, 71, 80, 111, 126, 130, 137–138, 156, 158, 176, 188, 208, 211–213, 220, 226, 231
Pavlov's dog experiments 260–261
PBS Teachers 64
PBS Teacher Source 296
Pearcy, M. 81
peer assessment 76
peer pressure 38, 146, 148
people, places, environments (NCSS theme) **20**
performance 72–73
personal actions (teaching values) 210–211
personal electronics 243
personal finance 237–240
personal goals statement 11
Piaget, Jean 24
picture definitions 89–90
picture pantomimes 171
pioneer 89
plagiarism 221, 223
planning social studies instruction 35–65; activities (development) 48–50; adaptation 55–56; concept webs 46–47, *48*; content description 49–50; content outline 46, *47*, 51; culminating activity 54; expanded textbook units 41–43; failure of teachers to plan 37–38; flowcharts 46, *47*; hallmarks 37; importance 36–37; long-range planning 39; objectives 46, 49, 51, 57; planning episodes 44–45, 50–55, 57–62; rationale 50; setting stage, creating environment 37; shorter instructional sequences 56–62; textbook-centered units 39; types of planning 41; unit elements format 49–50; unit planning (development) 45–46; unit planning (types) 41–43; unit topics 43–45
pluralism 195, 200, 207–208
Pogrow, S. 191
political science 30, 153
pollution 184, 189
popular culture 131
portfolios, success factors 72
positive interdependence 144
post-reading questions 101
power 196; authority, governance (NCSS theme) **20**
PowerPoint (Microsoft) 86, 157, 222, 258, 261, 282, 290
predictive skills 85
Prensky, M. 234
prescriptive issues 201
presentation 157
primary sources 296; reading levels 85
problem-centered group activities 152–153
problem-identification 123
problems approach to social studies 24–26; in classroom 25–26; definition of "problems" 25
problems-centered group activities, "about the process" 152
problem-solving xv, 13, 16–17, 68, 73, 76, 104, 119, 122–127, 129–130, 140, 162, 199; guidelines **124**; skill "most needed throughout life" 25; strategies **123**; teaching values 211–212; use of maps and globes 134
problem-solving tasks (types) 124–127; identifying all factors of problem 124–125; identifying purpose problems 126–127; multiple perspectives of problem 125–126; prioritizing problem 125;

problems with alternative solutions 126; problems with proposed solutions 127
problems, real-life 124
production, distribution, consumption (NCSS theme) **20**
production efficiency 242
professional certification 2–3, 31
professional development 6, 218–219, 225
professional organizations 6, **7**
programming director (television network) 126
project assessment 75–78; categories 78
projects 152–153
Promethean ActivBoard 233
pronouncements, rules, warnings 208–209
psychology 30, 255–261
psychology lesson plan #1 (sensation) 255–258; activating strategy 256; assessment 258; character education 258; closure 258; daily planner 256; diverse learners 258; guided and independent practice 256–257; instruction 256; materials and technology 258; objectives 255–256; standards 256
psychology lesson plan #2 (classical conditioning) 259–261; activating strategy 260; assessment 261; character education 261; closure 261; daily planner 259; diverse learners 261; guided and independent practice 260–261; instruction 260; materials and technology 261; objectives 259; standards 259
public issues, example 201; inquiry learning 200–201; questions (types) 200
publicity and review reports 100
public policy **22**, 200–201
Puerto Rico 286
Puritans 124–125
purposeful assignments 94
purposeful reading 95

quality reading (less can be more) 91–93; class divide-ups 93; student-written summaries 91–92; teacher-written summaries 91–92; textbook cut-ups 93; textbook highlighting 93; textbook write-ins 93
quantitative approach 29
question assignments, guidelines 101; "within reach" of students 101
question reversal 96
question words 96
quotes (powerful) 161

race 196, 296
racism 200, 207–208, 213, 229, 265
Randolph, Edmund 179
random groups 145
Rasinski, T. 166
Raths, L. 202, 215
readers' theater 98, 166, 191
reading: ability 74; adaptations, exceptional education students 114; drama through 162–166; questions 96; teachers 83; and writing assignments 83–84
reading and writing in social studies 82–108; classroom episode 104–105; collaborative writing (sample topic sentence set) **105**; connecting writing to social studies and reading 99–100; creative writing 103–104; cross-curricular connections 96; extended teacher definitions 89; organizing to write 100–101; quality reading (less can be more) 91–93; reading questions 96; research and reporting skills 102–103; story starter examples **105**; student-centered experiences 89–90; task statements 96; teacher-provided experiences 89; textbook-reading 93–95; trade books 96–99
reading skills 83; needed in social studies 84–85
real world 71
reasoning 203
record keeping 156
recruitment, type of interactional drama 173
Red Scare 265–269
Reel Character Education (Russell and Waters, 2010) 229
reenactment 172–173
references 142
reflective question 141
regulatory environment 243
relevance 204–205
religious studies, social science discipline 31
reports 75–78
Repositories of Primary Sources 107
research and reporting skills 102–103; principles 103
research case study 197
research, internet use 155
resources (economic) 242–243
resource units 63
retirement home **190**
Revere, Paul 165
Rights of People 283–288
Roberts, P. 65
Robin Hood 105
Rockefeller Foundation 17
Rocky Mountain Region 242
role models 209–210, 212
role-play 53–54, 169–170, 175–176, 189, 191
Rosenstone, R.A. 227
Rosenzweig, R. 233
Ross, E.W. 81
rote learning 72, 120, 133
Rubistar for Teachers 81
rubric assessment 54, 56, 74–76, 79, 81, 149, 239–294 *passim*; historical monuments (Grades 5 and 6) **77**
rumor 267, 269
Russell III, W.B. xv, 229, 296–297
Russell lesson plan (basic components) 56, 63
Russell model (use of film) 227–228
Ryan, K. 208

Sakurai, Gail: *Japanese American Internment Camps* 58–59, 61
sampling error 69
Saxe, D. 215

scanning 84, 130
schemata 120–121
school success 207–208
Schul, J. 159
Schweder, W. 118
science, technology, society (NCSS theme) **20**
scientific historians 29
scientific method 123
sea captain explorer 168
seamless web 27
self-assessment 76
Selfield, Henry of 181
self-motivation 130–131
self-selected groups 145
Selridge, Lady Jane 181
sensation 255–258
sensory meditation 257
sensory memory 132
separation of church and state 31
sequential case study 197
service learning experiences 189, **190**; long-term 189, **190**; short-term 189, **190**
Service, Robert 169
Sewell, A.M. 142
sexism 207–208
sexuality 196
shipwreck rescue 125
shopping center 181–182
shorter instructional sequences 56–62; activating strategy 59; brainstorming 60; character education 62; closure 60; cross-curricular connections 61; daily planner 58; evaluation 61; guided and independent practice 60; individual assessment 61; individual needs (diverse learners) 62; lesson plan 56–57; materials 61; objectives 57–58; small group instruction 59–60; spectrum vocabulary 59; standards 58; technology 61; visual 61; whole group instruction 59–60
short-term planning 63
Shotick, J.A. 171
Silk Road 275–279
Simon, S. 202, 215
Simpson, J.L. 84
simulation game, curricular purpose 177; example (President Washington's cabinet) 177–179; in-basket 182–183; real and hypothetical with one decision 180–181; single-choice decision based on vested interest 183–184; speculative information with many decisions 181–182
sketch units 45
skills, now viewed differently 68
skimming 84, 95, 130
Skype 103
Slatin, B. 117
slavery 86, 149, 174
Slavin, R. 150, 159; jigsaw process 148
small group instruction 60
smells 162–163, 256, 260
Smith, F.A. 94
Smithsonian (magazine) 166
Smithsonian Education website 296
social action project **190**
social climate 16, 18, 123
Social Education (journal) **9**, 36, 55
social interaction 102, 113, 146, 166, 174–175
social issues: case study 197; exploration with film 229
social justice 111, 153, 205, 212–213
social media 3, 157, 230, 232
social science materials (helping students to read) 85–88; classifying experiences 88; four-step strategy 85; Frayer Model 86–87, **87–88**; teacher explanation of meaning 86; vocabulary (development strategies) 85–86
social skills 144, 146–147
social standards teachers, NCSS national standards for preparation of (2018) 23–24
social status 148
social studies committees 63
social studies, cooperative learning 143–159; dilemmas 68; diverse learners 109–118; experiencing 160–191; goals 32, 195, 202, 212; learning and decision-making (issues-centered) 193–215; origin of term 17; primary purpose (NCSS) 119; purposes 32, 205; reading and writing 82–108; role of assessment 67–68; technology and media 217–234; thinking, problem-solving, skills 119–142
social studies curriculum, teacher input 63
Social Studies (journal) **9**, 36, 55
Social Studies Research and Practice (journal) 55
social studies teachers, entry into profession 1–12; impact on students 15–16; obligations to profession of education 4–5; obligations to public 4; obligations to students 3–4
sociodrama 170, 189
sociology 31, 262–269
sociology lesson plan #1 (imperialism and American society) 262–265; activating strategy 263; assessment 264; character education 265; closure 264; daily planner 262; diverse learners 264–265; guided and independent practice 263–264; instruction 263; objectives 262; standards 262
sociology lesson plan #2 (Red Scare) 265–269; activating strategy 266; assessment 267; character education 268; closure 267; daily planner 266; diverse learners 268; guided and independent practice 267; Mafia card game 266, 268; materials and technology 267–268; objectives 265; standards 265–266
sociometries of books 100
Socrative (app) 226
software 36, 131, 149, 154–157 *passim*, 200, 217, 222, 226
Soltis, J.F. 11
sorting activities 88, **121**, 131, 156
sound pictures 90
Southern Poverty Law Center 117
special-skill development groups 145
spectrum vocabulary 59
speculation 204
sports 101, 133, 135, 206, 220, 271, 288–291

Stahl, N. 159
Stahl, R. 159
standards 58, 63; technology and 219–220
standards-based teaching, assessment tools **69**; goal 76
state social studies organizations 6; listed (with web addresses) **8**
stereotypes 18, 164, 229, 269
stories: cards 172; geography 100; maps 121, 138; with morals or lessons (teaching values) 210; play 171–172, 189
storypath (Fulwer and McGuire) 174
storytelling 174–175; type of interactional drama **173**
stress 129–130
Strike, K.A. 11
structured drama techniques 169–171
student empowerment 102, 130, 246
student self-evaluation 69–71, 75, 151
students teaching students 89
student-written summaries 91–92
study skills, building desire to master 129–130
subjective assessment 73, 75–76
subject matter teams 42
"Successerella" 171
Supreme Court 158, 185

TACOS 292–293
tactile learners 115–116
task statements 96
taxation **22**, 153
Taymans, J. 147
teacher-developed units 43, 63
teacher-provided experiences 89
teachers: accountability 186, 202; authority 75; determination of grades 66; dismissals 3–4, 230; effective versus ineffective 2; observation 78–79; qualities 2; role models 209, 212; stage managers 162; standards 219–220; technology (basic skills) 218; training days 218–219
Teachers of English to Speakers of Other Languages (TESOL) 117
teacher-written summaries 91–92
teaching certificate 3
Teaching Channel, website 220
teaching magazines (commercial) 55
teaching objective 70
Teachings in Education 80–81
Teaching Tolerance (website) 117
Teaching Tolerance 117
teaching units 45
teaching values through, examining personal actions of self and others 210–211; examples and models 209–210; problem-solving 211–212; pronouncements, rules, warnings 208–209; stories 210
team interview 151
technology **21**, 61; committee 232; cooperative learning 154–157; and media 217–234; as productive tool 218–219; and standards 219–220; teacher unease 154
technology integration, challenges 230–232
technology uses 155–157; communication 156; presentation 157; record keeping 156; research 155
TED talks 215
telephone 126
television 25, 44, 54, 100, 103, 126, 133, 142, 173, 204, 209, 217–218, 222, 227
tests: assessment through 72–75; developing 74; "indicators of student progress" 67; normative performance 67; validity 71
test scores 67, 186, 202, 295; emphasized in schools 66
Texas 112, 242
textbook-based instruction (inadequacy) 36–37
textbook-centered units 39
textbook-reading 93–95; aiding predictions (helping student develop sense of "story") 94–95; purposeful 95
textbooks, 84, 130, 202; cut-ups 93; highlighting 93; steps towards effective use 94; teacher editions 41–42, 55, 63; teaching 55; units 63; write-ins 93
theater 37, 98, 166, 169, 171–172, 191
thinking skills 74, 120–121, **121**; incorporation into social studies 129
Thompson, K.L. 147
time 38
time, continuity, change (NCSS theme) **20**
Today in History (app) 225
topics-based groups 145
trade books 96–99, 106; biographies 97, **97**; fiction and poetry 98–99; nonfiction 97
transitional aspect 49
traditional teaching, assessment tools **69**
trend projection 205
Truman, President Harry S. 185, 198
truth 5, **99**, **121**, 161, 203–205, 209, 214
Turner, T. 296
Twitter 155, 230

unconditioned response (UR) 259–260
unconditioned stimulus (US) 259–260
understanding 132, 293
UNICEF 188
United States (U.S.) government 280–288
unit planning 64; meanings of "unit" 39; types 41–43
unit plans, development 45–46
units 63; culmination phase 48–49; developmental phase 48; evaluation process 49–50, 55
unit topics 43–45
University of Houston 224
University of Kansas, Latin American Studies Department 271
U.S. government lesson plan #1 (Declaration of Independence) 280–283; activating strategy 280; assessment 282; character education 283; closure 282; daily planner 280; diverse learners 283; guided and independent practice 281–282; instruction 280–281; materials and technology 282; objectives 280; standards 280

U.S. government lesson plan #2 (Voting Rights) 283–288; activating strategy 285; assessment 287; character education 288; closure 287; daily planner 284; diverse learners 288; guided and independent practice 285–286; instruction 285; materials and technology 287; objectives 283–284; standards 284
U.S. history 288–295
U.S. history lesson plan #1 (Play Ball) 288–291; activating strategy 289–290; assessment 290–291; character education 288; closure 290; daily planner 289; diverse learners 291; guided and independent practice 290; instruction 289–290; materials and technology 291; objectives 288–289; standards 289
U.S. history lesson plan #2 (WWII, American Involvement and Battles Chart) 291–295; activating strategy 293; assessment 294; character education 295; closure 294; daily planner 292; diverse learners 294; guided and independent practice 293–294; instruction 293; materials and technology 294; objectives 292; standards 292
using maps 135; *see also* maps

Vacca, J.L. 108
Vacca, R.T. 108
values 200, 212–213; alternatives available (and choice among them) 203; analysis 202, 211; character and (worldview perspective) 212; clarification 202, 215; dealing with evidence 204; decision-making skills 203–205; definition 193; integration 202; judgments 73, 203
Values and Teaching (Raths *et al.*, 1966) 202
values development 208–212; dilemma example 211
values education, definition 193
values teaching 205–208; living in democracy 205–206; school success and functional classroom 207–208; values implicit within multicultural society 206–207
Vansickle, R. 159
Viens, J. 117
Vinson, K.D. 81
Virginia Center for Digital History (VCDH) 224
visual aids 62, 89–90, 113–114, 157, 222–223, 232, 248, 288
visualizations 162
visual learners 245, 252, 258
visual literacy 222–223; definition 222
vocabulary 84, 90–91, 106; development strategies 85–86
Von Glasersfeld, E. 24
voting rights 283–288
Voting Rights Act 286

Wallerstein's world-systems analysis 246, 249
Walsko, G. 171
Washington, George 174, 205, 209; cabinet 177–178
Washington Journal 238
Waters, Stewart xv, 229, 296–297
WebQuests 225
websites 157, 220–221, 223–224, 295
Wessling, Sarah Brown 32
white boards 59, 154, 218, 226
Whitman, Walt 169
whole group instruction 59–60
Wilson, M. 81
Wineburg, S. 142
women 18, **97**, 149, 173–174, 180, 207; *see also* gender
Wong, H.K. 11
Wong, T.R. 11
word look-outs 90
working memory 132
worksheets 135, 146, 247–248, 293
world history 269–279
world history lesson plan #1 (Culture Cubed) 269–274; activating strategy 270–271; assessment 273; character education 274; closure 273; daily planner 270; diverse learners 274; guided and independent practice 272; instruction 271–272; materials and technology 273; objectives 269; standards 269–270
world history lesson plan #2 (Silk Road) 275–279; activating strategy 276; assessment 278–279; character education 279; closure 278; daily planner 275–276; diverse learners 279; guided and independent practice 277–278; instruction 277; materials and technology 279; objectives 275; standards 275
World War Two 291–295
writing: adaptations 114–115; connection with social social studies and reading 99–100; skills 102, 106, 265; teachers 166

Young, C. 166
YouTube 64, 80–81, 103, 107, 117, 191; geography 247